INTRODUCTION TO ECONOMICS

KENNIKAT PRESS SCHOLARLY REPRINTS

Dr. Ralph Adams Brown, Senior Editor

Series on

ECONOMIC THOUGHT, HISTORY AND CHALLENGE

Under the General Editorial Supervision of

Dr. Sanford D. Gordon

Professor of Economics, State University of New York

INTRODUCTION TO ECONOMICS

BY

ALVIN S. JOHNSON, Ph.D.

REVISED

KENNIKAT PRESS
Port Washington, N. Y./London

INTRODUCTION TO ECONOMICS

First published in 1922
Reissued in 1971 by Kennikat Press
Library of Congress Catalog Card No: 70-137949
ISBN 0-8046-1451-2

Manufactured by Taylor Publishing Company Dallas, Texas

KENNIKAT SERIES ON ECONOMIC THOUGHT,
HISTORY AND CHALLENGE

PREFACE

THE first edition of this book was prepared some twelve years ago, at the end of a long period of active theoretical controversy in American economics. It can not be said that the issues in dispute had come to rest in a general agreement. Rather, the majority of economists were wearied of controversy and sought an escape from it in concrete studies of the practical problems of economic policy or business technique. I sympathized strongly with the movement toward more practical inquiry. I believed that there was small profit to be had from further theoretical refinements; that what was especially needed was quantitative analysis of the living economic forces.

Long experience as a teacher of economics had, however, convinced me that the most satisfactory approach to the practical problems of economics is by way of a well coördinated statement of principles. The striking characteristic of economic life is its organic character; and the student who has not had the organic nature of the economic structure impressed upon his mind, runs grave risks of proceeding from his special problem to generalizations that are either hopelessly negative, or sentimentally Utopian. Every economic problem is tangled up with other problems. The living wage, for example, appears at first sight to be a fairly independent problem, to be handled in terms of the cost of housing, clothing, and food, with definite specifications as to the qualities as well as quantities required. But such an inquiry leads inevitably to practical conclusions. It is found, we will say, that three fifths of our workers fall short of a living wage. Is it human for an investigator to stop with the establishment of this fact, and to refrain from making recommendations for remedying the condition? Wages must be raised, he is pretty sure to conclude.

At whose expense, however: the employer's, or the consumer's; at the expense of capital, of the owners of natural wealth? Or is it possible that wages can be raised without expense to anyone? Obviously, our simple problem has plunged into a forest of other problems, and will pretty certainly be lost unless it finds a path blazed by principles.

It was such considerations that led me to believe that what the general student needed, as an introduction to economic science, was not a more or less loosely connected discussion of practical problems, but a system of principles developed just as logically and rigorously as pedagogic requirements would permit. As all economists agree, value is the clue to the general problems of the science. It is through repercussions on value that changes in any part of the economic system are transmitted to all other parts of the system. A student who can handle the problem of value can attain to tenable conclusions on any problem of economics, provided that he is possessed of the pertinent facts. One who can not handle the problem of value may have a world of facts at his command, and yet not be able to make of himself anything better than a barrier to clear thinking and sane policy. Therefore, I threw the problem of value into the foreground of my discussion, and spared no pains in exhibiting it in all its chief phases in the fields of price and distribution.

In the course of twelve years I have naturally been forced to modify many of my opinions on practical economic affairs and to reject altogether some opinions I once held. But I am now even more firmly convinced than before that the best approach to economics is by way of a thorough study of principles. And I think that many more teachers of economics will agree with me to-day than was the case in 1910, for the war and the reconstruction period have thrown into the focus of active popular interest a host of problems that demand the rigorous application of principles. The mechanics of international trade, problems of taxation and finance, of money and credit are now felt to be vital by millions of men. As always happens when economic problems acquire popular interest, there has been a great efflorescence of question-begging argument, of seductive conclusions, and Utopian schemes. And as the mist of confused thought begins to lift, it becomes clear that the solid contributions of economics in this period have been those which were built upon the accepted body of economic principles.

In this revision I have left the greater part of the text intact. Here and there I have inserted new material which seemed pertinent, and in one case a whole chapter, on Management. Innumerable minor changes have been made, usually with the object of clearing up obscurities that might confuse the student; occasionally with the object of softening the outlines of a conclusion which I now see was too absolute and uncompromising.

ALVIN S. JOHNSON

APRIL, 1922

CONTENTS

INTRODUCTION TO ECONOMICS

CHAPTER I

THE NATURE OF ECONOMIC SCIENCE

1. *The desire for wealth has in all ages been one of the principal motives of human action.*

From the earliest time of which we have record a great part of the activity of man has been occupied with the production or acquisition of wealth — material objects and personal services upon the control of which human welfare depends, or seems to depend. In the long ages of savagery and barbarism primitive man was engaged in a ceaseless struggle with nature for the bare means of existence — food, clothing, and shelter. Limited as were the supplies afforded by nature, a savage tribe never long enjoyed them in peace; other tribes coveted the hunting grounds, or the bays where shellfish abounded; the rich pastures, or the groves of fruit-bearing trees. Hence the difficulty of obtaining from nature the means of subsistence was aggravated by constant warfare between tribe and tribe. A struggle for mere existence against nature and against hostile tribes — such was the life of primitive man.

From century to century man learned to equip himself better for the struggle for existence. Tools, at first rudely wrought from stone, later from the metals, greatly increased his productive power. A yet greater step in advance was made when animals were domesticated, and a certain and steady food supply took the place of the precarious products of the chase. The cultivation of roots and grains that had in their wild state yielded scanty returns to the gatherer marked another stage of progress. Methods were crude, and the tasks of pastoral and agricultural life exceedingly laborious — a condition which gave rise to the enslaving of captives taken in war. With the increase in productive power, limited classes were freed from the economic struggle and were enabled to devote their energy to ends less intimately connected with the pursuit of wealth — politics, literature, art, religious organization. Every advance in the productive power of society has increased the relative number of those who are free to engage in activities that add nothing to the stock of bare necessities.

It remains true, nevertheless, that the great majority of men are mainly occupied with the pursuit of wealth. This is in large measure due to the fact that a man's desire for material welfare is capable of indefinite expansion. Merely to possess food sufficient to satisfy hunger does not content him; the food must be pleasing to the palate as well as nutritious. Warm clothing is an excellent thing; but civilized man demands that his clothes be of good appearance as well as comfortable. A sod house on the prairie is constructed with no great amount of labor and almost no expense; in such a house one may defy the worst storms of winter and the hottest winds of summer. Yet the modern dweller on the plains would scorn such an abode; his home must present an appearance of comfort and prosperity. To stand well with one's fellows is to most men hardly less important than life itself, and in all human history a significant factor in winning and retaining the esteem of others has been the possession of proper attire and other personal appointments. There is a standard of wealth consumption which each little group of associates in society is under some sort of compulsion to attain. If my neighbors and friends all have fine houses, I cannot enter my humble dwelling without a sense of inferiority. If they are well dressed, I desire to be equally well dressed. If they are wise or learned or cultured, I naturally strive to emulate them in this respect also. But one cannot be well clad or well housed, one cannot without great difficulty be wise or learned or cultured, unless one can command a fair amount of wealth, an amount far in excess of the bare needs of existence. Under modern conditions wealth has become a means — though, of course, not the only means — to most of the things which one can desire. And as it is not in the nature of man to be content for any long time with what he possesses and what he has attained, it is inevitable that his desire for wealth, which is so potent a means for further attainment, should continue unabated.

While to most men wealth is a means to the satisfaction of ulterior ends, it may become an end in itself. Not only to the mean spirited, who easily become infected with the miser's diseased yearning for wealth, but also to men of more active, more generous quality. It is necessary to allow for force of habit. A man has given the better part of his life, let us say, to establishing himself on a firm economic foundation. He has pursued wealth so long as a means that it becomes a habit with him. He finds satisfaction in still pursuing it, although he has no need for it.

2. *A man desires wealth not only for the satisfaction that it may give himself, but also for the satisfaction it may give those whose interests he regards as his own.*

Nothing is more common than to stigmatize the desire for wealth as a narrowly selfish motive. As a fact there are comparatively few men who desire wealth merely for the sake of the personal gratification that they expect to derive from it. The normal man is more desirous that his wife and children should enjoy the comforts of wealth than that he should enjoy them himself. There are some persons whose desire for wealth is animated chiefly by the needs of a group of persons in no way connected with them by ties of kinship. The founders of free hospitals, orphan asylums, sailors' homes, and the like are types of this class. Some persons have sympathies so broad as to include all the citizens of a country within the group for whom they desire the benefits of wealth. The greatness of Pericles consisted partly in his ardor for advancing the material prosperity of the Athenians, even through the exploitation of allied states.

We may therefore say that the desire for wealth animates the purest and most unselfish of men as well as the most sordid. The desire for wealth is a desire for means to ends, and these may be good or evil. The philanthropist who wishes to found a home for invalid children must have wealth, just as the voluptuary who desires a palace of all delights to please his jaded senses. The economic motive animates both; very likely the philanthropist desires wealth the more ardently. What differentiates the two is the end which the wealth is meant to subserve. To assert, then, that most men are in great measure actuated by economic motives is not to assert that they are selfish or sordid. It is merely to assert that wealth has been placed between man and the satisfaction of most of his desires; that as he seeks to attain any end whatsoever, he will seek to possess the means to that end.

The desire for wealth enters into the greater part of the activities of most men in modern society. But it is very far from the exclusive motive, even in activities that seem to have no other object than the acquisition of wealth. A very strong desire is to create: to stamp one's personality upon the environment. Often such desires can be satisfied through economic activity. The good artisan puts many refining touches on his product, not for the sake of the pay he receives, but to satisfy his own instinct of excellence. The captain of industry often loses sight of the fact that his business is primarily a profit-making enterprise and exults in it as a thing of beauty or power, worth heavy sacrifices, if necessary.

3. *Wealth consists of all material objects and human services which can be made subject to man's control and upon which man depends for the satisfaction of his wants.*

The apples in one's orchard are wealth; they are subject to one's control, and their consumption yields satisfaction. Even if their owner does not care for apples, they are wealth to him if through exchanging them he can gain control of other objects capable of satisfying his wants. The trees which bear the apples and the land upon which they grow are also wealth, as they are necessary means to the production of the fruit. Wealth, then, includes those things that satisfy desires immediately, or *consumers' goods*, and those things that serve as means for producing objects of immediate desire, or *producers' goods*. Both classes together constitute *economic goods*.

4. *Human services may satisfy wants directly or indirectly.*

The services of an actor, a musician, or an orator result in the immediate satisfaction of desire. The services of a mason, a plasterer, or a carpenter embody themselves in material form. Bricks in the form of a house have a utility superior to that of an equal number of bricks in a material yard, and the measure of this superiority is the measure of the services of the bricklayer.

In summing up the annual production of wealth of a given country, it is necessary to take account of the services yielding immediate satisfaction. It is not usually necessary to take account of the services resulting in the indirect satisfaction of desires, as these are as a rule embodied in material objects, which are always taken into account in estimating the production of wealth. The rule admits numerous exceptions. The services of instruction, especially technical instruction, are analogous to the services of those who construct machines and implements for use in production. A country has added to its effective wealth in the course of a year if through training it has embodied new productive capacity in its young men and women. A country with a generally skilled population is richer than one with a population wholly unskilled, just as a country possessed of abundant machinery and tools is richer than one without these. Usually, however, economists shrink from admitting human qualities, however acquired, to the category of wealth. The conception seems to smack of slavery.

5. *Nothing can be wealth unless the total supply is so narrowly limited that every part of it is necessary to satisfy existing wants.*

The sun in spring satisfies an intense want of mine; so also do showers in the dry season. But these things are not part of my wealth, as they are not subject to my control. The air I breathe satisfies my most intense want, but it is not wealth. Though my life depends upon a constant supply of air, it cannot be said to depend upon any specific part of the existing volume. If my fire consumes part of the oxygen in the air of my room, thus, for all practical purposes, destroying the air, a fresh supply flows in through the open window, without effort or thought on my part. Since no particular part of the supply of air is of any special importance, air cannot be wealth.

In a newly settled country standing timber is often so plentiful that all possible need for it for firewood or for lumber falls far short of absorbing the entire supply. In such circumstances standing timber can have no place in the list of objects composing wealth. If one man's wood were swept by fire he would find no difficulty in securing timber *gratis* from other men. When land itself is so plentiful, relatively to the need for it, that not all the best land is occupied, no man's welfare is dependent upon his control over a particular tract of land. If in the early part of the nineteenth century a squatter in the Ohio valley had been dispossessed from the land which he occupied, he would have lost nothing but the improvements which he had fixed in the soil. The land, therefore, was no part of his wealth.

6. *The wants that endow a class of objects with the quality of wealth may originate in present needs or in anticipated future needs.*

The coal fields of Utah are capable of producing a far greater supply of coal than the persons who now have access to those fields can possibly use. If man lived in the present alone, those coal fields could not be classed as wealth. But it is generally recognized that at some future time the mines in that region will be unable to supply all need for fuel. The anticipated future need affects the present calculations of men and leads them to class the coal fields among the objects at present constituting wealth. In like manner, land fit only for building sites in the vicinity of a growing city acquires a place among objects of wealth even when it is far in excess of the present needs of the population. Indeed, much the greater part of the wealth of a modern country is designed to satisfy future, not present, needs; and the greater the wealth and the business capacity of a people, the greater will be the proportion of its wealth deriving its value from future needs.

7. *Value is the one quality that all forms of wealth have in common.*

The various objects that compose the wealth of an individual or of a society form a heterogeneous mass, and, from a physical point of view, have no characteristics in common. What could be more dissimilar, physically considered, than a steam engine and the music of an orchestra? From the point of view of human need, however, they have something in common. Both may be desired; and the desire for one may be measured in terms of that for the other. Both are valuable; the one may be twice as valuable as the other. In this case we should say that the one represents twice as much wealth as the other. Value is the universal characteristic of wealth, and it is in terms of value alone that wealth can be measured.

8. *Economics is the science which deals with wealth in its most general aspect; namely, its value aspect.*

Gold and silver are forms of wealth. They have well-marked physical characteristics which distinguish each from the other and from all other physical objects. These characteristics are not, however, of direct concern to economics. Each possesses value, and this fact is of immediate importance to economic science. That an ounce of gold is worth more than twenty ounces of silver is an economic fact; that silver is harder or whiter than gold is not an economic fact. True, differences in physical characteristics may account in part for differences in value; but that physical differences are not a sufficient explanation of differences in value is clearly shown by the fact that the former remain constant, while the latter change from day to day.

There is a body of principles determining the proper use of each form of iron and steel. One kind of steel may properly be used for rails, another kind may not be.

These laws and principles, however, are not a part of economics. They fall properly under the science of metallurgy. The science of agriculture treats of the various economic plants, of the physical and chemical properties of agricultural products, of their distribution over the earth and of the uses to which they are adapted. This science, however, is no part of economics. An inquiry into the value of iron or of corn, or into the value of the indirect goods that are employed or used up in the production of iron or corn, would properly fall within the domain of economic science.

9. *Economic science derives many of its premises from the laws governing human wants or desires.*

Economics is the science of wealth. Nothing can be wealth — that is, possess value — unless it is desired, and the degree of desire determines in large measure the degree of value. There are some things that are desired intensely if their supply is narrowly limited, while, if their supply becomes very great, they are scarcely desired at all. Diamonds fall in this class. Other things are not desired very intensely even if their supply is small; if the supply is vastly increased, the desire for each part of the supply is not greatly reduced. This is especially true of things that can be used as substitutes for other things already widely used, as aluminum vessels for vessels of copper, iron, etc. With the progress in wealth some things come to be desired more intensely, other things less intensely. It has been told — probably by a romancer, but the point remains valid — that after the Russian Revolution a peasant was arrested for carrying to his home a lean joint of goat flesh, wrapped in a priceless painting cut from its frame in some pillaged palace. The peasant was arrested not for his mistreatment of the painting, but for having contraband meat wrapped in it.

If ever the peasant becomes rich he will look back with amazement to the relative values he fixed on meat and paintings, in the time of famine. Objects for future use are desired less intensely under one set of conditions than under another. We see, then, that in order to explain values it is necessary to take account of the laws governing human wants. These laws in so far as they are treated in economics are grouped under the head of the "Consumption of Wealth."

10. *Economics deals with the general laws governing the production of wealth.*

There are laws governing the production of wealth that are operative in all branches of industry, or at any rate, in a wide range of industries. Everywhere we find a tendency toward more narrow specialization of function on the part of the laborer; everywhere a tendency to substitute machine production for hand production. In a large number of industries we find the business establishment increasing in average size from decade to decade. In many industries an increase in the amount of product may be had only at a disproportionate increase in labor and expense. These laws and related ones are grouped by economists under the head of the "Production of Wealth."

11. *Economics deals with the distribution of wealth among the different classes of which society is composed.*

The most prominent characteristic of modern industrial life is that commodities are produced, as a rule, through the joint efforts of many individuals. There was a time when the blacksmith smelted his own iron and controlled each stage in the process until the finished nail or horseshoe was in the consumer's hands. To-day, probably a thousand men have coöperated in the production of even so simple an article as a horseshoe. The value thus produced must be distributed in some way among the various producers. Those who have contributed labor receive wages; those who have contributed capital receive interest. What determines how large a share of the total value shall go to the laborers, how large a share to the owners of capital? There are general principles governing this distribution, and these form perhaps the most interesting and important part of economics. These laws are grouped by economists under the head, "The Distribution of Wealth."

12. *Economics is a practical science; its chief function is to throw light upon questions of public policy.*

Economics as a distinct science took its rise in studies concerning taxation and public finance. In early modern times the expenditures of government in most European states were steadily increasing. The various princes vied with one another in the splendor of their palaces and in the number and brilliancy of their personal following; the cost of maintaining the tranquillity of the nation at home, and its dignity and influence in foreign lands, became heavier from decade to decade. More than all, methods of warfare by land and by sea were changing, and military success was coming to depend quite as much upon the size of the war chest as upon the valor of the soldiers. These new expenditures could be met only through taxation; accordingly, it became a very practical matter for the statesman to devise means for increasing the prosperity of a nation in order to increase its capacity for paying taxes. As the precious metals seemed to be the most convenient and the most stable form of wealth, it was the aim of the statesman to provide these in abundance. European countries, having no important mines of silver and gold, could secure these metals only through foreign trade. Hence the kernel of early modern economic policy was the regulation of foreign trade, with a view to bringing into a country large supplies of treasure. These regulations formed a system which in the end became burdensome in the extreme; their futility and injuriousness were exposed in the latter half of the eighteenth century by the *Economistes* in France and by Adam Smith in Great Britain, whose writings first placed economics on a scientific basis.

Through the nineteenth century economic discussion has progressed from one practical problem to another — money and banking, trade unionism, socialism, monopoly, etc. The chief function of the science is still, as in its earliest period, to ascertain what economic policy of government will be most conducive to the general welfare. Although it is known as the "science of wealth," it is not the function of economics to instruct individuals how they may best acquire wealth. Its principal aim has been attained when it has thrown all possible light upon the economic problems which a state, and its members as citizens of a state, may need to solve.

13. *Most of the political problems of the present time are economic in their nature.*

The importance of economics to the citizen of a modern state is clearly seen when we enumerate the issues that have held a prominent place in national politics. Since the founding of the republic there has been no presidential campaign in which the tariff has not been an issue. It is an active issue to-day. The relation of the federal government to the banking system was an important issue in the early nineteenth century, in the period of the Civil War and again in the first decade and a half of the present century. The money question was potent in national politics from the Civil War through the end of the nineteenth century. The trust problem, the railway problem, the shipping subsidy question, have exercised the last generation of legislators without ever attaining to a state of final rest.

The Great War, with its tremendous enthusiasms and zeal for sacrifice, was, viewed in the large, a colossal anti-economic phenomenon. Nevertheless, in every warring country economic policy was given its place alongside of military strategy in the national concern. Indeed, such phrases as "the economic front" became commonplace. The whole economic power of the belligerents had to be deployed in the struggle. The oversubscription of a national loan was hailed with the enthusiasm of a battle won. And since the war we have had it impressed upon us that no peace treaty ends the economic repercussions of war. Industrial and agricultural depression, a disordered state of international trade, taxation that presses heavily upon us, form the background of our political life to-day.

Most of us have at some time speculated upon the apparent injustice in the distribution of rewards and services under the existing economic system. Is it right that the unskilled laborers, whose hours are long, and whose toil is hard and uninteresting, should receive only the smallest pittance, while the successful lawyer or architect receives a princely income for work that may afford him the greatest pleasure? Many able thinkers have utterly condemned the existing economic system because of this inequality of rewards; they would substitute a plan of sharing which would give to each according to the time spent or according to the degree of exertion. Certainly, this would increase the welfare of many who now have far too little; it might not seriously injure those who have more than is necessary for comfortable existence. Yet could such a change be made without setting in motion influences which in the end would leave the rich poor and the poor more wretched than they now are? The question is one that cannot be answered without a thorough study of the laws governing the production and distribution of wealth under modern conditions.

It is now clear why economic study, though of recent origin, is prosecuted with more zeal than almost any other department of science. It is concerned with one of the most vital of all subjects — the general welfare. Without economic science the existing constitution of society cannot be understood; unless based upon an adequate understanding of economic laws, attempts at practical reform of recognized evils are likely to do more harm than good.

14. *Economics must ever remain a developing body of thought, since economic life, which it seeks to explain, is constantly changing.*

Had a Greek philosopher attempted a systematic treatise on economics, we should find in it comparatively little that would assist us in solving the problems of to-day. Such a treatise would have dwelt at length upon the proper management of slaves, and the principles governing their value. It would have paid slight attention to the principles governing wages, since free labor was comparatively unimportant in ancient Greece. It would have devoted very little space to capital and interest, as capital was slightly developed, and the taking of interest an infrequent phenomenon. Even exchange value, or price, would have received scant attention, since most commodities were consumed by the producer, instead of being placed on the market, as to-day. So we may surmise that the economic science of the present day will, some hundred years hence, prove almost devoid of practical interest. The economics of each generation must be based upon the prevailing system of wealth production and distribution.

15. *The fundamental characteristic of the existing economic system is that men produce goods, not for their own use, but for sale.*

Throughout the periods of savagery and barbarism men lived in small groups, which produced, through the chase, agriculture, and pasturage, practically everything that the members of the group consumed. Whether the group prospered or fared ill depended upon the weather, the fertility of the soil, the quantity and character of game, the relation to other groups — whether tribute was given or received. Within the group the relative welfare of each member depended to a certain extent upon his own prowess and efficiency; perhaps to a greater extent upon the tribal customs in accordance with which the common products of the group were distributed among its members. In the civilized states of antiquity a somewhat similar condition of affairs existed. Industry was based on slavery; the lord of a landed estate produced by slave labor almost everything that was needed on the estate. His welfare depended upon the amount and fertility of the land he possessed, the number of his slaves and his skill in managing them, the state of the weather, and freedom from hostile invasion. So, also, in the mediæval villages. They were self-sufficing; the welfare of the community depended upon natural forces and the energy of the members of the community and their capacity for coöperation. Each individual depended for his welfare partly upon the same conditions, partly upon village custom in the apportionment of services and rewards.

With the rise of modern trade a significant change took place in economic life. In greater and greater measure men engaged in production for distant markets, instead of for their own use. Under such conditions welfare depended not only upon the producer's energy and success in the creation of goods. It depended also in large measure upon the price of the goods which were sent to market. The transition from production for one's own use to production for the market took place at various times in different countries and in different industries. In some branches of production it is only recently that the change has been effected. Thus the production of bread, formerly almost everywhere carried on in the household for consumption there, has in the cities become an independent branch of industry, carried on for supplying a market, just as the production of shoes, cloth, or iron.

The striking characteristic of modern economic life, then, is that men produce goods for the market. The employee in a shoe factory will very probably never wear any of the shoes he helps to produce; if the maker of clothes ever works on garments for himself, this is the exception to the rule of his daily labor. The farmer consumes little, if any, of the wheat that he raises; the woolgrower rarely spins and works up into cloth for his own use the product of his flocks. The modern economic system is therefore called an exchange economy, for it is through exchange of goods that each man gets the commodities that he needs. And with the rise of the exchange economy a new set of laws of wealth and welfare has come into operation. The welfare of a farmer under modern conditions depends in some degree upon his own energy and intelligence, and in some degree upon the weather. But in a very large degree it depends upon the price at which he can sell his products. A high price of iron brings prosperity to all the classes engaged in the production of iron, as a low price involves them in loss and distress.

16. *A second characteristic of the modern economic system is competition in the sale and purchase of goods.*

When men first began to produce goods for sale, we may suppose that they had fairly definite views as to the minimum price they would take and the maximum which they might reasonably seek, and that the margin between minimum and maximum was not wide. At any rate we know that in mediæval times the producer was animated by the ideal of a fair and just price; to demand more than this was extortion; to accept less was a humiliation. This spirit prevailed, however, only in dealings with fellow-townsmen. To compel strangers to pay more than a fair price, and to force strangers to accept less than a fair price for their wares, was regarded as entirely legitimate. As trade developed it assumed more and more the character of trade between strangers, each party to a transaction seeking to gain the largest possible benefit from it.

Naturally that buyer was in the most favorable position who could pit one seller against another. Each seller would be forced to scale down his prices lest the other seller consummate an advantageous bargain. Similarly, that seller was fortunate who could pit one buyer against another. This was competition in its crudest form. In this form it exists to-day in auction rooms, stock exchanges, and in certain branches of retail trade.

A seller may find himself alone in the presence of a buyer, yet both may be subject to the influence of competition. The seller knows that the buyer can probably find another seller of the same or similar wares; the buyer knows that the seller can find other buyers. Accordingly, the action of each is controlled, in a measure, by the possible action of persons who are not present and have no knowledge of the particular transaction in which they are engaged. This form of competition is more or less effective according to the number of transactions of a given kind occurring in a community. No grocer can sell sugar at a price much in excess of that fixed by other grocers; no farmer can hold out for an excessively high price for his wheat. The seller of an old mansion is less narrowly limited in his demands by competition of this kind, as the buyer must choose between the mansion and some other kind of house. On the whole, it may be said that with the development of industry a constantly greater proportion of the goods bought and sold are of such a character that competition enters into the determination of their prices.

Competition may assume a yet subtler form. In small towns petty dealers often evince a spirit of hostility to the occasional circus, because the circus "takes money away from the town." It is clear that the money spent at the circus cannot be spent for candy and soda water and other similar goods. The circus is thus really a competitor of the petty trader. The latter must give goods of better quality, or goods at lower prices, to prevent pennies from being hoarded for circus day. The principle involved in this illustration is that every seller is a competitor of every other seller; every buyer of every other buyer. An exchange economy inevitably entails competition.

17. *Competition is always subject to more or less conscious restraint. Where this restraint is effective, monopoly exists.*

In mediæval and early modern times the producers and traders of each town claimed the right to exclude strangers from buying or selling within the town, except under restrictions that effectively prevented them from competing for the ordinary trade of the town. Each citizen was compelled by law and custom to refrain from acts that would impair his fellow-citizens' chances of securing "fair prices." Early modern trade with barbarous and half-civilized peoples was also carried on under regulations calculated to restrain competition. Each European country claimed the exclusive right of trading with certain regions — Spain with Spanish America, England with British America and parts of the East Indies, Holland with the Dutch East Indies, etc. Nor were all citizens of these countries permitted to participate in the trade with their respective colonies; companies of traders were formed and were given exclusive privileges, insuring them the benefits of non-competitive conditions. In recent years every modern nation has witnessed the formation of combinations of producers with the object of limiting competition. Many of these combinations are successful in controlling, to a certain extent, the prices of their products. These combinations are popularly known as monopolies. They are none the less subject to the form of competition last described in the foregoing section.

18. *A third characteristic of the modern economic system is the formation of classes based upon economic function.*

Every society which has passed beyond the most primitive stage has been composed of classes. Master and slave, lord and serf, Norman and Saxon — such are some of the class distinctions with which history has familiarized us. Under modern conditions class distinctions are formed on other lines. One class of men gain their livelihood by labor; another by the ownership of property; a third by placing labor and wealth in productive combinations — laborers, capitalists, and enterprisers. This differentiation of classes is by no means complete, and probably never will be. Most laborers own a little property; most capitalists perform labor; most enterprisers are at the same time both laborers and capitalists. Nevertheless, the differentiation is clearly enough marked for all practical purposes. It is a natural result of modern conditions of production. So long as each man produced goods for his own use, the tools and appliances which he used were of necessity simple. To cut enough wood for one's own use did not require a very expensive ax; to furnish boards for one's own dwelling required only a handsaw, to be worked by two men. Spinning wheels and looms were likewise of the simplest make. These tools and appliances could be made by the workman himself, or secured through exchange at small sacrifice. Accordingly, the laborer as a rule owned the implements he worked with. In early modern times, although production for the market had become fairly common, the means of production still remained in the worker's hands. The increasing demand for products, however, soon led to the introduction of more expensive tools, and at last to the invention of machinery. Every step in this direction made it more difficult for the worker to provide himself with the means of production. So these had to be supplied by persons of wealth — capitalists. Under present conditions manufacturing industry in almost all its branches requires so large an expenditure for equipment that no single laborer can own the tools and machines he works with; nor is it often possible for a group of laborers to equip themselves for production through combining their small savings. The capital outlay for a mill employing a hundred workmen is usually far in excess of what a hundred workmen can accumulate. Industry must therefore be conducted by wage laborers and employer-capitalists. In many cases those who possess capital are not in a position to use it directly in business. The widows and orphan children of wealthy men are the clearest case in point. But there are great numbers of men and women who simply prefer to devote their attention to other things than business operations. Possessing wealth enough for all their personal requirements, they may choose to live in luxurious ease, to try their fortune as sculptors or painters or poets, to engage in scientific research or polar expeditions. These persons form a class more or less distinct. As their capital is employed in industry without their personal management, we may differentiate them from the employer-capitalists and describe their economic position as that of capitalist pure and simple.

19. *The laws of price are the governing principle in modern economic life.*

A farmer or a manufacturer is popularly said to "put a price" upon his products. In the majority of cases, however, what the seller really does is to make a choice between selling at a given price or keeping his goods unsold. Except in comparatively rare cases there is a market price for goods which the buyers and sellers must accept if they desire to engage in business at all, and over this price no single person has any perceptible control. Yet prices do not exist apart from the action of men; they are the creation of man in society. Many persons, each acting with a view to his own interest, offer wheat for sale; many persons stand ready to buy it. The price of wheat is fixed as a result of the offers and demands of all persons who sell or buy wheat. It is therefore a social phenomenon — the creation of all society, or of a large part of it. And so it is with almost all prices. They are set by society. Hence the laws of price are properly called the laws of social economics, or of political economy.

Under modern conditions the prosperity of each industry as a whole depends largely upon the prices of its products. Within each industry the prosperity of each laborer, capitalist, or employer depends in great degree upon the way in which the total product of the industry is divided. And here again we encounter social laws. There is a general rate of wages, which the laborer must accept if he wishes employment. In the same way, there is a general rate of interest. No one man exercises any appreciable influence in fixing these rates; they are the resultant of the actions of all those who have labor to sell or capital to lend, on the one hand, and on the other hand, of those who desire to hire laborers or to borrow capital.

The influence of price extends even farther. In large measure the laws of price determine what each of us shall do; they fix one's place of residence as well as his occupation. If the price of glass is high, and remains high for a considerable period of time, high profits and high wages are possible in the glass industry. New establishments will be opened; boys and young men who otherwise would have engaged in other industries become glass blowers. By fixing a high price on glass, society, as it were, decrees that more persons and more capital shall be devoted to that industry. If coal and other sources of power are exceptionally cheap in a given locality, if conditions of transportation are exceptionally favorable, large profits may be made by manufacturers in that locality; they increase their investments and new capital flows in from less favored districts. A city is built, and the population that was formerly scattered in hamlets and country is under a sort of compulsion to congregate there. Why are our cities becoming greater and greater? The social laws of price decree it. If we would understand just why modern society presents a given form, our inquiry must take into account, as perhaps the most important factor, these laws of price.

20. *Summary.*

Economics is the science which treats of wealth — the material objects and human services which contribute to human welfare, and are therefore valued. The history of mankind is largely a record of progress in the power of producing wealth and the development of institutions for the distribution of wealth among the individuals composing society.

Economic science begins with a study of the desires which give rise to economic activity and the values which originate in these desires. It deals, further, with the general laws governing the production of wealth and its distribution among the various classes in society. The practical object of the science is the establishing of principles upon which organized society must act in order to maintain and increase the general well-being.

The economic problems of any historical period can be understood only with reference to the underlying conditions characterizing the economic life of that period. In order to appreciate the significance of modern economic problems, it is necessary to ascertain the fundamental characteristics of modern economic life. These are: (1) Production of goods and services, not for the use of the producer, but for sale; (2) Competition in the purchase and sale of goods and services; (3) The existence of classes based upon economic function—laborers, capitalists, and enterprisers. The last two characteristics are, in a sense, corollaries of the first.

The key to an understanding of the existing economic system is to be found in the laws governing the prices of commodities and services. The prices of goods are for the most part beyond the control of individuals; they may be said to be determined by society as a whole. The laws of price are therefore properly described as social laws; and the body of thought dealing with these laws is known as social economics.

CHAPTER II

UTILITY, VALUE, AND PRICE

1. *Economic evolution is, in large measure, dependent upon the development of wants.*

Man is distinguished from all other living creatures by the number and complexity of his wants. The lowest savage requires better shelter and more varied and nutritious food than his next of kin in the animal world. The wants of the savage are, however, few and simple as compared with those of civilized man. An extraordinary run of fish, an exceptionally good season for game, may leave the savage with all his wants practically satisfied. Men who have had occasion to employ workmen of half-civilized races complain that as soon as the workman has received wages enough to supply his wants for a few days, he ceases to take interest in his work, and very soon quits his employment, to resume it again only when driven by the goad of hunger. Civilized man, on the other hand, seldom suffers chronically from lack of means to satisfy hunger; he is, however, constantly aware of some want that remains unsatisfied, and the higher the state of civilization, the greater the number of wants that are effective enough to incite a man to activity. The normal man in an American city limits his toil only when he feels that this is necessary in order to preserve his powers for future labor, and in many instances does not limit it even then. He overworks, often, without any better reason than that he does not know when to stop. Even our pleasures are selected largely with a view to increasing our working capacity.

Not only do the wants of civilized man impel him to work harder than a savage would work; they also force him to take more careful thought in the application of his energies. Hence the invention of new appliances for production and better methods of organizing and directing productive power. As a rule, the more numerous and complex the wants of an individual, the greater are his exertions and the higher the skill and intelligence with which his energies are directed.

2. *Human wants differ widely in elasticity, the wants for luxuries being more elastic than the wants for necessaries.*

Every want of man is capable of complete satisfaction. But the different wants vary widely in their insistency and in the ease with which they may be entirely satisfied. The want for bread, for instance, is extremely insistent, yet easily satisfied. I must have bread, but I would not care to have even a petty baker's entire supply. Such a want is known in economics as an inelastic one. The people of the United States require a fairly determinate quantity of wheat for food, and this quantity they will strive to secure even at great sacrifice. Much more than this, however, would not be wanted at all, unless of course it could be sold in other lands, or some use other than the supplying of food could be found for it. On the other hand, the want for some classes of things is very hard to satisfy at all, although it is not absolutely essential that the want be satisfied. I can get on very well without possessing paintings, but I should like to have all there are in the Louvre. The people of the United States may live comfortably without having many art galleries, but it is almost inconceivable that they could have too many. Such wants, then, are elastic.

As the examples given indicate, it is the wants for so-called necessaries that are inelastic; the wants for luxuries are elastic. Civilization tends to develop the wants for luxuries of all kinds. Hence, it may be said that the higher a people stands in the scale of civilization, the farther it is from the complete satisfaction of all its wants.

3. *When a want is satisfied by the consumption of a succession of similar goods, the satisfaction derived from the first consumed is greater than that derived from the second, and that derived from succeeding goods grows steadily less. This principle is known as the law of diminishing intensity of wants.*

Every man wants enough food to keep him alive; a quantity sufficient for this purpose he desires intensely. An equal additional quantity will keep him in good condition; this quantity he desires only less intensely. Give him more food; it may still please his palate, and satisfy a want. But a point is soon reached where the man wants no more food at all.

So the want for a suit of clothes is hardly less insistent than the want for food enough for life. A second suit of clothes would be highly desired, even if of identical quality, as it may be worn when the first is soaked with rain or otherwise out of condition for wear. A third suit of the same kind would not be desired very intensely; a fourth, or at any rate a fifth or sixth, would be a superfluity. But if it is possible to vary the quality, the want becomes far more expansive. The social element becomes predominant; the man would dress at least as well as men in the social group to which he belongs, or of which he desires to become a member. Yet a point is eventually reached where neither increase in quantity nor improvement in quality is desired.

It may then be stated, as one of the general laws of human nature, that each want is capable of varying degrees of satisfaction, that with each increase in the means of satisfaction the desire for additional means grows less, until a point is reached where want is no longer felt.

4. *The capacity of a good for satisfying wants is known as utility.*

Whatever satisfies a want is a good, in economic terminology. The power of a good to satisfy wants is utility. It is, of course, plain that nothing has utility in this sense unless it is wanted. Utility is strictly parallel with want; human want for a certain object endows it with utility, and the degree of utility is measured by the degree of want. Before men knew the use of iron, iron ore was not wanted and had no utility at all; with every advance in the art of metallurgy, the utility of iron ore has increased. In the days of Marco Polo, the only utility that existed in the petroleum of Asia Minor arose from its use "to anoint camels suffering from the mange"; now the progress of science and industry has endowed the same material with a very high utility.

The same object may have far greater utility under one set of circumstances than under another. A tree on a mountain side may have utility as it stands, derived, of course, from some prospective use. This utility may be called *elementary utility*. When the tree is felled and carried by a stream to a saw-mill, its utility is increased by mere change of place. This addition to the utility of the tree may be called *place utility*. A further increase in utility appears when the log is transformed into boards. This increase is known as *form utility*. If the boards should be kept in a lumber yard for ten years, very likely, on account of the failing supply of timber, their utility would be considerably increased. This increase may be called *time utility*. It is to be remembered, however, that the foregoing terms do not represent different kinds of utility, but relate to the conditions under which utility comes into existence. Utility is the single, uniform quality of want-satisfying power.

Utility, it is to be borne in mind, is not identical with usefulness. Opium prepared for smoking, being ardently desired by the victims of the opium habit, has a very high utility, in the economic sense; but it is the reverse of useful. As a rule, whatever is useful has utility, but there is no close correspondence between the degree of usefulness and the degree of utility.

5. *When a man acquires goods of the same kind one by one, the utility of the first good acquired exceeds that of the second, the utility of the second good exceeds that of the third, and so on, each successive good representing a smaller utility. This principle is known as the law of diminishing utility.*

We have seen that wants are capable of varying degrees of satisfaction. As utility is strictly parallel with want, concrete goods, satisfying the different degrees of want, have different degrees of utility. Three bushels of wheat may supply me with bread enough to sustain life through a year; the utility of these three bushels — supposing I have no other source of food supply — is exceedingly great; I want them as I want life and all that life contains. It would not be easy to fix an estimate upon this amount of utility, but let us call it 1000*x*. Another three bushels would enable me to keep in fairly good physical condition; but their utility to me is evidently less; perhaps it would be 100*x*. Another three bushels might mean overfeeding; yet some persons are desirous of being overfed; hence I may still desire these three bushels, and thus endow them with utility, which may possibly be measured by 10*x*. With another three bushels I might feed a cat and a dog; it would give me pleasure to have these as pets; therefore I should desire the additional supply of wheat, and it might represent a utility of $5x$. An additional three bushels I could perhaps not use in any way giving me satisfaction. They would have no utility for me at all.

Suppose that I find a remarkably beautiful seashell. As it seems desirable to me, it has utility to me. The amount of utility may equal $10y$. Another shell will not be so much of an acquisition, but I shall still desire it. Its utility may perhaps be $9y$. Additional ones will give me less pleasure, but as the want for things of beauty is hard to satisfy, I may still experience a desire for a hundredth or a thousandth shell, and these would have some utility for me. There is, however, a point beyond which additional shells would merely cumber my premises; they would then have no utility for me.

These examples assume, of course, that I do not undergo a change while I am acquiring these goods. If repeated examination of the seashell inspires me with an increasing sense of its perfection of form, I may desire a second even more than I desired the first. Its utility will be greater than that of the first originally was, but not greater than the utility of a first shell would be in my present state.

So one's first experience of classical music may be less enjoyable than his second experience of the same kind of music. He has, in the meantime, become a more cultured person. But assuming that no opportunity for development in taste is permitted, the pleasure derived from the first hour of listening to good music will be greater than that derived from a second successive hour of equally good music. The utility of the second hour of music is less. And so we may accept it as a general rule that the utility of a unit of any kind of good diminishes as the number of such units in one's possession increases.

6. *The want-satisfying power of the least important unit of a commodity in one's possession is termed the final or marginal utility of that commodity.*

In the foregoing examples it has been assumed that the quantity of the goods increased until no desire for further units existed. Most of the things which we desire are not to be had in superfluous quantities. Instead of having five units, each consisting of three bushels of wheat, let us assume that I have but three. The third unit would still have a utility of $10x$. As this is the utility of the last or final or marginal part of my supply, it is called final or marginal utility. Suppose that I have only ten seashells, and that the utility of the tenth is $5y$. In economic language $5y$ is the final or marginal utility of seashells. Final utility, it is clear, is a very variable quantity; if the desire for a good increases, with no increase in the number of units of the good, final utility increases; if the desire remains the same, but the number of units of the good diminishes, final utility again increases. In the first example, if the third unit of wheat were destroyed, the marginal utility of wheat would at once become $100x$.

Conversely, marginal utility diminishes with decrease in want or increase in number of units. I might tire of collecting seashells, or the waves might wash up a wagonload of them. In either case the marginal utility would shrink — perhaps to zero.

7. *In effect, the importance of any unit of a commodity is determined by the want-satisfying power of the marginal unit. The importance of a unit, thus determined, is termed its effective utility.*

But does any man really arrange his wheat or other goods in series of units and say to himself: "This unit is worth 1000x; without it I should starve; this unit is worth 100x, as my comfort and strength depend upon it; this unit is worth 5x, for if I did not have it I should be compelled to do without my pets"? Not at all; the different units are just alike, and one is thought of as just as desirable as another. For practical purposes, the utility of one unit is the same as that of another. Let us suppose that there are four units of wheat, and that the last has a utility of 5x. What is lost if any one of the four units is lost? Simply 5x. What sacrifice would one make to prevent the loss of any unit, even the one which would have been used to sustain life, and by itself would be worth 1000x? A sacrifice not greater than 5x. For if any other unit is lost, the least important one will be substituted for it, and the effective loss will be properly placed at 5x.

The utility of the last and least important unit, then, exercises an important influence in determining what utility one will in effect ascribe to any unit. For practical purposes the utility of any unit is exactly equal to that of the least important one. The utility of a unit, thus measured by that of the least important one, is called "effective utility."

If the total number of units of a good is so great that the last one has no utility, the good has no effective utility at all. No one will do anything to prevent the destruction of part of his supply; no one will give anything to increase his supply. Thus water, although a single gallon would have indefinitely great utility if this were the only gallon available, is in most places so abundant that the last units of the supply have no utility. Therefore no unit has effective utility.

8. *A knowledge of the comparative effective utilities of different goods is essential to the rational application of means for the production or acquisition of goods.*

Almost every one who is about to engage in the production of wealth has several options as to the kinds of goods he may produce and as to the qualities or grades of each kind. A farmer may produce wheat or corn, cattle or hogs; he may produce a hard variety of wheat or a soft one; he may produce thoroughbred stock or grade stock. Every man who is at the point of making a purchase has numerous options as to the goods upon which he is to spend his money. Some options, naturally, offer greater advantages than others.

Suppose that a farmer can produce, with the expenditure of one day's labor, two bushels of potatoes or one bushel of wheat. Should he spend his time in producing wheat, or potatoes, or both? If the effective utility of two bushels of potatoes is greater than that of a bushel of wheat, the rational thing for him to do is to produce more potatoes and to spend less time producing wheat. In accordance with the law of diminishing utility, the effective utility of potatoes will decline as their quantity increases; at the same time, that of wheat will increase, as our example assumes that labor formerly occupied in wheat production is diverted to the raising of potatoes. A point will probably be reached where a day's labor will produce as much utility in one branch of agriculture as in the other; and until this point is reached, the cultivator has it in his power to increase his welfare simply by making a more rational distribution of his labor.

But before one can rationally distribute his labor or other resources, he must have a definite notion of the relative effective utilities of goods. He must measure the utility of one — the degree in which it seems desirable to him — in terms of the utility of another; or he must measure them all by a common standard. And this, of course, is easy to do. Think of any two objects. Which seems the more desirable? That one has the greater utility for you. How far would you walk in order to get good No. 1? If you would walk twice as far to get good No. 2, the latter has, for you, twice the effective utility of the former. Any good, or any sacrifice, may serve us as a standard for measuring the comparative utilities of goods. Under existing economic conditions, of course, the standard which most readily occurs to one is money. If one wishes to compare the utilities of wheat and potatoes, he naturally considers how much money he would give for a bushel of either.

9. *The utility of a good, measured by some standard, either of utility or sacrifice, is personal value. Personal value varies from individual to individual, and is constantly fluctuating.*

Now, the effective utility of a commodity, compared with that of some other commodity, or compared with some sacrifice which serves as a standard, is personal or "subjective" value. Value in this sense of the term is effective utility measured. And as effective utility is constantly fluctuating with changes in the amount of a good, or in the desire for it, personal value is also always fluctuating.

We often hear of the "real" value of a thing, or of the "intrinsic" value, as if there were some kind of value resident in a thing apart from man's desire for it. Thus a painting, picked up at an auction for say, $100, may be pronounced by an expert "intrinsically" worth $500. That is the expert's judgment of the market value of the painting under more usual conditions of sale. A stock-broker often assures his clients that a particular security, to be had, say, at 75, is worth "intrinsically" 100. That is his judgment of the prospective income yield and the price the investment market will at some future time place upon it. These "intrinsic" values, then, are nothing but assumptions as to the personal values that will emerge under different conditions and at a future time.

Values will naturally be different for different persons. What is the value of my grandfather's watch? To me, it may be equal to that of $1000. Perhaps you would not give $10 for such an antiquated timepiece. In less extreme degree the same thing holds of every good. Some will place a high value upon an object; others a low value; and the one is as properly the true or intrinsic value as the other.

But is there not a certain scale of values in which most persons agree, and has not this general value a claim to the title "true value"? There is indeed something like a scale of values established, as it were, by common consent; and the economic activities of each are, in effect, directed toward making his own scale of values conform to that of society. How this social scale of values arises out of the purely personal values just described, it will be our next task to consider. It is of course self-evident that the social value does so arise. One cannot conceive of society as establishing values and imparting them to individuals.

10. *Personal values are in some measure socialized through imitation.*

Utility, as we have seen, is a quality with which an object is endowed by virtue of a human want. This want may arise out of personal or out of social need. If a particular social need should disappear or change, certain of our wants would disappear or change. Certain classes of goods, destined to satisfy such wants, would lose their value, or undergo some change in it. There was a time when gentlemen clipped their own hair and covered their heads with wigs. To move in polite society, one had to follow this, as other fashions. Hence there was a want for wigs, and these were endowed with effective utility and value accordingly. As the wearing of one's own hair came into vogue, this particular kind of wig ceased to have either utility or value. Now it is clear enough that the great majority of those who followed the earlier fashion could have had no personal need nor want for a wig. They derived the want from their associates. The custom, I suppose, originated with some bald-headed prince who really needed a wig. And so it was transmitted from the court to the gentry, and persisted long after the reason for its existence had disappeared. The value of wigs thus arose from a personal need; it attained vogue through imitation, and, by a similar process, faded out and disappeared.

Suppose that I attend an auction of the effects of an eccentric gentleman, who has led a solitary life collecting odds and ends of all kinds, among them some things of value. I find a painting that pleases me. Say that I know nothing of art, and that all the painting represents to me is a group of dull, brutish persons, making unnecessarily hard work out of some simple agricultural operation. What is its value to me? It would be difficult to say; certainly in my own mind the value is something very tentative. But finding that the picture can be had for no great sum, I resolve to buy it. I hang my acquisition in an inconspicuous place, for I am not sure whether I should be proud of it or ashamed of it. A friend who knows something of art calls on me. Perhaps he takes merely a glance at the picture and says nothing. Its value to me shrinks to zero. But if he cries enthusiastically, "Ah! a Millet!" immediately its value to me expands in an extraordinary fashion; what had been scarcely a valuable object at all becomes a priceless treasure.

Here then is one reason why values for different persons tend to conform to the same scale. If I find that most of my friends think that a riding horse is dear at $300, I think so, too, although I might get more satisfaction out of the horse than they. Value is thus in large measure a matter of imitation. But before one can imitate, there must be something original to serve as a center of imitation; and in the matter of values, this must be the original personal value of some, arising out of effective utility to them.

Moreover, though imitation brings about a certain uniformity in the scales of values of different persons, it can not of itself make them absolutely alike. If most of my friends think that a particular horse is worth $200, I certainly would not value it at $300, unless indeed I am a connoisseur in horseflesh and my friends are not. But I may think the horse is cheap at $200, while my friends may think it is dear. And this shows that in spite of all tendency to conform, there is in my scale of values some part that is peculiarly my own.

11. *Personal values are profoundly influenced by the art of salesmanship.*

Because personal values are in most cases uncertain and fluctuating, readily susceptible to suggestion and imitation, it is always possible for a shrewd salesman to manipulate them to his own advantage. I enter a shop with the fixed purpose of buying a hat, and nothing else. I have a definite idea of the kind of hat I want, and the price I am willing to pay for it. Do I come away from the shop with just that hat and nothing else? Not unless I am of unusually decisive character, or the salesman weak in his art. In the ordinary case the salesman, by a gesture or tone of depreciation so slight that

I feel it rather than observe it consciously, raises a doubt in my mind whether the hat I want is really the best bargain I can make. Subtly he leads me to transfer my interest to another hat, more expensive or at all events affording him a larger margin of profit. Nor does he let me go with the hat, but manages to excite in me values I had not been conscious of, adhering to gloves, ties, or perhaps even a cane. When I entered the shop none of these things seemed for my purposes worth the money they cost. When I leave it some of them, at any rate, have assumed a higher value in proportion to money; and the proof of it is that I have parted with my money in their acquisition.

Modern salesmanship, in all its ramifications, is a mighty force playing ceaselessly upon all of us. Consider how the feeling has been built up in most of us that capacity for floating is an extremely useful property in a soap. A number of years ago the American people would not consume enough raisins to make the California grape growers prosperous. They organized an advertising campaign the object of which was to make us all place a higher personal value on raisins as food. The result was a great increase in the consumption of raisins, and at increased prices. There are many articles in general use whose values have been built up almost wholly in this way. More money may have been spent in attracting the attention of the consumer and manipulating his sense of values, than in producing the articles and in transporting them to the dealer's shelves.

12. *The most effective force making for socialization of values is exchange.*

So long as men lived in self-sufficing groups, producing whatever they needed for their own use, there was no other force than imitation which could make the personal valuations of one group correspond with those of another.

But in an exchange economy there is a much more potent force making for the socialization of values.

Suppose that two farmers, with adjoining fields, both grow potatoes and wheat, and suppose that they are so far from a market that they can exchange their products only with each other. Farmer A may consider that a bushel of wheat is worth two bushels of potatoes; Farmer B may consider a bushel of potatoes worth two bushels of wheat.

Assuming such a divergence in personal valuations the natural result will be, not that they will debate the relative justice of their views of value, but that they will trade. Farmer A can afford to offer Farmer B two bushels of potatoes for a bushel of wheat; Farmer B can afford to accept even a half bushel of potatoes for a bushel of wheat. Exactly how much A will at first offer, we cannot say, nor is that of much importance. What is certain is that he can, and probably will, offer terms that will be acceptable to B, and some bushels will be exchanged.

Now, as A parts with some of his potatoes, the effective utility, and with it the value, of potatoes to him increases. As he gets more wheat, the effective utility of wheat declines. And the reverse will be the case with B, who is increasing his stock of potatoes and diminishing his stock of wheat. It may still be worth while for the two farmers to exchange more bushels; but it is not so much worth while as it was at first. In the end, exchange must cease, for each will value wheat in terms of potatoes exactly as the other does.

Perhaps Farmer A has land that is very well adapted to potato production, while Farmer B's land is best fitted for the growing of wheat. In another year A will have a superfluity of potatoes and B of wheat, and the process of exchange will again be necessary to equalize values.

So in a developed economic system the value of wheat in regions where it is produced tends continually to fall below the value of it in regions where little wheat is grown; and this it is that keeps up a constant exchange between distant regions. And this constant exchange, in turn, tends to eliminate the discrepancies in values.

Returning to the case of the two neighbors, perhaps A has a cow which he does not care to keep, but which B would like to have; while the latter has a harrow which he does not need, but the former could well use. Possibly A values the cow at twenty bushels of wheat and the harrow at thirty; while B values the cow at thirty bushels of wheat and the harrow at twenty. Here is a good opportunity for a trade. Either one might give the other a certain number of bushels of wheat "to boot," in order to bring about the trade. At what terms will the exchange be made? We cannot tell. Nor will the exchange, at whatever terms, affect the relative values placed upon cows and harrows by either party to the exchange. It would be different if more cows and harrows were to be exchanged. In that case the scales of values of the two exchangers would tend to uniformity, as was the case with the potatoes and wheat. But very likely no further exchanges are to be made. So I may be able to buy for $25 a coat that I would regard as cheap at $50. Another coat at $25, however, might not seem worth more to me than $20; accordingly, I refrain from buying it. Hence the coat which I do buy retains a personal value for me in excess of the value placed upon it by the seller. It is a value that as a whole refuses to be socialized. A similar state of affairs exists wherever one buys single goods, not quantities of like units, as in the case of wheat.

13. *Personal values may be mere reflections from social values. Such personal values may be called personal or subjective exchange values.*

In the examples employed in the last section it was assumed that both parties to the exchange had personal values, arising out of their own wants, for both commodities exchanged. This may have been the usual case under primitive conditions; but now, when we produce almost exclusively for sale, the seller of a commodity must fix a personal value in some other way. Say that I am a dealer in women's shoes. For my personal use they have no value whatsoever. Yet when a prospective customer appears, I have just as definite a value, below which I would not sell the shoes, as I should have if I were trading off a pair of shoes that I might use myself. Whence do I derive this value? I know that if I do not sell shoes to this particular buyer I shall probably be able to sell them to some one else. And I will take no less for them than I think some one else will pay. If experience shows me that few persons will pay the price, I must alter my personal value, or the fashions will change, and I shall have a stock of unsalable leather on my hands.

Now it must be plain that this kind of personal value is entirely a secondary phenomenon. It is derived from the estimate of other men's personal values, arising from personal needs. It has its importance; but it does not explain the values that are actually placed upon goods. This explanation lies in the facts of direct personal valuation.

14. *Value expressed in terms of money is known in economics as price.*

In one's personal estimate of values one may employ as a standard of measurement any object having effective utility. The farmer may value a horse in terms of wheat or cotton; the ranchman in terms of cattle; the fisherman in terms of fish. The difficulty with such estimates is that they are not sufficiently intelligible to other persons. A traveler in the Orient writes that a certain rajah places the value of an elephant at 2000 yards of Japanese silk. Do you know whether the elephant is dear or cheap? If the valuation were made in terms of silver or gold, we should all have a fairly definite idea of the value placed upon the elephant, as we are daily using these metals and estimating their importance. In practice values are usually expressed in terms of silver or gold money. For convenience, economists use the term "price" as the equivalent of money value. There are personal prices and social prices, just as there are personal and social values. Social prices are practically determined by the action of buyers and sellers, and as these commonly meet in a market, social price is called *market price.*

15. *Market prices tend to a uniformity, and correspond with the personal prices of those who are least eager to buy or to sell but who nevertheless succeed in buying or selling.*

Personal values, as we have seen, naturally vary widely with different individuals. We need not believe that any two persons would affix exactly the same money valuation upon a particular horse. One man might value the horse, for his personal use, at $500; another at $50. Yet we find that for a certain grade of horses there is something like a uniform price. Perhaps this price is $250. In such case the personal values of $50 and $500 are both ignored. They have no influence upon the price actually set.

Personally I may abhor the idea of flying. If I were to place a value upon aeroplanes for my own use, it would be far less than nothing. Clearly my personal value of aeroplanes has nothing to do with their price, which for a given grade may be $5000. If I had a mild interest in this form of sport I might value an aeroplane at $1000; yet I should not influence their price. Were I so passionately fond of flying, and so plentifully provided with money, as to value an aeroplane at $100,000, this valuation would nevertheless be incapable of raising the price of aeroplanes much, if any, above $5000. It is clear, then, that some personal values count, and some do not, in the determination of prices as they are fixed in the market.

To show just what it is that determines what personal values count in fixing market prices, we may employ a somewhat artificial example which is the common property of modern text-books in economics. Let us imagine a horse market in which there are six persons with horses to sell, and six persons each of whom would like to buy a horse. We will assume that the horses are as alike as peas, so that each buyer would as willingly have one as another. Of course each buyer desires to buy as cheaply as possible, and each seller desires the highest possible price for his horse. Each buyer has in his own mind a top price — the most he would pay under any circumstances — and each seller has a bottom price, below which he would absolutely refuse to go. Being rational men, the buyers carefully refrain from letting their top prices be known; and in the same way the sellers keep their lowest prices a close secret. We shall assume the fiction writer's omniscience, and set down the top and bottom prices of the buyers and sellers respectively, as follows: —

Buyers		Sellers	
A	$100	M	$90
B	90	N	80
C	80	O	70
D	70	P	60
E	60	Q	50
F	50	R	40

How many horses will be sold, and at what price? Of course, if each of the buyers in the first column were shut up in a stall with the seller in the opposite column, all the horses would be sold, and at different prices. But we are assuming that all are in an open yard, and hear one another's bids and offers. Under these circumstances no buyer will pay more than another, nor will one seller take less for his horse than another. What price will actually be fixed can be seen by following out in detail the probable action of these buyers and sellers.

Suppose A, a buyer, offers $40 as his first bid. R could afford to take it; but as any of the other five buyers would be glad to get a horse at that price, they each offer a little more than $40. Competition for this horse goes on until the price is raised to $50. At this point two horses may be had; but there are six competing buyers, and the price goes higher. Thereupon F, who will pay no more than $50, drops out. He can exercise no more influence in determining the price of these horses than I can in determining the price of aeroplanes. Bidding goes on, and the price is forced up to $60. Three horses are to be had at this price; but as there are still five buyers the price goes above $60, and E drops out. At last the price reaches $70. There are now four sellers willing to part with their horses at this price; and four buyers willing to pay the price. Imagine that bidding goes on, and the price rises to $71. D would then drop out, and four horses would be offered, with only three buyers. Any one of the four sellers would rather sell at $70 than have his horse unsold; bidding among the sellers, therefore, forces the price back to $70. Under the conditions this price represents an equilibrium between the values of the buyers and those of the sellers.

Let us imagine, however, that before the sale is actually effected, another buyer, with a maximum valuation of $110, appears. The price will then be forced above $70, and D will drop out. It will not reach $80, however, for then five sellers would compete to meet the needs of four buyers. The actual price will be fixed somewhere between $70 and $80. If an additional seller, with a valuation of $30, were to appear, the number of buyers remaining the same, the price would drop below $70, but not quite to $60.

The seller who is least desirous of selling, but who nevertheless effects a sale, is known as the *marginal seller.* The buyer who is least eager to buy, but yet succeeds in buying, is known as the *marginal buyer.*

16. *Demand is the volume of purchases of a commodity that would be made at a given price. Supply is the volume of sales that would be made at a given price. Market price tends to fix itself at a point where demand and supply thus defined are equal.*

Every person who reads widely in economic literature, frequently encounters the statement that market prices are determined by demand and supply. It is therefore worth while to ascertain exactly what these terms mean. Demand is clearly not synonymous with want or desire. We may imagine a Hindoo grain dealer closing up his shop because there is no demand for grain, although he may be besieged by an army of starving people. Desire must be supported by purchasing power before it becomes demand. Supply does not mean the existing stock of a commodity. There may be a shortage in the wheat supply because those who have wheat are holding it for higher prices. The owner of a commodity must be willing to sell before the stock in his possession becomes part of the supply. It is evident that in most instances the lower the price of a commodity, the greater will be the demand for it and the less will be the supply, and *vice versa.* The demand for wheat at ten cents a bushel would be enormous, the supply at that price would dwindle to practically nothing. There must be some price for each commodity that will exactly equalize the volume of demand with that of supply. This price is the one that will prevail in the market.

At a given time the aggregate demand for wheat at $2 a bushel may extend to one million bushels; but the sellers of wheat may be willing to place on the market two million bushels at prices ranging from one dollar up to two. Manifestly $2 a bushel cannot be the price set by the market, for the owners of the second million bushels, not finding purchasers, will offer it for less. At a lower price, some sellers will drop out, and some additional purchasers will appear. At $1.50 a bushel, perhaps fifteen hundred thousand bushels will be offered, and the same amount taken. Then $1.50 is the price that will actually be set.

Those buyers whose personal valuations are the lowest, and who would be ready to drop out if the price rose, are the ones who at any particular time determine the volume of the demand. Those sellers whose personal values are highest, and who are ready to drop out if the price falls, determine, for the time being, the volume of the supply. The principle that the price is fixed at a point which equalizes demand and supply is therefore tantamount to the principle, given in section 15, that price corresponds with the personal valuations of those who are least eager to buy or to sell, or the marginal buyers or sellers.

17. *A particular set of marginal buyers and sellers control prices only for a brief time.*

While it is the buyers and sellers who are just ready to drop out with changes in price — the marginal buyers and sellers — who at a given time hold the price where it is, price changes may take place in spite of them, through changes in the wants of purchasers, or through the appearance of new sellers. The introduction of the automobile resulted in a new demand for gasolene, and as a consequence the price rose, eliminating the purchasers who had before been in a price-determining position. If alcohol came to be produced cheaply in vast quantities and ways were found for substituting it successfully for gasolene for the same purpose, the price of gasolene would fall, and a new set of purchasers, who formerly had nothing to do with fixing its price, as they did not desire it enough to buy it, would come to occupy the position of controllers of the price.

Under existing conditions we do not find ourselves in the presence of unpriced goods upon which a price is to be placed. Everything that one wishes to buy already bears a price; one accepts the price, or refrains from purchasing. I compare my personal value of anything — say a hat — with the value of the commodity in the market. If I decide that a hat is worth more than $5 to me, I purchase it if it is to be had at that price. As I part with some of my money, each dollar I have is worth more to me; and hats are worth less. Thus I make my personal value approximate that of the market. If I am a seller of hats, and I find that $5 is worth more to me than a hat, I willingly part with the hat at that price. As I have more dollars, one is worth less to me; having fewer hats, I am not so eager to part with one. Thus by buying and selling one makes his personal values conform more nearly to that of the market. At the same time, by taking a hat from the seller, I reduce by a trifle the number to be sold to other purchasers; I make the hat sellers less eager to sell, and contribute of my puny strength to draw up the general level of value of hats to my own personal value. So all of us who are purchasers are joining our efforts to raise prices to a high level, although what we desire is low prices; and all of us who are sellers are exerting our combined strength to pull them down, although our chief desire is high prices. Those of us who are least eager to buy or to sell exercise an equalizing function; when the buyers' side prevails, and prices are rising, the least willing buyers drop out; and similarly with the least willing sellers, when the sellers succeed in pulling prices down.

18. *Summary.*

Progress in civilization is attended by an ever-increasing number of wants. Of these, some are inelastic: though often very insistent, they can easily be completely satisfied. Other wants are elastic. Complete satisfaction of elastic wants is difficult. Wants of the latter class evince the greater tendency toward development with the progress of civilization. Wants of both classes admit of different degrees of satisfaction; in the case of every want successive increments in the means of satisfaction are desired with diminishing intensity.

Utility is want-satisfying power. Successive increments of any good diminish in utility as the want endowing them with utility diminishes in intensity. The least important of a number of units of a given good is known as the marginal unit; its utility is termed marginal or final utility. In effect, the utility of any unit of a given good is no greater than that of the marginal unit. The utility of any unit, thus reduced to terms of that of the marginal unit, is effective utility.

In order that a man may direct his economic activities to the best advantage, he must often compare the effective utility of one commodity or service with that of another. The effective utility of one good thus measured by that of another is personal value. Personal values vary from individual to individual; they may, however, be reduced to approximate uniformity through imitation or through exchange. When all the personal values in a social group have been reduced to uniformity, social values emerge. These values, expressed in terms of money, are prices.

In a market prices are fixed at a level corresponding with the personal valuations of those actual buyers who are least eager to buy and those sellers who are least eager to sell. From another viewpoint, it will be seen that prices are established when the amount offered for sale at a given price just equals the amount sought by purchasers at that price, or, in other words, where demand and supply are equal.

CHAPTER III

NORMAL COMPETITIVE PRICE

1. *The market price of the most important commodities is subject to frequent fluctuations.*

Since prices depend upon the valuations of the marginal buyers and sellers, or, what amounts to the same thing, upon demand and supply — factors that are constantly changing —we should naturally expect prices to fluctuate. That they do fluctuate is easily proved, either by our daily experience in buying and selling, or by an examination of price statistics. In the period from 1915 to 1921 the average annual price of wheat rose from $1.08 per bushel in 1915 to $2.32 in 1920 and declined to $1.49 in 1921. Corn rose from 66 cents in 1915 to $1.45 in 1919 and declined to 67 cents in 1921. Cotton rose from 6.6 cents in 1915 to 35.9 cents in 1920 and declined to 11.5 cents in 1921. The war and its consequences had much to do with these remarkable price fluctuations. But even in time of peace agricultural prices vary greatly from year to year, from month to month, and even from day to day.

We are, indeed, familiar with a large class of commodities the price of which never varies. Postage stamps are always sold at uniform prices. Many patented articles, especially goods for personal use, and most copyrighted books, are sold at unvarying prices. For long periods steel rails are quoted at unvarying figures. The explanation of such steadiness in price is always the same — monopoly, in one form or another. Where there is but one seller, and that seller resolutely refuses to change his prices, there can, of course, be no price fluctuations. We shall postpone discussion of monopoly prices to the following chapter; in the present we are concerned with the laws governing prices in the competitive field.

2. *The prices of perishable commodities fluctuate more widely than do the prices of those commodities that are relatively imperishable.*

Spectacular changes are not common in the prices of durable commodities whose production can readily be increased or diminished at will. The price of pig iron, copper bars, staple cotton or leather goods does not fluctuate widely in brief periods of time. These goods will keep. If there is no demand for them to-day, they may be held over for weeks or months or years. The producer will hold them for the recovery of demand, reducing his current production if necessary. If it happens that they are forced to unusually low prices, buyers can afford to lay in stocks, and their increased buying works to send prices up toward the usual level. The prices of such commodities as strawberries, fresh vegetables, and fresh fish may easily advance or decline 100 per cent in a single week. With progress in methods of preserving such commodities, the range of price fluctuations is reduced. We do not buy perishable commodities at such low prices, nor at such high prices, as were known before refrigeration came into common use.

3. *The range of price fluctuations grows less with improvements in transportation and the extension of the market.*

In the early part of the nineteenth century England, through the policy of levying heavy duties on imported wheat, forced her population to rely almost exclusively upon the domestic supplies of grain. As a consequence of this policy a good season meant very low prices, a bad season very high ones. In 1812 the price of wheat rose to $3.84 per bushel; in 1822 the price was $1.35. To-day such a range of wheat prices is unknown in England except when ocean transportation is disorganized by war. Wheat is imported from all quarters of the globe, and it is impossible that all the world should have a bad season at one time. If the American crop is short, it is highly probable that the crop of India or Argentina will be exceptionally heavy.

Improvements in railway transportation have made possible the carriage of perishable commodities over great distances. Fresh fish from the Columbia river on our northwest coast are now carried to England when the prices in the English market are high enough to justify the expense of transportation. This keeps the local price of fish from falling so low as it otherwise would, when the catch is heavy, and keeps the English price from rising so high as it otherwise would when the North Sea fisheries yield a short supply.

We are safe in saying that modern improvements in transportation and market organization tend to eliminate sharp fluctuations, limited to a small area, and to substitute more moderate fluctuations, extending over wide areas.

4. *Competitive prices tend toward a theoretical level which may be called the normal, since every deviation from this level is followed by a reaction.*

At times market prices rest at a level that every one knows is too high or too low to be maintained for any long period. Such prices we naturally regard as abnormal. A certain fabric comes into vogue; everybody must have it, and, as there is not an indefinite amount of it, the price rises. Perhaps it was worth $1 a yard before fashion touched it with its magic wand; the price may easily become $5. Now, is this price one that is likely to continue — even supposing that the fashion should be transformed into a custom, and the enlarged demand for the fabric should thus become permanent? Would it be safe for one to buy large stocks of this cloth, with the expectation of selling them at $5 a yard? Would it be wise for one to put up a mill for the manufacture of this kind of goods, with the expectation that the high price would continue? There are conceivable conditions under which one might prudently do these things; but in most cases this would be very bad business. Most probably, the price would sink again toward the $1 mark. In all likelihood $1 is about what that fabric will sell for in the long run.

If for any reason the price of wheat rises to $3 a bushel, we can predict with absolute certainty that the number of sellers will go on increasing until the price comes down; $3 for wheat is therefore an abnormal, or unnatural, price. On the other hand, if the price falls to fifty cents a bushel, we may be certain that in time sellers will drop out, and the price will rise. Fifty cents is an abnormal price, just as $3 is. Between the two prices must somewhere be one that is normal or natural. The market price will be constantly rising above or falling below it; yet there will always be an increase in selling when the price is above the normal, and a diminution in the number of sales when the price is below the normal; consequently the price will fluctuate about this point, never remaining long much above or much below it.

So it is with a large proportion of the commodities sold on the market. Their prices may at any time double; but in all probability this is a transient phenomenon. If anything is sold at an extremely low price — a price that has rarely been known before — probably this also is a transient phenomenon. And just as it would be bad business to buy large stocks, or build factories, in anticipation of the continuance of excessively high prices, so it would be folly to quit a business, or sell out all one's stock, because of excessively low prices. The business man who is most likely to succeed is the one who has a due appreciation of normal price and who directs his business, so far as it is concerned with a more or less distant future, in accordance with the laws of normal price. Accordingly great practical importance attaches to normal price. And in so far as it determines the direction of the productive forces of society, it is of the highest importance to the student of economics, as well as to the man of affairs. This is true even though actual prices may at any given time be above or below the normal, and may perhaps never remain for an appreciable time at precisely the normal level.

5. *The forces which cause prices to hover about a normal level originate in the field of production or supply.*

Prices, we have seen, rise or fall in consequence of changes either in demand or in supply. The most violent fluctuations in price are, as a rule, due to changes in demand. Consider the fall in price, in the early autumn, of summer clothing. Increase in supply has nothing to do with this price change; decrease in demand is the sole explanation. Compare the price of a striking style of women's hats, at the height of their popularity, with their price when another style of hat gains the ascendency. The forces of demand originate, in large part, in caprice, individual and social. Were prices determined solely by these forces it would be vain to search for a law of normal price.

The forces governing supply, on the other hand, admit of a reasonable degree of calculation. Supply is controlled, in a measure, by chance, as in the case of the products of the soil, which may be abundant or scarce according to the season. Far more important, in the control of supply, are the decisions of producers, and these decisions are usually the result of calculations, not caprice. A man raises hogs or peas or even roses, not because it pleases him to do so, but because he thinks it "pays."

The supply of most commodities may be increased or diminished at the will of the producers. Many producers are in a position to increase their output by slightly enlarging their working force, or by running overtime. Some producers are engaged in the manufacture of a number of different commodities, or of grades of one kind of commodity. By discontinuing the production of some of these and concentrating their energies on a single one, they exert an influence upon supply. Moreover, there are always some persons who are in doubt whether or not they shall enter upon a certain line of production; still others, now engaged in that line of production, are in doubt whether or not they shall go out of business.

When the price of a given commodity is very high, factories producing that commodity run on full time, or overtime; factories that would otherwise have produced several other commodities turn all their energies in this direction; manufacturers who were in doubt as to whether or not they should go on producing, find their doubt stilled; and new producers are lured into the industry. All this makes for an increased supply and a falling price. How long will the expansion of business continue?

6. *Normal price is that price which just covers the cost of production.*

The two factors determining the business conduct of a producer are price and cost of production. In the cost of production are included the value of materials used and the wear and tear and general depreciation of machinery, buildings, lands; interest on all capital used, whether borrowed or owned by the producer; wages of all labor, whether hired or that of the producer himself; premiums to insurance companies for the assumption of the risk of destruction of buildings and stock, or an equivalent return for risk if borne by the producer himself; taxes, water rates, etc. If the price of a commodity exceeds its cost, including in the term all the above-named elements, the supply of the commodity can be profitably increased. If the price just equals cost, there is no sufficient reason for either increasing or diminishing the supply. If the price is less than cost, the supply will diminish.

Suppose that it costs an average manufacturer $1 to produce a yard of woolen cloth. If he can sell it for $1, he will probably go on producing about as much this month as he did last. For this price enables him to pay his operatives, to pay interest on capital borrowed, to pay taxes and insurance premiums, etc. It also affords him as much of a reward for his labor of management as he could get if he placed his services at another manufacturer's disposal; and as large a return on his own capital as he could get from any other equally safe investment. But suppose the price rises to $1.10. For every yard he can sell he gets ten cents over and above all costs. This amount we shall call a net profit. Of course he desires to sell as many yards as possible. He works his mill to its fullest capacity; if he has looms that are nearly worn out, he makes haste to replace them with more efficient machinery; if he has been contemplating the erection of an annex to his mill, he pushes the work forward as rapidly as he can. Every other manufacturer in his line does the same, and in time the increased supply of the fabric forces the price down, until it reaches $1, where the manufacturer no longer has any reason for increasing operations. Possibly the price goes still lower and reaches ninety cents. This does not pay all costs, but the manufacturer may still continue to produce, as it may be better for him to pocket his loss than to let the mill stand idle. But it is plain that he will curtail operations wherever he can. He will discharge his least efficient workmen, and discontinue the use of his least efficient machines. Every other manufacturer, in greater or less degree, will do likewise. So the supply falls away and the price rises toward $1. This, then, is the normal price — a price that just covers cost of production.

7. *While it may be to the interest of the producers of a commodity, as a body, to limit production and so maintain prices at a high level, it is to the interest of each individual producer to extend his own production.*

If, then, the price of a commodity exceeds cost, forces are set in motion which tend to bring the price back to the cost level. Now, every producer desires an excess of price above cost, and the greater the excess, the better he likes it. If a manufacturer can produce a certain fabric at a total cost of $1, and can sell it at $1.10, he enjoys a very comfortable net profit; and the same thing is true of all other manufacturers in the same line, and they might continue to secure this net profit if each one would refrain from enlarging his output. There is, then, something illogical in the conduct of the several producers. Each of them is eager to get as large a sum of net profit as possible; but the result of their action is that nobody long continues to get any net profit at all.

The reason for this is that when producers are numerous, each contribut'ng only a small percentage of the aggregate product, no single one of them can exert a perceptible influence upon price through any practicable increase in his operations. Suppose our manufacturer increases his output 100 per cent. Probably this does not reduce the price one fiftieth of a cent a yard. Therefore he obtains nearly twice as large a sum of net profit as he would have done if he had kept his output unchanged in volume. The temptation to increase his output, then, is very strong; it is strengthened by the fact that he knows that every one of the other thousand producers is subject to the same temptation; some will yield to it, then others, finally all; and those who yield first will be the ones who will get the greatest sum of profit. Under the conditions, the best thing for the manufacturer to do is to yield to the temptation the moment it offers.

And this is what must inevitably occur where competition exists — where each producer may increase his output if he desires to do so. However much it may be against the interests of all the members of a group of producers to increase operations, it is to the interest of each one to increase his own operations, if the price of his products exceeds their total cost.

Often, in American history, have different classes of producers planned a universal curtailment of production, in order to force prices above cost level and hold them there. At one time the producers of raw petroleum, at another time the producers of wheat, at still another time the producers of cotton, have beguiled themselves with such plans. If each cotton producer would plant ten per cent less ground next year, the price of cotton would probably rise twenty per cent, and every producer would get more money for less labor. Suppose that the cotton producers make a general agreement to this effect. Well, every producer who violates his agreement, and doubles his acreage, will get the benefit of the high price, and the additional benefit from an unusually large quantity to sell. Each producer, having his own interest at heart, and suspecting the integrity of the motives of others, is under the strongest temptation to increase his output. Some will refrain from doing so; but enough will increase their acreage to keep cotton very near to cost price.

But let us suppose that the cotton producers are able to bind themselves legally to diminish production, ten, twenty, fifty per cent, or are able to form an association whose ruthless use of physical force terrorizes each individual into observing the restrictions on production fixed by the association, as has at times been done in the narrower field of tobacco production. In that case prices will cease to hover about cost of production. They will be such as always to afford a net profit. Such prices, in contrast with normal or competitive prices, are called monopoly prices. They are controlled by laws, but these laws are quite different from those which prevail in competitive industry.

8. *Deviations from the normal level of prices are quickly or slowly corrected according to the ease or difficulty with which expansion and contraction of production take place.*

If one out of a number of grades of ordinary cotton cloth rises to an abnormally high price, the supply of that grade of cloth increases almost immediately. The labor and machinery that have been employed in producing other grades are diverted to the production of the grade that is in demand. A few weeks or months probably suffice to bring the price back to the normal level. If the price of all grades of cotton cloth rises above the normal, a longer period of readjustment is necessary. New factories must be built; new workers trained for the industry. If the industry has been long established, indeed, expansion can take place in less time than would be required if the industry were newly established. Let us say that there are, in a long established industry, 1000 mills producing the same grade of goods and selling them in a common market at a uniform price. Fifty of these mills become so dilapidated each year, through age, that they are dismantled; fifty mills of equal capacity must be put up each year in order to maintain a constant supply of goods. If prices are so low that not all costs of production are covered, no new mills are erected to take the place of those which are abandoned, and a part of the supply fails. If prices are above cost, instead of fifty new mills, there may be 100, and the increased supply tends to draw prices back toward the cost level.

When an industry is new, to be sure, adjustment does not take place so automatically. All the mills are, by assumption, new, and presumably nearly equal in efficiency. If prices rise, new mills are erected, but if prices fall there are none that will be dismantled. All will suffer together. This is a condition which often occurs in countries like the United States where many industries are still in a state of rapid expansion.

9. *In agriculture, the uncertainties of the seasons often interfere with the operation of the laws of normal price.*

If the price of wheat is high this year, more than a normal acreage will probably be sown to wheat next year. The average yield per acre may, however, be low next year and the price of wheat may remain high, thus inducing farmers to sow a still larger acreage the year following. A succession of good years may then ensue, with the result that prices become abnormally low and the wheat acreage is much reduced. No evidence of over-production is conclusive enough to deter farmers from planting the crop for which their fields are most suitable. They sow in hope of high prices, only to be frustrated. Each season's low prices come upon the farmer unawares. He probably ascribes them to some cause other than the true one, and continues in his course of over-production, perhaps for years. Conversely, high prices may be ascribed to false causes — speculation, failure of crops abroad, etc. — and consequently fail to set in motion the corrective influence of expanding supply. It is only by keeping in view a number of years that we can discern a normal price level for agricultural products.

10. *Deviations from the normal price level are greatest where production requires antecedent preparations extending over a period of years.*

Every one who has lived in a fruit-growing country has had his attention drawn to the extraordinary returns sometimes secured by the owners of orchards. Some fifteen years ago the product of a cherry orchard in the Santa Clara valley was sold, on the tree, for $200 or more per acre, and a failure of the cherry crop is a rare occurrence. Land similar to that upon which the cherry trees were grown was to be had at $150 an acre; the cost of planting an acre, and caring for the young trees up to the time when they became productive, would probably have been covered by an equal sum. A $200 return on a $300 investment looks very attractive, certainly. Why did not more persons enter the business of cherry production? Because several years would have had to elapse before they could secure any returns, and in the meantime the price of cherries might have fallen so low that there would not have been even a fair return in their production.

In 1885 a Nebraska landowner planted 200 acres of catalpa trees. In 1907 he cut the trees and sold the product — posts, telephone poles, and wood — for a sum which, after paying at a liberal rate for all labor in the care of his trees and in cutting and marketing them, yielded over 10 per cent compound interest on his original outlay for land and for planting. This is an unusually high return on landed investment in that part of the country. Why then after this demonstration did not more men plant catalpa trees? Well, who could foresee the prices that would prevail twenty years later? It is entirely conceivable that for a hundred years or more those who plant trees will receive an abnormally high return on their investments. On the other hand, the business of tree planting may easily be carried to an extreme, with the result that for a long period of time those who plant trees will receive practically no return.

11. *Where several commodities are the result of a single process of production, it is impossible to determine the cost of each one separately. The group as a whole has a normal price; the separate commodities have not.*

Some commodities are invariably produced together, as beef and hides, cotton and cotton seed, wool and mutton. In most great industries, it is found possible to make use of parts of the raw material that are ordinarily regarded as waste. Thus, in the refining of petroleum, besides the main products, kerosene and gasolene, a host of by-products — lubricants, tars, dyes, etc. — are produced. How much does it cost to produce each of these? Nobody can tell. They could not be produced at all, in commercial quantities, were it not for the immense capital engaged primarily in the production of kerosene and gasolene. Part of the cost of the use of that capital ought to be counted as cost of by-products. But it is not possible to say how great that part should be. No one can say how much it costs to produce hides, or cotton seed, or wool. There is, of course, an ascertainable cost, and hence a definite normal value, of live cattle, of sheep, of unginned cotton, of petroleum products as a whole. If the price of beef, added to the price of hides and other by-products, is more than reasonable compensation for the cost of raising cattle, the business of cattle-raising tends to expand. And so with other cases of joint products.

The same principle is very clearly illustrated in the business of transportation. A ship or a railway train may carry passengers of different classes, as well as a wide variety of baggage and freight. How much does it cost a railway company to carry a particular passenger from Chicago to New York? From one point of view the cost appears to be almost nothing. The train would run even if this passenger remained in Chicago. An empty seat would be hauled from city to city, instead of an occupied one. The passenger adds his weight to the load that the engine must draw, but a few cents would easily cover this cost. What is true of one passenger is true of any other; he could be carried for nothing, if the costs entailed by his presence were alone considered. The cost of running the train, however, is a very large sum, and this is the immediate cost of carrying the passengers as a body.

But the cost of running trains is not the whole cost of the service of the railway company. The track must be kept in repair; interest must be paid on capital invested in roadbed, terminals, etc. How much of this cost is assignable to the passenger service, how much to the freight service? It is impossible to say. Of the total cost of operating the railway a certain percentage, usually a small one, can be assigned definitely to the cost of running passenger trains: wages of crews, wear and tear on engines and cars and interest on the capital invested in them. Another percentage may be assigned to the freight service. But the greater part of the cost will remain, to be distributed between the two services more or less arbitrarily. Railway accountants sometimes attempt to assign costs more definitely than this, but their results are artificial.

12. *The cost of production varies from establishment to establishment. At any given time normal price is determined by the costs of those who produce under the greatest disadvantages, or the marginal producers.*

Where the cost of a particular commodity is ascertainable, and any one is free to enter upon its production, the price constantly tends toward the level of cost. Cost, then, may be said to determine normal value. It is, however, to be borne in mind that cost itself is something variable and fluctuating. Cost of production in any industry is greater for some producers than for others. A given grade of cotton goods may be produced either in Rhode Island or in North Carolina. It may cost an average of ten cents a yard in Rhode Island, and nine cents a yard in North Carolina. Some Rhode Island factories are better than others; perhaps the cost of producing the cloth is eight cents in the best factories and twelve cents in the worst equipped ones. And similar gradations may exist in North Carolina. So when we say that normal price is fixed by cost of production, exactly what do we mean? Average cost? Greatest cost? Least cost?

It may be supposed that a factory which produces at a cost of eight cents will run on full time, and with full working force, if the price is $8\frac{1}{2}$ cents. If the price is ten or twelve cents, it can do no more, unless it can be expanded by the erection of an annex. Let us suppose that it would take a year to construct such an annex and get it into working order. In the meantime the factory produces as much as it can when the price rises; but so it would have done if the price had not risen. So far as this factory is concerned, the rise in price does not immediately create an expansion of supply that reacts upon the price. This factory, then, cannot be said to be in a position to control prices.

But let us suppose that there are other factories which produce at a cost of nine, ten, eleven, twelve cents a yard. So long as the price remains at $8\frac{1}{2}$ cents, none of these, we may assume, will be in operation. As soon as the price rises to nine cents, the factories producing at that cost will open their doors, and by increasing the supply of goods, will tend to check further rise in prices. If prices rise nevertheless, the factories producing at a cost of ten cents will begin operations, and will exert their influence on supply and on price. When the price rises to twelve cents, it will be the factories producing at this cost that will tend to check a further rise in price. When the price is twelve cents, the costs of production of the better equipped mills — those producing at eight and one half, nine, ten, and eleven cents — have little to do with the determining of price. If the price rose a little higher, or fell a little lower, these factories would continue to produce exactly as much as they do when the price remains at twelve cents. They do not, therefore, regulate the supply. This the twelve-cent mills do, since, if the price falls, they are ready to drop out, and reduce supply.

It is not to be understood, however, that a manufacturer can say: "I produce at a cost of twelve cents; I must have at least that price," and so force the price up to twelve cents. If the market demands that manufacturer's contribution to the supply, it must pay twelve cents for every part of the supply. The manufacturer in the least favorable position cannot fix the price at his cost. He can only withhold what he might have supplied, and so bring to bear upon the market some small pressure, making for higher prices.

It is only in a restricted sense, then, that we can say that normal prices are fixed by cost of production. Those who produce at a cost of twelve cents, by their action in placing a product on the market or withholding it, make an attempt at holding the price at that point. Perhaps the task is too great for them; the price slips away; and those producing at a cost of eleven cents make an endeavor, by the same means, to hold prices at their cost level. They also may be unequal to the task, but at last the price rests in the hands of producers who are just able to hold it at their costs. We may think of these as being on the fringe or "margin" of production; they are often called, in economics, the marginal producers.

13. *In the long run competitive prices tend toward the level of costs of the most efficient producers.*

The price does not, however, rest permanently with the same marginal producers. Those producers whose costs are less than the price are continually reaping profits; they invest them in new mills, equally well equipped, and borrow capital further to increase their productive capacity. In time they greatly increase their output, and this tends to reduce the price of the commodity. The marginal producers find the burden of holding the price at their cost level growing heavier and heavier; soon the price breaks away from them altogether, and is held for a time at the cost level of slightly more efficient producers. But the most efficient producers continue to enlarge their works; an increasing supply is thrown upon the market, and the price settles to a still lower level, where it equals cost to producers who formerly enjoyed a slight profit. In this way prices are continually gravitating toward the level of cost of the most efficient producers.

It may therefore be said that for a short period price is determined by the costs of production of those who produce at the greatest expense, but whose contribution to the supply is necessary in order that the existing demand may be met. In the progress of time, however, such producers are unable to hold prices at their cost level, and are forced out of business. The final adjustment — if it should ever be attained — would leave price at the level of cost to the most efficient producers, all of whom would stand on a plane of equality as to costs.

This does not mean, however, that the price of a given commodity must continue to decrease. The cost itself may increase, for the more efficient as well as for the less efficient producers. As we have used the term, cost includes the value of raw materials and fuel; interest on capital, whether fixed in land, buildings, and machinery, or invested in raw materials, etc.; wages of all labor employed; and a number of lesser items — taxes, insurance premiums, etc. Now, every one of these elements in cost is perpetually fluctuating in magnitude according to its own peculiar laws. The sources of raw material may be approaching exhaustion; wages and interest may be rising; taxes may be growing heavier. But while such an increase in costs may prevent the more efficient factory from producing as cheaply as before, it burdens the less efficient proportionately. It cannot, then, prevent prices from tending toward costs to the most efficient producer.

14. *Summary.*

The market prices of commodities are subject to continual fluctuations. These fluctuations are greatest in the case of commodities that rapidly deteriorate and that are dependent upon a local market. Despite such fluctuations there is a discernible tendency toward a normal level of prices. This level is determined by the cost of production. The force that causes market prices to hover about cost of production is competition between the several producers.

The ease or difficulty with which supply may be increased or diminished determines the degree of possible deviation of prices from the normal level. Marked deviations are frequent in the case of agricultural products, since unforeseen seasonal influences are constantly vitiating the calculations of the producers. Great deviations are possible where production is governed by calculations looking to the remote future.

The costs of production in every industry vary considerably from establishment to establishment. In short periods of time the costs of those establishments which labor under the greatest disadvantage play a chief part in determining prices. In the long run prices tend toward the level of cost of those establishments which enjoy the greatest advantages in production.

CHAPTER IV

MONOPOLY PRICE

1. *The price of a commodity may be controlled by dealers or producers through control of supply.*

As has been shown in the preceding chapter, the mechanism which keeps prices hovering about cost of production consists in the automatic adjustment of supply to demand. If price rises, supply increases, and thus price is forced down again. If then the supply of a commodity can be controlled by the producers, the price is, in some measure, also within their control. With this control, the producers are in the happy situation where they can, within limits, enrich themselves at their pleasure. It is no wonder, then, that producers and dealers from very early times have sought to bring supply under control. Joseph controlled the total supply of grain in Egypt, we are told; he was thereby enabled to charge whatever prices he pleased, and the prices he fixed were such that he got in exchange for his grain all the possessions that the Egyptians had. In ancient and mediæval times, when roads were bad and the costs of carriage prohibitive, whoever should buy up the stock of grain in a town would make himself practically master of the town. He could measure out the grain in small quantities, charging whatever prices seemed good to him.

To-day, as in earlier times, business men are constantly seeking to gain control over the prices of the commodities in which they deal. That some are at least partially successful in this is shown by the great number of articles the prices of which do not vary. Price control extends, however, far beyond the field of constant prices. A man who has absolute control over the sale of a commodity may be expected to fix high prices in times of prosperity, low prices in times of depression, and in many cases this policy appears to be followed by those men who now have practical control of the prices of the commodities which they sell.

2. *Power to control prices is commonly termed monopoly.*

In the strictest sense of the term, monopoly is the exclusive privilege of selling a commodity or a service. Most governments have a monopoly, in this sense, of the postal service. Some governments monopolize the sale of tobacco; others, the sale of salt; still others, the sale of spirituous liquors. The exclusive privilege of sale is sometimes granted by government to private individuals or corporations. A common example of this kind of monopoly is the patent by which an inventor is assured control over the use of his invention, or the copyright by which an author is given control over the sale of his book. In many cases a private corporation is given the exclusive right to supply a city with water, gas, or electric light. In some cities only one street railway company is chartered, and in some countries steam railway companies are given monopolies of the transportation service within specified areas. Monopolies created by law, then, are both numerous and important. In a democratic state they are not likely to grow into a serious abuse; in a state where the government is not really controlled by the people, such monopolies may become exceedingly oppressive.

3. *A partial monopoly can be established by private persons, through agreements fixing prices or limiting supply.*

Let us suppose that the producers of a given commodity agree among themselves not to sell below a certain price, or, what leads to the same result, not to produce more than an amount so small as to command scarcity prices. If producers are few — say half a dozen — such an agreement may stand. No one can materially increase his sales without attracting attention; moreover, no one can increase his sales without an immediate effect on price. If the producers number millions, such an agreement is empty words; almost any one can violate it without detection, and without any appreciable effect on price. And the number of violators of the agreement will be so great that no control of supply or of price can be exercised.

When the number of producers is small, then, there may be effective control of supply. But such control cannot long be retained unless new producers can be kept out of the field.

The producers of cotton yarn of the higher grades are not very numerous. It is therefore conceivable that they might agree to limit supply and force the price to a point paying a "fair" profit. But it is not a difficult matter to build and equip a mill to produce a given grade of cotton yarn. If, then, the price were forced to a high level, new producers would soon appear. These would enjoy the benefit of the high price, although to effect sales they would have to cut prices slightly. The original producers would have to reduce their prices; the new producers would then cut still lower, and so on until the price had reached cost of production. Indeed, the price would almost certainly go lower than this, for the number of producers, each striving to get more customers, would have increased. The last state of the cotton yarn business, accordingly, would be far worse than its first. We have had in America not a few examples of attempted monopolies which in the end merely intensified competition.

4. *Permanent price control may be secured through control over some element essential to production, such as labor, raw material, means of transportation.*

If the industry which it is sought to monopolize requires a very high grade of skilled labor, and the members of the combination control the whole supply of labor of this grade, the monopoly may rest secure until new labor can be trained for the shops of would-be competitors. If the only satisfactory way of training such labor is through apprenticeship under men already working in the trade, it becomes difficult indeed for a competitor to get an independent supply of labor. This situation might become a serious one in some industries were it not for the fact that it is not easy for one set of employers permanently to control their workmen. The latter know that at any time they can thwart their employers' monopolistic schemes by accepting employment with competitors; and this knowledge is made good use of, in forcing constantly higher wages. Where monopolies of this kind have arisen, they have usually broken down because of disputes between the employers and their workmen.

Some products depend upon supplies of raw material that are found in comparatively few parts of the earth, and in limited quantity. If a combination of producers can get possession of all or most of the mining or agricultural lands which are capable of yielding a certain product they may win their desired freedom from the danger of new competitors. Anthracite coal, for example, is found only in a restricted area in the United States. A combination of capitalists of very great wealth might with comparative ease control the total output — and indeed, something of the kind now exists. Such a combination has nothing to fear from new competitors, although of course it must meet the competition of producers of other fuels.

In the history of the American petroleum industry, there was a time when the Standard Oil Company, through ownership of pipe lines, enjoyed an immense advantage over its competitors, who were compelled to ship petroleum over the railways. The Standard Oil Company was not, indeed, enabled by this advantage to destroy competition entirely; its control over supply was, however, notably strengthened by the ownership of the pipe lines. And even when pipe lines were by law made common carriers, required to serve all on equal terms, their location, designed first of all to serve the Standard Oil Company, continued to afford an advantage to that company.

5. *Permanent price control is sometimes maintained through the systematic intimidation of competitors.*

Let us suppose that there is a combination of the more important producers of coal, who yet have nothing like complete ownership of the coal lands, and that there are a number of small competitors whose natural market is a city which we will call X. Other markets, we will assume, are so far distant that cost of transportation prohibits their supply from the mines of the small producers. The combine, let us say, has mines from which it can supply the market X, as well as a great number of mines supplying other cities. If, then, it desires to destroy the business of its small competitors, it may decide, for a while, to sell coal in X for less than the cost of raising it from the pit. This the combination can afford to do, because it is enjoying high profits from its monopolistic position in the supplying of other markets. Of course the small competitors can sell no coal at prices which will meet those of the combine; very soon they become discouraged and retire from business. Then the combine can raise prices of coal in X to a profit-yielding point. The small producers will probably not again attempt to compete, knowing that the same tactics will again be employed to destroy their business.

Of course, if coal were easy to transport, this method would prove very expensive to the monopolistic combination. An enterprising dealer in the town X, finding that the combination sold coal there at much lower prices than in town Y, might buy up coal in the former place and ship it to the latter. On every ton of coal sold in X, we have assumed, the combination is losing money; and every ton sold in Y helps to depress the price there, to the further disadvantage of the combine. In a sense, it would be underselling itself.

Accordingly, some other method of destroying competitors must be employed when the commodities which it is sought to monopolize are of little weight and bulk, as compared with their value, and hence easily transported. Suppose that a monopolistic combination controls most of the manufacture of cigars, and that an overbold outsider, eager to share the benefits of high prices, enters the field. He may place on the market an excellent brand of cigars, charging for them less than the combine charges for similar ones. The combine cannot lower the prices of all cigars in the competitor's vicinity, for in that case dealers will buy them up and express them to all parts of the country; and thus the combine will be inflicting losses upon itself. But there is another method which it may find efficacious.

Let us say that the independent producer calls his brand of cigars the "Rex." It is his all; his fortune is bound up with its fate. The combine has 500 brands; it makes profits on all of them. Accordingly, it can afford to put out a new brand of cigars — say the "Regina" — for half the price of the Rex, though of as good quality, and place it on the market wherever the Rex is sold. Before long the Rex is no longer purchased; its producer goes out of business. Then the combine puts worse tobacco into the Regina, until at last, like all its other products, this cigar is dear at the price.

6. *Monopolies that are not based upon privileges granted by government are rarely complete, and consequently are influenced in the fixing of prices by fear of competition.*

To destroy a competitor is a proceeding that almost always involves heavy expense. If a powerful combination desires to destroy a small but vigorous competitor, it is often obliged to sell below cost, not only to those persons who actually deal with the competitor, but also to many other persons in the same market. The combination can compel its competitor to lose money, but in so doing it loses money itself — sometimes ten dollars for every dollar its competitor loses. Accordingly, it is often cheaper for a combination to buy up the plant of a competitor, even at an unreasonably high price, than to force the plant to close down through price-cutting. If the competitor refuses to sell to the combination, the latter may adopt a "live and let live" policy, agreeing to respect the competitor's right to his territory and established trade, so long as he does not appear obnoxiously active in increasing his business. All the great American trusts have competitors toward whom they observe a policy of toleration. The trust sets a price upon its products, and the independent concern sells at the same price. If, however, this price is so high as to offer great profits, the independent concerns grow stronger and stronger, and in the end extend their business, encroaching upon the field of the monopoly.

It is not alone the competition of the existing independent concerns that a monopoly has to fear. Very high prices are likely to induce new competitors to enter the field. Such competitors must either be driven from the field by the expensive policy of price-cutting, or some of the business of the monopoly must be surrendered to them. In fixing prices, then, the monopolist must have regard not only for actual competition, but also for such competition as might arise, or *potential competition.*

7. *A complete monopoly will fix prices at a level that yields the maximum return above all costs.*

Suppose that a monopoly has complete control of the salt that is to be sold in the United States. It may cost one cent a pound to produce it. At what price will the monopoly sell it? If the price is one cent, perhaps one billion pounds can be sold. If the price were raised to two cents, who would eat his food unsalted? Who would economize salt in the least? It is safe to say that there are few persons in the United States so poor that they would not go on eating as much salt as before. And the same thing would be true if the price were raised to five cents a pound — a price of which four fifths would be monopoly profit.

But not all the salt is for table use; a large part of the total supply is used for live stock and for manufacturing purposes. If the price of salt rises, the use of it for these purposes declines. When salt is very cheap many farmers scatter it on the ground for their cattle, or leave it in troughs with no shelter, where the weather devours more of it than do the cattle. High price would mean economy. So, at two cents a pound, probably not more than 900,000,000 pounds will be used, instead of 1,000,000,000. At five cents a pound the amount taken might shrink to 800,000,000 pounds; at ten cents, to 700,000,000; at twenty, to 500,000,000. Were the price forced up to $1 a pound, very likely great economy would be exercised even in the use of salt in human food. Perhaps not more than 80,000,000 pounds would be used.

Now, while the monopoly would make the enormous profit of ninety-nine cents a pound at the last-mentioned price, this would be a very irrational price for it to set. The total profit from the sale of salt would, according to our assumed volume of sales, be $79,200,000. And this would be much better than selling 1,000,000,000 pounds at cost, or 900,000,000 at two cents. The latter price would yield just $9,000,000 profit. At five cents the monopoly would get a profit of $32,000,000; at ten cents, of $63,000,000; at twenty cents, of $95,000,000. So twenty cents is really a more profitable price for the monopoly than $1. At twenty-five cents, however, 400,000,000 pounds might be taken; and this would mean a profit aggregating $96,000,000. This, then, is a still better price than twenty cents, from the monopolist's point of view. Let us suppose that at thirty cents 300,000,000 pounds will be taken. The profit at this price would amount to only $87,000,000. This price, accordingly, is too high; and the best price for the monopolist lies between twenty-five and thirty cents.

Of course this would be an exorbitant price; and far more extortionate than any existing monopoly price. But given the conditions — a complete monopoly of salt — extortionate prices can be established. One must have salt; he must have a certain amount of it. There is nothing in the world that can be substituted for it. And even if the price were exorbitant, the cost of salt would form no very large item in any one's expenditure. No one would leave the country to escape the monopoly.

8. *The greater the elasticity of demand for commodities controlled by monopolies, the lower will be the price that yields the maximum monopoly profit.*

The demand for salt is peculiarly inelastic. To do without salt altogether is impossible; to reduce consumption always involves hardship. Most other commodities can be replaced by substitutes. One kind of food readily takes the place of another; cottons may be replaced by woolens, linens, and silks; wood for building purposes may give way, in large degree, to stone, brick, and concrete. There is almost always an ill-defined boundary between the consumption of one commodity and that of another, and changes in relative prices shift the boundary now in one direction, now in another.

Let us suppose that a monopoly has gained control of the entire supply of beef in the United States. Perhaps the cost price at which beef can be placed on the market is ten cents a pound. With beef at this price, the American people might conceivably eat 80 pounds per capita — 8,000,000,000 pounds in round numbers. At eleven cents, some of the poorest people would cease eating beef and use mutton or pork instead, or use less meat of any kind. Perhaps the amount consumed would fall to 7,000,000,000 pounds. That would give the beef monopoly a princely income — $70,000,000. At twelve cents the amount consumed might fall to 6,000,000,000 pounds; but this would yield a net profit of $120,000,000; and if the amount at thirteen cents fell to 5,000,000,000 pounds, the profit would yet amount to $150,000,000. Fourteen cents and 4,000,000,000 pounds would be still better for the monopoly — $160,000,000. But fifteen cents and 3,000,000,000 pounds would be a step backward, for the profit would be only $150,000,000. Fourteen cents, then, is the most that the monopoly could wisely charge.

Of course, if the demand does not shrink so rapidly as I have assumed, the maximum price can safely be placed at a higher figure. If the shrinkage is more rapid than I have assumed, fourteen cents is too high.

As the number of commodities offered to the public for consumption is continually increasing, it is safe to say that the average consumer grows less and less dependent upon any one. Demand, accordingly, grows constantly more elastic, and the power of monopolies to fix prices at a high level constantly diminishes.

9. *In fixing prices, a monopoly is more or less extortionate according as it pays less or more attention to the ulterior effects of high prices.*

If it is the intention of the monopolist simply to exploit the beef market for one year, — to corner the present supply, make the most out of it, and then retire to live on his plunder, — he may find that at fourteen cents there will be no greater shrinkage of demand than has been assumed in the foregoing example, and this will then be the best price for him to set. Most persons who are accustomed to this article of diet will continue to buy it even at the higher price. But in a year, more and more of them will form other habits. A corner in beef organized in the following year might not be able to charge more than twelve cents without diminishing total net profit; and in the third year a corner might not be able to charge more than eleven cents. Accordingly, a monopolist who does not mean to retire from business must generally avoid charging a price that would give the highest possible returns for one year. He must fix prices in such a way as to keep the bulk of his custom from year to year. And this is one reason why modern monopolists are less extortionate than the ancient and mediæval "engrossers" of the necessaries of life. As a rule, the modern monopolist hopes for steadily increasing profits from a growing business; he therefore cultivates his clientèle through prices that are moderate.

If a ring of speculators of immense wealth should buy up the entire American cotton crop, they could fix the price of cotton at twice the normal price, and yet sell most of it. Cotton fabrics would advance in price, but not proportionately, for many persons would go without cotton cloth rather than pay unreasonably high prices. The profits of cotton manufacturers would fall; wages of cotton operatives would be reduced. The cotton manufacture would decline; many cotton operatives would go into other employments. Cotton production in Egypt, India, and Australia would be stimulated. It would take more than a year, however, for such adjustments to take place. In the meantime the speculators would have sold their cotton at high prices, and reaped their extortionate profits. The injury occasioned by the changes in cotton manufacture would fall upon the producers of the succeeding American cotton crops.

If a combination of capitalists were to secure possession of the entire business of petroleum refining, it would be no less easy for them to obtain exorbitant profits for one year. But the decline in consumption that would follow, when time had been given the people to provide themselves with other sources of light and power, would seriously impair the future profits of the petroleum monopoly. Now, no profit, however exorbitant, on a single year's sales, is to be compared with comfortably high profits for an indefinite series of years. Great fortunes are to be obtained through the permanent monopolization of the means of producing a commodity, rather than through cornering the visible supply and exacting excessive prices, without regard to the effect of the policy on future sales. For this reason monopolies of the permanent kind are continually increasing in number and importance, while it is only rarely that a temporary monopoly is successfully carried through.

10. *In order to secure the maximum profit, a monopolist often endeavors to classify consumers, and to burden each class according to its ability to pay high prices.*

There are some classes of consumers who will pay increased prices without a murmur, while other classes will not only feel greatly aggrieved, but will even refuse to buy, when prices are appreciably increased. To the rich it makes little difference whether beef is high or low. If the monopoly can array its customers in groups, according to their readiness to pay high prices, it can grade its prices accordingly. The classes that will endure only a slight increase in price are given prices so moderate that they continue to buy, while the classes that are less apt to complain over an increase are forced to pay prices that yield a higher profit. This is much better for the monopoly than to fix an average price which drives away the former classes, and does not exploit the latter to the highest possible degree.

How, then, can a monopoly make such a division of its customers into classes according to their profit-yielding capacity? One way consists in different prices for different localities. If there is greater per capita wealth in California than in North Dakota, a monopoly would charge higher prices in the former than in the latter state, even allowing for all costs of transportation. Suppose that the cost of production of beef for North Dakota is ten cents, and the cost of transportation practically nothing; the cost of production of beef for California we may assume is the same, and the cost of shipping two cents a pound. The beef may be sold in Dakota for eleven cents and for fifteen in California — giving a net profit of one cent in the former state and three in the latter. Of course, the difference could be as great as this only in case shipping beef in small quantities is expensive; otherwise outsiders would buy beef in Dakota at eleven cents, ship it to California, and make a good profit. And here we have one limitation upon a monopoly's power to vary its charges for different localities. The difference cannot permanently remain at a figure which is greater than the sum an outsider would have to pay in transporting the monopoly's goods from the point where they are cheap to the point where they are dear.

In the case of many goods, however, different qualities are sold to different classes of consumers. The choicest cuts of meat go to one set of consumers, and the remaining cuts, in order of toughness, to the various sets of consumers who have less to spend. Now the consumers of the cheapest beef may stand a slight increase in price before substituting something else for beef; while those who consume the best quality may see the price double before substituting even a cheaper grade. The far-sighted monopolist, then, instead of increasing the prices of all grades at a uniform rate, will so distribute the increase of price as to burden each class of customers as much as they will bear without withdrawing their custom.

In some cases where no real differences in quality exist, the consumer is made to believe that there are such differences. Some years ago — and perhaps to-day — there were several grades of salt on the market, selling at different prices. The manufacturer who produced them has admitted that they were all exactly the same. The classes who could afford to pay high prices for salt bought the grade that was alleged to be the best; those who could pay less bought cheaper grades. Thus the manufacturer, who enjoyed a limited monopoly, was able to make each class of consumers pay according to ability. It is easy to see how far this principle might be carried in the case of such articles as soap, chocolate, canned goods. It is a wise man who knows what ingredients go into these commodities; and if the manufacturer, who must know, says that one is purer and more choice than another, what can you or I do but accept his statement and pay the higher price for the so-called better quality?

11. *A monopoly may maintain prices at a higher level in the domestic market than in foreign markets.*

A few years ago a New York dealer offered for sale a considerable stock of watches of a standard American make at prices far lower than are commonly charged by the manufacturer in the same city. These watches had been purchased in England at such low prices that the dealer was able to make a handsome profit in bringing them back to America and selling them at cut prices. It is well known that American agricultural machinery is often sold more cheaply in foreign countries than at home, in spite of the cost of shipping. Before the Great War the German steel combination sold steel to the British consumer more cheaply than to the German consumer, and the American steel trust has frequently been charged with a similar discrimination in favor of foreign purchasers. The principle is a fairly common one; it is probable that of the American monopolies that have invaded foreign markets there are few that have not in some degree employed this principle.

Such discriminations are to be explained by the fact that for one reason or another the domestic consumer can be made to pay higher prices than the foreign consumer will tolerate. In some cases the American consumer can be made to pay higher prices simply because he is more addicted to careless expenditure. This explains price discriminations in the case of such articles as watches, razors, pipes, etc. In other cases the foreign consumer is favored because he can avail himself of the competition of foreign producers, who are excluded from the American market by our customs duties. This explains price discriminations in such products as steel rails. In yet other cases the discrimination is explained by the fact that the foreign consumer has access to a greater number of substitutes than the domestic consumer.

12. *In railway transportation, the principle of discriminatory charges is very widely employed under the name of "charging what the traffic will bear."*

Almost every railway is, in a limited sense, a monopoly. It may encounter competition at important business centers, but most small cities and towns are absolutely dependent upon a single line. Leaving out of account public regulation of railway rates, we may say that the railway will burden each class of shippers according to the ability of that class to pay. The shippers of silks can be made to pay a high rate per ton mile; the shippers of bricks must have a low rate, or it will be impossible for them to remain in business at all. If allowed to pursue its own devices in rate making, the railway would naturally discriminate between the different producers of the same commodity. The owner of a well-situated mill would be forced to pay a higher rate than the owner of a mill badly situated. The owner of a rich farm would be made to pay a higher rate than the owner of a poor farm. The shipper who is in a position to avail himself of the competition of a rival line would receive better rates than the shipper who can use one line only. The last form of discrimination was once exceedingly common. It is under the ban of the law and is no longer of great importance.

13. *Monopolies must endeavor to preserve their customers' prosperity, and to assist them in meeting competition.*

In spite of the fact that railways hold a monopoly position, and avail themselves of the principle of discriminatory charges, it is very seldom that a railway secures excessive profits. This is because the demand for railway service is extremely elastic. A high general level of rates "kills business." The perishable fruit of Southern California must be carried to the Eastern market over a single line of railway. But that railway cannot raise rates on fruit to a very high level without destroying the business of fruit culture in California. Though the railway itself has no competitor, the fruit growers are engaged in an active competition with those of Florida and the West Indies, and the railway must make it possible for its customers to hold their own.

In like manner, a monopoly of anthracite coal must sell this fuel at a price so low that manufacturers using anthracite are not seriously handicapped in their competition with manufacturers in other parts of the country who use bituminous coal. A monopoly of tin cans would have to fix prices at a level low enough to permit the industry of preserving fruit to hold its ground against the business of drying fruit. The lumber dealers of a town may have an inviolable agreement fixing prices, but they will not often place prices so high as to handicap the town in its competition for population and business. Monopoly prices, therefore, are not likely to be ruthlessly exorbitant. They are usually not higher than the customers of the monopolies can pay without serious impairment of their power of survival. None the less they are higher than they should be, and enable those who hold a monopoly position to draw to themselves a larger share of the social income than their services justify.

14. *Summary.*

Monopoly is attained through the control of the supply of a commodity or a service. This control may be secured through governmental restrictions or through private agreements fixing prices or limiting output. Monopolies resting merely upon the agreements of independent producers are inherently weak.

If some essential element in the production of a good can be controlled by a single enterpriser or by a group of enterprisers who are able to work in complete harmony, a wellnigh impregnable monopoly may be established. A high degree of monopolistic control is often attained through intimidation of competitors. Monopolies are seldom entirely free from competitors, and hence are compelled to fix prices at a level which offers slight inducement to competition.

A complete monopoly will fix prices with a view to securing the greatest aggregate return from the entire business. The more elastic the demand for a commodity, the lower will be the price which affords the maximum net return. When it is the aim of a monopoly to hold permanent control of the supply of a commodity, it is necessary to fix prices at a comparatively low level, in order to prevent the demand from dwindling away in the course of time.

In order to gain the greatest monopoly return with the least shrinkage of custom, it is often advisable for the monopolist to discriminate in prices, burdening heavily those who can be made to pay high prices, while levying moderate charges upon those who cannot pay high prices. In railway transportation, this practice is commonly described under the name of "charging what the traffic will bear." No enlightened monopoly will charge prices so high as to handicap its customers in their competition with persons not subject to the control of the monopoly.

CHAPTER V

THE COST OF PRODUCTION

1. *A complete explanation of prices involves a statement of the laws governing the costs of production.*

The preceding chapters have shown that the costs of production play an exceedingly important part in determining the values of goods. Commodities produced under competitive conditions tend to sell at cost; commodities the production of which is controlled by monopolies sell above cost, as a rule, but at prices which usually stand in a close relation to the costs of production. In practical life, one rarely carries the analysis of value farther than this. Costs appear to the individual producer as something fairly definite and fixed, upon which he may safely base his calculations in deciding whether or not he shall enter a given line of business.

From a business point of view the cost of producing a commodity or a service consists in the aggregate price of the commodities and services used up in the process of production. The greater part of the cost of most commodities is made up of the price of material, the price of labor, and the price of the use of the capital invested in plant. These prices the individual producer must, as a rule, accept as he finds them, just as he accepts the price of finished products as he finds it. We have seen that by increasing or reducing the volume of his production, the individual business man exerts a real, though imperceptible, influence upon the price of finished products. It is obvious, at the outset, that the individual business man must exert a like influence on the price of the commodities and services that enter into his production. If he extends his business, he must increase his demand for labor, machinery, and materials, and this cannot fail to affect the prices of these factors.

2. *The materials of production have market and normal prices governed by the same laws as the prices of finished products.*

We may examine briefly the process by which cotton yarn, the material of the cotton-weaving industry, is valued. A multitude of weavers desire to buy it; some of them would pay a price of 10 x per hundred pounds rather than go without it; others would pay only 5 x per hundred pounds. A multitude of sellers stand ready to furnish cotton yarn; some may be willing to sell at 5 x rather than not sell at all; others may be willing to sell only if the price is 10 x. What price will actually be set? Just as in the case of commodities for direct use, the market price is fixed at a point where demand and supply are equal — that is, where the amount offered at a given price is exactly equal to the amount that will be taken at that price.

But the price fixed at any moment by demand and supply may exceed the cost of producing the yarn, even in the mills of those enterprisers who produce at the greatest cost. In such case the output of cotton yarn increases, and the price falls until it just covers cost of production to those who are producing at the greatest disadvantage. If the price were to fall still lower, these producers would have to quit the business; and this would reduce supply and thus of itself tend to force up the price of cotton yarn. But the same price may be high enough to give excellent profits to the more efficient producers; these continue to extend their business, and the increase in supply from this source may be more than an offset for the decrease resulting from the closing of the less efficient mills. Thus the price gravitates steadily downward, resting momentarily at cost of production to the least efficient producers; then sinking to the cost level of slightly more efficient producers; finally resting at the level of cost of the most efficient producers of all. Thus it appears that we need no new law to explain the action of buyers and sellers of cotton yarn. They act just as they would if they were buying and selling a commodity ready for consumption.

3. *Fluctuations in the price of a product are reflected, in greater or less degree, in the prices of materials employed in making the product.*

If, through a general increase in the demand for cotton fabrics, the price of cotton cloth everywhere rises, all the manufacturers of cloth at first enjoy a profit. To increase that profit each manufacturer tries to extend his business, and this tends to bring down the price of cloth. But in order to extend the cotton cloth manufacture, more yarn must be had. The cloth manufacturers are forced to bid against one another for the existing supply of yarn, and the price of yarn rises.

We see, then, that it is not merely because of competition in the sale of finished products that such products sell at cost; it is also because of competition in the purchase of the elements of production. If the price of cloth is for a time much above cost, the expansion of the cloth manufacture tends to lower the price of cloth and raise the price of yarn and other elements in cost, until the price of cloth and its cost are again nearly equal.

Looking now at the manufacture of yarn, we see that such an increase in the price as we have assumed will result in high profits throughout the industry, and consequently will give rise to an attempt on the part of each manufacturer of yarn to increase his output. But an expansion of the spinning industry involves an increase in the demand for raw cotton. And this tends to raise the price of raw cotton as well as to reduce the price of yarn.

If, on the other hand, the price of cotton fabrics were to decline, we should see this decline reflected in the price of cotton yarn, and later in the price of raw cotton. High prices of finished products thus tend to produce high costs. Rise of costs, however, encounters an opposing tendency in increased production of the goods that make up costs.

4. *The benefits of an increased demand for a finished product may rest permanently with the producers of the crudest materials that enter into that product.*

If the demand for steel rises, the steel manufacturer gains a profit, in the first instance. This benefit is soon passed on to the producer of pig iron, in the shape of a higher price for that product. An expansion of pig iron production follows, and this entails an increased demand and a higher price for ore. Thus increased cost deprives the pig iron producer of his profit, just as it deprived the steel manufacturer of his profit. The owner of ore mines can now demand a higher price for ore, as it is found in the mine. This ore has, strictly speaking, no cost; it is a free gift of nature. The owner of ore mines, therefore, cannot be compelled to surrender his gains to an antecedent producer. So long as the increased demand for steel exists, he enjoys the benefit of high ore prices, unless new mines are discovered to compete with him.

The relation to the price of finished products of the price of crude materials, as they exist in nature, is best illustrated by examples drawn from primitive conditions, where such materials first begin to bear a value. In a newly settled country, the cost of bricks would contain no element representing clay in the bank or trees on the hillside. It would consist solely in wages of labor employed in cutting and hauling the wood, in digging and mixing the clay and shaping the bricks, and in interest on capital invested in kilns and drying sheds, etc. Bricks might at a given time sell at a price in excess of these costs; but this would cause new brickworks to be erected, and the price of bricks would fall until bricks were selling at a price merely covering cost.

As population increased, the demand for wood for brickmaking would increase, as would also the demand for wood for other purposes. In time the proprietor of woodlands would see an end of the supply within easy distances, and would demand a price for wood in the tree. Here, then, would be a new element in the cost of bricks. Further growth of population might make the supplies of suitable clay insufficient to meet all demands, present and prospective. The owner of clay deposits could therefore demand a royalty for every cubic yard of this material. If the demand for bricks continued to increase, the price of wood and of clay would steadily rise, and thus a constantly increasing proportion of the selling price of the bricks would be absorbed by the cost of the raw material.

5. *The price for the use of land, suitable for one product only, fluctuates with changes in the demand for its product.*

In some of the countries of North Europe are found extensive tide-marshes noted for the production of exceedingly nutritious grasses. These lands cannot, without great expense, be put to any other use than that of producing forage. When the price of dairy products rises, the rental of these lands rises; when the competition of inland districts forces down the price of dairy products, the rental declines. Owing to the influence of custom in maintaining ground rents at a fairly stationary level, the rental of such lands is likely to rise only after the higher level of dairy products has been established for a considerable period. But in time the value of the final product is inevitably reflected in the rental of the land.

In most cases land may be put to a variety of uses. Corn land may be put under grass, fruit, or vegetables. The rental of corn land cannot fall below the probable rental that the land would yield under other crops. But often land is so peculiarly suited, by quality or by situation, for the production of a specific crop that the price of its use comes to depend upon that one crop alone.

Let us suppose that a beet sugar manufactory is established somewhere in the heart of the wheat belt. Naturally, if a farmer wishes to rent a field upon which to grow sugar beets, he will have to pay as high a rental as wheat growers in the vicinity pay for the same quality of land.

Beet growers may find, after paying all of the costs, that a considerable profit remains in their hands from the sale of their beets. In such case this form of culture will expand, and more and more wheat land will be devoted to the growing of beets. The increasing output of beets may conceivably reduce their price; but more probably, since an enormous increase in the sugar output of a given locality is yet a very small addition to the world's sugar supply, the price of beets will remain fairly constant. Accordingly, the expansion of the industry will continue until all the good lands within a reasonable distance from the factory are given over to this branch of agriculture. If the beet growers still have a surplus profit, they will compete among themselves for land, each desiring to increase his acreage. Higher rents will be offered, until the extra profits of the enterpriser are absorbed by this increasing element in cost. If for any reason the price of sugar rises to a higher level, the rental of beet lands must also rise.

6. *Under certain conditions the wages of labor are intimately connected with the price of a particular product.*

Let us imagine that a new branch of production arises — say, the manufacture of wrapping paper from cornstalks. A single factory is erected, and let us assume that it will be operated in the winter months only. The factory we may suppose is established in the country, near the source of raw material. And in the country there is a great deal of labor that is not employed in the winter months. At what rate will our manufacturer be able to hire this labor?

It is clear that the cost of living will have nothing to do with the wages fixed. Country laborers are paid enough in the open months of the year to carry them through the winter. What they earn in the paper factory is a net addition to their annual income. They can work for nothing, and be no poorer than they were before the factory was erected. The work in the factory may be pleasant rather than otherwise. Nevertheless, it is safe to assume that some rate of wages must be paid. Perhaps wages of fifty cents a day will provide the requisite amount of labor. If so, that is all the manufacturer will pay.

Now, if the manufacturer gets his labor at such a low rate, he may make extraordinarily high profits. In this case other enterprisers are likely to go into the business. If the industry assumes extensive proportions, it soon drains off the supply of labor that can be had for fifty cents a day. Further expansion becomes possible only through an increase in wages which will tempt into the industry workmen who regard their ease as worth more than fifty cents a day, or who are earning at least so much in caring for live-stock, etc. But profits may still be high, and new enterprisers may be continually entering the business. To secure laborers they are compelled to offer wages slightly higher than those paid by the enterprisers whose business is already established. The latter, in order to retain their laborers, are compelled to meet the bids of their new competitors. Thus wages for this kind of work go up, until all the enterprisers are fully supplied with workmen.

Any further expansion will be followed by a similar increase in competition among employers of labor, and a rise in the rate of wages will be necessary in order to induce less industrious workers, or workers having some alternative employment, to enter the factories. But each expansion of the industry means an increased product thrown on the market, and, other things equal, a lower price for it. What with the rising of wages and the falling price of paper, it is clear that the profits of the enterpriser must decline. Possibly the expansion will continue until wages have risen to $3. All depends upon the amount of paper that will be taken at a given price, and the amount of labor available.

7. *The price of labor depends not only on the price of the finished product, but also on the price of other factors in production.*

Let us assume that there is a city which has been devoted almost exclusively to the manufacture of iron and steel goods. A cotton manufacturer, visiting the city — Ironton, let us call it — shrewdly concludes that the iron worker must have a number of sisters and daughters and other female relatives, who are practically wasting their time, and who would be glad to earn a small income by cotton spinning and weaving. Accordingly he erects a mill at Ironton. Possibly he will get all the labor he cares for at a dollar a day, while his competitors, in the established centers of the trade, are paying two dollars a day for the same grade of labor. In this case the cost of producing a given grade of cotton at Ironton may be twenty per cent lower than the cost of producing the same grade in the older centers, while the selling price must be about the same since cottons are easily transported from one center to another. Of course this will give the enterpriser at Ironton large profits. Before long other enterprisers will begin to inquire why a cotton mill has been set up at Ironton; and finding what advantages that city offers in the way of low costs, they too will erect mills there.

The effect of the appearance of these new manufactures at Ironton is to increase the demand for cheap labor. Possibly there are so many women and girls who are ready to work for "pin money" that the new mills can be plentifully supplied with labor at the same price that has been paid by the enterpriser first in the field. But it cannot be a great while before the supply of dollar labor falls short of the demand; enterprisers erecting new mills will have to offer slightly higher wages to entice workers away from the older mills, and these will have to raise wages to the rate offered by the new comers. The competition will continue until wages are so high as to induce a new set of workers to enter the mills. Costs at Ironton may still be abnormally low after wages have risen, say, to a dollar and a half a day. In that case the cotton industry at Ironton will go on expanding, until at last aggregate costs are as great at Ironton as in the older centers of the trade.

The point that here needs emphasis is that the competition of different centers equalizes, not wages cost, but aggregate costs. Coal may be cheaper at Ironton than in other centers of the industry; mechanics' services in the erection of buildings and in the setting up and repair of machinery may also be cheaper. In such case cotton manufacturers at Ironton are not producing at cost even when the wages of textile laborers are as high as in other centers. There still remains a margin of profit, which leads to expansion of the industry and increased demand for labor. Under competition wages at Ironton must inevitably rise above the average in other centers. We may, therefore, formulate the principle that if competition exists among different producing centers, all supplying the same markets, wages in an industry in one center will rise or fall until, together with other costs of production, they equal wages plus other costs of production in the other centers where the industry is carried on. To give a numerical example: if in city A one hundred yards of cotton cloth cost $10, of which $8 consist of cost of materials, fuel, interest on capital, etc., and $2 of wages; and if in city B, which obtains the same price for cloth at the mill, all other costs amount to only $7, wages in B will rise, under competition, until labor cost amounts to $3.

Much attention has been given to the fact that in many branches of industry the American producer can meet the competition of the foreign producer, although the former pays higher wages than the latter. In many cases the personal efficiency of the American laborer is so much greater than that of the foreign laborer that wages cost, per unit of product, is less in this country than in foreign countries. Labor cost is thus higher only in appearance, not in reality. In other cases the low prices at which Americans can afford to sell are to be explained by the exceptionally low prices prevailing here for other cost factors — fuel, the use of land, etc.

8. *The dependence of the price of cost goods upon the price of finished products is usually obscured by the fact that most cost goods are demanded by more than one industry.*

In a large area of the Middle West, the soil is equally well adapted for the growing of corn and of wheat. If the price of wheat falls, the rent on land formerly used for wheat growing will not necessarily decline. The land will simply be taken over by corn culture, and continue to yield the same rent. Here it appears that the necessity of paying rent exerts a controlling influence on the supply of wheat, and hence on its price. The labor which can be used in farming can also be used for railway building and for much of the unskilled work in the cities. If, then, the prices of farm products decline, the wages of farm labor may decline only slightly, if at all, since any reduction in wages would drive laborers into other employments. In any single industry, the price of labor and of other cost goods is likely to be less subject to the control of the men engaged in the industry than is the price of the products of the industry. To double the output of a particular grade of cotton cloth would, under ordinary circumstances, reduce its price very materially. The expansion of the production of this grade of cloth would represent an increased demand upon the supply of raw material, of labor, and of fuel. But this increase might represent less than one ten-thousandth of the total demand for these factors in production, and would consequently exert scarcely a perceptible influence upon their price. It is natural, then, that practical men should regard costs as something fixed and independent of their control, while they regard the price of finished products as variable and dependent upon their action in producing or refraining from production.

That costs follow prices, instead of determining them,

is seldom evident at first glance in normal times. In times of great economic stress the principle is so obvious as to press itself upon the attention of even the most careless observer. In the second half year of the Great War, when the belligerent nations were importing vast quantities of industrial products and food supplies, prices in America set out on an upward course that continued until well after the close of the war. In most cases prices were doubled, in some trebled or even quadrupled, and very promptly costs began to rise. Wages doubled, even when there were no labor organizations to press for a rise; rents increased, the prices of coal and raw materials attained to higher levels than had ever been known. Then prices took a downward turn, with the post-war depression. Wages and other items of cost followed painfully after prices. After so colossal a demonstration of the principle it might be supposed that no one would ever again suppose that money costs have the power of determining the level of prices. Yet since costs will continue to determine at what price a given enterpriser can produce, and since few men look far beyond their own business, it will soon be stoutly maintained by many intelligent persons that what determines price is cost of production.

9. *Where two centers of production compete freely with each other, the one may be able to drive the other out of certain lines of industry. The one cannot drive the other out of all lines of industry.*

It is often said that the South can manufacture cotton more cheaply than New England, and that therefore, since both sections must sell their products at practically the same price, cotton manufacture in New England is doomed. The advantages of the South are said to be cheaper labor and cheaper power. Let us see how long the advantages can be retained.

As the South extends its production, the price of cotton goods declines. Possibly some New England mills are forced to shut down; others, while continuing in operation, reduce their output. The expansion of the industry in the South increases the demand for labor and tends to raise its price. The contraction of the industry in New England reduces the demand for labor, and tends to lower its price. Forces are therefore at work reducing the difference between the two centers in labor cost.

But the wages of cotton operatives depend not only on the fortunes of the cotton industry, but on the fortunes of other industries as well. A reduction in the wages of cotton mill hands in New England causes an efflux of such labor into other industries, and this tends to check the reduction in wages. In the South rising wages in the cotton industry is followed by an influx of laborers from other industries, and this tends to check the rise of wages. It is quite possible that, owing to the existence of other industries capable of absorbing labor on the one hand, or of yielding up labor on the other, the South will get a larger and larger share of the cotton industry, until it has taken over practically the whole business.

Now let us suppose that all the industries of the South are in competition with all the industries of New England, and that costs are lower in the former part of the country than in the latter. An attempt on the part of all Southern producers to extend their outputs immediately forces up the price of all producers' goods — labor, fuel, and water power, etc. A tendency on the part of all New England producers to restrict production immediately reduces the price of producers' goods. It is, then, only for a brief time that all costs can be higher in one section than in the other. The higher price of labor might indeed induce the whole New England working population to migrate to the South; but in no other possible way could the volume of New England industry be permanently restricted by Southern competition.

The same reasoning applies to international competition. After the Great War there was much talk of the danger that German competition might destroy the industry of England, Belgium and even of the United States. There is no doubt that after the collapse of the German money standard, the cost of production in Germany fell far below that of the other industrial nations. Wages, rents, coal and raw materials of German origin were to be had at absurdly low prices, measured either in gold or in international purchasing power. But the condition was one that could not last, once international trade got well under way. The export demand for German goods was bound to raise their prices, and with this rise, to draw wages and other cost items to a higher level. At the same time German competition was bound to lower the prices of similar goods produced in other countries, and eventually to lower wages and other items of cost correspondingly. Much distress accompanies such a process of readjustment, but in the end it is inevitable that a new balance should be established, in which most staple export goods are produced as cheaply in one country as in another. No nation can permanently enjoy the advantage of general low costs, because the costs themselves are ultimately adjusted, in the case of export industries, to the international price level.

10. *Some costs manifest a more direct dependence on the price of particular finished products than do others. The former are therefore said to be price-determined; the latter are said to be price-determining.*

In the making of bricks, the laborers employed are for the most part of a kind equally well suited for farm labor or for unskilled labor in the cities. The fuel used in burning the bricks might be put to a hundred other uses. The clay, on the other hand, can probably be used for nothing but for making bricks.

Accordingly, if the price of bricks rises, this is not likely to affect the price of labor or of fuel. For the price of these goods is derived from a wide range of production in which they are employed, and the making of bricks represents a negligible part of the demand for them. It is entirely different with the price of clay. If the available deposits are limited, this price may rise so high as to absorb practically the entire gains resulting from the rise in the price of bricks. If the price of bricks falls, the loss is borne chiefly by the owner of the clay deposit.

In a country whose agriculture consists almost exclusively in wheat raising, a rise in the price of wheat will raise wages of farm hands only slightly, as the rate of wages in agriculture must bear a close relation to the rate of wages in other unskilled pursuits. It will raise the rent of wheat lands, as the price of the use of such lands depends on their use for growing wheat, and on nothing else. It is easy, therefore, to see what the earlier economists meant when they said that rent is the effect, not the cause, of price. Rents, under certain conditions, rise or fall with the price of agricultural produce. Certain modern economists express the same thought when they say that rents are price-determined. Wages were regarded by earlier economists as the cause, not the effect, of price; they are said by some modern economists to be price-determining, not price-determined. As we have seen in the foregoing sections, a sufficiently broad view shows that the prices of all cost goods are derived from the prices of their products. And there are few cost goods so definitely restricted to a particular line of production that a reduction in their price in one industry does not result in a partial withdrawal of their supply, with a consequent reaction on price.

11. *Summary.*

Since prices normally bear a close relation to the costs of production, an ultimate explanation of prices involves an explanation of the forces determining costs. The general principle is that the prices of cost goods are derived from the prices of finished products. Accordingly, when the price of a finished product rises, this rise is reflected first in the prices of those goods that enter into its production, and later in the prices of goods entering into the production of the cost goods. Under competition the benefits from a rise in the price of a finished commodity rest ultimately with the factors in production that are limited in quantity, either by natural or by social-economic conditions.

If a production good is used in a large number of industries, a rise or fall in the price of any single commodity into which it enters will have little effect upon its price. For to reduce the price of the production good in one industry would result in diverting it to other industries. A condition of producing a finished commodity is a price sufficient to pay the usual rate for production goods of this kind. Such goods are therefore in a price-determining position. The production goods which can be used in only one industry rise or fall in price with the products of that industry.

CHAPTER VI

THE LAW OF DIMINISHING RETURNS

1. *Increase in the output of an industry is normally checked by increase in the cost of some factor in production, due to the difficulty encountered in increasing the supply of that factor.*

In the last chapter we saw that one of the forces limiting the expansion of an industry is the tendency of costs to rise to the selling price of the product of the industry. The American cotton-spinning industry may be very profitable one year — that is, the margin between the selling price of cotton yarn and the cost of producing it may be wide. But before long an expansion of the industry takes place; increasing demands upon the existing supply of skilled labor, of raw cotton, and of other factors in the production of cotton yarn force the expenses of the enterprisers engaged in the industry to a higher level.

We saw further that not all elements in cost show the same tendency to increase. In cotton spinning, part of the labor force is skilled, part of it unskilled. If the industry were to expand, say, by fifty per cent, a great strain would be put upon the supply of labor specially trained for cotton spinning. No perceptible strain would be placed upon the supply of unskilled labor, for outside of the spinning industry enormous quantities of unskilled labor are to be had. The skilled labor might therefore for a time enjoy a large increase in wages, while the wages of unskilled labor would scarcely be affected at all.

Similarly, such an expansion of the industry would represent a great strain upon the supply of raw cotton, which for a year could not be increased. Quite possibly the price of raw cotton would be doubled. The same expansion of the cotton-spinning industry would result in an increased demand for coal for power. But the use of coal is so universal, and the volume of its consumption so vast, that the increased demand from the cotton industry would be a negligible factor in influencing its price. Coal would probably not rise perceptibly.

2. *The individual enterpriser usually finds himself hampered in his efforts to increase his business by the difficulty of increasing his supply of some of the factors entering into his production.*

For a somewhat different reason, the output of a single enterpriser can often be increased only at increasing cost. It is true that one enterpriser out of a multitude cannot force up the wages of labor against himself, as a whole industry can do. Nor can he exertany perceptible influence upon the price of raw material and other supplies. But there are usually certain factors entering into his production that, so far as he is concerned, are either limited absolutely, or can be increased only at a disproportionately heavy outlay. In any agricultural section you may find an enterprising farmer forced to limit his operations to a single hundred acres. He can hire as many men as he pleases at $40 a month, the price he pays his one "hired hand." He can buy additional teams and additional machinery at no advance over the price of those he already has. Why does he not buy or rent additional land, and carry on a large scale business? Because all the adjoining lands are occupied by men who prefer to till them with their own labor and who would consequently demand a very high rental, if they consented to give up their land. Our farmer might be compelled to go a distance of three or four miles to get additional land at reasonable rates. Of course land cannot be advantageously cultivated from such a distance. Hence the farmer is forced to content himself with his own one hundred acres.

In almost any town you may find a bright and capable young grocer, conducting the pettiest corner grocery business. The possibilities of trade may be numerous; a store ten times as large might easily be supported by the potential custom. Why then do we find a little store? The young merchant might easily rent larger premises, without more than a proportionate increase in rent. He might hire as many clerks and delivery boys as he wished, without paying a rate of wages in excess of the rate he pays to the one or two already in his employ. What he especially lacks is capital. Perhaps he has $5000 of his own. The cost which the use of this capital represents is merely the interest he could get at a savings bank — say, four per cent. With $5000 capital of his own, he may be able to borrow another $5000 at six per cent. For an additional $5000 he would probably have to pay ten per cent, as the security he has to offer is not so good. It is unlikely that he can borrow more capital, no matter how high a rate of interest he may be willing to pay. The maximum business he can conduct, then, is one for which a capital of $15,000 will suffice.

A small stream, flowing between high, rocky banks, may offer an excellent opportunity for the establishment of a factory to be operated by water power. Let us suppose that a manufacturer, acquainted with the advantages of the location, decides to erect a mill. He may be able to command practically unlimited capital. Whether his mill will require one hundred hands or one thousand will make no difference in the rate of wages he will have to pay. Raw material can be obtained at least as cheaply in large lots as in small. Plainly, what will determine the size of the factory will be the power to be obtained from the stream. A ten-foot dam will give a certain power; a twenty-foot dam a much greater one, and every additional foot in height of dam means additional power. But there is an absolute limit to the height to which the dam may reach, without forcing the stream above its banks and ruining a large amount of property on the lower levels adjacent to it. There may also be limits of expense; after the dam has reached a height of twenty feet, a further addition to its height may imply such a great increase in its length and in the character of the materials required to stand the increased strain that the additional power is not worth its cost.

It will not be necessary to multiply instances further. If the reader will examine the various businesses with which he is acquainted, he will observe that in a large proportion of them it is difficult, if not impossible, to duplicate some of the elements in production without incurring disproportionate expense.

3. *In some cases an absolute limit is placed upon production when one of the factors cannot be increased in amount. In most cases, by the application of increased amounts of the other factors, production may be increased, but with constantly greater difficulty.*

Among the products of industry are many chemical compounds, the components of which are combined in perfectly definite proportions. A shortage of fifty per cent in the supply of any component entails a shortage of fifty per cent in the finished product. In most cases, however, the producer can vary the proportions in which economic elements in production are combined. A bushel of wheat may be produced on a relatively large area with the application of a small amount of labor, or on a relatively small area with the application of a large amount of labor. Cotton cloth may be woven with relatively small expenditure for labor and large expenditure for power and machinery, or with large expenditure for labor and small expenditure for power and machinery. Even a slight acquaintance with actual business conditions gives ample illustration of the fact that in every industry there is great variety in the proportions in which the various producing factors are combined. Accordingly, if a business man is confined to a limited supply of one factor, he may yet increase his operations by selecting a method which involves small use of the limited factor and large use of the other factors.

4. *An increase in the amount of labor and auxiliary capital employed upon a given area of land does not, as a rule, result in proportionate increase in product.*

Let us return now to the case of the farmer, confined to his one hundred acres of tillable land. By his own labor and with a single team and the appropriate machinery he may till the whole tract. Fifty acres, we may assume, are put into wheat, fifty acres into corn. In the time for sowing wheat, a few good days may be followed by a week of rainy weather. Half of the wheat field may be sowed in time to get the benefit of the wet weather; the other half of the field may have to be left until the ground is dry, and so this part of the crop will lose the advantage of an early start. Similarly, part of the corn planting may be belated, with resultant danger to the crop from early frosts. There may not be enough dry days in the late spring to enable the farmer to keep his cornfield free from weeds. In harvest time, the chances of loss from delays in cutting and stacking the wheat are still greater. Of course these adverse chances may not be realized. The weather may be dry just when it should be; the rains may come just when they are wanted. But experience proves that the weather is not thus happily regulated. One year with another, our farmer will be fortunate if he gets twelve bushels of wheat and forty bushels of corn per acre.

Instead of tilling the whole tract with his own labor, the farmer may hire a man to help him. He buys an additional team, plow, harrow, cultivator, etc., practically duplicating his stock of machinery as well as his supply of labor. The land can now be much more carefully tilled; it will almost surely yield a greater aggregate return. Will the return be doubled? It would be unreasonable to expect this. More probably, the wheat yield will increase to fifteen bushels; the corn yield, to fifty bushels.

Now let us imagine that the farmer employs a second hired laborer, and invests an additional $500 in a team and machinery. How much will be added to the crop? It is unlikely that the addition will be as great as that resulting from the employment of the first hired workman. We will assume that the wheat crop per acre is increased to seventeen bushels, the corn crop to fifty-five. With a third hand the crop of wheat would perhaps increase to eighteen bushels, and the crop of corn to fifty-eight. A fourth hand might increase the crop of wheat to eighteen and one-half bushels; that of corn, to fifty-nine bushels. There is no reason why every additional workman should not make some small addition to the crop, until the wheat crop had become fifty bushels and the corn crop one hundred and fifty.

An important principle, involved in this example, may now be stated. From a given area of ground, an amount of produce can be obtained increasing with every increase in the labor and auxiliary capital employed in tillage, but increasing less than proportionally with the increase in labor and auxiliary capital. This principle is called the *law of diminishing returns in agriculture.*

5. *Returns diminish more rapidly in some branches of agriculture than in other branches.*

Some crops are far more responsive to the efforts of the husbandman than are others. If a wheat field is well fertilized and properly prepared to receive the seed, it may yield twenty-five bushels per acre. An American farmer would find it next to impossible to raise the yield to forty bushels, even at the expenditure of almost unlimited pains. A similar field, prepared in the ordinary manner, may yield fifty bushels of potatoes per acre. By extreme care in selecting the seed and in keeping the field free from weeds and from insects the yield might possibly be raised to two hundred bushels, or even much more. It is more feasible to quadruple the potato crop than to double the wheat crop. In the production of many garden vegetables and small fruits, the returns to extraordinary care are often almost incredible. Indeed, it has sometimes even been doubted whether the law of diminishing returns is operative in the growing of such products. There can be no doubt that doubling the amount of labor expended upon a given area in gardening often increases the output by more than one hundred per cent. But it is self-evident that a point must eventually be reached where a doubling of the expenditure for labor will fail to double the output.

6. *If the amount of capital expended in improving a given urban building site is increased, the returns do not increase proportionately with the increase in capital.*

The principle of diminishing returns, as it operates in agriculture, was first formulated by economists more than a hundred years ago, although practical men have, of course, taken account of it in their business conduct ever since agriculture became man's chief source of food. The applicability of the principle to land devoted to trading and manufacturing purposes was for a long time ignored by economists. This may be explained by the fact that formerly urban land was so cheap that the small amount required for the erection of a shop or a factory represented an almost negligible element in the total costs of carrying on a business of this nature. The enterpriser rarely found himself forced to adjust his business with a view to obtaining the greatest possible use from a definite amount of land. If his capital sufficed for so large a business, he purchased or leased a city block on which to erect his buildings; if his capital was small, he limited his use of land to a few lots. To-day conditions have changed, in consequence of the extraordinary growth of the cities. The merchant who desires to carry on a business in the heart of the business district of a great city often finds himself restricted to a given number of front feet. The adjacent lots are taken up by establishments which show no disposition to remove. It is then a question how to conduct a maximum paying business upon a fixed ground space.

One way of overcoming the limitation of ground space consists in erecting a very lofty building. Instead of contenting himself with a building of six stories, the enterpriser may push the height to fifteen or more. Perhaps it costs $600,000 to erect a six-story building. An additional $100,000 may possibly give another story; but more probably the seventh story will, in effect, cost more than this. To raise the building materials to this height is more expensive than to raise materials to a lower story. Moreover, a seven-story building is not merely a six-story one with a floor superadded; in planning the taller building, it is necessary to allow for greater strength of wall in the lower stories, in view of the additional weight to be borne by them. Greater care must be exercised to reduce risk from fire. In addition to the increased cost of constuction, there will be greater costs in connection with the permanent use of the seventh floor than in connection with the use of lower floors. More labor will be spent in carrying up the goods to be exposed for sale, and in carrying down the articles sold. More numerous and more powerful elevators will be required for the higher building. We may therefore place the initial cost of the additional floor at $120,000.

An eighth floor would, in effect, cost still more than the seventh — $140,000, let us say. A ninth floor may cost $160,000; a tenth floor $180,000, and the fifteenth floor may cost $280,000. As there is no reason for supposing that the higher floors will accommodate more business than the lower, it is clear that the returns on capital invested diminish with each additional floor.

7. *The principle of diminishing returns is illustrated by the results of increasing the rolling stock of a transportation company without increasing trackage.*

In a certain city a street railway company, let us assume, has extended its lines of track through all the streets which promise any considerable traffic. The trackage is then a fixed element in the company's business, analogous to the land of the farmer or the floor space of the merchant. The variable elements are labor, fuel for power, and auxiliary capital in the shape of cars.

With one hundred cars in the entire system, running at intervals of twenty minutes, the company may carry an average of one hundred passengers per car per trip, thus earning $5. It is easy to see that the number of passengers carried would be increased if the service were more frequent. Persons who have only a short distance to go will form the habit of walking, if the alternative usually means waiting fifteen or twenty minutes for an overcrowded car. Quite possibly the company would get twice as many fares with two hundred cars, running at intervals of ten minutes. In this case the tendency of returns to diminish does not appear.

Imagine now that the company places a third hundred cars upon its lines, still further reducing the intervals between cars. In large measure these cars will simply carry passengers who would have been carried by the other cars; and this is, of course, no gain to the company. The greater efficiency of the system, and the greater comfort of riding in cars that are never overcrowded, will develop some increase in traffic. Possibly this increase will amount to fifty passengers for each of the new cars. Each of the new cars would thus represent an addition of $2.50 to the income of the company. An additional hundred cars may increase the number of passengers carried by an average of twenty-five for each additional car; still another hundred may increase the number of passengers carried scarcely at all.

8. *The principle of diminishing returns comes into operation when the amount of labor increases, while the amount of capital remains fixed.*

The element in production which operates to limit the expansion of a given business may be capital in its general form, not any concrete productive good. It is a fortunate business man who finds his capital limited only by the possibilities of profitable employment which he commands. In practical life a man can secure for use in his business, besides his own capital, only the additional capital for which he can give security. And this is usually limited to some proportion of the value of his own property.

Assuming that a manufacturer possesses a capital of

$50,000, and can borrow $50,000 more, the sum $100,000 limits his operations as narrowly as any other fixed element in his production could do. He has, of course, many choices as to the exact disposition of the capital. If he is engaged in cotton manufacture, he may use first-class machinery, or he may employ a poor grade of machines — perhaps machines that have been discarded in other sections, as was for a long time a common practice in the South. He may decide upon investing $50,000 of his capital in looms, and the remainder partly in the building and partly in materials, etc. With twenty-five laborers and high-grade looms, the output per laborer will be high; with fifty laborers and lower grade looms, the output per laborer will probably be less, although the total output of the mill will be increased. A third force of twenty-five laborers with a still cheaper grade of looms will add something to the total output, but the output per man will be still further diminished. Perhaps the output per man, when twenty-five are employed, will be $2000. With cheaper looms and fifty men, the output per man may be $1900. Seventy-five men, with the capital put into appropriate form, might produce $1800 per man. With one hundred men, the returns per man might be $1700, and with each further addition to the number of men a corresponding decrease in product per man might take place, until at last additional laborers added nothing to the output.

9. *The principle of diminishing returns is of universal application in the field of production.*

Wherever one element in production is fixed, while the other factors in production increase, the principle of diminishing returns inevitably operates. Wherever one factor in production increases, while the other factors increase at a more rapid rate, the law of diminishing returns operates, but in modified form. If the labor and movable capital of society increase while the natural resources at the command of society fail to increase, diminishing returns appear, as in the individual establishments of our examples.

We may now state the law of diminishing returns in its general form. *When any one of the several factors whose coöperation is essential to production is limited in quantity, either absolutely, or by conditions of increasing cost, while the quantity of the other factors may be increased practically without limit, every unit of increase in the variable factors results in an increase of output less than proportionate to the increase in the variable factors.*

10. *Economy in production is at its maximum when the final expenditure on the variable factors just equals the return to those factors.*

The manufacturer who erects a mill to utilize the power obtained by damming a stream, is limited in his operations by the power represented by the head of water. This is the fundamental limiting element in his calculations. But it is not to be supposed that the power which he will actually obtain is a definitely fixed quantity. Human ingenuity has devised no means whereby all the power actually resident in any natural source may be transmuted into a form which lends itself to use. All our devices for securing and transmitting power are imperfect; the best of them are only less wasteful of energy than the worst. Our manufacturer may install a mechanism which costs little but permits a large part of the power to go to waste, or he may install a more complicated and costly set of devices, which will come far nearer turning to account the whole power represented by the fall. We may think of the manufacturer as weighing the advantages of different kinds of power plant. The expenditure of $1000 will permit the utilization of, perhaps, one half of the power. A second

$1000 may make it possible to utilize two thirds of the power. With a plant costing $3000 perhaps three fourths of the total power will be utilized. A $4000 plant may utilize four fifths of the power, and so on. At what point will it be more profitable to let power go to waste than to incur additional expense to save it? One half of the power may have a value of $300 per year. Interest and depreciation on the $1000 necessary to obtain this power may amount to $150. The value of the power which would be obtained through the $2000 plant, on the basis we have assumed, would be $400; and the cost, figuring interest and depreciation as before, would be $300. The simple plant therefore would yield a net value of $150 above cost; while the more complicated plant would yield only $100. It would accordingly pay best to install the $1000 plant. If the value of the power should double, however, while the cost of the several kinds of power installations remained unchanged, the $1000 plant would yield a value of $600 at a cost of $150, leaving a net gain of $450; while the $2000 plant would give a power worth $800 at a cost of $300, leaving a net gain of $500.

The $3000 plant would yield a power worth $900, but at a cost of $450. The net gain is evidently diminished through the installation of the $3000 plant. The $2000 plant is, under the circumstances, the most economical available. Were the value of the power again doubled, the $3000 plant would yield the highest surplus above cost, and so would be the most advantageous economically.

Under present conditions it is an excellent steam engine which transforms into mechanical power one sixth of the energy of the coal which it consumes. A simple and inexpensive type of engine does not do nearly so well as this. At a given place and time, will it be more economical to employ an engine of the very highest type, and which naturally is very costly, or an inexpensive engine of a simple type? The former may transform into power fifteen per cent of the energy latent in the coal; the latter, only five per cent. If the additional power obtained through the better engine does not equal the excess of interest and depreciation charge on the more costly engine, the simpler engine is the more economical in spite of its wastefulness from the mechanical point of view.

A farmer should continue his application of labor and capital to land as long as the returns from additional units of labor and capital exceed their cost. If wages and interest decline, it becomes possible to increase the application of labor and capital to land without passing beyond the bounds of economical production. Similarly, cultivation may profitably be made more intensive if the prices of agricultural products rise. We have here an explanation of the fact that in old countries land is cultivated more intensively than in new countries. In the latter wages and interest are high and prices are low.

11. *The law of diminishing returns may be counteracted by improvements in production.*

Improvements in methods of production are constantly taking place, with the result that a given amount of labor or of capital increases in efficiency. If the amount of labor employed upon a hundred-acre field increases, the increase in product will not ordinarily be proportionate to the increase in labor. But if at the same time a new way of cultivating or fertilizing the soil is discovered, or if the quality of the seed is improved, the product may very well increase relatively to the amount of labor. This fact does not prove that the law of diminishing returns is non-existent. It merely proves that there are other forces at work which may, at times, neutralize its effects. These forces are, of course, of the greatest practical importance, and will later demand our attention.

Another qualification of the principle of diminishing returns consists in the fact that the very process of increasing the number of units of variable factors employed in connection with an unvarying factor may, under certain conditions, increase the productive efficiency of each unit of the varying factors. To employ two men on an acre of land that could be cultivated by one would result in a diminished return per man if each worked alone. But many tasks may be better performed when two or more men coöperate than when each works by himself. Accordingly, it may happen that an increase in labor which makes coöperation possible, or an increase in capital which makes possible better methods, may be accompanied by increasing, instead of diminishing, returns.

12. *Summary.*

In most businesses the enterpriser is subject to definite limitations in his control over one or more of the factors upon which his production is based, while he may be able to increase other factors without assignable limits. Such limitations upon some of the factors in a productive combination do not necessarily place an absolute limit upon the size of a business; they do, however, imply that after a certain size has been reached, further expansion involves disproportionate expense. This principle, known as the law of diminishing returns, is of universal applicability in the field of production.

The greatest economy in production is attained when the returns to the last units of the variable factors in a business just equal the cost of those factors. Every reduction in the cost of one of the variable factors extends the scope of profitable application of that factor.

The law of diminishing returns may often be counteracted by improvements in production; in some cases this counteracting influence may be brought about by the very forces that tend to bring the law of diminishing returns into operation.

CHAPTER VII

THE SPECIALIZATION OF ECONOMIC FUNCTIONS

1. *In primitive conditions all the functions of wealth production are performed by the single kinship group, or family.*

At the dawn of civilization men lived in small groups that were practically self-sufficing. Whatever work was to be done was executed by all the men in coöperation, or by any member of the tribe indifferently. There was naturally a distinction between the work of men and that of women; the former were in many cases engaged chiefly in hunting, the latter in root grubbing and in a primitive form of gardening. Economic differentiation, then, hardly existed. It is true that there was little occasion for the specialization of economic functions, since wants were few and economic functions were consequently simple.

In many cases civilized men have been placed in conditions that bear a superficial resemblance to those of primitive life. But the civilized man carries with him a great number of wants that the savage never experienced. We therefore find, in such conditions, a progress in the differentiation of economic functions taking place in a few decades, while, in the history of the human race as a whole, differentiation was the result of thousands of years of development.

In a frontier community, where almost the entire population consists of independent families living upon farms, the economic functions performed by each person are numerous and diverse. The frontiersman must, in the first place, be an agriculturist and a grazier. Each of these occupations includes numerous functions calling for different qualities, the agriculturist being a plowman, sower, reaper, etc. The frontiersman must also be a woodcutter at times, a carpenter, a mason, a cabinet-maker, a smith, a butcher, and a hunter, not to speak of a host of miscellaneous functions that he must occasionally perform. His wife probably has a no less varied array of occupations. She is a cook, a laundress, a seamstress, a nurse, a teacher and even a spinner and weaver. To survive on the frontier one must be a jack of all trades. And practically the same range of duties falls upon the strong and the weak, the intelligent and the dull, the man who quickly acquires skill and the man who acquires it with great difficulty.

2. *The first stage in the differentiation of economic functions is the exchange of services.*

Were the frontier community wholly isolated for many generations, a transformation of its methods of production would gradually take place. A person with more than the ordinary talent for building would be called upon to assist in the construction of his neighbors' houses, receiving in return assistance in work for which he had no special qualification. Little by little, occupations would be differentiated, and eventually the community would contain among its population carpenters, smiths, masons, weavers, etc. While these craftsmen might still own land, and spend their odd hours in agriculture, the main source of their livelihood would be the exercise of their several crafts. Specialization in the form known as *differentiation of occupations* would thus have come into existence.

So long as differentiation of functions rests upon a direct exchange of services, it cannot be carried far. A cobbler may need a gate built, but it is not a simple matter to find a carpenter willing to take his pay in shoes. A scheme of payments based on an accepted medium of exchange is requisite. Moreover, differentiation of functions presupposes a considerable number of people in easy communication with one another. Population would need to be fairly dense before a man could devote himself exclusively to the building of houses, even if he undertook the work of stone mason, brick mason, and plasterer in addition to that of carpenter. Such trades as that of locksmith could hardly exist at all, since a scattered rural population could not furnish work enough to maintain it.

3. *An important step in the direction of economic specialization was taken when men began to produce commodities for sale.*

In early modern times the development of trade gradually transformed production for the household or for the immediate neighborhood group into production for the general market. This change first attracted attention in the woolen industry. At first, we may suppose, only the surplus of domestic production was placed upon the market of the town, or carried to fairs where a larger concourse of purchasers was to be found. In time production for domestic use became a mere incident; the weaver came to depend on more or less distant markets for the sale of his wares. And this implied the purchase in the market of the materials of production. So we find German weavers in the fifteenth century carrying their wool from England and their finished products to southern and eastern Europe. Under these conditions there was no reason why a man should produce more than one kind of cloth. A great body of consumers was within his reach, and however special his product, he could devote himself exclusively to it.

In like manner, traders would soon appear in the frontier community of our example in the last section and carry away the lighter surplus products, giving in exchange the manufactured goods of older communities. A railroad would, in time, transform the frontier community into an integral part of the civilized world. Instead of weaving its own cloth, it would barter its surplus products of the soil for textiles produced in other parts of the world. The community as a whole would thus be specialized to the functions best adapted to its conditions.

As the community advanced in numbers and wealth one function after another would be taken out of the province of the man of all work, and given over to persons specially qualified by nature and training to perform it effectively. Each trade, again, would tend to subdivide. The carpenter would no longer plan the building upon which he worked, this function being given over to the architect. The planing of boards would cease to be a part of the carpenter's work, as planing mills would be established which would do the work far more economically. Even in agriculture some differentiation would take place; one man would devote himself chiefly to the growing of grain, another to dairying or market gardening. Owing to the seasonal character of agricultural labor, however, and the advantages of combining crops in such a way that the work may be distributed as evenly as possible throughout the open months, specialization in agriculture could not be carried very far. Indeed, even in the best developed agriculture, we do not often find some farmers wholly devoted to wheat culture, others growing nothing but corn, others potatoes or turnips. Agriculture by its nature precludes a high degree of differentiation of functions.

4. *Differentiation of function in production is in large measure dependent upon the character of the existing commercial organization.*

In the mediæval towns the artisan was at the same time a trader. He was compelled to supply himself with materials, often from distant sources; he was often compelled to carry his wares from place to place in order to find purchasers. The risks incident to procuring materials and marketing products weighed heavily upon him. Coöperation, as in the German Hanse towns, reduced his difficulties in some measure; nevertheless, under the conditions, comparatively few men could rely for their subsistence upon a single occupation. With the development of a merchant class, the producer was relieved of the labor and risks of assembling materials and marketing products. The accumulation of large and permanent stocks of material gave occasion for a constantly increasing number of occupations and subdivisions of occupations.

As an illustration of the effect of commercial development upon the division of labor, we may cite the industry of shoe manufacture. One hundred years ago shoe making was carried on by independent cobblers, supplying a local demand. Every cobbler made many types of boots and shoes. At a somewhat later period, shoes had become an article of commerce, and the cobbler ceased to be dependent on the local demand. In the next stage in the process of development, the commercial demand for shoes had become too important to allow the supply to remain dependent upon the enterprise of the independent cobbler. The merchant began to furnish material ready cut to be sewed and pegged by persons capable of doing the work, whether trained in the cobbler's trade or not. In this stage the simpler processes were performed by one set of hands, the more complicated by another. Thus *division of labor* had succeeded differentiation of occupations. Further improvements in methods of marketing the finished product led to still more minute division of labor, under the factory form of organization. To-day each shoe goes through scores of hands before it is placed on the market as a finished product.

A similar evolution may be traced in the ready-made clothing industry — a still newer field. The retail and wholesale clothing trade has grown up in the last seventy-five years; its increasing demands have given a stimulus to the differentiation of functions in the making of clothes. It is, of course, to be borne in mind that in all cases the development of trade and the differentiation of economic functions have proceeded concurrently. Each has been in part the effect, in part the cause, of the other.

5. *Improvements in transportation give occasion to increased specialization in industry.*

Division of labor first reached a high degree of development in centers enjoying water transportation. Until recent times, it was only at such centers that the more bulky materials of industry could be assembled in sufficiently large quantities to permit extensive subdivision of functions; furthermore, it was only from such centers that it was possible to carry bulky goods to a great number of consumers. The advent of the railway enabled inland cities to engage in highly specialized production. As railway service became better and cheaper, many forms of industry permitting a minute division of labor appeared. Until refrigeration had been reduced to a science, and the methods of transporting products preserved by ice had been perfected, every locality depended for its supply of meat upon the local butcher. If the consumers in the vicinity were few, they were ordinarily supplied by small shops which permitted only a low degree of division of labor. In the cities, the shops were larger, and division of labor was carried farther. To-day there is almost no limit to the market for a single establishment. Fresh meats from Chicago may be found in any city or town in the land. Fresh mutton killed in New Zealand and Australia finds a ready market in England. The parallel development of live stock transportation has given the slaughtering centers a practically unlimited supply of raw material. Accordingly, a minute division of labor has been evolved in the slaughterhouses. In the Chicago slaughterhouses the killing and dressing of a bullock is subdivided into fifty or sixty separate functions, each assigned to a separate set of workmen. Each set makes some small change in the material and passes it on to another set. Of course some functions are performed by single workmen, some by several. The laborers are organized in gangs of over 200 men, each gang containing just the appropriate number of men of each class.

6. *In the field of production at the order of the consumer, division of labor is dependent largely upon the density of population.*

Where the producer of a commodity deals directly with the consumer, the opportunity for minute division of labor is not so great as where the producer is brought into relation with the consumer through the intermediation of a general market. The amount of work that may be secured by a single custom-tailor's shop is limited by the number of purchasers of custom-made garments within easy distance. In a village this number may be so small that anything like subdivision of the tailor's trade is impracticable. In a large city the case is different. A single shop may easily find customers enough to keep twenty men at work. In the latter case division of labor is entirely practicable. If transit facilities in the large city are excellent, the number of men that may be employed by a single tailoring establishment may be one hundred or more, and labor may be as minutely subdivided as the employer desires. In the making of furniture at the order of the consumer, similar limitations upon division of labor are found. The small town is able to support only a small shop, where all the work is performed by two or three men, while the large city renders possible the large shop, with minute subdivision of labor.

7. *The degree in which the functions of production may be subdivided is dependent upon the prevailing form of economic organization.*

Where each workman is his own employer, as was generally the case in the mediæval industrial organization, labor cannot be very minutely subdivided. In such an industrial organization the spinner buys his wool and sells his product to the weaver; the latter sells the cloth to the fuller, who, in turn, sells it to the dyer. The product is again sold, perhaps, to the shearer, who in turn sells the finished cloth to the draper, who deals directly with the consumer. With such a form of organization much time is necessarily wasted in the buying and selling of the material in its several stages, and the greater the number of stages, the greater the waste from this source. Again, as each person follows his own taste in choosing his trade — subject, of course, to family tradition and trade restrictions — it is unlikely that the society will have just the right number of craftsmen of each kind. At one time there will be too many spinners, relatively to the number of weavers; at another time fullers will be so numerous that not all can be employed. And this element of waste also increases with increasing subdivision of labor.

Where, on the other hand, industry is carried on

under the factory system, the workmen are assembled under one roof, subject to the control of an employer. The material passes through the shop without interruption, and beginners are taken on in each branch in the proportions which experience shows to be most desirable. Of course this implies a large accumulation of wealth on the part of the employer, who must provide the premises, furnish materials, pay wages, and assume all other expenses of production. In fact, we may say that large capital and efficient management are prerequisites to a thoroughgoing system of division of labor. And, of course, efficient management on the part of the employer implies a corresponding readiness to submit to direction on the part of the employee. We might easily conceive of a society in which all other conditions requisite to division of labor might exist, but in which division of labor of an advanced type would, nevertheless, be impracticable on account of the restiveness of the working population under close direction.

8. *From a business point of view, the principal advantages of division of labor are* (1) *increased skill and speed in production;* (2) *fuller utilization of time;* (3) *greater ease of supervision.*

To enumerate all the advantages of the division of labor would require a volume; but we may group the more important ones under a few heads. In the first place, the limitation of the labor to be performed by one man to a single function, which involves the use of a single tool, and which may be reduced to a few simple movements, makes possible accurate workmanship and great speed, with relatively little weariness. The workman soon reduces his movements to a rhythm; he grasps each piece of material in the same way, delivering his strokes upon it in such a way as never to throw away his energy. Every one knows how much better results a trained oarsman secures from the expenditure of a given amount of muscular energy than the raw beginner, who puts forth his strength now on the water, now on the air, now in the right direction, now in the wrong one. The difference in effectiveness between the strokes delivered by the man who works with a single tool, and the strokes delivered by one who works with a dozen tools, is hardly exaggerated by the comparison.

Even the best workman loses some time in changing from tool to tool. It is not difficult to find a carpenter who spends many fruitless moments searching now for his saw, now for his hammer, while the whereabouts of a plane or square, when those implements are needed, proves a baffling, if not insoluble, problem. And this is the man who leaves his work with the loudest complaints of his weariness. A division of labor that holds a man so strictly to business that he never has a chance to stop to search for anything, contributes materially to reduce such waste of time and energy.

The simplification of the task of each laborer makes it a comparatively easy matter to ascertain how much any particular one is actually doing. One who has lived in the country has probably made the acquaintance of two types of laborers: the first, those who are always bustling about in a hurry and yet accomplishing little; the second, never in a hurry, yet showing, in the end, a good record of achievement. Because of the miscellaneous character of the work of the agricultural laborer, it takes a long time to measure the relative efficiency of different men. Where a man is compelled to repeat the same operation throughout the day, no show of bustling energy will create the illusion of achievement. The pieces of work done have simply to be counted to give an accurate idea of the laborer's efficiency. It is obvious, then, that the difficulty of supervision is greatly reduced by systematic division of labor.

9. *From a social point of view, the principal advantages of division of labor are:* (1) *that it affords a place of usefulness to many who would otherwise be of little use to society;* (2) *that it opens opportunities for special abilities; and* (3) *that it facilitates mechanical progress.*

Under frontier conditions, where each man must perform a wide variety of functions, some prove utter failures, wasting so much time turning irresolutely from task to task that they accomplish nothing. These same men might prove highly efficient workmen under different industrial conditions. If our frontier communities had kept detailed records, we should find that they contained many a man who would have made a good architect or engineer, many a woman who would have made an excellent modiste or teacher, but who proved hopeless failures in the environment in which they were placed. Architecture and engineering, designing of costumes and teaching of children, were indeed functions not wholly neglected, but they made up a very small part in the life of each family and gave little opportunity to any one for the full development of his natural talents.

Division of labor makes the attainment of a place of usefulness possible for persons who have not the time or the versatility to learn how to perform a variety of functions. There are many persons who cannot afford the time to learn the tailor's trade; many who have the time for apprenticeship, but not the general ability required for the making of a well-fitting coat. Few persons are so stupid that they cannot, with slight waste of time, learn how to sew a straight seam. If the work of making a coat is distributed among a dozen persons, each one can quickly learn to do well his particular part. Further, in the distribution of the work, each one may be given a task proportioned to his ability. The skilled cutter will not waste his time picking basting threads, and the person for whom the latter function is a sufficient profession, will be kept from spoiling material through attempting something more ambitious.

Perhaps the greatest advantage that arises from division of labor is the stimulus it gives to the invention of labor-saving machinery. A hundred years ago it would have seemed quite impossible to make shoes by machinery. The process of manufacture appeared so complicated that hand labor alone would answer. To-day shoes are largely the product of machines. Many forces coöperated, of course, to bring about this result, but only one of these concerns us here, the division of labor. When a complicated operation like the making of a shoe has been split up into several score of simpler operations, some of these are likely to prove so nearly mechanical that the idea of machines to take over the work suggests itself. If the process of production is divided into twenty-five parts, perhaps the third, and eleventh, and seventeenth are taken over by machines. In time division of labor still further simplifies the remaining operations; additional ones prove to be fitted for machine work, and thus more of the hand-workers are displaced. It is conceivable that in the end practically the whole process might be taken over by machines, while the hand-worker might be transformed into an attendant of the machine, so to speak, feeding it with material, and passing on the product to another machine.

10. *From a social point of view the division of labor is attended by serious drawbacks.*

The division of labor greatly increases the productive efficiency of the social working force, and this is from every point of view an advantage. It makes possible the utilization of many forms of labor that would otherwise find no place in the productive organization. This is an advantage when the form of labor utilized is incapable of development, as in the case of adults below the average in strength or in intelligence. Persons who would have to starve or beg under a system of complicated employments are often able to earn a fair living under a system of simplified employments.

On the other hand, the division of labor, and the accompanying development of machinery, give inducement to the employment of classes that should not be employed at steady and monotonous labor. Children and persons failing in health are drawn into the circle of sustained labor. The former should be allowed to develop their faculties in a natural way; the latter, to recover their health. When each employment required all the faculties of a normal man, there was nothing to tempt producers to employ laborers of this class. Since the introduction of division of labor, the evil of employing those who should not be employed has assumed serious proportions. Legislation has been invoked to limit the employment of children, but in few countries has child labor been subjected to wholly satisfactory regulation.

Another serious disadvantage of the division of labor is that it tends to reduce the pleasure men derive from their work. The artisan who produces a completed piece of work usually takes an active interest in it. The carpenter takes pride in the houses he has built; the cabinetmaker, in the furniture that has come from his shop. It is a common thing to find men belonging to these trades — representatives of the earlier order — reluctantly leaving their work when the whistle blows or the foreman shouts "Time up." Not so with the workman whose day is spent in performing some minute part of the work of producing each one of a multitude of like commodities. His part in production is merged with that of his numerous fellows. He may, if he is of sanguine temperament, take pride in the achievements of the establishment where he is employed; but for the most part his interest in the work is dependent on his prospect of receiving increased pay.

A further disadvantage of division of labor is that it renders the workman dependent on a certain kind of work, and therefore exposes him to the risk of unemployment when supplies of material are wanting or when markets fail. There are in most modern countries many men and women who are well-trained textile workers, but who do not know how to find other employment when a crisis causes a contraction of the textile industry. The higher the degree of specialization, the more serious are the effects of changes in industrial conditions.

11. *Progress in the specialization of economic functions is subject to a law of diminishing returns.*

We may now consider how far the principle of division of labor modifies the operation of the principle of diminishing returns, described in the last chapter. According to the latter principle, an increase in the amount of labor employed in connection with a limited amount of capital gives a return which is not proportionate with the increase in labor. But what if the additional laborers give opportunity for division of labor which had not before existed? Suppose that a tailor's shop with a capital of $20,000 formerly employed six men; it now employs twelve men. Division of labor can be carried farther with twelve men; hence is it not possible that the employment of the second six men will double the output of the shop? This is quite possible. An additional six men will give occasion to still more systematic division of labor, and so may still further increase the efficiency of each man. And so with a fourth set of six men. But it is evident that one cannot go on indefinitely subdividing the work of making a coat. Eventually a point will be reached where further subdivision of labor increases the efficiency of each laborer only slightly; still further subdivision, even less; finally a degree of subdivision will be found that will not pay. That is, the principle of division of labor is itself subject to diminishing returns. A practical illustration of this fact is to be found in the organization of the working force in many large establishments where much use is made of division of labor. The making of a complete article is not assigned to a single man; nor is it assigned to all the men in the shop. Each article is assigned to a "team," among the members of which the successive manipulations of the material are distributed. The entire working force may contain scores of teams. Now, the size of each team indicates the limits of the profitable division of labor. If an enterpriser limits each team to sixty men, this is proof that in his opinion a team of seventy men would not show so large a product per man.

We may grant that an increase in laborers employed in connection with a given capital may possibly result in an increase in product more than proportionate to the increase in labor. This may hold true until the number of laborers is sufficient to compose a team of maximum efficiency. If an additional team is engaged, without increase in capital, it is doubtful if returns will increase in proportion to the number of teams; a third team will show a return less than that of the second, and so on until the point is reached where it does not pay to employ an additional team. So far as the principle of division of labor is concerned, then, the only qualification to be made in the law of diminishing returns is that when we assume that labor increases, we must assume that it increases by teams, not by individual men.

12. *Summary.*

In the course of economic evolution, one after another of the functions of the primitive family group has been taken over by persons who make a specialty of it. The development of exchange has been a condition and a cause of the tendency toward specialization. The differentiation of economic functions may rest with the assignment to each individual of a particular trade, or it may be carried so far as to subdivide the work of a single trade. In the former case we have what is known as differentiation of occupations; in the latter, division of labor.

A high degree of division of labor presupposes a well-developed commercial organization. Improvements in transportation increase the number of fields in which the principle may operate, as does also increase in the density of population. In a society in which production is carried on by employer-capitalists with hired workers division of labor can be carried much farther than in a society in which the laborer works on his own account.

The productive power of society has been greatly increased by differentiation of functions. The subdivision of tasks makes it possible for each individual however limited his abilities, to find some task that he can execute successfully. Above all, it facilitates mechanical progress. On the other hand, it encourages employers to substitute child labor for the labor of men, and it destroys, in large measure, the pleasure that men find in their work.

Up to a certain point progress in the division of labor neutralizes the effect of diminishing returns. But division of labor is itself subject to diminishing returns; the earlier stages in the process are more fruitful than the later ones.

CHAPTER VIII

MANAGEMENT

1. *Management, under primitive conditions is a function usually attached to the ownership of capital.*

In the small industrial establishment typical of early nineteenth century America, the whole oversight of the productive and commercial operations devolved upon the proprietor. It was he who determined whether the margin between the prospective price of the product and the present cost of material, labor and power warranted production at all or required the temporary closing down of his establishment. The proprietor provided himself with such machinery as he thought he required and could afford, hired efficient labor at high wages or less satisfactory labor at lower wages and kept up such discipline as seemed to him effective. His self-interest sharpened his eye, and made him keen to avoid mistakes. But naturally he was not all-seeing. Usually there were many leaks that escaped his attention. Some proprietors were more competent in managing than others, and were more likely to survive in competition. There was accordingly a gradual progress of the bulk of industry toward better management, but it was painfully slow. We need no better proof of the general blindness of early nineteenth century managers than the fact that practically all of them worked their employees twelve, thirteen or fourteen hours a day, although it was being demonstrated by Robert Owen and other capable employers that in the long run more can be got out of a workman in a day of moderate length than out of an excessively long day.

It is not necessary, however, to go back to early industrial conditions to find examples of management attached incidentally to ownership. Almost the whole of American agricultural enterprise is still carried on under that system. So also are the innumerable small shops in village and city, much of the repair business, a large part of the clothing industry, and many other manufacturing enterprises of considerable importance. In all this vast field common sense, instinct and rule of thumb are characteristic of management. And everywhere there are leaks, which often become serious enough to end in business failures. Where the leaks are less grave they cut down, more or less severely, the returns on the proprietor's capital and efforts. This is especially the case in farming. When the farmer owns his land, free of encumbrance, and with the aid of members of his family does practically all the work on it, mismanagement can make him work unnecessarily hard for unreasonably small returns, but it can not ruin him. We find farmers who go to the trouble of maintaining dairies when the price of dairy products does not cover the cost of the forage and grain, reckoned at the prices prevailing in the local markets. One farmer will maintain horses enough to eat up the chief part of the products of his labor, while another will have too little horsepower to keep his fields properly tilled. One will have much more machinery than he can use to advantage, while another will waste his labor performing by hand operations that could be done more cheaply by machines. But still they survive.

The wastefulness of bad management brings its penalties in more striking form in commercial and industrial establishments. The street vendor who loses on bananas all he makes on peanuts is destined to be crowded out of business unless he drops the luxury of handling bananas. The owner of a "general store" who persists in loading up his shelves with goods that will not sell will sooner or later go into bankruptcy. The penalties of bad management are so drastic that it is easy for the student of economics to fall into the assumption that bad management can nowhere persist for any length of time. But it must be borne in mind that competition is not to be compared to a race between perfect athletes trained down to the last ounce of superfluous weight, but more properly to a free-for-all scramble among the handicapped, some lame, some broken-winded, some suffering from bad hearts, some inattentive and lazy. The less bad win, but the winners may still be very bad indeed, judged by any reasonable standard of perfection.

2. *In the more highly developed industry, management becomes a function differentiated from ownership.*

When a business attains to any considerable size, it is of course impracticable for the owner to keep a personal oversight of all the detailed operations. Instead of dealing directly with the individual workman, the owner acts through foremen, who are supposed to know the character of the work to be performed and to be capable of judging whether the workmen are putting forth their best efforts. The owner may remove himself a stage farther from the productive process by setting up a superintendent between himself and the foremen. He may further subdivide the management, placing one man in charge of the selling force, another in charge of buying materials and machinery, while a third manages the business of production. As a rule, the larger the business, the greater the subdivision of management and the greater the number of links between the owner and the men who actually manipulate the material.

Great variety naturally appears in the degree of responsibility reposed in the various managing officials. In some cases these can only submit recommendations. The owner reserves final decision to himself. But commonly all routine functions are settled definitively by the managers, and only the general strategy of the establishment is reserved to the owner. If times are bad and it appears that production may involve loss, the owner determines whether operations shall be restricted, and in what branches. If times are good, the owner determines whether new equipment or an extension of plant would be desirable. And of course he watches receipts and expenditures and forms his ideas as to whether the management is efficient or not. When he concludes that matters are not going so well as they might, he tries to determine where the source of the difficulty lies and replaces one official or another whom he judges incompetent. The superintendent or manager in charge of a group of foremen is likewise watching the results of each one's work, and if discretion lies with him, dismisses those who do not seem competent. And the foremen in turn keep watch of the workmen. Where the foreman has discretion, as he often has, he is expected to keep his eye open for slackers and trouble-makers, and replace them with a more useful personnel.

In this stage of development management is mainly a selective and disciplinary process. From the top down, men are chosen for their jobs with a view to their competence, and are held to successful performance by the penalty of dismissal. There may, of course, be additional disciplinary methods in use; extra pay for good workmanship, a system of fines for tardiness, irregularity, injury to machinery or waste of materials. But throughout, the process depends on the keenness of eye, the common sense and good judgment of the men holding discretionary power. Men are taken on and dismissed without anything like a systematic determination of their fitness or unfitness. There is no certain relation between the extra rewards for excellent work and the value of that work to the enterprise. Still less are fines nicely graduated to the delinquencies for which they are imposed. There is necessarily much room here for whim and personal likes and dislikes. Some check is placed upon the action of the foreman when the workers are strongly organized. Organization also places limits upon the discretion of the management in fixing the scale of wages and in establishing extra rewards and penalties. But organization does not affect the conditions of the higher grades in the management nor does it divest the system as a whole of its rule of thumb character.

3. *Under the scheme of management generally prevailing, American industry falls far short of any reasonable standard of efficiency.*

It is natural that Americans should regard with complacency the achievements of American business enterprise. As compared with earlier epochs, American business enterprise to-day has attained remarkable results. In spite of the fact that wages have risen and conditions of employment have been much improved, a great variety of products can be brought to market at lower costs than was possible half a century ago. As compared with business enterprise in other modern states, that of America can claim a certain preëminence. Nowhere else is the product per man so large as in America, nor the wages of labor so high. There can be no doubt that relatively to that of most other countries, American business management is highly progressive. American business men may cling too long to methods that are wasteful, but they do not match their foreign competitors in the conservatism that permits antiquated methods to survive.

But such comparisons should not blind us to the fact that the prevailing scheme of management does not by any means achieve the best results practically attainable. In a survey of six typical American industries conducted in 1920–21 by a committee of the Federated Engineering Societies, it was found that the average establishment fell 28.66 per cent short of a practicable maximum in the metal trades, the most satisfactory industry studied, and 63.78 per cent short in the men's clothing industry, the least satisfactory. In all the six industries, taken as a group, the average establishment did not attain to fifty per cent of its practicable maximum of efficiency. And that maximum, it must be observed, represents no theoretical best, but merely what could be attained if the best methods and practices actually in use somewhere in the industry were brought together and applied in a single plant.

It is not at all an unreasonable estimate that without any increase in labor or in the capital invested in machinery, the output of American industry could be increased twenty-five per cent or more by improved management. Every laborer and capitalist and enterpriser could enjoy a twenty-five per cent increase in the goods placed at his disposal. And this result would not presuppose any new inventions, or the devising of any new methods of management. It would presuppose only the general application of methods and technique already being successfully applied somewhere.

4. *An essential part of good management is the application of a rational system for determining costs.*

If you ask a farmer how much it costs him to produce a quart of milk, a dozen eggs, a pound of pork, the chances are a hundred to one that he can not tell you, or if he does give a definite figure, it will be a wild guess. He may be able to tell you how much the aggregate annual product of his farm has cost him — although it is not likely that he can — but he has no rational scheme for distributing this cost among the several products which he sells or uses at home. And yet it is of importance to determine this distribution. If the farmer knew that he was losing money on milk and making money on hogs and poultry, he would cut down his dairy herd and devote himself to the more fruitful part of his production. But since his farm provides his housing and the better part of his food supply, he may afford the luxury of carrying on branches of husbandry that do not pay.

What is far more surprising is that a great many manufacturing and commercial enterprises have no system of cost accounting to guide them away from unprofitable undertakings. For example, in a small town, a dealer in lumber, coal and feed may keep no books that indicate precisely how much each part of his business costs. For all the proprietor knows, he may be losing money on feed and making up his loss on lumber. He might be better off if he dropped feed from his list. A hardware manufacturer often does not know what his saws, chisels, hammers and axes cost him. Very likely one or another of these items costs more than the price at which he sells it.

What complicates the problem of cost accounting is the uncertainty that clouds the proper distribution of various items in cost. Let us suppose that a hardware manufacturer is considering whether he can afford to make an ax which he can sell to a jobber for one dollar. It is easy to determine the cost of the material that goes into the ax. We will put that item at twenty-five cents. The labor directly employed in making the ax costs, we will say, another twenty-five cents. Allow ten cents for fuel and wear and tear on the machines and tools used; there still appears to be a surplus of forty cents. But have we allowed for all the items in cost? No. The manufacturing business as a whole has to pay interest on capital invested in ground, buildings and machinery. It has to pay wages to managers and superintendents; it has to pay taxes, costs of advertising, etc. All these charges that do not distribute themselves directly — known as overhead charges, or simply as "overhead" — ought to be borne in some fair proportion by all the items sold. For the ax the overhead may exceed the forty cents of apparent surplus. Then it does not pay to produce the ax, unless of course nothing that will pay can be produced by the machinery which produced the ax. But if such is the case, it was a mistake to buy the machinery at all. Good management will equip a plant only with machinery designed to turn out products that pay their own direct costs together with their due proportion of overhead.

5. *Good management applies expert attention to the problem of saving material.*

Turn five equal bolts of cloth over to five fairly skilled tailors with instructions to cut the cloth up into sleeve pieces of a given pattern. Will the number of sleeve pieces be the same for all of them? Far from it. The variation in number may be ten per cent or more. And probably even the best one will leave ten per cent more of the cloth in the form of worthless scraps than is really necessary. The housewife who makes clothes at home may afford to waste cloth by haphazard cutting. Not so the clothing manufacturer. All his profit will be carted out in the scraps, unless he takes heed. And indeed this happens at times. The best managed clothing plants have definite systems of measurement that insure the fullest possible utilization of the material. But there are others which leave the matter to the judgment of the individual cutters with consequent serious loss of materials. The same conditions appear in the shoe making industry. The report of the Committee of the Federated Engineering Societies on Waste in Industry states that in cutting leather for uppers, it is not unusual for one cutter to use up a hundred dollars' worth of leather a week in excess of what another cutter uses up in producing an equal number of pieces of the same grades of stock.

Analogous differences in the use of fuel affect every industry. One manager, by close attention to furnace equipment and methods of firing, will get ten, fifteen or twenty per cent more power out of each ton of fuel than another. What is essential to good management here is close antecedent study with time and money spent, if necessary, on careful experimentation, and systematic training of the men who are to apply the methods which have been found most economical.

6. *Good management involves careful planning of the production process so that it may move forward smoothly without clogging at any point.*

Most products placed upon the market are the outcome of a large number of operations which must be executed, as a rule, in series. In the clothing industry, for example, from 80 to 150 operations are required to make a sack coat. Unless the whole system of operations is nicely planned, the material will clog at one stage or another, leaving part of the working force and the machines idle. In the best managed shops the planning is done well enough so that all the workers and machines are kept uniformly busy, but in the majority of shops that is by no means the case.

The building industry, since it is carried on under the

eyes of the general public, offers the most familiar instances of the losses due to imperfect planning. Say that you are having a house built, and visit it day by day, eager to have it finished so that you may move in. You visit it one morning: a half dozen hammers are tapping merrily. Suddenly the sounds cease; you make your way to the living room where the floor was being laid and find the carpenters packing their kits. There is no more flooring on hand, they explain; perhaps additional flooring will be delivered the next day or the next week. Or one day you find a troop of new men in spotted overalls sitting on nail kegs and gossipping with the plasterers. The painters; they have come too soon, and will have to go off to another job, to reappear in a week or two, after the operation has stood dead for several days waiting for them. Of course you may say that in such a case it is not the building contractor — the enterpriser — who loses money because he failed to plan his work well. It is you, the consumer of services, who pays. Very well. But consumers become discouraged when vexations and exactions are too numerous. The volume of building is kept down and the business of the building contractor languishes.

7. *Good management does not leave the choice of tools and methods of using them to the chance preference of the worker, but is at pains to secure satisfactory adaptation.*

If you were required to cut a half cord of wood daily, do you know just what kind of ax would enable you to do it in the least time? Say that you have a dozen to choose from, with a dozen differences in weight, in width of edge, in length of helve. If you have never used an ax regularly, you will have only the vaguest notion as to which one would best suit your requirement. But you must select one. You try one with a fairly heavy head and long helve. After some days you try another. In the meantime you have adjusted your muscles to the first, and that prejudices you against every other. And so, unless you made a very bad mistake in your first choice, you will return to it; and the longer you work with it, the more you will be inclined to favor it. If you break it, you will select another very much like it. Yet it may be that if at first you had selected another ax, your average efficiency would be ten per cent greater.

The principle involved in this example is that in matters of manual technique, wrong choices tend to perpetuate themselves through habit. When I write these lines, do I keep my paper and pen in just the relation that makes writing easiest, the physical obstruction to the flow of my ideas least? It is a hundred to one that I do not. I am working in a deep worn channel of habit, a channel first traced out, I suppose, by a teacher who wanted me to hold my hand in writing just as some extinct authority, with a different constitution of bone and muscle and nerves, was supposed to have held his hand. When you read these lines, do you hold the book in just the best relation to your eyes and the light so that the physical friction to the flow of your ideas is at a minimum? A hundred to one, you do not. It does not make a great difference to us. We do not read or write enough to make us old before our time. But the man who has the wrong habit of using his ax or shovel or wheelbarrow — usually the wrong type of implement besides — does grow old before his time and achieves too little.

The writers on the art of management — scientific management most of them prefer to call it — have filled volumes with the striking results that can be attained, and have been attained, through the application of rational management to the equipment and manual habits of workers. They have shown how the average bricklayer can double or treble his performance by a better adjustment of scaffolding which allows him to eliminate excessive stooping, by closer attention to the consistency of his mortar, by learning how to pick up a brick and how to lay it down. One might suppose that this last part of the art of bricklaying would have attained to perfection within the trade in the time that has been given to it since the construction of the Tower of Babel. But no, the scientific managers have demonstrated that bricklayers do not know how to pick up bricks. It remains for good management to teach them the art.

Neither do professional shovellers know how to shovel coal. Polakov's "Mastering Power Production" cites an instance in point. Four men each working twelve hours a day, were required to move by shovel and wheelbarrow, 180,000 pounds of coal a day. They could not stand the work long, and gave it up. A little intelligent thinking was then applied to their equipment. They were found to be working with short handled shovels of sixteen pounds capacity and wheelbarrows of 250 pounds, built so as to throw an excessive weight on the arms. In place of this equipment, they were given long handled shovels of 21.5 pounds capacity and wheelbarrows of 400 pounds capacity, but lighter on the arms. In consequence of the change, the men found themselves able to move 65,000 pounds each in eight hours instead of 45,000 in twelve. Moreover there was no longer complaint that the work was too hard.

It would be going too far to say that all manual equipment and all manual habits are wrong. But it is not going at all too far to say that wrong equipment and habits are so general and so much of a handicap to efficiency, that a golden harvest awaits the managers who can make substantial progress toward substituting the right equipment and the right habits.

8. *A prerequisite to good management is securing the good will and coöperation of the workmen employed.*

Many improvements in management can of course be made without directly involving the relations of employer and employee. Whatever these relations, good planning, proper choice of equipment, systematic accounting, will stop many leaks and often substitute profits for losses. But the greatest leak of all is the active discontent of labor, with its consequences, lack of diligence and attention, and frequent changes in the working force. The management may do its very worst in the way of imposing fines and holding the threat of dismissal over those who do not come up to the standards; but the best work is simply not to be got out of an unwilling workman. It was not to be got out of slave labor, with all the atrocities of that system. Still less is it to be got out of free labor.

It has been pointed out that in the early period of American industry the working day was much longer than even the interest of the employer, if it had been enlightened, would have fixed. Employers, like manual workers, form bad habits. They adjust their operations to the premise that they may command a certain number of hours of the workers' time, and they stick resolutely to the view that they benefit by holding firmly to every hour. Yet there is abundant evidence that in a wide range of industry, a worker will in the long run accomplish more in an eight hour day than in one of ten or twelve hours. During the Great War, the British Ministry of Munitions assumed for a time that in the national emergency it was justifiable to remove all restrictions on overtime and hold the munitions workers to ten, twelve and occasionally fourteen hours. The immediate result was a speeding up of production. But presently chronic fatigue supervened, and the working day had to be cut back toward the eight hour limit, simply in the interest of maximum production.

There is, of course, no specific number of hours that represents the most effective working day for all classes of labor. In general, employments that involve a heavy drain upon the attention require a shorter day than those in which operations are so mechanical that one can attend them satisfactorily while his wits go wool-gathering. But it is probably true that as a rule, the working day is too long. It is to be borne in mind that all our industry grew up with the habit of the long day taken over from the more primitive, less nerve racking conditions of agricultural life, and that employers as a class have steadily opposed every change to a shorter day. Undoubtedly there are still innumerable vestiges of the the destructively long day, which it is the business of good management to excise.

Still more vital than the question of hours is the question of wages. It is vain to expect maximum performance from workers who are housed in hovels, clad in rags, fed on innutritious fare. They could not do good work, even if they had the will, and the will is not in them. An adequate standard of living is just as much in the employers' interest as efficient equipment. A copious encyclopedia would be required to record the instances in which an increase in wages was accompanied by a more than proportionate increase in efficiency. We are constantly hearing of the menace to American industry of the cheap labor of Europe and the Orient. But the fact is that except in industries specially circumstanced, high priced American labor is cheaper than the low priced labor of foreign countries. China, for example, has excellent deposits of iron ore, and vast beds of the best coal. But Chinese steel rails do not threaten to drive

American rails off the international market. The Japanese, with their favorable commercial position, have made great inroads into the market for cheap cottons in China. In better grade cottons, Japan does not compete successfully in the international market with higher priced occidental labor. When oriental labor becomes dear enough to afford a good standard of living, we shall perhaps have reason to fear its competition.

In the matter of wages, as in that of hours, the industry of today is still afflicted in some measure by bad habits taken over from the original rural environment. Industry found labor cheap and adjusted itself to that cheapness. It has resisted every rise in wages, crying ruin whenever the movement for higher wages became formidable. Wages have risen and the ruin has not supervened. On the contrary, prosperity has ultimately been advanced by rising wages. It may be and indeed it is very probable, that in many occupations a further increase in wages could be granted with more than proportionate increase in efficiency. Good management will detect such points, and both increase efficiency and improve the attitude of labor.

When labor is discontented, it shifts constantly from one employer to another, except in the occasional crises of unemployment when men cling desperately to their jobs. This shifting of personnel, it has come recently to be understood, is an extremely wasteful process. Every new man taken on by an establishment has to be broken in, even if he is familiar with the general processes employed. While this breaking in is going on, his value to his employer is often less than his wages. Some industrial managers have placed the cost of adjusting a new man to his place at hundreds of dollars. It is, then, a great handicap to an establishment to have men continually leaving to try their luck elsewhere. Yet many managers have tolerated a shifting so rapid as to replace their entire working force on the average twice a year, or even more frequently. Such a replacement is known as a "labor turnover." The frequency of the "labor turnover" is one of the tests of the quality of management. A good manager will devise means for holding his labor beyond the term customary with the industry. And that involves a systematic study of the attitudes, habits and aspirations of labor that few managers have as yet undertaken. It involves a readjustment of wages systems, as well as a sympathetic attitude toward the organizations on which laborers are more and more relying for the defence of their interests.

It is not to be supposed that laborers will take kindly to the remoulding of their manual habits unless they are to share the benefits of the increased production. The scientific managers have worked out a great many schemes of bonus payment for exceptional performance, designed to secure the coöperation and good will of labor. Some of these schemes have worked well, for a time, and then have failed. It may well be doubted that it will ever be possible to institute a mechanical scheme of wages payment that will insure permanent harmony and good will. What is needed is a continuous personal relationship between management and labor which will establish in the minds of the laborers a confidence in the management and a belief that the interests of labor are given full consideration, along with the interests of the capital of the enterprise.

9. *A consequence of the general improvement in management is to provide more goods and hence to increase the social welfare.*

In working to improve his art of management the enterpriser is aiming at increasing his profit. He does not lower prices to the consumer simply because he is able to produce at lower costs. But if he has found a system which insures him a comfortable margin of profit, he naturally increases his output, and in so doing tends to bring prices lower. As other enterprisers in the same industry copy his methods or work out equally effective methods of their own, prices tend more strongly to fall.

But improvements in the art of management, like improvements in the methods of utilizing fuel, are not restricted by nature to any one industry, but, with appropriate modifications, may be applied generally. Accordingly, any cheapening will affect not one product alone, but most of the other products for which it is exchanged. With the increased product of their industry, the employers and employees engaged in manufacturing clothing are able to buy a larger volume than before of the products of other industries affected by improved management. Progress toward better management is, then, an important interest of society as a whole. It works toward placing at the disposal of everyone a more adequate supply of the necessaries and comforts of life.

10. *In some cases improvements in management can be instituted only through collective action, often taking the form of standardization.*

Just as within each industry there are usually a number of operations that must be executed serially, and that necessitate careful planning, so among the several industries there are serial relations that demand collective planning. Thus the lumber industry, transportation and the building industry form a series demanding coördination. No matter how well the building industry is planned, stoppages will be inevitable unless the railways bring forward steadily the products of smoothly functioning lumber mills. The printing trades, transportation, the paper mills and pulp mills form a similar series.

Almost every industry takes its place in some such series.

Since each industry is conducted by numerous independent concerns, there is likely to be much that is haphazard in the interrelations of the industries. Every paper mill, for example, tries to make a product that is in some degree distinctive, so that a printing establishment which has once become its customer will be bound to it. Consequently there has grown up a vast variety of papers differing in weight, sizing, color, and dimensions of sheets. The great purchasers of paper, newspaper, magazine and book publishers, form their own distinctive ideas as to the dimensions of sheets, the weight and finish of paper. We have in the United States some six thousand brands of paper, about half of which are not much used. It is of course plain that the differences between these grades must often be so minute that only an expert could detect them. Fifty or sixty grades would probably satisfy whatever natural demand for variety exists.

The consequence of this multiplicity of brands is that every important paper dealer has to keep on hand an immense stock of paper. The customers destined to call on him for immediate shipment in the next month may want only grades 1, 40, and 300, but he can not be sure that they will not demand any one of the numbers between the first and the last and additional numbers besides. He must, therefore, have stock of all grades on hand. And that means a great deal of capital tied up, accumulating interest charges to be passed on to the printer and finally to the buyer of printed matter.

Nor is this tying up of capital the whole of the difficulty. No paper dealer can keep on hand enough of all these grades to meet any possible demand for one. Hence it must often happen that printing is held up, workers thrown out of employment, and the profits of the enterprise jeopardized because the right kind of paper is not to be had, until some factory has had time to make it. And at other times, a paper mill has to close down because the market, though hungry for other brands, does not want the kind this mill is prepared to make.

Similarly in the lumber industry, a great complexity of grades has developed where simplicity would be of great value to both the builders and lumber manufacturers. Say that a contractor has undertaken to lay hardwood flooring in a large hall. The specifications call for a given grade and thickness. In the progress of the work, the contractor finds that the grade he was relying on is exhausted in the local lumber yards, but another grade similar in every respect except that it is slightly thicker is available. What shall he do about it? He will either wait for another shipment or lay the thicker lumber and dress down the extra thickness by hand. In either case there is serious waste, to increase the cost to the owner or diminish the contractor's profit.

Such meaningless handicaps upon industry are a proper object of public inquiry or semi-public intervention. During the Great War, when productive power was at a premium, many manufacturers proceeded on the recommendation of officers of the government, to reduce excessive variations in products through the application of rational standards. After the war, this movement was taken up by the Federated Engineering Societies, whose report on Waste in Industry has already been cited in this chapter. The progress that it is possible to make through associated action under a public spirited impulse is indicated by an agreement that was reached among the makers of vitrified paving brick. There had been over sixty grades on the market, to confuse the public purchasing agents and cause frequent stoppages of work for lack of material. It was agreed to reduce the number of brands to twelve or less. This means less individual character in paving bricks, but no doubt more good paving.

11. *Summary.*

Management, originally an undifferentiated incident of ownership, has developed into a specialized function, with an organization which tends to grow steadily more complex. The owner becomes separated by a chain of increasing length from the workmen directly engaged in production. The traditional form of management, which still prevails in American industry, is built upon the principles of selection and discipline. The present state of management in America, though more efficient than that of an earlier epoch, is far from satisfactory, as measured by the best practicable standards.

A properly developed management is premised upon cost accounting. It devotes systematic attention to the saving of material; to the planning of production in order to insure continuous functioning; to the proper adaptation of implements and habits of work. Good management secures the good will and coöperation of labor, partly through a rational limiting of hours of labor and provision of as adequate wages as possible, partly through a systematic effort to understand the point of view of the laborers and to safeguard their legitimate interests. Improvement in management is a public concern of great importance, and justifies public intervention where the difficulties to be overcome are external to the single establishment and involve a whole industry or group of industries. In recent years, such intervention has taken the form of applying pressure to induce industries to apply standardization to their products.

CHAPTER IX

THE CONCENTRATION OF INDUSTRY

1. *The average size of the business establishment is steadily increasing.*

It is a matter of common observation that to launch a business to-day a larger capital is required than was the case a generation ago. An examination of the census statistics of manufactures shows us how strongly marked this tendency toward larger establishments has become. From 1880 to 1914 the number of establishments making agricultural implements decreased from 1943 to 601, while the aggregate capital of the industry increased from $62,000,000 to $338,000,000. The following table illustrates the same tendency in other industries: —

	1880 Number of Establishments	1880 Capital	1914 Number of Establishments	1914 Capital
Boots and Shoes	4,959	$42,000,000	1,355	254,000,000
Chemicals . .	595	28,000,000	395	224,000,000
Furniture . .	5,227	44,000,000	3,192	267,000,000
Lumber . . .	25,758	181,000,000	27,229	916,000,000

In many other industries, while the number of establishments increased during this period, the capital increased far more rapidly. The number of establishments making cotton goods increased from 1005 to 1328, but the capital increased from $219,000,000 to $899,000,000. Silk manufacturing establishments increased from 382 to 902; their aggregate capital increased from $19,000,000 to $210,000,000. There is hardly a single branch of manufacture in which the average establishment has not increased in size very markedly. The same thing is true even in greater degree in the business of transportation, both by rail and by water. It may seem that the successful competition of motor trucks and buses with steam and electric railways offers an exception to this rule. But as motor transport develops, "fleets" of motors press hard upon the owner of the single vehicle. In retail and wholesale trade, in banking, and in insurance, we find the same general tendency toward an enlarging business unit. The present may therefore justly be characterized as an era of business concentration.

In order to understand this tendency, we must acquaint ourselves (1) with the external conditions making large scale business possible, and (2) with the advantages that enable the large business enterprise to prevail in competition with the smaller one.

2. *The size of the business establishment is limited by the facilities for assembling raw material.*

Among the industries showing least tendency toward increase in the size of the individual establishment is that of canning and preserving fruits and vegetables. In 1880 the average capital of an establishment engaged in this industry was $20,000; in 1914 it was $40,000. A cannery must depend for its material upon the products of a relatively small area, since fresh fruits and vegetables cannot be carried far without deterioration, except at great expense for packing and icing. The size of an establishment for the making of butter and cheese suffers under the same limitations. The same thing was formerly true of the slaughtering of cattle and swine; but in these industries a radical change has occurred in recent years.

For an analogous reason no marked tendency toward

concentration has appeared in agriculture. In that industry, an important element in success consists in keeping the dwelling place of the laborers so near to the fields that no great amount of time is wasted in going to and from the work. It is also essential that the barns and granaries be near enough to the fields to obviate excessively long haulage of the products. It follows, then, that the number of acres that may be managed from a common center is somewhat narrowly limited. An apparent exception to this rule is to be found in the great wheat farms of the Pacific States, the Dakotas, and the Canadian Northwest. Here the land is level and free from stones and stumps of trees; the natural fertility is great, and evenly distributed over large areas. Cultivation consists simply in plowing, sowing, and harvesting, and this can be done by aid of the highest type of agricultural machinery. As soon as the natural fertility of the soil is exhausted, however, a more intensive tillage will be necessary; fertilizers will have to be applied; rotation of crops will succeed continuous wheat-cropping. For such tillage the immense unbroken fields are not well adapted. The "bonanza" farm is a transient as well as an exceptional phenomenon.

3. *The size of the business unit is further dependent upon the facilities for marketing products.*

Some products deteriorate so rapidly that they cannot be produced in large masses and distributed over wide areas. Baker's bread will serve as an example of this type of commodity. It would be useless to erect a bakery so large that it could not find a sufficient market for its wares within easy delivery distance. The production of many kinds of fresh fruits and vegetables is similarly dependent on a local clientèle for a market, and the size of the establishment is limited accordingly. Some products are limited to a narrow local market because they are too bulky to justify transportation over long distances. Common bricks and firewood fall in this class. In both classes, the denser the population, the larger the business establishment that can be successfully operated.

4. *Every improvement in transportation and reduction of charges makes possible an increase in the size of the average business establishment.*

Reduction in the charges for carrying wheat and flour, both by rail and by water, have resulted in an extraordinary concentration of the business of grinding grain. Low rates on stock cars, and the development of the refrigerator car and refrigerator storage on shipboard, have made possible the centralization of the slaughtering business. Reductions in the rates on furniture have enabled Michigan furniture makers to send their goods to the most distant parts of the United States. There is scarcely a single manufacturing enterprise in the United States which has not been brought within reach of a wider market by the recent progress in transportation. Mercantile establishments find their sphere enlarged in similar manner. Rapid transit for passengers, and the advent of the motor delivery wagon, have enabled many retail stores to expand far beyond the requirements of the territory they originally served.

5. *Where industry is carried on by individual enterprisers, business concentration depends upon the concentration of wealth.*

Before the middle of the nineteenth century the typical business enterprise, both in the United States and in foreign countries, was owned by a single individual or by a partnership consisting of a small number of individuals. Large scale enterprise, then, was possible only where individuals had gained possession of fairly large fortunes. In countries where there was little inequality in wealth, as in France, the concentration of business could not be so marked as in countries where inequalities were greater, as in England. In the newer and more democratic parts of the United States, enterprise was conducted on a smaller scale than in the older parts, where wealth had been accumulated in fewer hands.

6. *The corporate form of business organization makes possible a higher degree of concentration than is possible under a system of individual enterprise.*

A business corporation, or joint stock company, is an association of individuals authorized by government to carry on an enterprise and endowed with certain special privileges, the most important of which is the right to be treated in law as a single person. Members of the association are such by virtue of ownership of shares of stock in the corporation. In the simplest form of corporation all shares of stock represent equal shares in the control of the corporation and equal claims upon its profits. The stockholders elect a board of directors and other important officers; employees of minor rank are usually appointed by the president, or by the president and directors. All business of the corporation is carried on by its officers and employees; shareholders, as such, cannot engage in business in the name of the corporation.

When a member of a non-corporate business association, or partnership, dies or withdraws from the business, it is necessary to wind up the affairs of the association. When a holder of stock in a corporation dies, his shares descend to his heirs, like any other personal property; when he wishes to withdraw from the corporation, he merely sells his shares. Changes in the personnel of the stockholders do not affect the business of the corporation. Therein lies the great superiority of the corporation over partnership associations. The former, when not limited by law, has perpetual life, and can therefore undertake policies looking to distant gains; the partnership, on the other hand, is subject to dissolution at any time, and is therefore unsuited to large and permanent enterprises.

Wherever the corporate form of organization is well established, large enterprises become possible even in communities where there are no individuals possessing great wealth. A steel plant requiring an investment of $6,000,000 may be erected in a city where no man has more than $10,000 to invest. Capital secured from a thousand different persons thus acquires the same effectiveness as a vast capital owned by a single individual.

7. *The large establishment can make the most extensive use of the principle of division of labor.*

As we saw in an earlier chapter, manifold advantages spring from the division of labor. The establishment to be launched must be at least large enough to make the fullest practicable use of this principle. Perhaps this end would be attained, so far as the working force directly engaged in the process of manufacture is concerned, in an establishment with a capital of $100,000 and with 100 laborers. A second 100 laborers, supplied with an equal amount of capital, might double the output, but they would not increase the efficiency of the first hundred men. So with a third and fourth hundred men. No further economy in concentration arises under this head.

In addition to its manual laborers, the establishment must have an "office" force; possibly it may have buying agents, who travel long distances in search of the various materials, and selling agents, likewise compelled to travel about in search of buyers. A small establishment could support only a small number of employees of these classes; there could be no extended division of labor among them. An establishment of larger size might be able to assign one man exclusively to the purchase of one kind of material, another to the purchase of another kind, and so enjoy the advantages of specialized skill. Similar division of labor might be effected among the selling agents and among the members of the office force. In this way a very large establishment could assure itself that every commercial situation arising would receive expert attention. There is, of course, no theoretical limit to the possible gains from this source. An establishment might be so large that it could have a man devoting his full time to the purchase of machine oil for its use, and something would doubtless be gained through the skill he would develop. But in practical life such trifling gains would have little effect in determining the size of an establishment. They are too small to make a perceptible addition to dividends.

8. *In the large establishment it is possible to make use of the most perfect mechanical equipment.*

The process of manufacture may involve a score or more of manipulations of the material, and at each stage several machines may be drawn into use. A number of different types of machinery are on the market, some performing the function required with greater celerity and certainty than others. The better machines, naturally, represent a larger investment. To equip a factory throughout with the best machinery would require a large capital, even if the process could be reduced to a series of steps occupying one set of machines as long as another. Such a division of the process is not ordinarily practicable; some machines contribute only very slight changes in the material, delaying it but a moment as it passes through, while other machines subject the material to more important changes and delay it for a longer period. In order that the machines may all be used to their full capacity, there must be a number of machines engaged in the slower parts of the process to one engaged in the part which can be performed quickly. And this involves a still further increase in the capital of the establishment.

In most industries, the general progress of invention is in the direction of more costly machines, and this is one of the more important reasons for the trend toward industrial concentration. At a particular time, however, there is a theoretical size of business which permits full equipment with the best machines then available. An increase in the establishment beyond this point brings no advantage in the direct process of manufacture. There may, however, be other important advantages to be gained through such enlargement of plant.

9. *The large establishment enjoys the advantage of cheap power.*

The providing of power, in most manufacturing industries, is one of the most important of technical problems and here the large establishment usually has decided advantages. The larger the power plant, in general, the cheaper can power be furnished. There is not so much heat wasted in a large furnace as in a small one; a large power plant can be so arranged as to prevent much of the waste of power in transmission that usually takes place in a small establishment. Here it would be difficult to find a theoretical limit to the advantages that follow from an increase in size of plant. In practice, however, the economies to be gained in this way are not very important after a moderate size of plant has been reached. We do not find men constructing huge factories merely to obtain the advantages of cheaper power, although these advantages are not to be overlooked in determining the size of a business to be established.

10. *The large establishment wastes less material than the small one.*

In the early history of the American iron industry the waste of fuel and metal was enormous. Present-day iron manufacturers find it worth while to resmelt the masses of slag left as worthless by the early smelters. The increase in the size of the blast furnace has reduced by over fifty per cent the amount of fuel necesary to produce a ton of pig iron. The wastefulness of small scale industry is strikingly illustrated in gold production. In one gold mining district of Mexico it is estimated that $120,000,000 worth of metal has gone down into the streams in the mud and sand from which the gold is washed. Modern large scale methods would have recovered practically all of this gold.

Furthermore, much material which would be absolutely useless to the small producer is made to yield a profit to the large enterprise which is adequately provided with equipment. On the Snake River in Oregon are large deposits of gold-bearing gravel, but the amount of gold contained in the gravel — about twenty cents per cubic yard — would not pay the small producer for the trouble of getting it. A gold-dredging enterprise has secured an enormous profit — in one year, 128 per cent on its capital — from this gold deposit.

11. *The large enterprise can often utilize, for by-products, what the small enterprise rejects as waste.*

In almost every industry the material undergoes some shrinkage in the process of manufacture, through the removal of parts not fitted to enter into the main product. These parts are waste in a small establishment, and the problem of getting rid of them is often a serious one. In the large establishment they accumulate in enormous quantities, and the question whether they could not be utilized in some way readily suggests itself. Through successive experiments, one element after another ceases to figure as waste, and is transformed into a by-product. Thus forty years ago much of the residue of the small oil refineries was allowed to flow away in the streams. The same material to-day is the basis of scores of by-products, the value of which is an important element in the profits of the petroleum industry. Compare the methods of waste disposal of the small butcher shops of to-day with those of the great packing houses. To the former from forty to sixty per cent of every animal slaughtered is sheer waste, to be got rid of in whatever way the public health authorities will permit. This waste in the large establishment is transformed into over a hundred by-products, practically no part of it being considered wholly valueless. Such utilization of waste requires the investment of a considerable capital in various kinds of appliances and the employment of a large body of laborers who have nothing to do with the main product. Some of the by-products take from the mass of waste only insignificant elements; hence their utilization is possible only when waste accumulates in enormous quantities. It is obvious that only a very large establishment can carry on a thoroughly systematic plan of developing by-products. An establishment large enough to enjoy all the advantages of division of labor and of costly machinery may not be one tenth large enough to gain all the profits of waste utilization.

12. *The large establishment can secure materials at lower prices, and sell its products at higher prices, than is possible for the small establishment.*

It has already been pointed out that an important advantage of the large establishment is the possiblity of organizing its buying and selling agents in such a way as to develop special skill for each kind of transaction. A further commercial advantage consists in the fact that purchases can be made on a large scale, and therefore, generally, on especially favorable terms. The dealer in raw material can afford to sell at an unusually low price to a customer whose purchases may mount up into millions. The same thing is true of all other dealers who supply the large establishment. There may, indeed, be a combination among such dealers, fixing the margin of profit at which each must sell; but such a combination can do little toward extorting high profits from an enterpriser who can, if he chooses, dispense with the middleman altogether, and deal directly with the producer of the materials. The maker of machinery is likewise compelled to content himself with a small profit when dealing with a concern which has capital and enterprise enough to make its own machinery, if it finds a profit in so doing. In its sales, the large establishment enjoys similar advantages. It can provide each purchaser with such quantities and such qualities as he may desire. If part of the product is to be exported, the large establishment can afford to send agents to foreign countries to find out what qualities are desired, and in what form the product will be most acceptable to the foreign taste.

The large enterpriser, further, can make a more systematic study of the market than can the smaller one, and so can make his purchases and sales when the markets are most favorable.

13. *The large establishment often enjoys exceptionally low rates on its shipments.*

Since the large enterprise commonly secures its supplies, and ships its products, in large quantities, it can more frequently avail itself of the low rates on carload lots than can its smaller competitors. More important still, it can often force transportation companies, in so far as they are not narrowly controlled by public regulation, to discriminate in its favor in fixing charges. Formerly this was done openly by the railways. When laws were passsed forbidding discriminating rates, the large enterprise was given secret rebates, which often represented a very material reduction in rates. This practice is relatively infrequent now, but there remain indirect methods of gaining favorable rates. There can be little doubt that in the past railway discriminations have played an important part in hastening the concentration of industry.

14. *The large enterprise usually pays a lower rate of interest on loans than the small enterprise.*

No matter how large the capital of an enterprise may be, there will at times be need of borrowing money. At a particular time the market for materials may be so favorable that it will be profitable to purchase large supplies beyond current needs. An active business will not have on hand any large amount of idle cash; hence the necessity for borrowing. As a rule, bankers lend money at a lower interest rate to a large enterpriser than to a small one. The principal reason why they do this is that the large establishment appears to offer better security than the small one.

15. *The advantages of business concentration vary in their nature from industry to industry.*

The foregoing is of course very far from an exhaustive statement of the advantages of the large enterprise as compared with the small one. Other advantages will readily occur to any one who observes the economic development of the locality in which he lives. It will be observed that some of the advantages are prominent in one industry, some in another. In the manufacture of cotton cloth, for example, there are no important by-products to be utilized. The market for ordinary grades of cloth is well developed; the jobber takes the product from the manufacturer's hands and disposes of it to the retailer, charging a commission so low that it would hardly pay the manufacturer to develop selling agencies of his own. Neither the material nor the product is very bulky, in comparison with its value; hence the advantages enjoyed by the large concern in the matter of freight transportation are not likely to be of very great importance. To equip a mill thoroughly with the best machinery in the market does not require a very large capital; nor does an establishment have to be very large to enjoy to the full the advantages of division of labor. Certain advantages do indeed attend mere size, even in this industry; but they are not so important that they may not be counterbalanced by slightly better management on the part of the smaller establishment.

In the iron and steel industries, on the other hand, a complete equipment of machinery is usually very costly. A large capital is required to keep every important machine in constant use. The transportation of materials and products is expensive, and a great part of the profit of an establishment may depend upon the kind of contract that can be made with the transportation companies. By-products are not very important, but the larger establishment can secure large economies through making the best use of its material. Fuel is of course an immensely important item in the industry, and decided advantages are to be obtained through purchases on a large scale. Furthermore, the larger the establishment the greater the economy possible in the use of the fuel. Accordingly, in this industry a very large plant will have substantial advantages over one of moderate size. In the meat packing industry, so far as the use of machinery is concerned, there is no important advantage enjoyed by the very large plant of which a plant of moderate size could not avail itself. Economy of fuel is another minor consideration in this industry. The important advantages of the large plant consist in more systematic division of labor, better utilization of by-products, better conditions of transportation, and more effective advertising. In the refining of petroleum almost every form of advantage that has been mentioned favors the large establishment.

It is not to be inferred that the advantages of the large establishment are confined to manufacturing industry. Mercantile business shows much the same tendency toward concentration. In the retail trade, the large establishment enjoys great advantages in the purchase and sale of goods; it not only buys more cheaply, but it is better able to cater to the tastes of its customers than the small store. It can afford a style of advertising that reaches the public, while the small establishment is likely to throw away the money it spends in advertising, not succeeding in impressing the conviction of its merits upon the prospective customer.

16. *The gains from concentration are subject to a law of diminishing returns.*

Theoretically it is difficult to establish a point beyond which further enlargement of a business establishment would be unprofitable. Every enlargement of a petroleum refinery, for example, makes possible some new economies. After a certain size has been reached, however, an establishment is able to enjoy most of the known advantages of large scale production. In some industries, this involves an investment of $500,000; in other industries, perhaps, of $50,000,000. A capital of such size the enterpriser will vigorously strive to bring together. A profitable business may perhaps be conducted with a much smaller capital; but it will be more and more seriously handicapped as time passes, and the average size of new competing establishments increases.

There is of course no reason why an establishment should not be much larger than is necessary to obtain practically all the benefits of large scale production known at the time. Say that a $2,000,000 plant offers all these advantages, there is no reason why a $4,000,000 or a $6,000,000 plant should not be established. But capital cannot be got together without effort; and unless substantial advantages are to be gained through the larger investment, the enterpriser is likely to rest content with the smaller one.

As we have seen, the expansion of businesses already established, in whatever branch of industry, is confined to narrow limits by the law of diminishing returns. There is a similar law which confines within narrow limits the size of a new enterprise in an industry dependent upon local supplies of material, or a local market for its products. With such enterprises, a point is reached where increasing business is attended by increasing cost, transportation generally representing the expanding element in cost. Finally, we have the new enterprises in industries which are practically independent of local supplies of material and of the local demand for products. In these enterprises we may assume that no element in production is as yet fixed. They may, within limits, assume such magnitude as will give them command over all the economies of large-scale production. These economies have a determining importance in the choice between a small business and one of moderate size; they are of less importance in the choice between an establishment of moderate size and a large one; with further increase in size of establishment their importance dwindles. Perhaps there is no point at which further economies cease; but there is a point at which they become practically negligible. In economic language, the economies from concentration of industry are subject to a law of diminishing returns.

17. *Summary.*

Concentration, or increase in size of the business establishment, is a characteristic of the existing stage of economic development. A partial explanation of concentration is to be found in improvements in transportation, which make possible the assembling of raw material and the marketing of finished products. A prerequisite to concentration is the control of great wealth by single enterprisers. Such control may result either from the growth of large fortunes or from the adoption of the corporate form of business organization.

The advantages of large-scale production are: (1) more thoroughly systematized division of labor; (2) better mechanical equipment; (3) cheaper power; (4) utilization of waste; (5) lower prices for materials and higher prices for finished products; (6) lower charges for transportation; (7) lower interest rates. All these advantages are subject to a law of diminishing returns.

CHAPTER X

BUSINESS COMBINATIONS

1. *In many branches of trade and industry the several establishments are united in combinations that limit in greater or less degree the independence of action of each one.*

In the last chapter we saw that the average industrial establishment is steadily increasing in size. In some industries concentration has already gone so far that a small number of establishments control the greater part of the output. A movement that is even more striking than the concentration of industry is the formation of combinations among the enterprisers controlling an industry. This movement is, in part, a direct result of concentration. When the number of producers becomes small, it is relatively a simple matter to unite them for a common purpose. The tendency toward combination is, however, not a necessary result of concentration; we may therefore best treat the two movements separately.

Combinations are most frequent in the fields of transportation and manufacture. Most of the railways of the country are combined in a few great systems; the manufacture of steel is dominated by one great combination and a half dozen lesser corporations of very considerable capital. A similar condition exists in the manufacture of illuminating oil, tin plate, sugar, and in a great variety of other industries. The production of copper and the smelting of silver and gold-bearing ores is largely controlled by combinations. A combination of great capitalists controls the mining of anthracite coal; in some parts of the country the mining of bituminous coal has fallen under the domination of combinations. Indeed, we may say that the tendency toward combination manifests itself in practically every branch of economic life.

2. *Combination may take the form of a union of producers that, as independent units, would be in active competition with one another.*

The combinations that first attracted serious attention in the United States were organized in the field of railway transportation. Two roads, uniting the same terminals, instead of competing recklessly for business, often formed agreements dividing the traffic on what appeared to them an equitable basis. In most of the early industrial combinations, the members forming the union were engaged in the same stage of the process of production, and hence were active competitors until the combination was formed. Such were the steel rail, the tin plate, and the wire nail combinations in the iron and steel industries. Similar combinations have existed among the paper manufacturers, the smelters of the more valuable metals, the distillers, and the binding twine manufacturers. It is associations of this kind that are commonly designated by the term *combination.*

3. *Combination may assume the form of a union between establishments engaged in different stages in the process of producing and marketing a commodity.*

One of the earlier phases in economic development was the distribution of the various stages in the production of a commodity among a number of industries or sub-industries. The manufacture of woolen cloth represented several independent industries: washing and sorting wool, carding and spinning, weaving, fulling, dyeing. The distribution of the product to the various consuming centers gave rise to another independent line of business, the wholesale trade. The work of placing the finished product in the hands of the consumer was taken over by another business, the retail trade.

In recent years an opposing tendency has made its appearance. The entire work of preparing and distributing a commodity is, in many cases, undertaken in a combination of establishments representing a single enterprise. One company mines coal and iron ore, transports these materials in its own ships and over its own railways, transforms the materials into pig iron for use in its own steel plant, and sells the finished product — rails, structural material, etc. — directly to the final purchaser. There are furniture makers that advertise the fact that every stage in the process of production, from the felling of the tree to delivery at the customer's door, is under their control. Shoe manufacturers own the tanneries that supply them with material, and chains of retail stores that place the product before the consumers. This uniting of all the stages in the process of production in one combined enterprise is known as the *integration of industry.* Integration and combination in the restricted sense often go hand in hand. The United States Steel Corporation is a combination of producers in the final stage in production, as well as a combination of producers in different stages of the process.

4. *Some combinations are temporary in their nature.*

Even in an industry which is apparently so unfavorable to combination as agriculture, temporary combination is becoming fairly common. Farmers often combine for the purchase of machinery, seed, or other supplies, or for the shipment of their products to distant markets. Similarly, petty retailers combine in the purchase of goods from the manufacturers, thereby gaining the benefits of purchasing in large quantities. A number of newspapers unite in sending a correspondent to a war or other center of popular attention. Groups of financiers form combinations, known as "syndicates," to subscribe a loan which would tax too seriously the resources of any one. Combination of the nature here described is often termed business coöperation. It is to be carefully distinguished from labor coöperation, a system under which the laborers seek to rid themselves of the control of an employer, and from consumers' coöperation, a plan by which consumers seek to get rid of the middleman, or merchant, and eliminate his profit.

Another form of temporary combination has for its purpose common action in fixing prices. On several occasions in the last two decades producers of cotton and tobacco have attempted to effect combinations for holding out for what they considered remunerative prices, and in the period of agricultural depression following the Great War similar combinations were sporadically attempted by wheatgrowers. Competing railways frequently agree upon charges for a limited period of time. Groups of speculators often combine to force up the prices of commodities or securities over which they hold a temporary control.

5. *Some combinations, though permanent in nature, include in their scope only a small part of the activities of their several members.*

In many parts of the country the growers of fruit have formed associations for the purpose of controlling the marketing of products. In his business as a fruit grower, each member of the combination is entirely independent; each member endeavors to excel his fellows in quantity and quality of output. Long experience of the exactions of the transportation companies and the commission merchants has led to united action in the marketing of products. Some of the larger associations have agents who visit all the important consuming centers and make the most favorable terms with the merchants who deal with the consumer. They also have agents whose duty it is to watch over the movement of cars bearing the products of the association, and to take note of the condition of the products at the time of delivery. In some countries dairymen and poultry producers have organized similar associations.

Most of the newspapers of the country are combined for the purpose of gathering news. This work has become so complex that a paper which cannot avail itself of the service of one of the great news gathering companies, like the Associated Press, operates under very grave handicaps. The value of these services is indicated by the fact that the mere right to use the service of the Associated Press is reckoned at $400,000 in the assets of a daily paper in New York City. In every large city the banks maintain a clearing house, where the claims of the various banks upon one another are settled. So important is this function of settlement that a bank which is excluded from the clearing house is seriously handicapped in its business. In some German industries the several establishments, while acting independently in the domestic market, maintain common agencies to handle the export trade. So advantageous did such combined action in international trade appear that Congress has enacted a law permitting American corporations to combine for the purposes of carrying on business abroad.

In many cases in American industrial history attempts have been made to control by combination the aggregate output of an industry, and so to fix prices. The several enterprises were left free to pursue their own policies in matters of production; in matters pertaining to the marketing of products they were subject to the control of the combination. This form we shall consider further in a later section.

6. *A combination may merge the several establishments into a single enterprise. This form of combination is known as a consolidation.*

In the great industrial enterprises of to-day, such as the United States Steel Corporation, the Standard Oil Company, and the American Sugar Refining Company, the separate establishments have completely surrendered their independence of action. Each establishment has its own officers, but these are chosen by the combination, or "parent" corporation, which thus determines their policy in every important respect. Several hundred combinations of this nature have been organized. So important are these combinations that many persons believe that the days of individual enterprise in the field of industry are numbered.

7. *The earliest effective form of permanent combination for purposes of price control was the "pool," an agreement distributing the amount of business to be done, or the receipts from the business, among the several enterprises.*

In the period following the Civil War competition became so keen in many lines of business as to force prices to the cost level, or even lower. This was especially the case in railway transportation. At first an attempt was made to maintain rates through formal agreements; but each railway, in its zeal for increased business, was strongly impelled to cut rates in spite of its agreement to maintain them. Various devices were employed to restrain this tendency toward cutting rates. The most successful of these were the "pools." A number of railways, competing for traffic between two centers, would agree upon a division of the traffic ("traffic pools") or upon a division of the receipts from the traffic ("money pools"). Thus in 1870 the three railways connecting Chicago and Omaha made an agreement by the terms of which each road was to accept whatever through business was offered, at a rate set by mutual agreement. Each road was to retain for itself 45 per cent of the earnings of the through passenger business and 50 per cent of the earnings of the through freight business. The remainder of the earnings was to be placed in a fund to be shared equally by the three companies. This arrangement remained in force for practically fourteen years; it was finally destroyed by hostile legislation.

A similar plan was adopted by the Bessemer Steel Pool in 1896. Each mill was assigned a certain percentage of the total amount of steel that was to be produced by the association. If any mill exceeded its allotment, it was required to pay $2 a ton on the excess to the treasury of the association, and an equal sum was paid those members of the association who fell short of their allotted output. In this way a restraint was placed upon the more active producers, and prices were maintained at a decidedly profitable level. This pool, like the great majority that were formed, was short-lived. Some of the more powerful members became dissatisfied with the percentage of output allotted to them and withdrew, leaving the pool too weak to maintain prices.

8. *A stronger form of combination was created by placing a majority of the shares of stock in each constituent company permanently in the hands of trustees. This form of combination is known as a trust.*

In 1882 the stockholders of the leading petroleum refining corporations, which had for many years operated in harmony under informal agreements, placed a majority of their stocks in the hands of nine trustees. For the stock surrendered to the trustees, the owners received certificates entitling them to shares in the profits of the combination. The power to vote the stock was transferred irrevocably to the trustees, who were thus in a position to determine the policy of each company. This form of organization was adopted by several other powerful combinations. By a federal law of 1890, known generally as the Sherman Anti-Trust Law, the trust was made illegal, so far as it affected interstate commerce, and most of the states have passed laws prohibiting trusts. This form of combination, therefore, has been destroyed.

9. *A permanent combination may be established through the formation of a corporation holding a majority of the stock in each of the companies which it is sought to combine. Such a corporation is properly termed a holding company; in popular speech it it called a "trust."*

When the trust form of organization became outlawed, men who sought to attain the same end hit upon the device of organizing a corporation with power to purchase and hold the stocks of other companies. Accordingly, when a group of powerful producers desire to form a permanent combination, they secure a charter from whatever state happens to be most kindly disposed toward that sort of business, authorizing the formation of a corporation with extensive powers, including the essential one of holding stocks in other companies. They then exchange their shares in the business corporations which they control for shares in the new company, and endeavor to induce other persons interested in the same industry to do likewise. Or the new corporation may place its shares on the market, and use the proceeds in the purchase of shares of producing companies. In this way it is possible to bring a large part of an industry under a single control. The process of thus merging a number of enterprises into one is known as "consolidation."

The so-called trusts of to-day are organized in the way described above. In some cases the holding company, instead of buying shares in a producing company, buys its plant outright. In many cases it fails to secure a majority of the stock in such a company, but secures a sufficiently large minority of stock to make its influence decidedly felt. For a long time the legal status of the holding company was extremely uncertain. The analogies with the trust, which had been outlawed, were very close, and it was an open question how far the courts would be beguiled by a mere change in appearance. As a fact the Standard Oil Company was found unlawful and ordered dissolved; the Steel Corporation was judged to be within the law. The distinctions drawn by the court are highly technical. But it is a fair view of the situation that holding companies aiming primarily at control of prices and actually exercising control are unlawful, while companies aiming at more efficient production are not.

10. *Consolidation increases the productive efficiency of the several establishments.*

Where a number of establishments are competing, it is to the interest of each to retain exclusive possession of such improvements in methods as it may succeed in making. If an improvement consists in a mechanical invention that can be patented, the establishment which secures it is protected in its monopoly by the law. It is conceivable that each one of a score of competing companies may thus retain exclusive possession of a device that the others could use to advantage. Consolidation permits each company to make use of all the patented devices originating in the establishments of the other companies.

The United States Steel Corporation erected at Gary, Indiana, a steel-making plant which was to embody every idea that had proved profitable in any of the plants of the company. It was anticipated that steel would be manufactured more cheaply at the Gary plant than was possible in any other steel works, and with certain qualifications, this expectation has been realized. No company not having the combined experience of the Steel Corporation could hope to establish a plant of equal efficiency.

The manager of one out of a number of competing establishments knows only in a general way what success his rivals are enjoying. One establishment may produce steel at slightly less cost than another, without attracting special attention. When one plant in a great combination shows a lower cost per unit of output than do the others, the fact is at once known to the officers of the combination, who naturally seek to learn the causes of this superior efficiency, in order to introduce improvements in the establishments of less efficiency. Thus in a consolidated enterprise there is a resistless tendency to force every establishment to keep pace with the one which displays the greatest efficiency.

11. *Consolidation encourages a higher degree of specialization in production than does the system of competitive enterprise.*

An independent establishment, in order to retain its customers, is often compelled to cover a comparatively wide range of production. This involves keeping on hand a large amount of machinery which can be used only for a small part of the time. It also involves, in many cases, the production of goods for which the supplies of material upon which it relies are not especially well adapted. A consolidated corporation can send orders received to those plants which are in the best position to execute them promptly and efficiently.

12. *Consolidation makes possible the supplying of each customer from the plant nearest to him, and thus reduces cost of shipment.*

Where an industry is competitively organized, there is a tendency for each producer to invade the territory naturally belonging to his competitors. Castings for use in Alabama should naturally be made in Alabama; castings for use in the Pittsburg district should naturally be made there. But if there is competition between makers of castings in the two centers, some of the products of Pittsburg will be sent to Alabama, and *vice versa*. This is sheer waste, and consolidation puts a stop to it, to the advantage of the producer and of society as well.

It is true that under the competitive *régime* informal agreements among producers to respect one another's territory kept this form of waste within bounds. But there was always disputed territory, in which freights were uselessly carried back and forth. Consolidation has eliminated cross freights, except in cases where real differences in quality make supplying from a distant mill necessary, or where the nearest mill is temporarily overwhelmed with orders.

In recent years the benefits from this practice of supplying customers from the nearest mill have in some cases been appropriated entirely by the producer, not shared with the consumer. Thus certain steel products, though made in Gary or South Chicago, are made to bear a price equal to the Pittsburg factory price plus cost of transportation to the Chicago district. That is obviously a disguised form of monopolistic price fixing. It would be impossible if the industry were conducted on a competitive basis.

13. *Consolidation reduces the chances of loss from oversupply or undersupply of the market.*

When an industry is carried on by a large number of competing employers, each one is in greater or less uncertainty as to whether he can market his products at remunerative prices. The causes for uncertainty are first, possible changes in the demand, over which the industry has no control, and second, changes in the combined output of the competing establishments. When a consolidation is formed, the second of these causes is eliminated. The producer knows exactly how great a volume will be placed upon the market. There is consequently less chance that huge stocks will accumulate at a time when the demand is slackening. When the volume of orders increases, the full extent of the increase is readily calculated, and preparations may be made for a correspondingly greater output, if an industry is consolidated. If an industry is not consolidated, each producer, although receiving an increased volume of orders, is uncertain whether the expansion of the business is general or not, and so delays preparations for increase of output, with the result that at the height of business expansion he must turn away orders at profitable prices.

Herein lies one of the chief advantages of the form of consolidation which we have described as industrial integration. When the steel industry was competitively organized, there was at one time overproduction of ore, at another time overproduction of pig iron, at still another time overproduction of steel billets, even when there was no overproduction in the final stages of the industry. Under present circumstances all stages in the industry keep pace with one another. If the demand for finished products appears to be on the increase, a symmetrical increase is ordered in the production of ore, pig iron, crude steel, and finished products.

14. *Consolidation reduces the expenses incidental to the marketing of products.*

The marketing of products is, in many lines of industry, a very complicated process, requiring great expense for advertising and for the services of trained salesmen. A manufacturer must often make special concessions in prices or in conditions of payment in order to introduce his goods; under competition he is always in danger of losing custom because of the efforts of his rivals to introduce their goods. Some efforts are of course necessary under the most favorable conditions to attract the attention of purchasers. But it is manifestly a more difficult problem to attract the attention of purchasers away from a rival's wares than to attract their attention to the general class of goods. Consolidation results in important economies in this respect. In many cases consolidated companies have been able to dispense entirely with the traveling salesman, since purchasers, having no choice, are compelled to resort directly to the producer.

One of the more important sources of loss to the competitive producer is the failure of purchasers to pay for goods secured on credit. The producer can not refuse credit, since by doing so he is likely to lose customers. The consolidated company can safely insist upon cash payment, since it has few competitors to take its customers away from it.

15. *The consolidation can usually borrow money on more favorable terms than any one of a number of competing producers.*

As a result of the manifold advantages of the consolidated company, the chances of its failure are reduced to a minimum. If it is conservatively managed, loans made to it possess a high degree of security, and consequently bear a low rate of interest. Moreover, the mere fact that the consolidation represents a vast aggregate of capital places it in an extremely favorable position in the loan market. Every one has heard of the Standard Oil Company, the United States Steel Corporation, the Harvester Trust, the great packing companies. Every one has formed an estimate of the financial standing of these companies. Consequently the man who has loaned capital to one of these companies can easily sell his claim upon it whenever he desires to regain possession of his funds. A small refinery or slaughtering establishment may hold a position that is financially as sound as that of one of the great companies mentioned. But this fact is not generally known, and those who loan money to the lesser companies find far greater difficulty in disposing of their claims when they desire to do so. For this reason they demand a higher rate of interest than they would be willing to accept from the great consolidation.

16. *The most important advantage arising from consolidation is the control over prices that it makes possible.*

All the advantages that have been enumerated would probably have been insufficient to cause an extensive movement in the direction of consolidation. Most of them could have been secured through a form of combination that would have left the independence of the individual establishment practically unimpaired. Combinations of independent establishments for purposes of price control are, under the American system, opposed to the spirit of the law, and for this reason could not be satisfactorily maintained. In Germany, where such combinations are recognized by law, there was no active tendency toward complete consolidation until after the war, when the disordered state of the whole national economic life placed a premium upon every manifestation of power, such as the great combinations organized by Hugo Stinnes presented.

It is still a disputed question whether consolidation has resulted generally in a material advance in prices. There are a number of cases in which it can readily be shown that these vast combinations have taken advantage of their monopolistic position to maintain prices at a level considerably above the competitive level. In other cases, consolidation appears rather to steady prices, preventing very low and very high prices, than to raise the average level. In any event, the rise in prices due to consolidations has been far less than a consideration of the monopoly position of these aggregations of capital would lead one to expect. The checks upon monopoly power, described in Chapter IV, appear therefore to be very effective.

17. *Summary.*

There is at present a tendency toward the formation of combinations of business establishments. The term combination is properly applied to unions between establishments in the same stage in the production of a commodity or service; it is, however, also applied to unions of establishments in successive stages in the production of a commodity. The latter form of combination is also termed industrial integration. Combinations may be temporary or permanent, partial or complete. The permanent and complete combination is known as a consolidation.

The chief forms of combination have been the pool, the trust and the holding company. The pool and the trust have been outlawed; existing combinations, commonly called "trusts," are of the holding company type. The holding company is a corporation which holds the stock of companies that are consolidated, and so controls their policy.

The advantages of consolidation are (1) the increased technical efficiency of each establishment, through application of methods developed in other establishments;

(2) greater opportunity for the specialization of each establishment to particular grades of the commodity produced; (3) reduction in transportation charges; (4) avoidance of oversupply and undersupply; (5) reduction in cost of marketing; (6) reduction in interest charges; (7) control of prices.

CHAPTER XI

COMPETITIVE WAGES

1. *Labor is the application of human faculties to the production of wealth.*

We have found frequent occasion in earlier chapters to touch upon wages and interest. Wages and interest are parts of the cost of production of commodities, as we saw in Chapter V, and as such have an important part to play in determining values. In the present and the following chapters we shall endeavor to ascertain the laws determining the rates of wages, interest, and whatever other forms of social income may remain after the shares of the laborer and of the capitalist are paid. In other words, we are entering upon a study of the distribution of wealth, or, more properly, of the distribution of the social income.

Every expenditure of human energy having for its chief purpose the production or the preservation of economic goods, or the increase in the valuable qualities of existing goods, is labor, in the economic sense of the term. Labor includes not only the exertions of the manual workers, by whom actual changes in material commodities are wrought, but also the exertions of the foremen, superintendents, managers, under whose direction the manual tasks are performed. It includes the activities of police, of judge, and of legislature, upon whose efficient performance rests the possibility of continued production in most of the existing branches of industry. Labor does not include, however, efforts undertaken for their own sake, without regard to economic result. The amateur football team spends an immense amount of energy, and gets its reward in the spending. The amateur hunter often cares little or nothing for the birds he brings down; his reward is the gratification of the prehistoric thirst for blood. The professional football player and the professional hunter, on the other hand, are laborers. They put forth their efforts for the sake of producing goods or services having a definable value and selling price.

2. *Wages are the income received on account of labor performed.*

As the term "wages" is generally used, it signifies the money or other things of value paid by an employer to those who serve him in capacities of inferior dignity; employees of higher rank receive "salaries." Political economy does not recognize any such distinction as this, based as it is upon the pretended social status of the recipient, rather than upon a difference of economic function. The ten cents a day paid to a child slave and the $100,000 a year paid to the president of an insurance company are alike wages in the blunt speech of the economist. Moreover, in economic language, the term "wages" extends to part of the income of a workman who is his own employer. One peanut vender may be working for a push-cart enterpriser, receiving three dollars a day for his efforts. This sum, all will agree, is nothing but wages. At the opposite corner of the square you may find another peanut vender, who is his own employer. The latter may gain, over and above the cost of raw nuts, gasolene, push-cart hire, etc., just three dollars a day. The two men then receive equal rewards for identical services. Possibly the second vender calls his income "profits." Political economy cannot afford to use two different terms to designate essentially the same thing, especially when one of the terms, "profits," is commonly employed in a quite different sense. Whatever a man receives simply as a reward for his exertions, whether directly or through the intermediation of an employer, is wages.

3. *Contract wages involve more important economic problems than does the wage income of the independent workman.*

While we cannot properly exclude from the term wages so much of the income of an independent workman as arises from his personal exertion, we are nevertheless justified in devoting our attention almost exclusively to wages as determined by contract between employer and employee. An increasing proportion of the world's work is being done under this system, and many of the most important economic problems of the day are concerned with it. Who ever heard of a "labor problem" in an agricultural community where every farmer relies exclusively on his own two hands? In such a community, what importance attaches to the general movement of wages, whether upward or downward? Indeed, who can determine, in such a society, how much of the total income of each farmer is wages, how much interest on capital invested in the farm? Wages have existed ever since our first ancestors were condemned to eat their bread in the sweat of their brows; but it is only under modern conditions, where one man pays another to work for him, that it comes to be of great importance to ascertain what laws govern the rate of wages. We shall therefore confine our study to that part of the economic field in which differentiation between employer and employee has taken place — where the "wage system" exists — and shall endeavor to ascertain the laws operative therein. These laws, indeed, exert an influence in the rest of the economic field as well, and are in turn influenced by forces lying outside of the field in which the wage system prevails. What a man could get as his own employer helps to determine how much he must have as a mere wage-earner; what he could get as a mere wage-earner helps to determine what he must gain as an independent workman.

4. *The returns resulting from the employment of a given amount of labor vary according to the conditions under which labor is employed.*

Let us set before ourselves, in imagination, an agricultural community in which all the land is owned by a small class of men who do not themselves engage in tillage, but hire the landless population to work upon their fields. And let us further assume that this population is unable or unwilling to migrate to other communities in search of employment. Whether there are many workmen or few, they must all seek employment upon the land, or starve.

Some of the land in the community is fertile, some of it barren. Some of it requires a large expenditure of labor for every bushel of wheat or potatoes produced; some of it yields rich crops with little labor. Every good field yields a moderate crop with a small expenditure of labor; if a larger crop is sought, it must as a rule be at the expense of a disproportionately large application of labor, as we saw in the chapter on Diminishing Returns.

Accordingly, we may safely lay down the proposition that the results arising from the application of labor to different fields, and in different methods of cultivation, will be unequal. Good land, in extensive cultivation, may yield three bushels of wheat per day's labor expended, while poorer land yields, perhaps, two bushels, and yet poorer land one bushel. Adding one day's labor to the amount previously spent on a piece of the best land may add only two bushels to the product, and adding still another day's labor may add only one bushel.

5. *Equal wages for equal tasks is the rule of competitive industry.*

However unequal the results of labor on different fields and under different methods of cultivation, the reward of labor — wages — will tend to be uniform, allowance made, of course, for differences in the physical efficiency of different laborers. Suppose that a farmer has ten fields, of different degrees of fertility, and employs one man to cultivate each, the work on the different fields being uniformly arduous. He would be a very unusual employer if he should propose to pay the men different rates of wages, according to the fertility of the field upon which each is employed. The probable result of such a plan would be that competition would arise among the men to win the employer's favor, each one desiring to be employed on the best field; and in the end we should probably find that the better fields would be apportioned to the men who would agree to perform for the employer various miscellaneous services which would, generally speaking, be equal in value to the advantages they enjoyed in the way of higher remuneration. How this would work out we might consider at greater length if we did not know by experience that no employer possessed of practical sense is willing to grade the wages of his men on any other basis than their personal effort and skill. If two workmen of equal skill put forth equal efforts, one with an old-fashioned, broken-down machine, the other with a new and efficient one, would any employer think the one deserved higher pay than the other? Certainly not. Cases of unequal rewards for the performance of equal tasks are of course to be found; but for these cases the explanation, as we shall see later, is of a wholly different nature.

Just as uniform wages will be paid for like tasks by any one employer, so uniform wages will be paid by all the employers in the community. No employer can stay in business long unless he pays as good wages as other employers. If any one raises wages slightly, he will attract to himself an increasing number of workmen, and he will soon get all he cares to have. In an earlier chapter we saw that there cannot be different prices for the same commodity in the same market. This law holds good for labor as for anything else one buys or sells.

6. *The wages of any one of a number of laborers of equal efficiency will not exceed the addition to product made by the laborer whose services are least important to the employer.*

Of ten fields, the best one, when cultivated by one workman, may yield a product worth $500; the worst one may yield only $150. What will be the maximum wage that the employer will pay? Not more than $150. For he will not pay any workman more than the entire product created by the aid of that workman, and he will not, of his own volition, pay one workman more than another. Nor can any workman compel the employer to pay him more than the one on the worst field receives. Suppose that the one employed on the best field insisted on a wage of $200. The employer would dismiss him, and place on that field the laborer formerly employed on the worst field. And so with any one of the ten laborers. What the employer would lose, if any one of them should leave him, would be simply the product of the worst field — $150, according to our premises.

If we assume that the ten fields are owned by different men, we arrive at an identical result. The employer who owns the poorest field cannot possibly pay more than $150 to the workman who tills it. If a workman on a better field demands more, his employer will dismiss him, and put in his place the workman formerly employed on the poorest field, whom he can easily induce to change employers by offering him a trifle more than the owner of the poorest field is able to pay. The dismissed workman must live; probably he will have to seek employment on the abandoned field, and content himself with the wages that the owner of that field can pay.

If we assume, instead of ten fields of varying fertility, one large, fertile field, giving employment to ten men, we see exactly the same principle at work. One of the men, cultivating the land extensively, may produce $500; a second may add to this product $450; a tenth may add to the total product of the nine previously employed only $150. The employer will not pay the first $500, the second $450, and so on down to $150. He will pay each one not more than $150. If any one should demand more, he would be dismissed, and his functions performed equally well by the man who otherwise would have added only $150. What the employer loses, when he loses any man of the ten, is the product created by the least important one of them all.

7. *The wages of any one of a number of laborers of equal efficiency cannot, under competition, be permanently less than the marginal product of labor, or the addition to product made by the laborer whose services are of least importance to his employer.*

We have, then, an upper limit of wages above which an employer cannot be compelled to go: the addition to the total output created by the man who works at the greatest disadvantage. Is there, similarly, a lower limit? In the situation we have assumed — a number of competing employers, each able to increase his employment of men through breaking up new, though less fertile, lands, or through more intensive tillage of lands already under cultivation — it is unlikely that any employer will make a large net return on the last man he employs.

Let us assume that the uniform yearly rate of wages is $120, while the product of the least important man varies from $120 on the least fertile farms to $175 on the most fertile ones. The man who has a fertile farm can increase his net income by offering a little more than $120 for an additional workman. Such a workman will not add $175 to the total output — the law of diminishing returns forbids this — but he may add $170. As the employer on the least fertile field secures a product of only $120 from his last man, he is compelled to let a man go. Perhaps the man who now becomes his least important hand is worth $125 to him, and $125 may be what the man on the next better field is worth. It still pays the farmer with the best fields to seek additional hands. The wages he must now offer are more than $125, — let us say, $130. And the additional men will be worth less to him — perhaps $165 each. Competition will still go on between the employers having the better fields and those having fields that are not so good, each rise in wages affecting, of course, the wages of all the workmen in the community. At last a point is reached where no employer can take a workman away from his competitor without offering wages so high as to outweigh the advantages to be derived from an additional employee. Here, then, wages will tend to remain stationary. Each employer will be paying his least important man so much that any increase in wages would make that man an unprofitable member of his working force. No employer would care to take on an additional man at the existing rate of wages. This means that on every farm the least important workman adds to the total product just enough to cover his wages. The addition to product made by the man working under the least favorable circumstances is, then, not only the maximum that the employer can be compelled to pay; it is also the minimum which he cannot avoid paying. If we describe as the "product of labor," that amount of valuable product which is brought into being by the presence of any particular laborer, we may say that, under competition, wages are determined by the product of the laborer working under the least advantageous circumstances (in this case, on the poorest land). This laborer is known in economics as the marginal laborer, as he is on the "margin" or fringe of employment, as it were — in a position where his continued employment is almost a matter of indifference to the employer, since his presence means neither profit nor loss. In the customary economic formula, *wages, under competitive conditions, are determined by the marginal productivity of labor* (i.e., *the productivity of the marginal workman*).

8. *An increase in the number of workers tends to reduce marginal productivity and wages.*

Now let us assume that the number of workmen in the community is increased by the immigration of equally efficient workmen from another part of the country. The new men must have employment; and there is plenty of work in the community for them to do — on one condition, however. They must accept employment on fields yet poorer than any now cultivated, or they must be added to the force at work upon the better land, occupying themselves with tasks that formerly were neglected. In either case they will add less to the product than was created by the marginal workman before the arrival of the new hands. They must accept a rate of pay lower than that which formerly prevailed, else no employer could afford to hire them. And as there will not be two rates of wages for equally efficient men, the general rate for all the workmen originally employed in the community must be reduced. If the immigration continues steadily, other things remaining the same, the marginal product of labor, and with it the rate of wages, must steadily sink.

If, on the other hand, some of the original landless population should move away, some of the worst fields would be abandoned, and it would become impossible to cultivate the better fields as intensively as before. On each field the importance of the marginal man would increase. If any employer should persist in paying the old rate of wages, his competitors, by offering a little more, would entice his men away. The tendency for wages to rise, with decline in the laboring population, would be as irresistible as the tendency for wages to fall with an increase in population.

9. *Improvements in methods of production tend, as a rule, to raise wages.*

Let us suppose that in this community are found extensive tracts of marshy land of practically no economic importance. A competent engineer enters the community, and at a comparatively low expense drains these lands and transforms them into the very best quality of tillable soil. The owners of the drained lands must have labor, and can bid a higher price than prevails generally. If the laboring population remains stationary, the effect of the new demand for labor is to withdraw men from the least favorable situations and place them upon the new land. On every farm the product of the marginal workman is increased, and wages rise accordingly. If immigration of laborers is going on, the new demand for labor counteracts the effect upon wages of the new supply; if emigration is taking place, the rise in wages that would otherwise occur is emphasized.

A similar influence may be exerted by a general improvement in agricultural practice. It is said that by the use of seed corn which has been grown in an isolated field from which all barren stalks have been removed before maturity, the average yield of corn may be increased from ten to thirty per cent. This increased yield is obtained without additional labor, excepting a small amount entailed by the care of the seed corn field. The use of such seed corn in the community we are studying would increase the product of every laborer, that of the marginal ones as well as that of the rest, and the competition of employers with one another would force them to raise wages in the measure of the increased marginal productivity. The introduction of a new forage plant, like Kaffir corn or alfalfa, might have a similar effect in increasing the productivity of the marginal laborers. So also might the use of a new kind of fertilizer, or the invention of a new agricultural implement. Almost all agricultural improvements, in fact, are likely to have the effect of increasing the productivity of labor and the rate of wages.

It is not in the least necessary that such improvements find general application. An improvement increasing the productivity of labor on one tenth of the farms will generally lead to an increased demand for labor on those farms. The demand is met by the withdrawal of labor from the farms not affected by the improvement; and this results in raising the productivity of the least favorably situated laborers on those farms, and so raises general wages.

10. *A reduction in the rate of interest tends to raise wages.*

One other influence needs to be noted here; namely, a fall in the rate of interest. There are few farms that could not be made to yield a much larger product, if abundance of auxiliary capital were to be had at a low rate of interest. If a farmer must pay ten per cent on borrowed capital or can get ten per cent on his own savings if he lends them, he will not build a good barn or drain a marsh unless he sees a fair prospect that the resulting increase in his income will be at least equal to ten per cent on the investment involved, together with wages at the current rate for all additional labor required in using the improvement. This means that when interest rates are high a great many opportunities for enterprise and the employment of labor must lie untouched. The competition of laborers for the relatively small number of jobs available keeps their marginal productivity and wages low. If interest falls, one improvement after another becomes economically possible and creates new opportunities for employment. The demand for labor withdraws part of it from the points of least productiveness and raises the general level of wages.

11. *Wages are dependent in part upon personal efficiency.*

We have seen that wages must vary with the circumstances in which labor is employed. Whatever the average personal efficiency of the workers may be, the rewards of labor will tend to rise if the supply of labor decreases and to fall if the supply of labor increases. If the capital increases and interest falls, wages will rise; if the process of production improves through new inventions or better management, wages will, as a rule, be raised. But within the lines drawn by such external circumstances as these, wages will vary according to personal efficiency. Whether the general level of productivity is high or low, the man who can do the work of two will get the reward of two, if competition works well. This is commonly the case where wages are paid according to the piece rate system. Where men are paid by the day or the month, it often happens that the more efficient workman gets no more than the one who is barely efficient enough to keep. But even here there are certain advantages that go with superior efficiency. The better man is retained when the condition of the market forces a curtailment of production. He has more chances of promotion, and of considerate treatment in case of illness or other misfortune. Where these disguised rewards are too insignificant for consideration, what is likely to happen is a levelling of efficiency. The man who can do the work of two gradually learns how to keep his output down to the average.

The average personal efficiency of labor naturally varies from time to time and from country to country, and wages vary with it. The average efficiency of the Russian farm laborer in the time before the Great War was remarkably low as compared with that of the American farm laborer. The defective equipment of Russian agriculture had much to do with the inferiority of labor, but the spirit of the laborer and the intelligence with which he directed his efforts bore also their share of the responsibility. That this was true was demonstrated clearly in the case of Russian farm laborers who emigrated to America. It was a matter of several years to bring them up to the American standard of quickness of movements and intelligent application of physical strength. Most immigrants to America have found at first that much more effort was expected of them in America than in Europe or Asia. This superiority in personal efficiency is one of the factors making for the superiority of the American wages level.

High personal efficiency is a cause of high wages, but it is also frequently an effect of high wages. When wages are so low that the worker can afford no other food than a bowl of rice, it would be foolish to expect the same capacity for hard physical labor as may be found where wages are high enough to give the worker a rich and varied diet. It has long been known to railway builders that it is impossible to get as much work out of East Indian coolies as can regularly be got out of occidental laborers. Although American railway laborers may be paid ten times the wages of laborers in India, the wages cost of constructing a mile of track in America will probably not exceed three times the cost of constructing a mile of track over a similar terrain in India. Where the initiative of the laborer is drawn upon more heavily, the superiority of the higher paid labor is likely to be still more pronounced. There are relatively few modern industries that can be advantageously transplanted from high wages countries to those in which low wages prevail.

The effect of high wages in increasing efficiency makes itself felt in a very short time. Japanese and Hindu immigrants in the Pacific States quickly respond to American conditions and put forth efforts beyond the measure of which they were capable in their countries of origin. But the full effect of high wages requires a generation or more for its development. In a region of high wages children are well fed, warmly clad and comfortably housed and grow up sounder physically and more alert mentally than the children born in a region of low wages. As a rule, the children of immigrants in America are physically superior to their parents and capable of developing greater economic efficiency. Often, to be sure, they lack the industry and patience of their parents and fail to make their superior advantages count. But this is very far from the general rule.

12. *In a complex industrial society, laborers fall into many classes between which there is no direct competition.*

We may now sum up the results of our study of wages under the assumed conditions. Wages are determined by the marginal productivity of labor, but marginal productivity itself is subject to many and varied influences, such as arise from increase or decrease in number of laborers; increase or decrease in the amount of available land; the progress of improvements; the fluctuations in the interest rate; changes in the personal efficiency of labor. Let us now see how far we can apply the same reasoning to the determination of wages under conditions more like those of modern industry, confining ourselves, however, to those parts of the industrial field in which competition exists among employers on the one hand and among workmen on the other.

The first fact that we must take into consideration is that we cannot assume that in this wide field of industry every workman can enter into direct competition with every other workman, and thus bring about an immediate equalization of wages. The journeyman tailor cannot be replaced by the excavator nor by the farm hand; the cotton-mill operative cannot take the place of the iron and steel worker. At any given time, then, there must be many rates of wages, not one universal rate.

As we enter upon a study of the forces which are responsible for the differences in wages in the various trades and occupations, we encounter a difficulty which has not hitherto arisen to vex us. How can we say what differences in general rates really exist? In all our discussion up to this point, we have spoken of equal rewards for equal services. Of course if one bricklayer does twice as much work as another, he is likely to receive twice the wages. But if a tailor receives twice the wages of a bricklayer, how can we say that it is because he does twice as much work. What common measure can we find for tailor's labor and bricklayer's labor? There is none.

13. *Through the apportionment of new additions to the working force, wages in different occupations requiring equal natural endowments tend toward an equality.*

Let us suppose that there are half a dozen occupations in a community, all of which require of beginners about the same degree of intelligence, dexterity, and strength, although they differ as widely in their nature as bricklayer's and tailor's labor, so that no direct comparison of wages is possible. Is there any reason why differences in wages per day should exist? At first, we should expect, the choice of occupations would be more or less a matter of chance. A boy would enter one of the trades because his father followed it; another, because his best friend intended to enter it, and so on.

Once in the trade, a man would have to remain there, unless he wished once more to go through the tedious tasks of a beginner. The different trades would thus be walled off, as it were, one from the other. Mature reflection might convince a man that he had made a mistake in choosing his trade; but this would not mend matters. His earnings would be wholly subject to the laws of his trade. If many men happened to be in the trade, and the demand for their services was limited, some of them would have to be set at unimportant tasks, which could not be well remunerated. And competition among the men would force wages down to the level of remuneration of these. If the trade were but scantily supplied with men, all might be employed at work that could pay a high reward, and so a high rate of wages would prevail. In each trade the rule that marginal productivity determines wages would apply; but marginal productivity would be unequal, for men of equal native ability, in the different trades.

In every trade, however, a constant supply of new recruits is necessary to keep its ranks full, and the prospective apprentice has a certain measure of freedom of choice. In one trade, he finds men discontented and impoverished; in another trade, he finds every appearance of prosperity. Unless he is very blind, he will choose a trade in which the latter condition prevails. So the tide of apprentices sets steadily away from the underpaid trades, and in the direction of the better paid ones. Failing numbers, in the former trades, raise the marginal productivity of labor; increasing numbers, in the more prosperous trades, reduce wages there. Whether this process will continue until perfect equality of rewards is established for men of equal native ability in different trades, we cannot say. The equalization depends upon the good judgment of the prospective apprentices in their choice of trades; and these, like all men, are likely to err. But gross inequality, under the circumstances, could hardly long persist.

14. *Permanent differences in competitive wages correspond with differences in the marginal productivity of labor, originating in influences affecting the distribution of the supply of labor.*

Some of the differences in wages actually existing appear to be fortuitous, as those assumed in the foregoing example. But many of these differences are clearly connected with the personal qualifications of the workman — his strength and skill, his intelligence and reliability. Others are connected with the different degrees of risk, agreeableness, and dignity of the employment itself. Still others depend upon trade union requirements or legal restrictions. What we are concerned with here, however, is not to classify the causes of differences in the wages paid in different occupations, but to see exactly how these causes operate.

We know, for example, that a dangerous occupation is likely to carry with it a higher remuneration than a safe one; that an occupation requiring a long apprenticeship is ordinarily better paid than one requiring practically no training. Why may we not say, then, that a part of a man's reward is for labor, part of it for risk?

If a tedious apprenticeship is necessary, may we not say that part of the reward of the journeyman is a compensation for the time and trouble spent in learning the trade? Such an explanation would be quite satisfactory if we actually found that, other things equal, wages were nicely graded according to risk or to the length of the period of apprenticeship — if, for example, we found that a workman in an occupation involving no appreciable risk received wages represented by x, an equally efficient workman in an occupation involving a considerable risk received $x+y$, and a third workman, in an occupation twice as dangerous as the second, received $x+2y$, and so on. But we do not find in real life any such simple rule as this. Dangerous occupations, we often find, are very ill paid in comparison with occupations requiring no greater natural ability and entailing no risk worth speaking of. Almost the least remunerative occupation that an able-bodied citizen of the United States can engage in is that of soldier, and this in spite of the fact that the Federal government prides itself upon being a liberal employer. Certainly the risks of the occupation are considerable. Trainmen on the American railways incur far greater risks of injury and violent death than most workmen in factory industry, the hand trades and commerce. Yet we do not find that railway men are better paid than other workers of equal skill, intelligence and energy. What we really find is that in some cases no allowance appears to be made for risk; in more cases some allowance is made for it, but there is no apparent tendency for this allowance to vary regularly with the degree of risk. Similarly with different degrees of skill. Ordinarily, the skilled laborer, who has undergone a long apprenticeship, receives a higher reward than the unskilled laborer of equal native intelligence. In some cases, however, this does not appear to hold true; and it is idle to attempt to show that there is any ascertainable proportion between degrees of skill and differences of remuneration. So also with disagreeableness of work. Little, if any, allowance is ordinarily made for it in wages, although in some cases it seems to play a very important part. Clearly, then, it is not enough to say that wages are affected by risk, by skill required, by disagreeableness of occupation. We must know how these causes operate, and why they operate with such irregularity.

Let us see if a concrete example will not make clear the relation risk actually bears to wages. Imagine that a gunpowder factory is erected at a distance of a few miles from a city of some size, and let us suppose that five hundred workmen will be required, and that they will be of a grade of skill that would command an average of $5 a day in perfectly safe occupations. How much will it be necessary to add to this sum, to induce them to enter the powder works?

Now, the first question that is likely to be asked is, How much danger is there that the works will blow up? You do not know this, neither do I; nor, we may venture to say, do the workmen whom it is sought to employ. Perhaps there is no danger at all in the present stage of the powder manufacture. Powder mills have often blown up, however, and most of us would prefer to stay out of them.

In every community there are some men who do not seem to be in the least afraid of danger. They may know that destruction has befallen others, but, each argues, everybody can't be killed; why should I be? Such men have supreme confidence in their luck. Danger, real or imputed, does not influence their conduct. Now, if there are a thousand men of this kind in the city, it will be quite possible to man the powder mill without offering any more of an advance in wages than would have to be offered by an enterpriser who proposed to establish a new shoe factory or nail mill. The powder manufacturer, as any one else starting a new enterprise, will offer wages a little higher than those prevailing in the city — twenty-five cents more per day, perhaps. Not every one will jump at the chance to improve his wages; but the men who despise danger will one by one leave their former employments and enter the doors of the powder mill. Presently wages will be reduced to the general level. No man will for this reason leave the mill, nor need the enterpriser care if a few should do so, for there are still plenty of men in the city who are not disturbed by fear of accident.

But suppose that instead of one thousand such men, there are only one hundred. The powder manufacturer will find that twenty-five cents extra a day fails to bring the full complement of men. Perhaps he will offer fifty cents extra; and this may bring another hundred men, who fear for their lives, indeed, but desire the additional income extremely. An additional twenty-five cents may bring another hundred, more timid or less eager for high wages. At the rate of $1 a day above the prevailing rate, the enterpriser may be able fully to man his works.

Now, we may ask ourselves, is this extra dollar a compensation for risk? Remember, there may be no real risk at all, and it may be that it is nothing but the name of powder that has kept the workmen back and forced up wages. And how is it that a powder manufacturer is able to pay men for risk, at their own estimate — very likely a mistaken one, too? Well, the powder manufacturer is experiencing the ordinary incidents of his business. Everywhere powder manufacturers have to contend with the same indisposition on the part of the ordinary workman to enter their mills. Everywhere the amount of available labor is limited, relatively to the demand for it. And so the productivity of a laborer, measured in value of powder produced, is high, and wages may be high accordingly. If, however, the number of men who do not mind the danger were sufficient fully to man all the powder works, more powder would be produced, its value would be less, and the productivity of labor, in value, would fall until it corresponded with that of labor in other occupations requiring equal skill.

If the risks to life and limb undergone by locomotive firemen and engineers were reduced by fifty per cent through the introduction of better safety appliances, the improvement of track, etc., how much could wages be reduced? I have never heard of a railway president who proposed to spend the company's money in reducing the chances of accident with the expectation that part of the cost might be met by a reduction in wages. Nor do we find that wages are especially high in the sections of the country where transportation is conducted at the greatest cost in life and limb.

In recent years there has been a tendency in every country to saddle the risks of injury and death upon the employer through workingmen's compensation laws. Where these laws have attained to their full development, every injury to a workman not the result of gross negligence on his own part has its price. Have employers been able to reduce wages as an offset to the new burden imposed upon them? Not at all. And now when the employer actually has to bear the burden of accidents, he finds it to his business advantage, as he never did before, to install all manner of safety devices. But the installation of safety devices is nowhere accompanied by a reduction in pay. Laborers did not as a rule, demand pay for risk. They will not cut their ordinary demands when risk is reduced.

15. *The standard of living affects wages directly through affecting efficiency and indirectly through affecting the supply of labor.*

What one requires to live on in accordance with one's established conceptions of comfort and decency is one's standard of living. Since most men have families to provide for, the standard of living is usually conceived in terms of the requirements of the average family unit. It is in this sense that we shall conceive it here.

So conceived, the standard of living would appear at first to be something extremely variable and fluctuating. Each family will have requirements differing from those of every other family. One family must have a spacious house in order to consider life worth living; another family can be happy in an apartment of three rooms. One family is certain that the world owes it a Rolls-Royce car; another feels favored of Providence if it can command any kind of rattling old car that will make a hill and hang together for the descent, and a third feels lucky if it can spare the sums necessary for occasional excursions by street car or bus.

When standards of consumption are so individualistic as in the cases cited they are of very little economic significance. There are standards, however, that are of a more general character. In a working class community there are certain standards of housing, clothing and food that one must live up to if he wishes to escape the pity and contempt of his fellows. These standards differ for different classes of labor. The skilled workman must make a better showing than the unskilled worker; the clerk must make a better showing, at least in clothing, than the skilled laborers; the professional man must make a still better showing; the business man, above all, must live in a way to offer presumptive evidence of prosperity. Wherever men live in sufficiently close association to be concerned about "appearances," there are standards of consumption formed or in process of formation.

Standards of living vary widely not only from class to class but from country to country. In America, for example, abundant wheat bread and sugar, and the daily consumption of fresh meat are parts of the standard of living of the average workman. In Japan rice, with occasional fish, is counted a sufficient diet. Leather shoes are an essential part of even the lowest American standard. In parts of Europe wooden shoes are regarded as satisfactory by the rural laborer and by some of the poorer classes in the towns. If we take as our base of comparison the standard of the ordinary laborer, we should find that in America it involves, on the whole, a greater command over the comforts and necessities of life than in any older country. Put in simple terms, it costs the American workman more to live than it costs the workman of France, Italy, Japan or China.

How does the standard of living affect the rate of wages? We have already seen that high wages may be a cause, instead of a result, of high personal efficiency. The workman who has been accustomed to wages high enough to provide his family with nutritious food, comfortable clothing and hygienic housing is able and willing to work harder than the workman who is reconciled to seeing himself and his family half starved and in rags. The former is more likely to bring his children up to a high standard of efficiency than the latter. And thus a standard of living, whether high or low, tends to be transmitted from generation to generation. The high standard of living became established in America when the wealth of virgin land offered a comfortable living to everyone strong enough and energetic enough to occupy it. And the standard thus established has survived the epoch of free land chiefly because it has been translated into personal efficiency.

The indirect influence of the standard of living is bound up with its actual or possible control of the supply of labor. So long as immigration was unrestricted, every period of prosperity and rising wages was characterized by a heavy influx of immigrants. At such times aliens already established in America would write to their kindred and friends of the high wages and pleasant conditions of employment they had found here. The heavy immigration resulting had the effect of checking the rise in wages, but did not immediately lower the standard of living. In the ensuing period of depression, when earnings proved insufficient to maintain the standard of living easily, a note of discontent and distress from the American working class was heard across the seas and checked the flow of immigration, for the time. If the American workman had been without standards, reconciling himself to low wages when high wages were no longer to be had, it may be assumed that immigration would not have felt the effect of his discontent until the wages levels of Europe and America had been fairly equalized.

The most potent influence of the standard of living, however, is exerted through its influence upon the growth of population. In a country where the average age of marriage is low the natural growth of population is likely to be very rapid. In the colonial and early national periods of American history, the population doubled by natural increase every twenty-five years. Such a rate of increase, at that time, was not incompatible with a steadily rising level of comfort. But it is plain that it could not continue indefinitely in any country without producing the severest pressure upon the means of production and consequent poverty among the most numerous classes of the population.

When standards of living are firmly established the tendency of population to increase beyond the means of subsistence meets a check short of universal poverty. Men will not marry and rear children unless they can foresee a fair possibility of maintaining the standards of living to which they are accustomed. The average age of marriage will be raised and the birth rate will be reduced. Where the standard of living of the working class includes nothing beyond the barest subsistence, as in China and India, there appears to be no escape from a state of extreme poverty for the masses of the population.

The standard of living exerts a powerful influence upon wages, as we have seen. But whether it operates directly or indirectly, it operates through the productivity of labor. In its direct operation, this relation to productivity is too evident to require further discussion. In its indirect operation, the relation is easily seen. The standard of living prevents that indefinite increase in the labor supply that would thrust the margin of production into barren fields, into the leaner mines, into industries of low utility, where only low wages could be paid.

16. *The special standards of living of the various professions and trades operate, as a rule, only indirectly and uncertainly.*

If you are planning to become a physician, you are likely to seek the counsel of some who are now practicing the profession. You will probably receive some such advice as this: "Whatever you do, don't make a physician of yourself. A physician must dress well; he must live in a good house; he must keep a car; in short, he must live at great expense, and, in the majority of cases, he will find great difficulty in obtaining an adequate income." Now, what this means is that physicians have a comparatively high standard of living, and that their average incomes are scarcely sufficient to meet all the demands upon them. You may not be deterred by the doleful account of the physician's financial difficulties. But is it not probable that, in the length and breadth of the land, hosts of young men are in this way turned to other professions? If, on the other hand, the majority of physicians were recommending their profession as one in which a good living was assured, is it not likely that many young men would be attracted to the profession? In the former case the average income of the physician would be likely to be increased by the growing scarcity of competent medical men; in the latter case it would be likely to be decreased by increase in numbers.

If, then, the earnings in a profession or trade are not sufficient to command, on an average, the necessaries and comforts that are deemed essential to happiness, a certain influence is exerted upon those entering the profession or trade, and thus upon the level of earnings.

In the example just given, the effectiveness of the standard of living in one profession depended upon the absence of a similar standard in other professions. Suppose that after getting the opinion of a physician as to the advisability of entering his profession, you apply to a lawyer for his opinion on law as a profession. "Whatever you do, avoid the law," he will probably tell you. Next, you go to one who has chosen journalism. "I pity a young man who selects journalism as his profession," is probably what you hear. Then you go to a teacher. He shakes his head. "If I were a young man, I should choose some other profession." Indeed, if you do not happen upon one of the few optimists who still survive, you are likely to conclude that you may as well choose the profession toward which you were originally inclined, since all professions seem to be inadequately paid. The fact is that most of us think that we need more than we get; and the result is that no one profession is able to frighten aspiring youths into choosing some other line of activity. We cannot therefore say with any certainty that such differences as we find in professional and craft earnings are determined by antecedent differences in the standard of living.

17. *Summary.*

In the widest sense, wages include all incomes originating in labor. In a narrower sense wages are the price paid by one person for another person's services.

While the productivity of labor varies with the conditions under which labor is employed, wages for tasks of equal difficulty tend toward a uniform level. This level is determined by the addition to product made by the laborers who might be most easily dispensed with, or the marginal laborers.

Wages tend to rise or fall with increase or decrease in the personal efficiency of labor. An increase in the labor supply, other things equal, reduces wages. Improvements in production usually tend to raise wages, as does also reduction in interest rates.

There is little direct competition between laborers in the several occupations; but the apportionment of the supplies of new labor tends to prevent any great inequality in the rewards of men of equal natural ability. Permanent differences in wages are the result of barriers preventing the free flow of labor from one field to another, such as a long period of apprenticeship, risk, trade regulations.

The standard of living affects wages, directly and indirectly, through affecting productivity. A population living on a high standard is more efficient, as a rule, than one living on a low standard. A high standard tends to check the growth of population whether by immigration or by natural increase, and so prevents the supply from outrunning the means of employment and subsistence.

CHAPTER XII

WAGES AS AFFECTED BY LABOR ORGANIZATION

1. *In industry at large the forces of productivity and competition are paramount, in determining wages. But organization is necessary to place labor and capital on a parity in bargaining.*

In the last chapter we saw that wages, in so far as they are determined by competition, tend to conform to the productivity of labor. It was recognized that competition works uncertainly, tardily and even in cases injuriously. Low productivity and low wages, temporarily established in an industry by competition may conceivably produce a permanent lowering of efficiency, with the result that the low wages may become permanent. None the less it was maintained that in the large, and in the long run, there can not be a wide gap between wages and marginal productivity. And the reason is that every employer who is incurring loss will reduce his working force while every employer who makes an important net gain on his marginal labor will try to increase his working force, and the competitive tugging and hauling of employers on the one side and workers on the other will force wages toward the productivity level.

But as we look around us in industry to-day, do we see competition working in this way to determine wages? Do we not rather see a body of employers doing their best to keep wages down and a body of organized workmen trying to raise them? And does not this observation incline us to the view that wages are determined by struggle, and will be high or low according as the one side or the other is the better organized and the more competently led? It would not be unnatural if we inclined to this view. But we ought to bear in mind that in economics there is often something very deceptive about first appearances. Let us see whether we can not gain a surer insight from an examination of the results of the greatest economic experiment of our time, the industrial movements of the Great War.

After an initial period of demoralization, prices in the United States began slowly to respond to the increasing demands of the belligerent nations. Placing the average prices of 1913 at 100, average prices in 1914 were 100.6, in 1915, 102.5, in 1916, 113.4, in 1917, 136.1, in 1918, 160.8. There was naturally great irregularity in the operation of this price increase. Some commodities rose hardly 25 per cent, others more than 200 per cent, but practically all commodities rose in some measure. If wages could have been kept at the 1913 level there would have been huge profits for employers as a class. But wages could not be kept there. According to the calculations of the Bureau of Economic Research, published in "Income in the United States," average annual wages for all employments rose from $723 in 1913 to $1078 in 1918.

What made wages rise? It may be said that wages went up automatically because prices went up. It cost the laborer more to live; therefore he had to have more wages. But the matter is not so simple as that. There is no general arrangement between employers and employees under which wages are marked up whenever the cost of living rises. Left to himself the average employer will not add a penny to wages on account of increased living costs, unless it appears profitable, or unless he is compelled to do so. The greatest employer in the United States, and we should suppose, the most generous and public spirited, is the government itself. How much did the government raise wages in this period of mounting living costs? Six per cent; and the increase in living costs was more than 60 per cent. Compare this increase in government wages with 80 per cent for agriculture, 78 per cent for railways, 70 per cent for mining, 63 per cent for factories, 60 per cent for the hand trades. Is it not sufficiently clear that the rise in wages can not have been an automatic response to rising living costs, nor a mere exercise in generosity on the part of the employers?

Wages rose either because the labor organizations forced a rise or because the employers found it profitable to raise them. Of these two possible explanations, which looks the more plausible, on the face of the figures? The greatest percentage of increase occurred in agriculture, where there is practically no organization. The next greatest occurred in railways, where the organizations are very strong. The hand trades are better organized than the factory workers or the miners, but their wages advanced only 60 per cent, as compared with 63 and 70.

What really happened was this: As the war demands developed, the industries catering to those demands found that they could make enormous profits if they could supply products in sufficient quantity. In order to do this they had to have more labor, and they proceeded to bid for it whatever price was necessary. They drew labor away from other industries not yet affected by war demands, and forced employers in those industries to choose between raising wages or closing down their shops. Where labor was well organized it was quick to perceive the fact that the employers could be made to pay more, and presented demand after demand. Usually it got what it demanded.

As the foregoing account shows quite conclusively, the primary force making for higher wages, both in the organized and the unorganized employments, was the increased demand for products and the high prices. In money terms, labor was worth more to the employer. He did not want to pay more, but he had to do so, or gradually lose his men to other employers, or still worse, find a strike on his hands.

War economics is, of course, pathological and we should fall into grave error if we applied the results of our study without qualification to the conditions of peace. We are, however, justified in drawing the inference that the forces of productivity and competition operate even under conditions of organization. They set limits, not easily defined, to be sure, to the efforts of organized labor to raise and of organized capital to depress wages. But within these limits there may be considerable latitude for combined action, on either side.

2. *A labor organization may conceivably increase the wages of its members (a) at the expense of some other participant in the productive process or of the consumer, or (b) through increased efficiency without cost to anyone.*

Let us assume that all the labor engaged in the manufacture of shoes is united in a hard and fast organization, powerful enough to prevent anyone not a member of the organization from working. And let us assume further that the organization has decided to raise its wages ten per cent. Who will meet this additional cost?

Of the net value product of our manufacturing industries about three fourths is paid out in wages and salaries. Or to put it specifically, in the period from 1909 to 1918, the share in the value product paid out in wages and salaries ranged from 68.7 per cent in 1916 to 77.8 per cent in 1914, according to "Income in the United

States," already cited. Now it is possible that an additional ten per cent for labor could be drawn from the twenty-five per cent of the value product retained by the employers as profits and interest on capital. But unless the industry is enjoying an especially favored position, such a reduction in the share of the employer would bring his returns below the prevailing level and drive capital out of the industry.

If capital is driven out of the industry the volume of product will shrink and its price will rise. Thus part of the additional charge for labor will be passed on to the buyer of shoes. The demand for hides and skins will be reduced and their price will fall. Thus part of the ten per cent increase will be reflected back upon the suppliers of these materials. We could pursue the analysis farther, to show how the burden would be diffused among the tanners, the butchers, and the cattle men and how, further, it would be distributed between labor and capital. But we need not trace out these ramifications. It is already sufficiently plain that the question of the ten per cent increase in wages does not lie exclusively between the employers and employees, in the shoe manufacturing industry alone. It may be one of far wider concern.

But neither the employer nor the general public is concerned primarily in wages per day or per hour. What is of concern to both is the cost of labor according to efficiency units. As we saw in an earlier chapter, well paid labor is often cheaper, in the long run, than badly paid labor. If we may assume that wages in the shoe manufacturing industry were insufficient, before the hypothetical increase, to afford adequate nutrition, clothing and housing, or though sufficient for these purposes, inadequate to produce the atmosphere of contentment and buoyancy in which men do their best work, it is entirely possible that a part, or even the whole of the ten per cent increase will be compensated for by increased efficiency. There is not the least doubt that labor could make itself ten per cent, or even twenty-five per cent more efficient in the average American industry, if it found this worth while and set resolutely about it.

But does organized labor wish to make itself more efficient? Or does it not rather cherish the doctrine that the less work each man performs, the greater the chance that there will be jobs for everybody and hence good pay for all? The latter view has, unfortunately, been widely accepted by the working class. But the contrary view is rapidly gaining adherents. At least one important American trade union avows publicly the doctrine that the organization should make itself responsible for production standards and do its best to increase output. Similar views are generally held by the most influential labor leaders in Europe. And if ever we reach a condition in which every workman must do his best in order to hold the esteem of his fellows, we shall enjoy a prodigious increase in production and an adequate basis for meeting all the reasonable demands of labor.

But even as matters stand, with no direct indentification in the laborer's mind between increased efficiency and increased wages, it must often be the case that an increase in wages pays for itself in the long run through better work. Why then does not the employer grant it without pressure from the union? Partly because he has the bad habit of confusing low wages with cheap labor. And chiefly because the cost of higher wages makes itself felt immediately, while the improvement in efficiency will not make itself felt for months, for years, or even within a generation. Raising the wages of the present body of laborers enables them to bring up their children better and promises a more efficient people, say, twenty or thirty years from now. Is the employer of to-day to be blamed if he fails to see why he should pay for this future public advantage out of his private pocket? But the impartial outsider ought to bear in mind this possible advantage when he is passing judgment on the rights and wrongs of the labor struggle.

3. *Existing labor organizations fall far short of the position of power assumed in the preceding section. Much of their policy is directed toward establishing such a position.*

There is not in America, so far as the writer knows, a single branch of industry which is completely organized. In some branches the organization members represent only a small fraction of the persons working in the industry or trade; in other branches the organization may make up the majority. Whatever the organization may do, some part of every industry will be operated in spite of its decrees. Therefore the organization must endeavor to keep its demands within the limits of moderation. A ruthlessly monopolistic policy would open the way to the rapid development of such parts of the industry as lay beyond the control of the organization.

The chief objects of labor organization are better wages, shorter hours, and pleasant and wholesome conditions of employment. But as means to these ends the organization naturally works to secure the adherence of all persons working in the trade it seeks to control and strives to keep the trade free from over-crowding, and whenever possible, to gain the support of other organized bodies of labor in its struggle with the employer.

4. *The typical form of labor organization is the trade union, an association of laborers employed in the same trade.*

In a trade which has become well established, a natural basis for organization is found in the mutual sympathy of those whose lives are passed under like conditions. One carpenter knows how to evaluate the problems of life and work of another carpenter. Even where there is no formal organization in a trade, we find a tendency among the members to work in harmony. They assist one another in finding work; members of the trade who are prosperous contribute to the support of those members who fall ill or are otherwise overtaken by misfortune. Moreover, the typical workman is reluctant to underbid a fellow-workman of the same trade in his dealings with an employer. Competition, then, is materially restricted even in trades without a formal organization.

With the appearance of a class of large employers, the inchoate organization of labor developed into the formal organization which we call the trade union. In its simple form, the trade union is an association of all, or of a large proportion, of the men exercising a trade in a given locality. The association has regular meetings where the conditions of employment are discussed, and rules are adopted governing the conduct of members. Officers are elected for the purpose of systematizing the work of the association, and of enforcing its rules.

It is rarely if ever the case that all persons in the trade are members of the union. Some workmen are averse to the restrictions upon their personal liberty that unionism represents; some are unable or unwilling to assume the financial responsibilities that membership entails; still more lack the courage to join in the struggles with the employers that every organization must face, sooner or later. Where the strife between the workers and the employers is not intense, the relations between members of the union and non-members may be entirely amicable. The non-members work alongside of the members, and demand and receive the same wages. Where the union laborers are engaged in a conflict with their employers, they usually manifest hostility to the non-union men, since the latter may accept employment, to the great injury of the cause of the union, and in any event fail to carry their fair proportion of the burden of the struggle though hoping to profit by it.

5. *As a matter of practical policy, a strong trade union usually endeavors to induce all men exercising a trade to become members of the organization. Sometimes union men are forbidden to work for employers who employ non-union men. This is known as the "closed shop" policy.*

The presence in an industry of a large number of men who take no part in the existing labor organization materially weakens the position of the organization. The union may, therefore, use every means to persuade all persons in the trade to become members of the organization. If any refuse, and the union possesses the necessary strength, it may endeavor to force them to become members by harassing employers who admit the non-union men to their shops. This policy is often denounced by representatives of the employing class as an unwarranted interference in the rights of the non-union men. It is further denounced as an attempt to compel the employer to assist the union in controlling its membership. Whether the closed shop policy is justifiable or not depends entirely upon the general policy of the union. If it admits to membership all men having the necessary qualifications for the work to be done, upon payment of reasonable membership fees, it is difficult to see how the men who are compelled to become members have any real grievance. So long as the demands of the union for higher wages or shorter hours are moderate, the impartial outsider cannot censure the organization for trying to make its position as strong as possible. In recent years, the closed shop policy has been relegated to a position of secondary importance. The closed shop is still the ideal of trade unionism, but it is seldom found worth fighting for. In some industries a compromise has been effected in the "preferential shop." The employer agrees to give the preference to union men, but reserves the right to take on non-union men when not enough union men are available.

6. *The trade union, whenever possible, places limits upon the number of persons admitted to the trade.*

If the wages of skilled workmen in any trade rise much above the general level, there is likely to be an influx of laborers from other employments, whose presence in the trade has the effect of reducing wages. In some cases the free admission to a trade of all who desire to exercise it would reduce wages below the normal level. In the building trades, for example, wages appear to be higher than they really are. The members of these trades receive high wages for the time they are employed but employment is very uncertain. In the greater part of the country, the winter represents a slack season in which very few members of the building trades find steady employment. This irregularity of employment does not receive due consideration from young men who are about to choose a trade; hence unrestricted admission to the trade might easily depress annual earnings below the normal level.

Restrictions upon entrance to a trade may take the form of apprenticeship regulations that are sufficiently onerous to reduce the number of beginners. Formerly, a seven-year apprenticeship was required in many trades. During the period of apprenticeship, the worker received no wages, and this in itself narrowly limited the number of persons who could afford to enter a trade. In some trades, an apprenticeship of three or four years is still required. Another method of limiting the number of apprentices is to prescribe the proportion of apprentices to trained workmen that an employer may have in his shop. It is easy to see that through such restrictions upon apprenticeship an artificial scarcity of labor in any one trade may be created, and wages may be kept at an abnormally high level. Those who are prevented from exercising the trade are forced into occupations where such limitations upon the labor supply are impracticable, thus depressing wages in those occupations. Consumers of the products of industries in which labor holds a monopolistic position are forced to pay abnormally high prices. There are, however, very few trades strong enough to raise wages much above the level that the degree of skill necessary would, in the long run, command, even if admission to the trade were perfectly free.

7. *The position of a trade union is greatly strengthened by the accumulation of funds for the relief of members in time of sickness or unemployment.*

The mere wage earner is at all times exposed to the danger of want as a consequence of accident, sickness, or prolonged unemployment. What he can save individually is seldom sufficient to carry him through a long period of time in which he earns nothing. The trade union, by collecting contributions from those members who are receiving wages and by distributing the money among those who are in need, greatly reduces the uncertainties of the laborer's lot. A plan of mutual insurance binds to the union many who would otherwise hold themselves aloof from it. Moreover, it keeps those who are out of work from offering their services to the employer at a reduced rate of pay, and thus prevents the demoralization of the labor market.

But the most important object to be attained through

the accumulation of funds is the strengthening of the union in a dispute with the employer. With a large fund, a union may be able to keep its members from accepting work through a period of several months — long enough to inflict serious losses upon a recalcitrant employer. A union without funds may be easily starved into submission to the employer's conditions.

8. *The position of a union is strengthened by an alliance with unions in related trades, or even in unrelated trades.*

Such trades as the carpenters, the masons, the plasterers, and other building trades, have much to gain through working in harmony. At one time the carpenters may have a strong organization, and the masons a weak one; at another time the reverse may be true. On one job a small number of masons may be needed, and a large number of carpenters. In such cases, the union masons could perhaps be replaced by the non-union masons that are to be found in every city, while it would be more difficult to secure a sufficient number of non-union carpenters. The building contractor must have men of each trade, and if he engages in a dispute with the union whose position is weak, pressure can be brought upon him by the union whose position is strong. A harmonious organization of allied trades can thus always place its strongest forces at the front.

An advantage of a different nature arises from an alliance of unions in unrelated trades. The cigar makers' union can bring no direct pressure to bear upon the employers of garment workers; but when garment workers are thrown out of employment by a strike, the cigar makers can contribute to their support. At another time contributions from the garment workers may assist the cigar makers in securing better terms from their employers.

9. *A trade union in one locality is strengthened by an alliance with unions in other localities.*

In a period of such easy communication as the present, a purely local labor organization can accomplish little. In a dispute between a labor organization and an employer, the latter can quickly import laborers from other localities to replace his former employees. Apprenticeship regulations in one locality are enforced in vain, if in other localities the labor market is overstocked through unrestricted apprenticeship.

Even when no importation of labor takes place, the union confined to a single locality finds difficulty in raising wages or reducing working time. Such measures usually represent cost to the employer, and if the product is cne which must enter into competition with like products from other localities, the concessions that the employer can make to his employees are narrowly limited. If the textile workers of Fall River demand higher wages, the employers may be unable to grant the demand without raising the price of cloth to such an extent as to encourage the competition of other textile manufacturing districts.

The importance of a central organization appears nowhere more clearly than in the case of industries in which extensive consolidations have been formed. If the laborers in one steel plant demand higher wages, the plant can be closed down, and the orders executed in other works where there is no trouble with the laborers. The employer loses practically nothing, and the laborers are in the end compelled to return to work on such terms as the employer may dictate.

In any event an organization covering a wide range of territory affords an excellent means of raising funds for local organizations in time of labor disputes. When the cigar makers of New York are on strike, the cigar makers in Philadelphia, Boston, Chicago, and other cities raise funds for their support.

The foregoing considerations have led to the formation of national or international unions in almost every important trade. In government these organizations are sometimes loose federations, sometimes strongly centralized bodies. In the centralized union the local union is required to obtain the consent of the national union before inaugurating a strike; the national officers can call a strike in any locality, even if the members of the local organization are content with their condition. The essence of the power of the national union is its control over the funds that are accumulated for emergencies. A local union which goes on strike without proper authorization forfeits its claim to strike benefits from the national organization; a local union which refuses to strike when ordered to do so is suspended or expelled from the national union, and is subjected to more or less severe discipline before it is reinstated in the organization.

10. *National organizations have much to gain through a central organization covering the whole field of industry.*

In the United States most of the national unions are associated in a great central organization known as the American Federation of Labor. This organization furnishes a means by which the support of the entire trade-union world may be given to unions engaged in an extended contest with their employers. The American Federation pretends to no direct control over its constituent members, but unions about to engage in a labor dispute naturally consult with the officers of the Federation and seek the coöperation of that body. The American Federation collects information relating to the entire field of labor and assists in organizing unions in new fields.

When disputes arise between different labor organizations, the American Federation officials act as arbitrators; when factional strife causes the disruption of a union, the officers of the Federation are active in effecting a reorganization.

11. *The principal weapon in the hands of organized labor is the strike. A strike is a concerted suspension of work for the purpose of enforcing some demand upon the employer.*

Sometimes the mere fact that demands are presented to the employer by an organization including his entire working force leads to concessions that would never be made to isolated employees. In many cases, however, the employer refuses to consider the demands of his employees, and a strike is called. It is possible that the employer would be unable to grant the demands even if he desired to do so. In perhaps a majority of instances the demands could be granted in part or wholly without serious loss to the employer. At all events the laborers believe this, and in suspending work they feel that they are merely stopping operations long enough to reach a satisfactory adjustment of the matters in dispute. Sometimes the employer also takes the same view of the matter and makes no attempt to replace his striking workmen.

If the employer feels that the demands of the men are wholly unreasonable, or that even if they are reasonable the union is not strong enough to enforce them, he is likely to attempt to fill the places left vacant with laborers who are not controlled by the organization of the strikers. This the latter must prevent, if they are to have any chance of winning. If there is nowhere to be found an adequate number of laborers willing to work as strike breakers, the strikers may be content to allow the employer to experiment with inefficient men. If the efforts of the employer to secure laborers appear to be successful, the strikers endeavor to persuade the strike-breaking laborers to join in the suspension of work. Pickets are stationed at the entrance to the works, to inform all men coming to their tasks that a strike is in progress. If the strike breakers do not yield to peaceable persuasion the pickets often resort to intimidation. Where the contest becomes very bitter, the strikers sometimes employ violence to frighten the strike breakers from their work. The employment of violence is discountenanced by the leaders of the strike; nevertheless, a great strike has seldom been entirely free from instances of injury inflicted upon strike breakers. While the right of workingmen to strike is recognized under American law — except in Kansas — the tradition of violence which has gathered around the strike has led to the employment of the legal device of the injunction, often to the serious disadvantage of the strikers. They may be enjoined from picketing, from using even peaceful persuasion to dissuade other workers from taking their places. Thus the court often, in effect, throws its weight on the side of the employer.

12. *A second possible weapon of organized labor is the boycott. A boycott is an association having for its purpose the destruction of the business of an employer through pressure brought to bear, directly or indirectly, upon those who have business relations with him.*

When men are on strike, they naturally refrain from purchasing the products of their former employer, and persuade their friends to follow the same course of action. This is a simple form of the boycott; it may be fairly effective when the product is destined for local consumption by the working class. An employing baker, for example, may be brought to terms in this way. Where the product is placed upon a general market the boycott takes a more complex form. The whole trade-union world may be warned not to buy the products of the offending employer. Such boycotts are illegal, under the present interpretation of American law and can be employed only by indirection. Their effectiveness is therefore slight.

Sometimes the boycott takes a very roundabout course. A merchant is boycotted for handling the products of an "unfair" shop; laborers are boycotted for buying goods from such a merchant; men who employ these laborers are boycotted, and so on. These roundabout boycotts are not very frequent nor very important. They are of doubtful value to the laborers' cause, as they inflict more hardship upon innocent parties than upon the persons against whom they are ultimately directed. Since such boycotts are illegal, their employment is pretty certain to bring the courts into the field on the side of the employer.

13. *Strikes and boycotts may be carried on by workmen who have no formal organization.*

We have spoken of strikes and boycotts as the weapons of organized labor. As a fact, however, a great many strikes take place in trades that are not organized in unions. For the purpose of carrying on a strike a temporary organization is effected which may be abandoned when the strike is won or lost. Boycotts, under one name or another, have often been employed by unorganized laborers.

It is not certain whether the formation of trade unions leads to an increase or to a reduction in the number of strikes. It is undoubtedly true that a permanent organization results in a reduction in the number of strikes having no adequate cause. A trade union develops responsible leaders who do everything in their power to prevent a strike when the chances of winning are small.

14. *In many trades where powerful organizations have been established, the terms of employment are fixed, not by bargaining between the employer and the individual workmen, but by agreements between representatives of the laborers, on the one hand, and representatives of the employers, on the other. This plan of fixing the terms of employment is known as collective bargaining.*

In the bituminous coal district of the North Central states representatives of the miners and representatives of the mine operators meet annually to determine the rate of wages to be paid. In these meetings all the circumstances of the industry are fully discussed, — the prices that the product is likely to command, the cost of placing it on the market, the cost of living of the workmen, the wages paid in other districts, etc. As a result of the discussion each side gains a fairly clear understanding of the position of the other. It becomes impossible for the laborers to insist upon terms that the employers cannot possibly grant, as not infrequently happens where no machinery for collective bargaining has been established. Differences of opinion as to what constitutes a fair wage naturally arise; but through full discussion and mutual concessions these differences are prevented from causing a rupture of negotiations. Since the adoption of the plan of joint conferences agreements have always been reached, and have in most cases been loyally observed by both employers and employed.

In a number of other American industries similar methods of collective bargaining are employed, and in England, where trade unionism is more powerful than in any other country, all the great industries establish the conditions of employment by collective bargaining.

It is clear that in a complex modern industry, only the

more general conditions of employment can be fixed by such agreements. Minor disputes will constantly arise relating to the interpretation of the general agreement. Provision is usually made for the settlement of such disputes by a committee representing both the workmen and the employers. Where such a committee is unable to reach a decision, resort is had to the services of an impartial outsider who acts as arbitrator.

In some industries there is a general understanding that if no agreement as to the renewal of the contract can be reached, the matters in dispute shall be settled by arbitration. Such arbitration, however, is not always successful, since either the laborers or the employers may prefer to submit to a trial of strength rather than accept the onerous conditions of the arbitrators' award.

15. *When a strike has been in progress for a long time, and both parties to the dispute are thoroughly wearied with it, though either is unwilling to surrender its claims, resort may be had to arbitration.*

In perhaps a majority of the important strikes of recent years each party to the controversy has taken a position which is not wholly defensible. The demands of the men are excessive, and the terms that the employer insists upon are unnecessarily onerous to the men. Negotiations are broken off and a strike follows, to the serious injury of both parties. As the burdens of the struggle grow heavier, each party sees that its original position was untenable, but shrinks from making concessions, fearing that to do so would be to confess itself worsted in the struggle. The only way in which the difficulty can be settled without loss of prestige to either party is through submission of the matters in dispute to arbitrators mutually agreed upon. Both parties bind themselves to accept the award of the arbitrators in good faith, and instances are rare in which this agreement is disregarded. The award of the arbitrators is seldom anything more than a balancing of concessions; it usually satisfies neither party, but is accepted as a lesser evil than a continuance of the struggle.

16. *Arbitration may be forced upon the parties to an industrial dispute by the pressure of public opinion.*

While the persons most seriously injured by the continuance of an industrial dispute are the laborers and employers directly involved, no important strike can be conducted without injury to the public. A strike of railway laborers almost inevitably injures innocent parties more than it injures the railway companies against which the strike is directed. The blocking of the street railway system of a great city through a strike inflicts immeasurable injury upon the general public. A strike of coal miners necessarily produces great distress among the poorer classes who are seldom in a position to keep a reserve of fuel; the resulting high price of coal causes the closing down of many shops and factories with consequent losses in wages and profits. In almost every great strike instances of violence are frequent, and the charges upon the public for maintaining the peace are greatly increased.

Accordingly there are the best reasons why persons representing the interests of the public should undertake the task of bringing about a reconciliation between the employers and their striking employees. In some cases those who undertake this task limit themselves to inducing the disputants to meet in conference to discuss the matters at issue. This may of itself lead to a settlement of the dispute. Such intervention is known as *conciliation*. In other cases an attempt is made to force the disputants to submit to arbitration. Often the movement to force arbitration is initiated by the party to the dispute whose sufferings are greatest or whose prospects of victory are least promising.

17. *It would be a great gain to society if industrial disputes could be submitted to arbitration as soon as they arise, instead of toward the close of a long contest.*

No argument is necessary to show that a strike is a wasteful way of establishing the conditions of employment. Since a settlement is likely to be effected by arbitration, why is a long and expensive struggle necessary? Why do not the disputants resort to arbitration at the outset?

In most cases an industrial dispute is based upon irreconcilable differences of opinion. The employer offers what he considers as good terms as he needs to give; he believes that the laborers will be compelled to accept these terms in the end. The laborer demands what he regards as the lowest wages that he can be compelled to accept in the circumstances; he believes that the employer will in the end concede his demands. Arbitration would almost certainly result in terms that each party to the controversy would regard as unfair to itself. Consequently each party prefers to resort to a trial of strength. After the struggle has continued for some time, and each party has gained an insight into the real strength of the other, the necessity of mutual concession becomes apparent to every one concerned. Terms that would, at the outset, have been spurned by both parties can be accepted, though perhaps reluctantly, by both the employer and the employee.

It is accordingly clear why a plan of purely voluntary arbitration is ineffective as a means for preventing strikes. Many of our states have created commissions or boards of arbitration with authority to settle industrial disputes upon the application of both contestants. The services of these officials are not often requested.

In New Zealand employers and organized laborers are required by law to settle their disputes without recourse to strikes. The colony is divided into districts in each of which a board of conciliation exists which is authorized to inquire into all labor disputes with the purpose of effecting a settlement by mutual agreement. If the parties to the dispute cannot be brought to an agreement, the dispute is referred to the court of arbitration, which hears both sides and renders a decision which is binding. Under the New Zealand system the strike has been eliminated. An analogous plan has been introduced in the state of Kansas, where a Court of Industrial Relations has been created to hear and determine disputes between employers and employees. No strike in an industry vital to the public is permitted. Whether the plan will prove successful in the end even in a state so slightly industrialized as Kansas, and whether it would work successfully in more highly industrialized states, remain open questions.

18. *The organization of labor modifies the operation of the competitive law of wages, but does not subvert that law.*

It has often been noted that in times of prosperity labor organizations are usually able to force a rise in wages; in times of depression such organizations are unable to check a decline in wages. In times of prosperity the trend of wages, both of organized and of unorganized labor, is upward; in times of depression it is downward. In economic terms prosperity means an increase in the value product of labor, and the laws of competition compel the employers to raise wages accordingly. Depression means a reduction in the value product of labor, and hence results in a reduction in wages.

But the competition of employers is never very acute, and for a long time they may fail to raise wages, although the general circumstances of industry justify higher wages. It is only as increased profits lead to an expansion of industrial operations and an increased demand for labor that the competition of employers takes the form of an increase in wages. Labor organization may force an advance in wages long before the competition of employers would lead to the same result. By virtue of organization the laborer shares more promptly, and probably more liberally in the increased productivity of industry than he would if he relied upon his individual bargaining power.

While we must grant to labor organizations an important influence in maintaining a high level of wages, we must not forget that this influence may easily be overestimated. Wages are higher in America than in England, not because our labor organizations are stronger than those of England, — for the reverse is true, — but because labor is more productive in this country than in England. Wages will remain at a high level in this country so long as the high productivity of labor is maintained; and no form of organization can long maintain wages in the face of declining productivity.

19. *Summary.*

While the forces of productivity and competition determine broadly what wages may be paid, there are limits within which labor organizations can work effectively to improve the condition of their members. Such improvement may take place at the expense of other participants in the process of production, or of the consumer, or it may result in an increased efficiency that provides the means for satisfying the requirements of labor.

The trade union is an association composed of workmen employed in the same trade. When such an organization is formed an attempt is made to induce all the men practicing the trade to become members. After the organization gains practical control of a trade, it may endeavor to limit the number of men admitted to the trade, in order to maintain a high level of wages.

A trade union's position is greatly strengthened if it undertakes the relief of its members in time of sickness, accident, or unemployment. The principal function of trade union accumulations is the maintenance of the members of the union in time of strike. Each local union, further, is greatly strengthened by alliances with other unions in the same locality or in other parts of the country.

The chief weapons of the trade union are the strike and the boycott. Where trade unions are strong they are often able to make satisfactory terms with their employers without resort to the strike. In many cases the terms of employment are established by agreement between the employers on the one hand and representatives of the trade union on the other.

Disputes between employers and workmen are sometimes settled by arbitration, without resort to a strike. In cases of prolonged struggles between employers and employees, public opinion may compel a submission of the matters in dispute to arbitration. In New Zealand all disputes between employers and organized laborers must be settled by arbitration. In Kansas disputes in industries supplying a vital public need are subject to the jurisdiction of the Court of Industrial Relations.

CHAPTER XIII

THE PRODUCTIVITY OF CAPITAL

1. *The term "capital goods" may be employed to designate objects of wealth that yield an income.*

Men who are engaged in business commonly divide their material possessions into two classes; those that are held for the money income they yield, and those that are held for the immediate satisfaction they afford. The objects composing a merchant's stock in trade, his buildings and fixtures, belong to the former class. The merchant's watch, the clothes he wears, the horse he rides for recreation, belong to the latter class. The former class we shall call "capital goods"; the latter, "consumer's goods." When a man buys capital goods, he is commonly said to "invest money." When he buys consumer's goods, he is said to "spend money."

The distinction, it is true, is not so easily drawn as might at first appear. Is a man's house to be classed with his capital goods? The income that it affords is primarily one of satisfaction, like that afforded by a watch or a saddle horse. The possession of a house saves the payment of rent, and to this extent adds to one's disposable income.

Reflection will show, however, that goods yielding an income of direct satisfaction are normally distinguished by their owners from goods yielding a money return. The standards governing purchases of goods for business purposes are adequacy and sureness of return; the standard governing purchases of goods serving personal uses is what one can afford. A home is seldom strictly a "business proposition," and for this reason may usually be excluded from the rank of capital goods. And the same thing is true of other goods yielding an income, not of money, but of satisfaction.

2. *The permanent fund of productive wealth which capital goods represent is known as capital.*

The great majority of capital goods are perishable in their nature. The capital goods of a merchant, so far as they consist of merchandise, are destined in a very short time to pass into the hands of the merchant's customers, where they cease to be capital goods. So far as they consist of buildings and fixtures, they may endure a generation or more; but in the end the buildings depreciate and the the fixtures become antiquated. It would be next to impossible to find a business establishment which has precisely the same capital goods it had a year ago. It is an easy matter to find an establishment which is said to have the same capital that it had a year ago. A merchant starts in business to-day with a capital of $100,000 invested in building and stock. At the end of a year we ask him what his capital then is. Very likely it will still be $100,000. Now, is this the same capital, or is it a new one? The merchant certainly will say that it is the same capital — unless, of course, he has lost, in the course of the year, his original capital and has replaced it from some new source. But how can the capital be the same after the lapse of a year? Nearly all the things that figured in the first inventory except the building, have been replaced, in the second inventory, by objects which may be of a quite different character. In the first inventory, perhaps, cheap grades of goods preponderate; in the second these may be largely replaced by higher grades. However this may be, there can be no denying that the goods have changed, yet the merchant says that the capital is the same.

Perhaps we are making ourselves unnecessary difficulties in our endeavor to arrive at the merchant's meaning when he says that his capital remains the same even after most of the things originally composing it have left his possession. Possibly he means simply that he has as large a capital at one time as at another. Two things that are equal in magnitude are of course not the same thing, but we often speak of them as if they were.

Yet if we reflect upon it, this does not appear to be what the business man means. Suppose that fire or flood had destroyed his store and stock, and that a rich relative, to set him on his feet again, had given him $100,000 to replace them. The merchant would not say that he was continuing in business with the same capital, although in magnitude it would be the same. Clearly, a business man thinks of his capital as something that is capable of remaining permanently the same although the goods that compose it are constantly changing. The popular conception of capital is a fund of productive wealth, which has the power of self-perpetuation. This conception we may accept as one of the simplest that have been proposed.

3. *The permanence of capital depends upon the economic power of capital goods to replace their value either through sale or through assistance rendered in production.*

An enterpriser possessing $100,000 in cash proposes to establish a clothing store. The first thing he must do is to find a place where, he has reason to believe, the goods in which he proposes to deal will sell at a higher price than that which he must pay for them. This, of course, is comparatively easy to do. Goods, as they come from the factory, may in a physical sense be ready for use; economically, however, much remains to be done before they can be placed where they will fulfil their ultimate purpose — the direct satisfaction of human wants. They must be conveyed to places where they are accessible to the consumer; they must be so arranged that inspection is easy. Expert salesmen must be at hand to point out their good qualities and explain away their bad ones. This means that a considerable addition to the value of goods may be made after they have left the factory; and this addition, properly speaking, is the product of the mercantile establishment.

Each item of the stock normally sells at a price which will at least replace that item with one of equal value, together with a surplus which will cover the cost of labor employed in handling it, and which will also make some contribution to the expense of keeping up the building. Any item which does not do this not only yields nothing toward interest on the capital invested in stock and building; it is carried at a loss; and a business man who should continue to carry such items would see his capital diminish, and perhaps ultimately disappear. Some parts of the stock may afford a far larger surplus, and the aggregate income of the establishment may be much more than enough to keep stock and store intact, after paying for all human services directly employed. The nature of this excess of income above outlay we shall consider at a later point. For the present we are concerned primarily with the fact that the first demand upon the business is that each item shall maintain itself — *i.e.*, through sale, reproduce itself together with auxiliary costs connected with it.

It must now be clear how it is that a fund of capital persists. Each capital good, before it is sold or worn out, produces a sum of value that enables the owner of the good to purchase or make another good of the same character, which in its turn possesses the power of replacing itself by a successor of equal value. The capital goods of this year are, therefore, not merely the successors in time of those of last year, now mostly destroyed; they are, economically, the offspring of the capital goods of the earlier period, and they have the same power of replacing themselves with other goods having the power of self-replacement.

It is, of course, to be understood that this self-replacement is neither automatic nor inevitable. We may say that under certain conditions a particular capital good will add something to the total product of an industry, but not enough to keep itself in repair and replace itself when worn out. Under other conditions a capital good will just do this; under still other conditions a capital good will add to the product of an establishment not only enough for its own repair and replacement, but a surplus besides. Experience has taught enterprisers how to avoid the employment of capital goods that do not maintain themselves, and of those that do nothing more than this. Mistakes are of course sometimes made, but not so frequently as to invalidate the statement that capital goods, as a rule, reproduce themselves economically through the values which they create. Intelligent action on the part of the owner of such goods is essential to the truth of this proposition; but such action may generally be taken for granted.

4. *What is capital to the individual may not be productive wealth from the point of view of society.*

A government may sell its bonds in order to raise funds to carry on a profitless war. The money raised is spent on powder and other munitions of war, which are soon destroyed. The wealth furnished by the purchasers of the bonds has simply been wasted, and cannot contribute to the payment of interest on the bonds or of the principal when it falls due. Interest and principal are, indeed, paid, but from the proceeds of taxation. The bondholder regards his bonds as capital; they are wealth that yields an income, as he views the matter. But we can easily see that it is not the bonds that produce the income; it is the labor and wealth employed in production that do this. If all the bonds were destroyed, the aggregate social income would be not in the least reduced.

Capital of this kind may be called "purely acquisitive

capital." It enables its holder to acquire an income; it does not produce an income. Capital which actually participates in production may be called "productive capital." The laws which we shall discuss in this chapter relate only to productive capital.

5. *Productive capital may be embodied in goods that are the product of industry, or in goods that are the free gift of nature.*

A generation ago practically all economists restricted the term "capital" to productive wealth that has been produced by industry, such as machines, stocks of materials, etc. Productive wealth the origin of which cannot be traced to man's industry was usually classified under the heading "natural agents," or simply under "land," since land is by far the most important good in this class. This terminology is still widely used by economists. In everyday language men speak of investing capital in land, as of investing capital in buildings or machinery. This usage will be followed in this book; wherever it is necessary to distinguish between the two classes of productive wealth, we shall call the one artificial capital, the other natural capital.

6. *Artificial capital originates in saving.*

It may at first appear that capital comes into existence whenever a productive instrument is created. Reflection shows, however, that this cannot be true, for a new capital good often merely replaces a capital good worn out in the process of production, and may be said to embody the same capital.

When a man employs, in producing a tool or a stock of the materials of production, time which he would otherwise have used to procure for himself the means of immediate enjoyment, he is creating capital. These capital goods are not merely replacing capital goods previously existing; they are a net addition to the stock of productive wealth at the command of society, which, like other capital goods, will for the future maintain themselves. When a man uses, to employ workmen in the production of capital goods, a part of his income which he would otherwise have spent for consumer's goods, he is causing new capital to be created; or, we may say, he is indirectly creating capital. When he uses part of his income to buy capital goods that are already in existence, he is creating new capital by a still more indirect process. Thus if a man buys a threshing machine out of his savings, he places in the hands of the manufacturing company purchasing power with which the company can hire men to make another machine. The process of creating new capital may take a yet more roundabout course. The man who saves may invest his savings in a share of railway stock — which is nothing more than an evidence of ownership of capital goods already existing. The man who sells the share of stock may use the proceeds to buy a share in a manufacturing company. Here again it is evident that nothing new is created. The seller of the manufacturing stock may, however, use the money to buy a share in a new manufacturing company, and this company may employ the proceeds to hire men to produce new capital goods for use in its business. Evidently it is the man who saved the money in the first instance who is the true creator of the capital thus added to the stock of society.

Under present conditions the process of creating capital is usually indirect. One man saves and other men produce the concrete capital goods in which the savings are invested. Of course it sometimes happens that such a complicated process fails to attain its proper end. One man may save $100 and buy a share of stock from another man, who uses the proceeds to meet his current expenses. In this case no new capital is created. What has happened is that a part of the existing fund of capital has changed hands. But normally men avoid trenching upon their capital; accordingly, we are justified in regarding each act of saving as the creation of new capital.

Just as it is improper to regard the creation of a capital good as in itself a creation of capital, so it is improper to regard the destruction of a capital good through ordinary use as the destruction of capital. For during its lifetime a capital good produces, as we have seen, a replacement fund. After the capital good has been destroyed, the capital exists under another form — as money or as other productive goods.

7. *Natural capital increases with the development of society.*

Until the frontiersmen crossed the Appalachian Mountains, the land of the Mississippi Valley, with the timber upon it and the coal and other minerals beneath its surface, was scarcely to be classed as wealth at all. At best, it was potential wealth, not actual wealth. The settlement of the country and the development of means of communication transformed this potential wealth into an immense fund of productive wealth, or capital. Every increase in population, every improvement in methods of agricultural production, increases the importance, and with it the value, of the natural resources of a country. Measuring the capital represented by these natural resources in terms of value, we see that it is constantly growing with the progress of society. The introduction of durum wheat raised the capital value of lands in part of the arid belt from practically nothing to $10 an acre or more. New processes of steel manufacture have endowed iron ore deposits originally worth very little with the character of highly productive capital.

8. *The productivity of a capital good can be ascertained only through experimentation.*

In order that a man may conduct his business successfully, he must be able to form a fairly accurate estimate of the productivity of each class of capital goods which he uses. In the case of some classes of capital goods productivity is easily determined. Thus if one wishes to know how much a ton of fertilizer will produce, he has only to apply it to one of two equally productive acres of ground. The difference in the product of the two acres, less the cost of labor employed in applying the fertilizer, is a fair test of the productivity of a ton of fertilizer. We may term this the gross product of the capital good. After deducting from this product a sum equal to the cost of the fertilizer, whatever remains is the net product of the capital good.

Some capital goods, however, do not readily admit of any such process of experimentation. Thus it might be difficult to determine the productivity of a field, apart from that of the seed, fertilizer, machinery, and labor employed in connection with it. Of course one acre might be left untilled, and all the labor and auxiliary capital might be employed on the rest of the field. The total product would be less than it would have been had all the field been tilled; and this diminution in product would indicate roughly the productivity of an acre of ground. This method would be clumsy and expensive; it is, moreover, unnecessary, since the productivity of labor and of auxiliary capital employed upon the land may be determined, for the most part, by the method already illustrated. Hence we may arrive at the gross product of the field by subtracting from the total product of the farm the values produced by the labor and the auxiliary capital. By subtracting from the gross product of the land a sum of value sufficient to replace the elements of fertility destroyed in the course of the year, we arrive at the net product of the land.

9. *The net product of capital goods is commonly known as the product of capital.*

Capital goods obviously must vary widely in their gross product. Some must be replaced daily, some yearly, some at the expiration of a decade or more; a few classes, like land, are practically permanent. Until full replacement of goods used up has been made, a fund of productive wealth, or capital, cannot be said to be productive. A manufacturer who finds that the receipts from a year's business are just sufficient to maintain intact his building, machinery, stock of material, and fuel, cannot say that his capital has added anything to his income. Capital which produces nothing is obviously not worth having; and the mere fact that men make sacrifices to possess themselves of capital shows that, as a rule, capital may be expected to yield an income.

When a man is considering whether he shall invest his capital in one kind of capital goods or in another, he may usually take the fact of self-replacement of goods for granted. The net productivity of capital goods, or, to use a simpler term, the product of capital, is the determining factor in his calculations.

10. *The productivity of capital invested in any one class of goods is measured by the addition made to product by the last or marginal unit of capital thus invested. Other things equal, the productivity of capital in any one form shrinks with increase of capital in that form.*

Let us suppose that a farmer possesses ten fields, varying in natural fertility from a very high degree to a very low degree. And let us assume that $1000 worth of capital in the form of machinery, live stock, etc., or auxiliary capital, is necessary for the tillage of any one of the ten fields.

If the farmer has control over only $1000 worth of auxiliary capital, he will of course place it upon the best field. If from the gross product of that field he deducts the cost of labor employed in connection with it, together with a sum sufficient to cover the cost of upkeep of land and auxiliary capital, he arrives at the net product of his agricultural capital — that is, of his investment in both field and auxiliary capital. How much is due to the bare land, how much to the auxiliary capital? This it would be difficult to say, as neither would have produced anything without the other.

Now let us suppose that the farmer gets possession of another $1000 to invest in auxiliary capital. He may now till the field which is least inferior to the first one cultivated. The joint product of this field and of the $1000 of capital will be less than that of the first field because of the difference in natural fertility. Shall we say that $1000 is more productive on one field than on the other? The two units of capital are just alike; the two fields are unlike. So it would seem to be more reasonable to assign the difference in productivity to the fields, not to the auxiliary capital. And this is what a practical man would do. If the first field produces $1000 and the second $900, he would say that at least $100 of the product of the first is the product of the land, apart from that of the auxiliary capital.

Is the $900 produced on the second field the product of the auxiliary capital alone? In a physical sense, certainly not; in an economic sense it is. This sum is what the additional $1000 worth of auxiliary capital adds to the farmer's income; $900 is what he would lose if he were deprived of either of his two units of capital.

With another $1000 the farmer is enabled to till a third field, which is somewhat less fertile than the second. Perhaps this field produces $800 net. If this is the case, the farmer will no longer regard the total product of the second field as the product of the auxiliary capital alone. This auxiliary capital is credited with no larger product than that of auxiliary capital on the third field — $800. The other $100 now comes to be considered as the product of the land. At the same time, of course, a second $100 is subtracted from the product of auxiliary capital on the best grade of land. And as the farmer adds unit after unit of auxiliary capital and opens field after field to tillage, the productivity of auxiliary capital steadily shrinks and that of the better land as steadily increases. Perhaps the tenth field yields a net return of only $100. In such case no one of the ten units of auxiliary capital can be said to yield more than this. The use of no one of the units is worth more to the farmer than $100, for if any one were taken away from his control, he would replace it with the one employed in connection with the poorest field.

In a grist mill the amount of capital which may be invested in machinery varies within wide limits. Once the mill is equipped with machinery, it would be difficult to increase greatly the amount of capital invested in machinery, since not more machines, but better ones, would here be the result of increased investment. We may, however, suppose that in determining upon the kind of equipment to be employed, an enterpriser goes through some such calculation as the following: —

Given a building and a certain minimum of auxiliary capital invested in machinery — say $10,000, an annual return of $10,000 may be secured. How much of this is the product of the building? how much is the product of the machinery? No one can say; neither form of capital would produce anything without the other. Increase the capital in machinery by another $10,000 unit; the net return increases, we will say, to $15,000. The sum added by the second unit of auxiliary capital is $5000; as the two units of auxiliary capital are interchangeable, neither will be credited with more than this. Thus $5000 detaches itself from the joint product of building and machinery, and is credited to the building. Add another $10,000 unit in the form of machinery. The return increases to $17,000. $2000, then, is the product that can be credited to this unit of auxiliary capital, and no one of the three units will be credited with more than this. The building thus comes to be credited with $11,000, the sum remaining after the product of the three units of auxiliary capital has been deducted.

The principle involved in this example may be stated as follows: The productivity of any unit of capital embodied in a given class of capital goods is measured by the amount added to the aggregate net product of a business by that unit which it is least worth while to employ.

11. *An increase in the capital of any establishment, attended by no parallel increase in labor, reduces the productivity of capital and increases that of labor.*

Suppose that a farmer can command practically an indefinite amount of agricultural capital, whether in the form of land or in the form of movable capital goods, but that the amount of labor that he can secure is limited to ten men. With $5000 invested partly in land, partly in movabie capital goods, he may be able to produce $5000 net. We should here find difficulty in determining what part of this sum is produced by the labor, what part by the capital. An additional $5000 of capita! may increase the aggregate product of the business by $4000. This sum we should properly ascribe to the new capital. And as this second unit of capital does not differ in any essential respect from the unit at first employed, and as the removal of one unit of the two would have the same effect as the removal of the other, we may properly regard them as equally productive. The extra thousand appearing in connection with the first unit must then be credited to the other factor in production — the labor. If a third unit of capital increases the product of the business by $3000, this amount will measure the importance of any one of the three units of capital. This is what the farmer would lose if he were deprived of the use of any of the units. If a fifth unit adds only $1000, the product assignable to any unit shrinks to that figure. And of course with each reduction in the product assignable to capital, the product assignable to labor increases.

12. *If the capital of an industry, or the capital of all society, increases, the productivity of capital declines.*

Up to the present point our study of the productivity of capital has been confined to the single business establishment. We must now consider whether similar principles are applicable to an industry in its entirety. The iron and steel industry of the United States may serve as our type.

Let us say that the capital engaged in the production of iron and steel is $3,000,000,000, the number of men, 400,000. Now let us suppose that without any revolutionary change in the demand for iron and steel the capital of the industry is increased by $100,000,000. What will be the effect upon the productivity of capital in the industry?

It is fair to assume that before the increase in capital those branches of the industry promising the highest profits were already well developed; that the richest deposits of ore and coking coal were already being exploited; that the best manufacturing sites had been selected. To what use, then, will the new capital be put? Some of the enterprisers may attempt to duplicate existing plant. This requires additional labor, and such labor is to be had only by inducing new men to enter the industry or by enticing men away from other iron manufacturers. In either case an advance in wages will follow, which will soon become general throughout the industry. In the old establishments as well as the new this will obviously reduce the share of the aggregate product which capital will receive. Again, the increase in iron and steel products thrown upon the market will lower prices. Thus, while the wages bill of an establishment per unit of product will increase, the value of each unit of product will diminish.

If all the new capital is used simply to duplicate existing plant, wages will rise to a decidedly higher level. The industry will need one tenth more men than it has at present, and these will be slow to appear unless they are offered high wages. The fall in prices, moreover, will be a serious one, as the output will be increased about ten per cent. But when the prices of the staple products of an industry fall, it often pays to develop new branches of the industry that under earlier conditions were not profitable. When wages rise, it pays to introduce machinery that saves labor. Part of the new capital will be absorbed in these ways, and thus the productivity of capital will be prevented from sinking to as low a level as would otherwise be the case. The fact remains that the capital will be less productive after the increase than before it; wages will be higher and prices lower. The increase in the aggregate capital of the industry, other things equal, will reduce the productivity of each unit.

The same principle is still more clearly applicable to industrial society as a whole. The iron and steel industry can relieve the pressure upon its labor supply by inducing men to leave other industries. If the capital of society as a whole increases, a pressure is placed upon the labor supply, for which there is no ready means of relief! The existing capital is normally sufficient to provide every one who desires to work with the necessary appliances. If, then, the capital of all industries increases more rapidly than the population, the average capital employed with each laborer must increase. Such increase in capital must be embodied in improvements upon existing appliances, and, owing to the operation of the law of diminishing returns, will increase the product of industry less than an equal amount of capital does when the social fund is smaller.

13. *The opening of new opportunities for investment may counteract the effect of increase in capital.*

There are of course conditions under which an increase in capital may not be followed by a reduction in the productivity of capital. If, for example, the labor supply increases as rapidly as the supply of capital, there is no reason why the productivity of capital should decline. Again, suppose that some practical method of draining extensive swampy regions or of irrigating vast tracts of arid land were discovered. The new capital might be absorbed by the opening of these fields. In the last century, though capital has increased enormously, there has been a corresponding enlargement of the field of investment; accordingly, the productivity of capital has declined little, if at all.

14. *An increase in artificial capital, while reducing returns on that form of capital, is likely to increase the returns from natural capital.*

It has already been indicated that by placing more and more auxiliary capital upon a given area of land one must ordinarily reduce the productivity of auxiliary capital and increase the productivity of land. It will naturally be the aim of the business man to keep his capital uniformly productive; if he has too much auxiliary capital he will endeavor to get more land, and *vice versa.* He will ask himself: Would it pay me better to invest my next $1000 in land or in auxiliary capital? And he will continue to direct his investments toward whichever of these classes of capital goods is for the moment the more productive, until the superiority of that class disappears.

Similarly, an entire industry may expand with more or less symmetry, distributing its new capital among the various classes of capital goods of which it stands in need. If the beet sugar industry expands, not only are more factories constructed, more machinery for the cultivation of beets purchased, but more land is drawn into the service of the industry. This land is, of course, taken away from other industries — from wheat culture, dairying, etc.

When the social fund of capital increases, on the other hand, it is not possible for a symmetrical increase in all classes of capital to take place. The land, we may suppose, is already almost all in use; the best mines are opened; the most available courses for railways and canals are already occupied. These things the new capital cannot duplicate; their relative importance, therefore, steadily increases. On the other hand, steel rails, locomotives, factory buildings and thousands of other forms of capital goods are readily duplicated. The marginal productivity of capital in these forms naturally declines, and a larger part of the product is left to be divided between labor and natural capital.

15. *When the return to natural capital varies from the return to artificial capital, equalization is commonly brought about by revaluation.*

When, however, we speak of the productivity of capital in general we usually take as our test the productivity of new capital — and this, we see, is practically the capital in goods which are capable of duplication. And instead of thinking of the old capital in nonduplicable goods as more than normally productive, we are likely to revalue the capital in such forms. Ten years ago, let us say, a five-acre lot gave as large a net product as a threshing machine. To-day the same piece of land yields twice as large a net return as a threshing machine equal in value to the one of ten years ago. We might say that the capital in land has doubled in productivity. But it is more usual to say that to-day the land represents twice as much capital as the threshing machine, although it represented no more capital than the threshing machine ten years ago. By a similar process of revaluation, the productivity of all capital which is abnormally productive is reduced to the general level. This process of revaluation will receive our further attention in the next chapter.

16. *The productivity of artificial capital varies at any particular time from industry to industry, but tends constantly toward a uniform level.*

Even capital which is embodied in capital goods that are capable of reduplication may at any given time vary widely in productivity from establishment to establishment, or from industry to industry. It is only by experimentation that the actual productivity of capital can be determined, and owing to the changing character of modern industry the process of experimentation must go on without ceasing. Accordingly, there are always chances of mistakes in investments. A cotton manufacturer may overestimate the productivity of capital in a given type of loom; after purchasing and installing the machine he must content himself with what it will produce, even though he knows that the same amount of capital would in another form yield a far higher return. Cotton manufacturers as a class may overestimate the future demand for cotton goods, and so may be led to invest heavily in buildings and machinery which prove incapable of returning the normal rate of interest on capital. At the same time the shoe industry may be undersupplied with capital; for a time, at least, every one hundred dollars invested in the industry may yield an abnormally high return.

Such disparity in the productivity of capital in the two industries would, however, tend to disappear. The capital invested in new cotton mills would, of course, be fixed in the industry for a long period of time. But in the industry as a whole there are always some mills that are about to be dismantled, having reached the limit of their useful existence. These mills have presumably earned in the past a sum sufficient to replace themselves with new mills of a value equal to that of the original ones. If the cotton industry is suffering from a depression while the shoe industry is highly prosperous, the replacement fund will be diverted to the latter industry. Through the reduction of capital in the cotton industry the productivity of capital in that field is increased; through the increase of capital in the shoe industry the productivity of capital is reduced in that industry. It is easy to see that if this process continues for any length of time the original disparity in productivity must disappear.

The equalization of productivity is hastened by the

disposition of new accumulations of capital. The fund of capital, under modern conditions, is constantly growing in magnitude; consequently industries are, as a rule, expanding. The new capital naturally seeks the most productive fields. If, therefore, the rate of return in the cotton industry is abnormally low while that in the shoe industry is abnormally high, the new capital will avoid the former industry and seek investment in the latter. The influx of new capital into the shoe industry reduces productivity there, until at last capital is no more productive in the one industry than in the other. When this point has been reached, further additions to the supply of capital are divided impartially between the two industries, reducing productivity uniformly.

It is, of course, possible that the productivity of capital in the two industries may never be absolutely equal. While the tide of new capital is setting steadily toward the shoe industry, a new demand for cotton goods or a new method of manufacture may appear and raise the productivity of capital in the cotton industry above that of the shoe industry. Some time will elapse before the change in the relative positions of the two industries is generally known; in the meantime the flow of new capital into the shoe industry continues. Eventually the new capital is diverted to the cotton industry; it may continue to flow in that direction after the cotton industry has lost its relative superiority. We can only say that a tendency toward equalization of productivity exists; not that equalization is ever exactly realized.

17. *Any barrier preventing the free flow of capital into an industry makes possible an abnormally high return on capital in that industry.*

It is, of course, to be remembered that the productivity of capital is not the only thing that an investor takes into account in deciding in what industry he shall invest his savings. In some investments the danger of losing all or a part of the capital invested is great. Capital employed in developing the oil fields and timber resources of Russia may be highly productive; but the existing government of Russia from which the right to exploit oil or timber is derived, may be overturned, and a new government may confiscate the capital invested in the business. Capital invested in street railways may be very productive. But if cities do not follow a consistent policy in chartering new companies, it is possible that at any time rival lines may be established on parallel streets and, if unable to make large returns themselves, they may, nevertheless, reduce the return on capital invested in the original lines to almost nothing. The capital still remains in the possession of the investor, but it is "dead capital." A merchant's capital, invested in a fancy fabric, may promise high returns; but a sudden change in fashion may force the merchant to sell the goods at a price which not only yields no return on the capital invested, but which entails an actual impairment of the capital fund itself.

Some risk, it is plain, inheres in every business; in some fields of investment, however, the risk is so small as to be negligible, while in other fields no prudent investor can disregard it. Other things equal, the vast majority of investors will prefer to invest in the safer fields. A disproportionately large share of the capital of society, therefore, seeks the safer investments, and as a result the productivity of capital in such investments falls below the rate of return to capital in the more hazardous investments. And thus it is that there appears a regular variation in the productivity of capital corresponding with variations in risk.

It is, of course, clear that it is not actual risk, but estimated risk, that affects the distribution and hence the productivity of capital. It is quite possible that the risk of losing capital invested in banking in Texas is less than the risk of losing capital similarly invested in New York. But if most of the persons having capital to invest mistakenly believe that the reverse is true, a disproportionately large part of the flow of new capital will enter the New York investment field and reduce the productivity of capital there below the level prevailing in Texas.

In an earlier chapter we saw that risk affects wages only in so far as it affects the distribution of labor; further, that if enough reckless workmen can be found to man the dangerous trades, risk will not affect wages at all. Exactly the same thing is true of capital. If there were enough investors who always chose the more remunerative employments for capital, regardless of risk, the hazardous fields would soon be so well supplied with capital that they would yield no higher returns than the safer ones. As a rule, however, capital is far more timid in assuming risks than labor. It is therefore more anomalous to find capital in a hazardous field yielding only normal returns than it is to find workmen in dangerous occupations receiving only normal wages.

Risk, then, may be regarded as a barrier which prevents capital from flowing freely into some of the more productive fields. It is of course not the only natural barrier affecting the flow of capital. If a particular industry is subject to the universal moral disapproval of a community, most capitalists will refuse to invest in it. Those who are unscrupulous enough to do so may enjoy the high returns that flow from an industry that is undersupplied with capital. Thus, high returns are often obtained from capital invested in contraband stills, gambling dens and opium "joints." It is, of course, possible that the investment institutions of a country may be of such a nature that a man can hold stock in disreputable enterprises without the knowledge of his associates, and that investors who have no personal scruples are numerous. Under these conditions the productivity of capital in such ventures will eventually fall to the normal level.

18. *Summary.*

Material goods which serve as means of production are known as capital goods. In the normal course of industry, each capital good, before it is sold or worn out, makes at least a sufficient addition to product to replace itself with an equally valuable capital good; and under normal conditions, each capital good, when worn out, is actually replaced. Capital goods may therefore be regarded as a self-perpetuating fund of productive wealth. This fund is termed productive capital; it is to be distinguished from those forms of wealth, also commonly termed capital, which add nothing to the product of society, although they enable their owners to secure an income. Under certain conditions, it is necessary to distinguish between that productive capital which is the product of industry and that which is the free gift of nature. The former may be termed artificial, the latter natural, capital.

The productivity of each capital good can be ascertained only through experimentation. A distinction must be made between the gross product of a capital good — the total value product originating in it — and its net product — the sum of value remaining after deduction of the expense of repairs or replacement. The net product of capital goods may be regarded as the product of the fund of such goods, or capital.

The productivity of capital invested in any class of goods is determined by the addition to net product made by those goods of the class that perform the least important functions. Every increase in the amount of capital invested in a given class of goods tends to reduce the productivity of each unit of capital in that class, and to raise the productivity of capital invested in other classes of goods, as well as the productivity of labor. Natural capital often fails to increase as rapidly as artificial capital; consequently, for long periods of time the productivity of natural capital goods tends to increase, while that of artificial capital goods tends to decline. Equalization of returns to the two classes of capital can be brought about only through revaluation of the natural capital goods. The earnings of capital in the different classes of artificial capital goods tend, under competition, toward a uniform level; in many cases, however, barriers preventing the free flow of capital keep the earnings of capital in one field permanently higher than in another.

CHAPTER XIV

RENT, INTEREST, AND CAPITALIZATION

1. *Rent, in everyday speech, is a payment for the temporary use of durable goods.*

In popular usage the term "rent" is applied to any payment which one person makes to another for the temporary use of a concrete good or group of goods. Thus rent may be paid for the use of a farm, a house, a piano, a square yard of advertising space on a bill board. In the nature of the case, only those things can be rented which remain practically intact through the period of use. One never rents a bin of coal or a stock of merchandise. Nor does one ever rent goods which can serve their purpose only by entering into permanent combination with other goods. No one would think of trying to rent steel beams to be used in the construction of his house. The more nearly indestructible a good is, and the more perfectly it yields up its services without losing its identity, the better is it adapted to the renting contract. Thus a field, being practically indestructible, may very well be rented for a period of years, although if its cultivation requires the incorporation of a large amount of auxiliary capital in the soil, in the form of drains or irrigation ditches, the field and the auxiliary capital must usually be rented together. A piano, which is much more likely to be injured, nevertheless lends itself fairly well to the renting contract because no other capital good enters into permanent combination with it in use.

2. *The term rent has been commonly used by economists to designate income arising from natural agents.*

In the classical economic terminology, rent included all income from permanent natural agents, whether these agents were leased or employed in production by their owners. A field, a building site, or a waterfall, it was said, yields rent. Incomes from houses, machines, and other reproducible goods were called interest on capital. The word rent is used in the classical sense by a large number of our living economists. While the term will be given a different meaning in this book, we shall recognize rent in the traditional sense under the name ground rent.

3. *The term rent in its broadest sense includes the products of all capital goods, whether rented by the enterpriser or owned by him.*

If a man owns and manages a farm which he could let at a rental of $1000, we may say that $1000 out of his income is really the rent of his farm. True, he does not pay this sum to any one; but neither does he pay any one wages for the labor which he himself performs. It would be absurd, however, to say that a man earns no wages when he is working for himself. As employer he pays himself wages as workman. In like manner, the man who cultivates his own field may be thought of as paying rent, as cultivator, to himself, as landlord. So, if an ocean transportation company owns and sails a ship which it could let for $5000 a year, we may regard $5000 out of the proceeds of the company's business as the rent of this particular ship. In this broad sense of the term, rent may be defined as that part of the proceeds of a business which is economically due to a particular capital good. It is the economic product of a capital good, regarded as a lump sum. And as even the most perishable of capital goods yield a product which may be measured in this way, we may strain the ordinary meaning of the term rent so as to include the concrete products of all capital goods whatsoever.

4. *For practical reasons, a study of rent may best be confined to the products of goods that have a high degree of permanence.*

While the term rent may, as has been said, be applied to the product of any concrete capital good, we shall in this chapter confine our study to the rent of those classes of goods that are of such a nature as to permit the transfer of their uses under renting contracts. The distinguishing characteristic of this class of goods is that the capital embodied in them is fixed there, for a considerable period of time at least. It takes perhaps ten years before the capital invested in a boat can migrate to some industry upon the dry land. That is the time necessary for the funds accumulating for the replacement of the ship to equal its original value. The capital embodied in a well-built house may be fixed there for fifty years; and the capital invested in a field, in a tunnel, or in an excavation must remain where it is forever. It is true that you may take *your* capital out of a field; this you do when you sell it. But what you really do when you sell the field is to transfer to another person your claim to the capital it represents. The capital in the field is the same after the transaction as it was before it. Such permanently invested capital may be contrasted with the capital invested in transitory forms, as coal, raw materials, merchants' stocks. The capital invested in these forms returns to its owner in a relatively short time in the form of purchasing power, and may be reinvested in any one out of a thousand different classes of capital goods. The return to such transitory goods is most conveniently calculated as a percentage return to the capital invested in them. It is natural to think of the return to a farm or a building as a certain sum of money, or a rent. One may, of course, translate the rent into terms of interest on the capital invested in the farm or building. On the other hand, it is natural to think of the return to a merchants' stock in trade as interest on the capital invested in the stock, although it would be quite possible to arrive at the returns to the stock by adding together the net products of all the capital goods whose services have been used.

5. *Gross rent is the total product of a capital good; net rent is whatever remains of the product after deductions have been made for the repair and replacement of the capital good. Net rent is identical with interest.*

We must be careful to distinguish between the total product of a capital good, or its gross rent, and that part of the product remaining after the cost of depreciation of the capital good has been deducted, or net rent. To arrive at the net rent of a house we must deduct from the gross rent a sum sufficient to meet the cost of repairs, together with a year's proper contribution to a fund for the replacement of the house when it shall cease to be habitable. Even the payment for the use of a field is a gross rent. The field wears out — that is, it loses through cropping a part of its original or acquired fertility. The owner of the field must, therefore, set aside a part of the product of the land to restore the fertility of the soil.

It will be noted that net rent, in the sense in which the term is used here, is nothing but interest under another form. We will say that a house yields a net rent of $1000. This $1000 is the sum of interest on the capital invested in the house. If this capital is $10,000, each $100 of it yields an income of $10. In other words, the rate of interest is ten per cent. In general, if we reduce the rent of a group of capital goods to a percentage of the capital embodied in them, what we have is interest on this capital.

6. *The rent of the permanent goods used in an enterprise is most conveniently treated as a residue remaining after the wages of labor, charges for the use of capital in perishable forms, and the cost of materials and other perishable goods have been deducted from the total product of the enterprise.*

In the last chapter we saw that there are two ways of arriving at the product of a concrete capital good, or its rent. One way is to withdraw the capital good from the productive combination into which it enters, noting the shrinkage in product that follows. The other way is to deduct from the gross receipts from a group of several goods the shares (if these can be independently ascertained) that are due to all of the goods except one. What is left is of course the product or rent of the remaining good. Either method may be employed in ascertaining the rent of many capital goods; but the latter method is most frequently employed in the case of goods that lend themselves readily to the renting contract. If one wishes to rent a steam thresher, for example, he will first of all inquire what the gross earnings from the operation of the machine are likely to be. Perhaps such earnings will average $40 a day. In order to operate the thresher, it is, of course, necessary to employ labor and auxiliary capital goods — as coal and machine oil — in connection with it. The labor must be paid for at the prevailing rate of wages; coal and oil must be paid for at the market price. There are accordingly definite sums that must be deducted from the gross receipts from the operation of the machine Whatever is left after these charges have been met — possibly $20 — is the gross rent of the machine for the day.

In the foregoing example the cost of labor, of coal, and of oil were regarded as preferred charges upon the earnings of the enterprise, and this indeed they are. The operator of the threshing machine must pay at least the prevailing rate of wages, or he cannot get labor to run the machine. Similarly, he must pay the market price of coal. Labor and coal have a multitude of uses outside of the business of threshing; if not properly rewarded in that business they go elsewhere. The machine, on the other hand, cannot seek other employment. It is committed to a particular function; consequently it cannot enforce any claim for a specific remuneration. The machine is, as it were, a residuary claimant; and this is more or less true of most of the capital goods that are actually rented. Economists therefore find it convenient to treat rent as though it were always determined in this way.

A steamship building company, not having sufficient orders on hand, launches a freighter on its own account, trusting to the chance that some ocean transportation company will be ready to pay a fair rental for its use. What will determine the rent that the transportation company will offer to pay? The managers of that company can probably estimate pretty accurately what the gross receipts from a year's operation of such a ship would be. Let us say that the estimated gross receipts are \$35,000. From this sum must be deducted the wages of officers and men, \$7000; charges for pilotage, harbor dues, etc., \$1000; the cost of coal and provisions, \$10,000; miscellaneous expenses, \$1000. Nor is this quite all. The \$10,000 invested in coal and provisions — supposing that the transportation company must purchase the whole amount at the beginning of the year — is capital that would in any other field earn \$500 interest. This sum must therefore be added to the preferred charges of operating the ship. The \$15,500 remaining out of the estimated gross receipts is the maximum rent that the transportation company can pay for the use of the ship. This sum, the gross rent of the ship, includes, however, payment for the depreciation of the ship through one year's use. If this amounts to $10,000, we have remaining the sum of $5500 as the net rent.

Similarly, the gross rent of a farm is found by deducting from gross receipts a sum that is sufficient to pay the wages of all labor employed in cultivating it; to replace all capital goods used up; to keep up the efficiency of all live stock and machinery, together with interest at the prevailing rate on the capital invested in such movable capital goods. To arrive at the net rent we must deduct from the gross rent thus determined whatever may be necessary to keep buildings, fences, etc., in repair, and to restore to the soil any elements of fertility that have been destroyed in the year's cropping.

7. *The rent of any one out of a number of classes of goods united in a permanent combination may be ascertained by comparison with other productive combinations in which some, but not all, classes are represented.*

In the cases that have been given the rent-yielding object is a group of capital goods, more or less securely bound together in use. The farm, for example, may be analyzed into several distinct factors. One factor is the bare land; another factor consists of improvements merged in the soil, as drains or irrigation ditches; a third factor consists of farm buildings, fences, tree plantations, etc. Some part of the rent must be ascribable to each one of these factors. The productivity of such a factor cannot be found by withdrawing it; nor can it be found by treating it as a residue, after ascertaining the shares of the other factors combined with it, for these shares cannot be ascertained directly. There remains the method of comparisons. How much more will a well-drained field yield than another field in the vicinity, of apparently equal natural fertility, but without drains? By such comparisons it is usually possible to tell pretty nearly what each factor in a permanent combination of capital goods is producing. One may distinguish in this way between the rent paid for a city house and the rent paid for the ground it stands on, although the two rents usually make parts of a single payment. Find an equally spacious and costly house in a suburb, where a building lot is to be had for practically nothing. The difference in the rent of the two houses is a fairly accurate measure of the rent of the city lot.

8. *The rent of an artificial capital good tends, in the long run, to equal interest, at the current rate, on the cost of duplicating the capital good.*

The rent of a ship, a building, or a machine, may, as we have seen, be ascertained, in the first instance, by subtracting from the gross receipts arising from its operation a sum covering all other expenses connected with its use. The value of such a rent-bearing object does not immediately affect the amount of rent it yields. A ship that yields a net surplus of $5000 above operating expenses may be worth $50,000 or $100,000. The value of the ship has nothing to do with the amount of rent that its owner will receive in the immediate future. But a ship is a capital good that requires periodic renewal. Out of 1000 ships sailing the ocean to-day probably fifty are near the end of their economic existence, and will have to be replaced by new ships if the existing tonnage is to be maintained. Now, if the rent of ships happens to be so low as not to pay the ordinary rate of interest on the capital represented by the cost of building them, no new ships will be built to take the places of those that are no longer seaworthy. The aggregate tonnage will thus be reduced; freights will be advanced until the rent of ships rises to a figure which affords a normal return to shipping capital. If, on the other hand, the rent of ships represents an abnormally high return to capital, more ships will be built, and freights will decline until the rent of ships is only sufficient to pay a fair rate of interest on the capital invested in them. And this is in general true of the rents of all capital goods requiring periodic renewal. For a time the rent may be too high or too low to afford just a normal return to the capital invested in such goods. In the long run, however, the rent is controlled by the prevailing rate of interest.

9. *The rent of land is dependent, in large measure, upon the rate of wages and of interest on auxiliary capital.*

We have seen how it is possible to distinguish the rent of the bare land from the rent of the improvements fixed in it. The rent of land as such is of great practical importance, as land is more frequently held under lease than any other class of capital goods. For this reason, and because land rent displays certain peculiar characteristics, it is worth while to devote especial attention to a study of the laws determining it.

Let us assume that the construction of a railway throws open to exploitation a large section of territory in the Canadian Northwest, and that all the land is at once bought up by wealthy persons who intend to hold it permanently, parceling it out in tracts suitable for tenant farmers. We shall further assume that the owners of the land leave its equipment with auxiliary capital goods entirely to the tenants, and that deterioration of the land through cropping is so slight as to be negligible. Whatever the tenant can be made to pay, under these conditions, is practically the rent of the bare land.

In making up his bid the tenant will have to estimate, on the one hand, the gross receipts from the land which he expects to occupy, and on the other hand, all expenses of cultivation, including the wages of all labor employed, his own as well as that of hired hands; interest on the auxiliary capital which he furnishes, whether his own or borrowed capital; and a sum sufficient to replace or repair capital goods destroyed or impaired through use. Let us suppose that all these items of expense amount to $1000. If the tenant has reason to believe that one year with another the gross receipts from the farm will be only $1000 he will pay nothing at all to the owner of the land for its use. If on the other hand he believes that the gross receipts will be $2000 he will be prepared to pay a rent of $1000.

It is obvious that what the tenant can afford to pay for the use of the land depends, in large measure, upon the rates at which he must reckon the wages of labor and interest on auxiliary capital. If these rates are high, the deductions from gross receipts to be made in calculating rent will be large. Accordingly, in order to arrive at the forces determining the rent of land in the section which we are studying, we must examine the influences affecting the local rates of wages and interest.

Land in the Canadian Northwest, as in every other part of the world, varies in natural fertility and in accessibility. If the supply of auxiliary capital and of labor is very small, only the most fertile and most accessible lands will be cultivated. The owners of slightly poorer or slightly less accessible lands will of course derive no revenue from them; they could afford to let such lands for a nominal rent. On these lands, then, labor and auxiliary capital are free to divide between them whatever they can produce. The labor and auxiliary capital employed on the better land can demand at least as much for themselves;

if this is refused, they will migrate to the unoccupied fields.

Now let us suppose that a new body of laborers, bringing with them the appropriate auxiliary capital, enter the region. These occupy the lands which in fertility and accessibility are least inferior to those first cultivated. If after this accession of labor and capital any one is dissatisfied with wages on the better lands, he may, as before, migrate to land still remaining unoccupied. But the unoccupied land is now more remote and less fertile than was that existing before the accession of the new labor and capital, and the product of labor and capital on such lands will be less. The cultivator of the better grade of land will therefore not have to pay so much for either factor as before. A larger share of his gross receipts may therefore be paid out in rent. And with every increase in the labor and auxiliary capital of the community, remoter and less fertile lands are brought under cultivation, with consequent decline in wages and in interest on auxiliary capital, and increase in the rent of all the better grades of land. At any particular time we may say that in this community the wages of labor and the interest on auxiliary capital are determined, respectively, by the productivity of labor and of auxiliary capital on the poorest land actually cultivated. This is of course only a special instance of the law stated in earlier chapters, that wages and interest are determined by marginal productivity.

From the fact that when labor and capital flow into a new region the rent of land steadily rises, it is often assumed that the aggregate of land rents is constantly increasing. But it is to be borne in mind that when labor and capital are drawn into a new region, the older communities may come to be less fully supplied than before. And this would increase the shares of labor and of auxiliary capital in those communities, and reduce the share that is assigned to land. The increase in rents in America, in the last half century, has in some measure been offset by a decline in rents in Europe. If, however, population and capital in reproducible forms continue to increase, without any corresponding increase in the amount of land accessible to the cultivator, and without improvements that increase the general productivity of labor and capital, the aggregate of land rent must increase.

10. *A rise in the prices of agricultural products usually raises the rent of land.*

In the foregoing example we have assumed that the value of the product of a farm remains fixed, while the rates of wages and interest vary. Let us now see what would be the effect on rent of an increase in the value of the product — which we shall assume to be wheat. Such an increase might be brought about by a reduction in the cost of transportation. For the local price of wheat is practically equal to the price in England, the great wheat market of the world, less the cost of transporting the wheat thither. If the cost of transportation is reduced five cents a bushel, the local price of wheat will rise five cents a bushel.

If the growers of wheat are forced to rely upon the local supplies of labor and capital, the effect of the rise in the price of wheat will be an increase in wages of labor and interest on auxiliary capital as well as in the rent of the land. For under the conditions assumed, wages and interest are determined by the value of the product of these agents on the poorest lands in the community actually in use. The value of this product will be increased by the rise in the price of wheat; hence wages and interest will rise throughout the territory. Since there has been no increase in the amount of labor and capital, no more land can be cultivated than before. The better lands can claim no larger a return, measured in wheat, than before; but this return now commands a higher price.

If, on the other hand, close relations have been established between this region and the rest of the world, so that wages and interest are determined by the general influences prevailing in society, practically the whole of the advance in wheat prices will be applied to rent. For suppose that at first wages and interest are raised above the general level. Additional labor and capital will flow into the region; competition will arise for employment on the better lands, or worse lands will be put under cultivation. Thus the marginal productivity of labor and of auxiliary capital will be reduced and the rent of land will increase until labor and capital are rewarded no better than they were before — that is, until land rent has absorbed the entire benefit of the increase in price. It is true that the withdrawal of labor and capital from the general field that this movement implies will tend to raise the rewards of these agents slightly. But this influence will be hardly perceptible.

We can now understand what it is that forces up agricultural rents in the vicinity of a growing city. The value of the gross product of a given area is constantly increasing, as a result of increased demand, while the charges to be deducted, wages and interest on capital in reproducible forms, are controlled by general laws which are affected only slightly, if at all, by the growth of this particular city. We can explain in the same way the rise of rent of city lots. The aggregate return from the business that may be transacted on a given ground space increases with the growth of a city, and as wages and interest on reproducible capital do not increase in equal degree, a larger surplus is left for the owner of the land. In the same way the rent of a railway or a canal in a rapidly developing region steadily increases. The railway or canal is a capital good which cannot readily be reproduced. Accordingly, if the aggregate business to be carried on increases, an increasing share of the value product of the business will take the form of rent on the irreproducible elements.

11. *Growth of population and increase in accumulations tend to raise ground rents generally.*

In all the cases that we have examined, an important factor in raising rents of land and similar capital goods is the influx, or possibility of influx, of capital and labor from the general field. If we view society as a whole, there is, of course, no possibility of a similar influx of labor and capital from outside regions. Nothing can transfer to the owners of land the benefits of increased value product except increase in the aggregate supply of labor and auxiliary capital. If these agents remain stationary in quantity, while the progress of improvements raises the productivity of the units that are placed at the greatest disadvantage — that is, if general wages and interest rise — it is obvious that the rent of land may fall. So also if population and auxiliary capital decrease in amount. If, on the other hand, labor and auxiliary capital increase so rapidly that wages and the interest on such capital fall, land rents must in general rise. It is, of course, possible that increase of capital and of labor may be attended by such great improvements in methods of production that wages, interest on reproducible capital goods, and land rent will all increase. This has been more or less true of the economic development of the last century.

•**12.** *The process of computing the amount of capital in a good from its net rent is termed capitalization.*

Given the net rent of a capital good which cannot be reproduced and the current rate of interest on capital, it is an easy matter to ascertain the amount of capital invested in the good. Multiply the sum representing the usual net rent by the quotient arrived at by dividing 100 by the number representing the rate of interest. If the net rent of a farm is $2500 and the current rate of interest is five per cent, the capital value of the farm is $\frac{100}{5} \times \$2500$, or $50,000. This process of computing the capital through the net rent is known as capitalization. If a building earns $10,000 a year, and there is good reason for believing that it will continue to earn the same net rent indefinitely, the simplest way of ascertaining how much capital is invested in the building is to find how large a sum of capital, in general investments, is required to earn an equal sum. If the general rate of interest is ten per cent, this sum will be $100,000. If the rate of interest is five per cent, the sum will be $200,000. In the one case the rent is capitalized at ten per cent, in the other case at five per cent.

13. *The amount of capital in a reproducible capital good is determined by its cost of duplication. The amount of capital in capital goods that cannot be replaced is determined by the capitalization of their rent.*

In the case of reproducible capital goods, the net rent alone is no sufficient indication of capital value. The cost of producing similar goods must be taken into account; indeed, this is by far the more important element in the computation. A ship, for example, may yield a net rent of $10,000 at a time when the current rate of interest is five per cent. He would, however, be a reckless business man who would assume, from these data, that the ship represented a capital of $200,000, and that he could afford to pay that sum for it. If a similar ship can be built for $100,000, this sum is the true measure of the capital invested. The net rent of $10,000 merely indicates that capital in ships is, for the time, highly productive. Soon the supply of ships will, doubtless, be increased and the net rent will fall to about $5000. It may be a year before the decline will take place; in such case the buyer of a ship already afloat can afford to pay about $105,000 for it. This sum may be analyzed into two parts; $100,000 for the capital in the ship, and $5000 for the transfer of the extra productivity of the ship through one year. If several years must elapse before the net rent of ships falls, the second element in the price of the ship will be placed at a higher figure; and if in some way this extra productivity could be made perpetual — if the ship, worth originally $100,000, could be made to yield indefinitely $5000 in addition to the normal earnings of the capital invested in it — the buyer could afford to pay as much for this extra product as for the original capital. That is, he would arrive at the value of the ship, not through a computation of its cost of production, but through a capitalization of its entire net rent.

Now, a tract of land is a capital good in a situation analogous to that of the ship in our hypothetical case. The capital invested in the land, in the first instance, may have been nothing at all. But if the land yields a net rent of $5000 a year and there is good reason for believing that this rent will be maintained, that fact is the only one that buyer or seller will need to consider. For it is not possible that the supply of similar pieces of land at the command of society will be so increased that the net rent will shrink to zero, as would be the case with a reproducible good originally costing nothing. Because of the natural limitation upon the supply of land, there is good reason for supposing that the existing rent will continue to be paid indefinitely. The right to receive the $5000 land rent for all time is therefore worth just as much as the possession of a capital in reproducible forms yielding $5000 interest annually. If capital in reproducible goods yields, as a rule, ten per cent, the rent of the land will be capitalized at $50,000; if the current rate on such capital is only five per cent, the rent will be capitalized at $100,000.

There is, of course, always a possibility that land rent may decline and its capital value shrink accordingly. Something of the kind happened to the rents and land values of Western Europe in the last quarter of the nineteenth century, when the competition of American grain lowered the prices of the European product. Toward the close of the Great War and in the period immediately following, the rent of wheat and corn land in the Middle Western States rose to remarkable levels because of the high prices paid for grain. The value of land rose correspondingly, to sink back painfully with the fall of agricultural prices in 1920 and 1921.

Shall we say that a tract of land that yields $5000 rent, and is capitalized at $100,000, is really a capital of $100,000, or shall we say that the real capital in the land is only the sum originally employed to clear it and render it fit for economic use? If we adopt the former mode of expression, we shall regard the capital in the land as no more productive than capital in any other form. If we adopt the latter mode of expression, we shall regard the capital in the land as extraordinarily productive. Business men, and many modern economists, adopt the former mode of expression. A property that yields regularly the income of a capital of $100,000 *is* a capital of $100,000.

It matters little what mode of expression we employ so long as we bear in mind the fact that the value of the land is merely the capitalization of its rent at the current rate of interest; that with an increase in the rent of a given tract of land, if interest on capital in reproducible goods remains unchanged, the capital value of the land automatically increases, until the ratio of the capital value of land to its net rent is the same as the ratio of the capital value of a group of typical reproducible capital goods to their net rent; that with a decline in the interest rate on capital in reproducible goods, the value of land yielding a given rent increases until the rate of interest on so-called capital in land is no higher than the rate of interest on other forms of capital. If the rate of interest on capital in reproducible capital goods falls, it is because the earning power of such goods declines. If the rate of interest on capital in land declines, it is usually because the land is revalued at a higher figure — that is, counts for a larger sum of capital.

14. *Increase in the capital of society causes the value of land to rise for two reasons,* (1) *because it raises the rent of land, and* (2) *because it lowers the rate at which a given rental is capitalized.*

We have already seen that with increase in the social fund of reproducible capital the productivity of such capital declines; the rate of interest falls, and a larger share of the product of society takes the form of ground rent. This of itself would have the effect of increasing the capital value of land. The decline of the interest rate affects the value of land further through lowering the rate at which a given rent is capitalized. If the current rate of interest is ten per cent, a certain field may produce a net rent of $1000. This sum, capitalized at ten per cent, gives a value of $10,000, which we may, if we choose, call the capital invested in the field. At the end of two decades the current rate of interest may have fallen to five per cent. This would naturally increase the rent of the field in question — perhaps to $2000. This rent we must now capitalize, not at ten per cent, as formerly, but at the new current rate of five per cent. The value of the land thus comes to be $40,000.

15. *Summary.*

Rent, in the most general sense of the term, is the product of any concrete capital good. For practical reasons, however, a study of rent may best be limited to goods of a fairly permanent character. The gross return to a capital good may be divided into two parts, one of which serves to replace the good when it is worn out, while the other is a net income to the owner of the good. This net income, or net rent, may be regarded as the sum of interest on the capital embodied in the good.

In practice, the rent of a durable capital good may conveniently be treated as a residue remaining after the cost of labor and of perishable goods has been deducted from the aggregate product. Where several durable goods enter into a permanent combination, the rent of any one may be determined by comparison with other combinations into which this particular good does not enter.

The rent of reproducible capital goods tends, in the long run, to equal interest, at the current rate, on the cost of duplicating such goods. The rent of goods that cannot be duplicated, such as land, can be arrived at only through a study of the forces determining wages, interest on reproducible capital, and other outlays in production. As wages and interest fall, or as value of product rises, the rent of such goods increases. The value of irreproducible capital goods is arrived at through a capitalization of their rent at the current rate of interest. In a developing country land values rise on account of increase in rent and on account of decline in the interest rate serving as a basis of capitalization.

CHAPTER XV

ENTERPRISE AND BUSINESS PROFITS

1. *Exceptionally favorable opportunities for the employment of labor and capital are to be found in every progressive society.*

In many parts of the United States a careful observer of business conditions will note neglected opportunities for the production of wealth. In one section of the country there is a great demand for thoroughbred stock; very high prices are paid for such stock, yet men are slow to equip themselves for meeting the demand. Another section of the country is known to present excellent opportunity for the production of high grade fruit, yet it has few orchards, and these of indifferent quality. Fertile lands are to be found that yield scarcely anything for lack of water, yet plenty of water for irrigation is at hand in a near-by stream. Waterfalls offering abundance of cheap power remain for years unutilized.

Nor are exceptional opportunities for wealth production limited to the exploitation of neglected natural sources of wealth. The richest opportunities are often those of organizing in a more effective way businesses already existing. In a dairying district, when each producer works in ignorance of what other producers are doing, he must learn through experience many facts concerning methods of production and marketing that could be learned much more cheaply through the experience of others. Moreover, the product of such a district lacks uniformity and its supply is very irregular, with the result that prices are unnecessarily low and fluctuate seriously. An organization of the producers may decidedly increase their income. In a certain city there is a corner lot, now occupied by a tumble-down dwelling house, that would furnish an excellent location for a grocery or hardware business. A block of ground in the residence part of the city, now occupied by a few old cottages, could, in view of present conditions, be profitably cleared and sold in large lots to persons intending to build expensive homes.

In earlier chapters we have seen what advantages flow from the concentration and combination of production. At a particular time there is one form of organization best adapted to the circumstances, and to introduce this form of organization offers an opportunity for rich reward to the man or men who are enterprising enough to undertake the task.

It may be said, in general, that whenever a new business is undertaken, it is with the purpose of exploiting a preëxisting opportunity for exceptional returns. The same thing is true when an established business enters new fields of activity.

2. *The function of combining labor and capital for the purpose of exploiting a business opportunity is known in economics as enterprise.*

In a growing town the time has become ripe for the establishment of a wholesale grocery business. Months and years may pass before any one undertakes to supply the need for such a business, but eventually a man of sufficient business prestige to command confidence proceeds to get together the requisite funds for launching the business. He may be rich enough to supply the necessary capital himself; he may supply a part of it and borrow the rest; or he may associate with him in the enterprise other persons having capital. The organizing of the business involves labor on his part, and some of it of a very high order. The essential part of his activity is not, however, the labor involved. What differentiates him from a laborer working in a routine way is the fact that he sees a new opportunity clearly and takes the steps necessary to utilize it. And the reward which he anticipates consists, not in wages for his labor, but in the exceptional returns to all labor and capital he employs, from which he expects to retain a share for himself.

The man who performs the function of combining labor and capital for the exploitation of an opportunity is known in economics as the enterpriser, or *entrepreneur.*

To illustrate the functions of the enterpriser, we will suppose that a man of known integrity and business capacity decides to establish a manufacturing business. He borrows at a stipulated rate of interest all the capital that the enterprise requires. The actual work of the business man himself, we will say, is a negligible minimum. His secretaries collect the information on which he acts in deciding to found such a business. His attorneys arrange the details of the loan contract; his banker finds for him the persons who have capital to lend. Even the work of selecting a building and choosing a responsible manager is given over to salaried employees. What, then, is the connection of the business man with the enterprise? He lends it his name, he assumes legal responsibility for the conduct of the business, and he reserves to himself the ultimate power of approving or vetoing proposals made by his staff. These are the only functions that the enterpriser must necessarily retain.

In real life it would be difficult to find a man who is an enterpriser and nothing more. It is rarely the case that a man without capital can borrow any considerable amount of it. Lenders demand the security that only the owner of independent resources can give. He would, moreover, be a fortunate enterpriser who could find secretaries and managers who could be trusted to the extent we have assumed. A part of the labor of oversight must ordinarily be performed by the business man himself. The fact that the same man usually combines in himself the functions of enterpriser, laborer, and capitalist does not, however, make the functions indistinguishable.

3. *Opportunities for enterprise are most common where economic conditions are rapidly changing.*

When the population of a city increases rapidly, opportunities for new business enterprises emerge one after another. Profits are to be made by converting residential districts to business uses, and by opening up new residential districts upon lands adjacent to the city. Increase in the number of large incomes in a city offers opportunity for businesses catering to the tastes of the rich. The increasing number of persons without means renders possible the establishment of new manufacturing enterprises. A multitude of business opportunities arise when a new railway line is opened; when improvements are made in the means of producing or transmitting power; when the tastes of consumers undergo a marked change.

War, however destructive to the general welfare, naturally opens an enormous number of opportunities for profit. Arms, munitions and supplies must be provided in vast quantities, whatever the cost. After the outbreak of the Great War immense profits were to be won by every enterpriser who could supply promptly the requirements of the belligerent nations. Existing factories were worked day and night, and new factories sprang up like mushrooms. In the vicinity of the expanding war industries there was a great demand for housing, which offered golden opportunities to owners of real estate and construction companies. All prices rose, and those who were in a position to buy stocks of goods and hold them won easy profits. War millionaires multiplied in every country, neutral or belligerent, in spite of the general impoverishment produced by war.

4. *Enterprise often entails risks, but this is not necessarily the case.*

An enterprising person, struck by the natural beauties of a mountain valley, decides to erect a summer hotel. He sinks his own capital and whatever capital he can borrow in erecting a building and in improving the grounds about it. The outcome may greatly exceed his expectations; throngs of patrons may seek admission to the hotel, enabling him to fix his charges at a very high level; and even this may increase the popularity of his house, since high charges are often accepted as a guaranty of exclusiveness — the quality for which men are most willing to pay liberally. The event may, however, be far less favorable; a few straggling seekers for rest and quiet may be the only patrons secured, and these may hardly pay the running expenses of the business. In such a case the enterpriser loses not only his prospects of prosperity; he also loses, for all practical purposes, whatever capital he has embarked in the enterprise.

Many enterprises, however, involve no risk. When a railway opens a new country, much of the land along the route is certain to rise in value, and those who are enterprising enough to buy before the rise are assured of a substantial return. The success of many enterprises involving organization is capable of almost mathematical demonstration. The exact measure of profit is usually uncertain, but that such an enterprise will afford the requisite minimum of return, may be predicted with certainty. The highest type of enterpriser is the one who places nothing at stake until his calculations prove that there is practically no chance of loss.

5. *The existence of valuable opportunities involving no risk implies the fact that competition does not operate freely.*

The question naturally arises, how can opportunities involving no risk, or little risk, be found? If competition were keen, each opportunity would be seized upon as soon as the chances of gain seemed to outweigh the chances of loss. But competition seldom operates perfectly. Many men are conservative, and show a preference for the well-established routine. These men overlook most of the opportunities within their reach. Other men see the opportunities, but through lack of capital, business prestige, or managing ability, are not in a position to avail themselves of the opportunities that are presented. This is especially the case where the initial outlay required is a large one. You may know of an opportunity for the profitable investment of $100,000; but if you have no capital of your own, you will find it almost impossible to induce other men even to listen to your project. The opportunity will probably wait for the man who has both enterprise and $100,000, or sufficient business prestige to induce other men to intrust him with their capital.

6. *The income which originates in enterprise is known as profit. It may be defined as a surplus remaining after costs, including interest on all capital and wages for all labor, have been met.*

In earlier chapters it has been shown that the returns to the average business enterprise must be sufficient to cover all costs of production, including under this head not only actual outlays, such as prices paid for materials, wages of hired labor, and interest on borrowed capital, but also ordinary returns on the capital owned by the business man himself and reasonable wages for his labor. An exceptional opportunity is one that will do more than this. A surplus remains in the hands of the enterpriser after all costs have been met. This surplus is known in economics as "pure profit," or more simply, as "profit." We must be careful to distinguish profit in this sense of the term from the income known as profit in the language of business. In the latter sense profit often includes interest on the enterpriser's capital and wages for his labor. Profit in the economic sense of the term is not essential to the continued operation of an established enterprise. Profit in the business sense of the term is a necessary income, since no one would remain long in a business unless he obtained a return representing interest on his capital and wages for his labor.

7. *The profits from an enterprise are commonly due to the fact that labor and capital in that enterprise are unusally productive, but are rewarded according to the standards generally prevailing.*

In any important industrial center the productivity of labor and of capital may at a given time vary from industry to industry, while the wages of labor and interest on loanable capital vary little, if at all. We may arrange the different industries of such a center in a series, according to the degree of productivity of labor and capital in each one. Labor and capital will, as a rule, receive no higher rewards in any industry than in the one that stands lowest in the series. If we assume that in this least productive industry labor and capital receive all that they produce — and we cannot assume that they receive more than this — we see clearly that in all the industries higher in the series they must receive less than they produce. In the more productive industries the products of labor and capital afford a surplus above wages and interest, which takes the form of a profit to the enterpriser.

Let us suppose that the American public, awakening to the significance of the ghastly record of railway accidents, forces through Congress a law requiring the railway companies to replace all remaining wooden passenger cars with cars of steel. The demand for steel cars would become enormous. The car-building companies, for a time, could sell their output at very high prices. The productivity of labor and capital in such establishments, measured in terms of price, would be abnormally high. But the wages of laborers engaged in building steel cars would be practically no higher than the wages of equally skilled laborers in any other branch of the iron and steel industries. There would accordingly be a surplus above costs, or a profit to the enterpriser. The car-building companies would pay no higher rate of interest on borrowed capital than any other manufacturing companies in the vicinity. A surplus originating in the abnormally high productivity of capital would thus be added to the profit from labor.

In any industry the productivity of labor and capital may vary from establishment to establishment, although there may be no variation in the rates of wages paid. We may, if we like, arrange the establishments in a series, according to the degree of productivity of labor and capital, just as we did in the case of industries of varying productivity. No higher wages or interest will be paid by any establishment than by the establishment working at the greatest disadvantage. As this establishment will pay to labor and capital no more than these agents produce, it follows that the better establishments will not need to pay out in wages and interest the whole product of labor and capital. A profit is left over for the enterpriser.

8. *Profits, in some instances, are explained by the fact that labor and capital, though not more than normally productive, are secured at abnormally low rates.*

Certain classes of laborers are in an exceptionally weak position, and may be compelled to accept wages decidedly lower than the prevailing rate. Immigrants from countries with a different language and a lower standard of life must often accept conditions of employment that are exceedingly unfavorable. Where employers are of one race and employees of another, a set of institutions may develop which give the employer whatever remains of the product of labor above a mere minimum of subsistence. In some parts of the United States convicts and persons condemned to the workhouse are farmed out at rates that enable the employer of such labor to reap large profits. Women employed under the sweating system, and, to a less extent, women employed in factories and shops, are often paid less than their labor is really worth, according to competitive standards. In the history of every industrial country, instances have appeared of large profits founded upon the exploitation of child labor.

A similar exploitation of capital sometimes occurs. Not many years ago, in some of our states, persons intrusted with public funds habitually employed such funds for their own advantage. Such a course of action, even when not unlawful, was generally disapproved, and hence was kept secret, so far as possible. Loans of such funds were made at rates low enough to purchase silence from the borrower, who, accordingly, was placed in a position where he could make large profits. Trustees having little interest in their wards have been known to lend the funds intrusted to them at abnormally low rates. Instances of this kind are by no means so rare as they are generally supposed to be; but recognition of this fact must not lead us to the view that profits are normally the result of conscienceless exploitation.

9. *Profits may arise from the transportation of labor or capital from regions of low returns to regions of high returns, under contracts in which rewards are based upon standards prevailing in the regions of low productivity.*

Let us suppose that employers of large numbers of unskilled laborers in the United States were free to send agents to Europe, or the Orient, to obtain a supply of labor. What the agent would offer for, say, two years' labor would be the local rate of wages for that period of time together with such a premium as might be necessary to overcome the reluctance of laborers to leave their native land. The cost of labor in this case would be determined chiefly by the standards of productivity prevailing in the countries from which the laborers were imported, while the value of the labor to the enterpriser would be determined by American conditions of productivity. By virtue of the labor contract the employer would thus be enabled to retain for himself a part of the product of the labor.

It is obvious that the possibility of obtaining a profit of this nature depends in large measure upon the character of the laws relating to labor contracts. If the enterpriser cannot enforce the contract by law the laborers whom he has imported may desert him before their services have yielded adequate compensation for the cost of bringing them to the country. In the United States to-day, not only would such a contract be unenforcible, but the importation of laborers from foreign countries under such contracts is a punishable offense. This was not formerly the case, and one of the important sources of profits in early American economic history was of the character that has been described. In many parts of the world, especially in the tropics, the contract labor system is still widely used. There are companies which make it their sole business to supply enterprisers with contract laborers from China and India. Such companies derive their profit from the product of the laborers, part of which is made over to the company by the enterpriser who employs the laborers.

We need not here consider the reasons that have led to the general condemnation of enterprise that relies for its profits on contract labor. What we are more immediately concerned with is the possible extent of profits of this nature. Let us suppose that the Chinese coolie in his own home can obtain an annual wage of $50, while his services on a Spanish-American plantation or other enterprise are worth $250 per annum. Allowing $150 for bringing the laborer from China and for his return, and $50 a year to overcome his reluctance to leave his native land, there would remain, on a two-year labor contract, a profit of $150 to the enterpriser, if he imports the labor directly, or to be divided between the enterpriser and the coolie labor company, if the latter acts as intermediary.

We may apply the same reasoning to the case of profits arising from the transfer of capital from regions where its productivity is low to regions where its productivity is relatively high. A mortgage loan company may borrow capital in New York at five per cent interest and loan it in Texas at seven per cent. The loan company thus receives a profit of two per cent. How is this profit produced? Clearly it is a part of the product of the capital set at work in Texas.

10. *Profits may arise when commodities which sell at prices covering costs in high wage-standard regions are worked up in regions having a low wage-standard.*

The prices charged by American bookbinders for the binding of books are based upon the cost of labor in this country, which exceeds the cost of equally efficient labor in foreign countries. There are men who ship books from the United States to Paris to have them bound, as the cost of transportation is not high enough to equal the saving in wages. The net saving represents a profit to the enterpriser. There are metropolitan publishing houses that have printing done in small towns, where rates of wages for printer's labor are less than in the large cities. The profits of Southern cotton manufacturers were for a long time dependent upon the fact that, while the prices they received for their products were held at a level sufficient to cover costs in New England, the wage level in the South was lower than that of New England. Great profits were gained by Japanese cotton manufacturers by virtue of the fact that while the prices of cotton goods in the Orient had to be sufficient to cover the high labor costs in America and England, labor could be had in Japan at very low wages.

Profits may also arise through transferring an industry from a region of dear coal to a region of cheap coal. If a commodity is expensive to transport, profits may be made by removing the industry producing it to a point near the centers of consumption; if the materials entering into the production of a commodity are exceedingly bulky, profits may be made by removing the industry to points near the source of supply of materials. With changes in the technique of transportation and in charges for carrying goods, there are changes in the relative advantages of different producing centers; and those enterprisers who can adapt themselves quickly to these changes are able to gain profits.

11. *Under certain business conditions, enterprisers as a class may reap profits, owing to the fact that the rates of wages and interest are slow to change.*

In times of business prosperity it often happens that the prices of almost all commodities rise; or, what amounts to the same thing, the products of labor and capital, measured in terms of price, increase. For a time enterprisers fear that the rise in prices is a merely temporary phenomenon, to be followed, perhaps, by a fall of prices to a level lower than that existing before the rise. So long as enterprisers maintain this attitude, they naturally refrain from enlarging their businesses. No enterpriser attempts to entice away the workmen in the employ of other enterprisers, as he would do if he believed that the high level of prices would be maintained, nor does he increase his demands upon the fund of loanable capital. There is accordingly no reason why wages and interest should rise. The effect of the rise of prices is thus to increase the price of the products of labor and capital without increasing the cost of labor or of the use of capital. If before the rise in prices labor and capital received the whole value of their products, it is obvious that they receive less than this after the rise. A part of the product of labor and of capital remains in the hands of the enterprisers as a profit.

During the Great War, while wages increased, they did not increase so rapidly as the prices of the products of labor. In all American employments, wages represented on the average 55.6 per cent of the value output in 1913. In 1914 the share of labor was 54.7; in 1915, 53.6; in 1916, 51.9; in 1917, 51.6; in 1918, 54. A greater part of the product of industry must therefore have taken the forms of interest and profits. As interest responds very slowly to changes in economic conditions, we may safely assume that during those years there was a substantial increase in the aggregate profits of enterprisers.

12. *Profits are, in most instances, a temporary form of income.*

The sources of profit that have been described have one characteristic in common: they cannot flow for a very long period of time. An importer of coolie labor may, for a time, make large profits; but if he does so, other importers appear, and either force up the price of this kind of labor at its source or depress the value of the services of coolie labor in the importing country. Sweat-shop contractors may make large initial profits out of underpaid labor; but in the end the number of contractors increases, and this either raises the wages paid to this kind of labor, or, what is more commonly the case, reduces the prices that are paid to contractors. Profits depending upon local cheapness of labor eventually disappear on account of increase in competition for such labor and rise in its price, except in cases where the supply of labor is practically unlimited, as in the Orient. In these cases the industry must eventually develop to such an extent as to create a large increase in the product, with a consequent reduction in its price; and thus, in the end, a level of prices of finished products is established which corresponds with the lower cost of labor, and leaves no margin for profits. If profits depend upon superiority of methods, these methods, in time, are universally adopted, and prices fall accordingly. If profits depend upon industrial misadjustments that leave some industries undersupplied with labor and capital, they are eventually eliminated by migration of labor and capital from the fields that are oversupplied to those that are undersupplied. The general profits that attend business prosperity are wiped out by readjustments in the prices of products and in wages and interest.

A particular enterpriser may, indeed, obtain a continuous income from profits. When he finds that one source of profit is running dry, he searches out another. This implies a rapidly developing state of industry, such as one finds in new countries like the United States. In this country it is not difficult to find instances of men who have enriched themslves now from one source of profit, now from another.

13. *Profits dependent upon the various forms of monopoly may display a high degree of permanence.*

One of the most important sources of profit is the introduction of new and more fruitful methods of production. So long as such a method is confined to one out of a number of competing establishments, prices remain at a level which covers cost of production in the establishments which do not employ the new method. If the new method of production is really an innovation in industry, and if it is of such a nature as to admit of definite description — as, for example, a mechanical device for saving labor — the person who invented it may take out a patent, which will assure to him the exclusive right of using it for a period of time — seventeen years, in the United States. During this period he may continue to enjoy the profits arising from the use of the method. He may, of course, sell the right of use to other persons, in which case he makes labor and capital more productive in the establishments buying the right, reserving for himself, in the shape of payments for the use of the patent, a part of the product of these agents of production.

Somewhat analogous to the profits arising from a patent are the profits arising from the use of a trade-mark or from the "good-will" of a concern. A certain brand of soap has, let us say, a reputation for purity, established by long years of honest business. Another soap bearing another name may be just as pure; but the consumer has no adequate means of determining qualities, and therefore prefers the brand which he has always believed to be good. It is evident that the manufacturers enjoying such a firm hold on the popular favor can charge somewhat higher prices for goods of a given grade than can manufacturers who have their reputation yet to establish. So a merchant who has established a reputation for upright dealing, or who has succeeded in attracting to himself the patronage of the wealthier classes of a city, can charge somewhat more than can his less fortunate competitors. The public esteem which an enterpriser enjoys — the good-will of the business — is sometimes only an insignificant source of profits. Sometimes, however, it is an exceedingly important source. In many cases the good-will of a manufacturing or mercantile establishment is worth more than its aggregate tangible assets.

The profits arising from patented processes and from the good-will of an establishment fall under the general head of monopoly profits. The surplus returns to an ordinary monopoly may be described in the same way. Let us suppose that all the manufacturers of tin plate agree to reduce output twenty per cent in order to force up prices. If the various producers can be held to their agreements, and if new producers can be kept from entering the field, there is no reason why every enterpriser in the business should not enjoy a permanent profit. In the chapter on monopoly price we saw how this can be done. What the monopolists do, from the point of view of distribution, is this: A group of allied enterprisers throw a fence, as it were, around a particular field of industry. They limit the amount of labor and capital admitted to the field, so that the productivity of these agents remains higher than in the unmonopolized fields. Consequently, there remains in the hands of the monopolistic enterprisers a surplus or profit.

14. *Monopoly profits may be capitalized in the same way as other permanent incomes from property.*

We saw in the last chapter how it is possible to arrive at the value of a capital good, such as a field, by capitalizing the income at the current rate of interest. Permanent profits may be reduced to a capital value in the same way. If the profit from a monopoly is $100,000 a year, and if there is good reason for believing that it will continue to be the same from year to year, the monopoly itself is worth as much as a sum of capital that will yield $100,000 interest per annum. If capital generally yields five per cent, the monopoly is worth $2,000,000. If the enterprisers having such a monopoly were to sell out their interests, they would demand that sum over and above full payment for all the buildings, machinery, and other tangible assets of their business. The same thing is true of the profits arising from the good-will of a business. These profits will be capitalized, and the buyer of the business will have to add the capital value of the profits to the value of the tangible capital goods.

The value of a patent is found in a similar manner. The only difference is that the profits from this source cease upon the expiry of the patent. What the buyer pays for is the right to a certain estimated income for a definite number of years. If the annual income is estimated at $5000 a year, and the patent has ten years to run, the simplest way of arriving at the value of the patent is to find the present value of each year's income, and add these sums together. If the current rate of interest is four per cent, the present value of $5000 due in one year is obviously equal to a sum which, plus interest for a year, will amount to $5000. That sum is about

$4807. $5000 to fall due two years hence is worth a present sum which together with compound interest at four per cent will in two years amount to $5000 — $4625. By a similar process — known as discounting — the value of each year's income may be ascertained, and by addition, the present value of the patent is established.

15. *Profits usually play an important part in promoting economic progress and in directing the distribution of the productive resources of society.*

All profits, whether monopolistic or not, are, from the point of view of distribution, a part of the product of labor and capital which various circumstances enable the enterpriser to retain for himself. It may therefore appear, at first thought, that the existence of profits is evidence of injustice in the distribution of wealth.

Upon reflection, however, we see that this is not universally true. Profit in many cases plays an important part in stimulating economic progress; in many other cases the existence of profit serves as a means of distributing the agents of production in such a way as best subserves the interests of society. An income that must exist if society is to be progressive and if the best disposition is to be made of its productive resources can hardly be regarded as unjustifiable.

It is the hope of profits that induces the enterpriser to devise improved methods of production, or to adopt improvements devised by others. In doing this the enterpriser increases the productivity of labor and capital, reserving for himself, as long as he can, the benefits of this increased productivity. But sooner or later the new method finds general application in the industry, and the enterprisers are forced to yield up the benefits arising from it to labor and capital, in the form of increased wages and interest, or to the consumer of commodities in the form of lower prices. In the latter case all laborers and capitalists gain by an increase in the purchasing power of their incomes.

When profits arise from a general increase in the demand for a commodity, the ethical title of the enterpriser to the income is not quite so clear. But such an increase in demand shows that the amount of labor and capital devoted to the industry affected by the increased demand should be increased. Under the competitive system this result can be brought about only through the action of enterprisers. Now, if enterprisers received no profit from enlarging old works and establishing new ones, why should they trouble themselves with doing this? If, on the other hand, they may for a time keep for themselves as a profit a part of the price of their products, they will naturally endeavor to enlarge their works as quickly as possible. When at last as much labor and capital is devoted to the industry as is socially expedient, profits cease through rise in wages and interest or through fall in prices.

Of the forms of profit that are classed as monopolistic, those arising from patented inventions and from good-will need no defense. The former is the reward for one of the most important services to society. The inventor can never get for his services, at any time, more than they are worth to society; at the expiry of the patent the invention becomes the common possession of all. The profits arising from good-will, in the literal sense of the term, are a reward for honorable business dealing, and can be retained only so long as the enterpriser is worthy of them.

16. *The profits of an ordinary monopoly cannot be ethically justified.*

The profits of an ordinary monopoly, so far as they are true monopoly profits, stand on an entirely different footing. The productivity of labor and capital in the field controlled by the monopoly is rendered abnormally high, not merely through superior organization and combination of these factors in production, but largely through the maintenance of an artificial scarcity of them, which is directly opposed to the interests of society. While the action of any one out of a number of competing enterprisers, each striving to increase his own profit, usually operates to increase the aggregate wealth produced by society, the action of a combination of enterprisers striving to secure a monopoly profit operates to reduce the aggregate wealth production of society. Through his anti-social conduct the monopolistic enterpriser receives a permanent profit, the fruits of other men's labor and capital. The enterpriser who carries on business under conditions of competition receives, as a reward for his important services to society, only a temporary profit.

It appears, therefore, that the elimination of monopoly profit through legislative action, if possible, is eminently desirable. It is, however, to be borne in mind that this cannot always be done without injustice. We have seen that monopoly profit, being permanent, may be capitalized. If a combination of manufacturing enterprises makes possible a monopoly profit of $100,000, the selling value of the combined enterprise — or of the capital stock representing it — is increased by the capital value of an income of $100,000. Now, the original promoters of the monopoly do not continue to own it forever. Some of the stock in it may pass to their heirs; some of it may be sold to persons who do not know that a great part of its value is merely the capitalization of a wrongful monopoly profit. If, then, the profit of the monopoly is eliminated, the latter class of persons find themselves deprived of an income the right to which they purchased in good faith as an income from capital.

17. *Profits, in time of economic emergency, may lose all practical relation to productive efficiency and become in effect a form of of exploitation. Such a degenerate form of profit is popularly known as profiteering.*

It has already been indicated that opportunities for profit become very common at times of great economic changes or readjustments, such as take place, for example, during a great war. Economically, war represents a tremendous shift in the character of the products of industry in demand. Plowshares must be beaten into swords. The sums which private individuals would have spent for all the miscellaneous commodities of peace, are taken from them by the government by means of taxation or through the flotation of loans and lavished upon arms, munitions and other military supplies. With an army in the field the government must have these things, and usually in vastly greater volume than can be supplied by existing facilities of production. Factories that had been equipped to produce locomotives must be converted to the production of field guns. Watch factories must be converted to the making of time fuses. Great difficulties present themselves in this process of conversion. Old machinery must be torn out and new machinery installed. The working personnel must be trained to new kinds of work. The government might take over the factories and convert them to such uses, or erect new ones, and produce the goods it requires. But in time of war a government usually has all its abilities severely strained in organizing armies, managing transport, etc. Therefore it relies upon private enterprise to provide war material. This means that a price must be offered that will tempt enterprise and stimulate maximum efforts. That is likely to be a generous price, offering liberal profits.

Within limits, private enterprise is justified in demanding the profits, because there are serious risks of loss involved. But the limits of reasonable profits are easily exceeded. The purchasing agents of a government at war are little concerned over prices. They must get the supplies; few questions will ever be raised as to the prices. Enterprisers are thus often in a position to charge about what they please, and many of them take full advantage of their position. During the Great War such abuses were common in every belligerent country. Naturally, there was great popular hostility to men who thus enriched themselves at a time when the people as a whole were meeting the heavy sacrifices of war.

In supplying the civil population, also, numerous opportunities for excessive profits arise during war time. There may be wheat and meat and sugar enough for all ordinary demands, but a panic may arise among consumers which leads to excessive bidding and a rise in prices for which there is no real justification. The public, too, gets accustomed to an order of things in which everything goes up in price. Merchants find it easy to mark up their prices, and thus make large profits. Rather late in this period of rising prices, partly because civil construction ceases in war time, rents go up, sometimes to exorbitant levels. If these successive price inflations resulted in an important stimulus to production they might be accepted by the public with philosophy. In many cases, however, they result in no increase in production at all, and seldom is the stimulus sufficient to compensate the public for the burdens thrust upon it.

When the evil of excessive profits or "profiteering" becomes intolerable, the government usually makes an effort to remove it by fixing prices. But the administration of price fixing is very difficult. The methods of evasion are numerous and subtle, and no government has yet found an adequate remedy for the disease of profiteering.

18. *Summary.*

In a progressive society exceptional opportunities for the employment of labor and capital are continually presenting themselves. The act of seizing upon such opportunities is known as enterprise; the income arising from enterprise is pure profit. The existence of profitable opportunities is evidence of the fact that competition does not operate freely.

From the point of view of distribution profit is an income created by labor and capital, but retained by the enterpriser. When labor and capital are abnormally productive, but are paid at normal rates, a surplus remains for profit; when labor and capital are normally productive, but are paid at abnormally low rates, a similar surplus appears. The importation of labor and capital from regions of low productivity to regions of high productivity, with the maintenance, in the latter regions, of the standards of pay established in the former regions, is one source of profit; the transfer of an industry from a region in which standards of pay are high to a region where such standards are low is another source of profit.

As a rule, profit is a temporary form of income. Monopoly, in its various forms, gives to profit a fair degree of permanence. Monopoly profit is therefore capitalized like any other form of permanent income.

Since profit is an income produced by the labor and capital of one set of men and enjoyed by another set of men, it appears to demand an ethical justification. Competitive profits may be defended on the ground that they serve as an incentive to improvement, and help to adjust the supply of each commodity to the demand for it. Such forms of monopoly profit as the royalties of an inventor and the receipts from the good-will of a business are easily defended. The profits of an ordinary monopoly cannot be defended, ethically; their continued existence depends upon a calculated misadjustment of demand and supply. In war time opportunities for profit are multiplied and lead to a condition of profiteering for which no satisfactory remedy has been found.

CHAPTER XVI

MONEY

1. *Money is anything that practically all men are ready to accept in exchange for their goods, with the expectation of employing it in the acquisition of other goods.*

In the foregoing chapters frequent use has been made of the term price, which of course implies the term money, since price is nothing but exchange value, expressed in terms of money. It has been tacitly assumed that money is in general use and that its value remains constant, price fluctuations being due to changes in the conditions of production or consumption of other things. The latter assumption, as every one familiar with recent discussions of economic policy is aware, cannot pass unchallenged. The value of money, like the value of all other things, is subject to continual fluctuations, and these fluctuations give rise to some of the most important problems of practical economics.

We may profitably begin this part of our study by considering what it is that the plain man regards as money. Anything that is accepted by practically every one in exchange for his goods or services, with the sole intention of exchanging it ultimately for other goods or services, is popularly regarded as money. This view, which is also that of many of the ablest writers on money, we may safely adopt as our own. Under different conditions of economic development, different concrete things have served as money, — shells, beads and other ornaments, bits of metal coined or uncoined, and even such commodities as cattle and furs. With the evolution of trade, a corresponding evolution of money has taken place, and those forms of money which were fitted for use when trade was merely an incidental part of economic life have given way to forms of money adapted to a complex system of commerce.

2. *The origin of money is to be sought in a gradual and unconscious evolution in which certain articles of direct use came to be more and more frequently accepted in exchange merely as a means of acquiring other articles of direct use.*

The origin of money antedates all historical records. Nevertheless, we know enough about the life of primitive man to construct a plausible view of the circumstances under which money must have come into existence. In the earlier stages of human evolution exchange, at least in the modern sense of the term, was unknown; hence, of course, money could not have existed. When it first became customary to make exchanges, goods were doubtless bartered directly for goods, as is sometimes the case even to-day. Certain articles, however, were more frequently the objects of exchange than others, as, for example, strings of seashells, articles of copper, silver, and gold suitable for personal adornment. Such articles, unlike the common necessaries of existence, could not be produced by any one desiring them. Not being essential to life, they would naturally be sacrificed by their possessors in time of need. The desire for such articles, on the other hand, could not be readily satiated. We can easily see, therefore, why articles of this nature should have been among the earliest to be freely purchased and sold. We can also see why persons having ordinary commodities to dispose of should have been willing to accept such articles with at least a half-intention of exchanging them later for other commodities. Men desiring such articles, and willing to make sacrifices to obtain them, could easily be found.

Just at what point articles of personal adornment, as, for example, silver bracelets, ceased to be ordinary commodities and became money it would of course be impossible to say. At any stage in this development some men may have accepted them solely with a view to a further exchange, while others may have accepted them primarily with a view to further exchange, yet with the alternative of personal use before them; and still others, with no intention of exchanging them for something else. To the first class of persons, the bracelets would have been money; to the second, neither money nor ordinary commodities but something half way between; to the last class they would have been merely ordinary commodities. If the last two classes were relatively insignificant, the bracelets would properly have been called money. We do not hesitate to call nickels and dimes money, although certain of the aboriginal inhabitants of the United States perforate all they can obtain and hang them in strings from their ears.

3. *The functions of money are* (1) *that of medium of exchange;* (2) *that of store of purchasing power;* (3) *that of measure of value; and* (4) *that of standard of deferred payments.*

When a farmer exchanges a load of wheat for money, and immediately exchanges the money for household supplies, the money so far as he is concerned serves merely as means for exchanging the wheat for household supplies. If the farmer does not immediately purchase the supplies, but keeps the money in his strong box against future needs, we may say that the money serves as a convenient means of keeping the purchasing power originally represented by the wheat through a period of time, or as a store of purchasing power. If the local dealer is at once a grain buyer and a dealer in household supplies, no money may actually be used in effecting the exchange. The value of the grain is estimated in terms of money, as is also the value of the household supplies, and the one quantity of money value is set against the other. In this case money is used solely as a measure of value. If the farmer delivers his wheat, but "trusts" the dealer with its value the future obligation of the dealer to the farmer is reduced to definiteness in terms of money. The farmer is credited, not with forty bushels of wheat, but, we will say, with $50. In this way money serves as a "standard of deferred payments."

The primary function of money is that of medium of exchange, and from it are derived the other three functions. Money serves as a store of purchasing power because of its universal acceptability in exchange. It serves as a measure of value because men are constantly weighing the value of other things against that of money. And for the same reason it serves as a standard of deferred payments. If you promise to deliver to me one thousand bushels of wheat a year hence, I have no very definite idea as to the sum of value I am to receive. If you promise to deliver to me $1000 a year hence, I have a definite idea as to the sum.

4. *Anything serving as money should present in a high degree the qualities of uniformity, stability of value, and adaptability to transactions of varying magnitude.*

In the early modern commercial centers traders were always seriously handicapped by the great variety of coins used as money. In every business transaction it was necessary to examine the money offered in payment almost as carefully as the quality of the articles offered for sale. In many cases gold and silver coins passed by weight; but even in such cases there was always some question as to the real value of the money, as the coins of different countries were of different degrees of fineness. It is hard to exaggerate the advantages presented by a monetary system like that of the United States of to-day, in which one dollar represents the same value as any other.

Hardly less important than uniformity is stability of value. If money is to serve as a store of purchasing power, its value must not be subject to rapid fluctuations. If it is to serve as a standard of deferred payments, stability of value is of extreme importance. Imagine the inconvenience of a standard fluctuating in value as widely as do most of the commodities of common use. A man borrowing money for a six-months period might find himself, at the end of the period, compelled to pay back twice as great a sum of value as he borrowed; or he might escape with paying half as great a sum. With such a fluctuating standard all contracts involving future payments of money would become highly speculative.

What really happens when the value of money fluctuates widely has been amply exhibited in the economic history of Central Europe since the outbreak of the Great War in 1914. The German mark, worth 23.8 cents in 1914, had fallen to one and three quarters cents in February, 1921, and one half a cent in February, 1922. The Austrian crown worth 20.3 cents in 1914, was worth a quarter of a cent in February, 1921, and four hundredths of a cent in February, 1922. Any long term loans contracted before the war and due in 1922 could be paid off with a sum representing, in Germany, one forty-seventh, and in Austria, one five hundredth of the value originally loaned. With a ten dollar bill an Austrian house owner could extinguish a five thousand dollar mortgage contracted before the war. And even one year loans, contracted at the beginning of 1921, could be paid off, in Germany, with money worth one-third, in Austria with money worth one-sixth of the sum loaned.

For an advanced commercial nation, adaptability of

money forms to transactions of varying magnitude is of great importance. In the rural districts of China, where trade is chiefly local and the articles of trade of low value, coins of one kind, and these of very low value, meet practically all needs. In a country like our own, with the greatest variety of business transactions to be performed through the medium of money, a wide variety of forms of money is required. For the smallest transactions it is necessary to have coins of a value which is low, relatively to bulk, as bronze cents, nickel five-cent pieces. For slightly larger transactions, coins of silver, which represent a greater value per unit of bulk, are more convenient. For transactions involving still greater values, gold coins are better adapted than silver; for the largest cash payments, paper money, which may be of any denomination, is the most convenient of all. How important is this variety in forms of money will be understood by any one who happens to be engaged in business in a town where at times the supply of small coins is not sufficient to meet the needs of petty trade.

5. *Uniformity in the medium of exchange depends upon effective governmental regulation.*

From very early times it has been recognized that the coinage of money is a business of such great public importance that it cannot be left to unregulated private enterprise. The private coinage of gold and silver has indeed sometimes been tolerated. In the United States as late as 1860 privately coined gold was to be found in circulation. But experience showed then, as it had often shown in earlier periods of the world's history, that private coinage results in serious evils. Coins that circulated as of equal value differed as much as ten per cent in their gold content. Those who were least able to judge the probable value of such privately issued coins were likely to be cheated in trade with those who were better able to judge the value of these coins. Because of such evils the issue of coins by private individuals has been prohibited by law. All coins are issued directly by government, and measures are taken by every well-regulated state to insure uniformity of value of money thus issued.

6. *The function of government in issuing money may be* (1) *to stamp the weight and fineness of metal in a coin; or* (2) *in a restricted sense, to determine the value of money regardless of the material composing it.*

The government may hold its mints open to private owners of precious metal, coining on their account all the metal they offer for coinage. Thus any holder of gold bullion can take it to the Unites States mints and have it made into coins. In such case it cannot be said that the government determines the value of the coins issued. If there is a large production of gold, there is likely to be an increase in the amount of gold taken to the mints for coinage, and, as we shall see later, a tendency toward a decline in the value of the coins. The government assures the recipient of a gold coin that it contains the requisite amount of pure gold; practically it assures him of nothing more.

When a metal is freely coined on individual account, there can be no perceptible difference in value between a given amount of the metal in the form of coin and an equal amount in the form of bullion. In the United States an ounce of uncoined gold is worth just as much as an ounce of gold coined. If for any reason gold in the form of coins should become more valuable than gold in the form of bullion, more bullion would be taken to the mints, and the difference in value would disappear. If uncoined gold became more valuable than gold in coins, coins would be melted down, and again the difference would disappear.

A government may accept for coinage on individual account either gold or silver, or both metals. When gold alone is freely coined on individual account, the monetary system of a country is said to be based upon *gold monometallism.* When both gold and silver are freely accepted for coinage, the monetary system is based upon *bimetallism.* The bimetallic system was generally employed in modern times until the nineteenth century. Early in that century Great Britain adopted gold monometallism, and in the latter half of the century the same system was adopted by all other important commercial nations.

When a monetary system is based upon gold freely coined by government on individual account, the needs of trade require the presence of money composed of other materials, such as silver, nickel, bronze, and paper. The value of such forms of money is said to be determined by government, since it bears no fixed relation to that of the material from which it is made, as is the case with the money made from a metal freely coined. As a fact, the government issuing such money usually adopts measures designed to maintain a fixed relation between its value and that of gold. The government of the United States regulates its currency in such a way that a five-dollar bill, or five silver dollars, or five hundred bronze cents are always equal in value to a five-dollar gold piece. Gold coin, which serves as a standard, may rise or fall in value; all other forms of money rise or fall with it. All the non-standard forms of money are said to be maintained at a parity with the standard form.

7. *The only practical way of maintaining all the forms of money at a parity is through provision for the exchange of any form for the others at the option of the holder.*

If a government issues a limited amount of paper money and makes it *legal tender*, that is, receivable at its face value in payment of all debts, public and private, such money may circulate at par, with no further provision for regulating its value. If I am offered a piece of paper which I am certain will be equivalent to $10 in gold in the payment of taxes, or in the payment of my debts to other persons, there is no reason why I should not accept it as readily as $10 in gold.

If much of this kind of money is issued, however, every one may hesitate to accept it in lieu of gold. Dealers may refuse to accept it in exchange for their goods; accordingly, it may depreciate in value in spite of the fact that it is receivable at par in payment of public dues and existing debts.

To make certain that non-standard forms of money shall not fall below their face value in gold, it is customary for governments to make provision for redeeming them in gold on demand. In the monetary system of the United States are to be found coins of gold, silver, nickel, and bronze, as well as paper money. Part of the paper money consists of gold and silver certificates; a small part of it, of treasury notes, issued in payment for silver bullion; part of it of "greenbacks" — promissory notes of the government, a legacy of the Civil War. All these forms of money are maintained at an absolute parity by the government. The gold certificates cannot fall below the value of gold coin, because for every dollar of such certificates there is a dollar's worth of gold coin or bullion in the United States Treasury, payable to the certificate holder on demand. The silver certificates are likewise secured in value by treasury holdings of silver. In the war emergency some part of the silver holdings of the Treasury were sold to supply the demands of oriental countries. This left a part of the outstanding stock of silver certificates uncovered by actual silver, a point of no especial consequence, since no one desires to exchange silver certificates for silver in any notable quantity. But the act authorizing the sale of the silver also provided that after the emergency was over the silver hoard should be restored by new purchases. It is a part of the settled policy of the United States to maintain the silver dollars at a parity with gold; and although no specific provision is made by law for the exchange of silver dollars for gold at the treasury, the privilege of making such an exchange would be accorded the holder of silver dollars if the latter showed any tendency to depreciate. A reserve of $150,000,000 in gold is held by the treasury for the purpose of redeeming any greenbacks that may be presented for redemption. Any one who desires may exchange the lesser silver, nickel, and copper coins for gold by presenting them in suitable quantities at the treasury.

8. *If a government fails to maintain all its forms of money at a parity, those forms that become depreciated tend to drive those that are not depreciated from circulation. This principle is known as Gresham's law.*

Let us suppose that the government of the United States issues a large volume of paper money, and makes no adequate provision for exchanging gold for such paper at the option of the holder. The value of this money would be very likely to depreciate, in terms of gold. After depreciation, every person who has payments to make in which the form of money is not specified, naturally uses whatever paper money he has in his possession, and retains his gold. If he has nothing but gold in the first instance, he exchanges it for paper, since he can get more than $100 in paper for $100 in gold, and then makes his payments in paper money. Thus gold ceases to pass freely from hand to hand; if it is used at all, it is as a commodity, valued in terms of paper money. Thus the paper money issued by the United States in the time of the Civil War expelled gold and silver from circulation. When gold and silver were both freely coined it was impracticable for a government to maintain the two forms of money at an absolute parity. At one time an ounce of gold might be worth sixteen ounces of silver; if then silver and gold were coined at a ratio of sixteen to one, — that is, if a dollar in silver contained sixteen times as much pure metal as a dollar of gold, — the two forms of money circulated at par. Changes in the relative production of the two metals, or changes in the demand for them, over which no government had complete control, caused silver to rise or fall relatively to gold. Since the value of coined metal, when coinage was free, could not differ perceptibly from the value of uncoined metal, a rise in the market value of silver, relatively to gold, raised the value of silver dollars above that of gold dollars. In such case the gold displaced the silver from circulation. A fall in the market value of silver resulted in a displacement of gold from the coinage.

In the monetary history of the United States, silver was at one time overvalued, in terms of gold; at another time it was undervalued. As a result there was at one time a tendency for gold to displace silver from the coinage; at another time silver tended to displace gold. The impossibility of keeping freely coined gold and silver at an absolute parity was one of the principal causes for the general adoption by the chief commercial nations of the monometallic system.

9. *The value of money is its purchasing power.*

Under present conditions all men accept money in exchange for their possessions solely with reference to its employment in the purchase of other things. We may, therefore, define the value of money as its power to command other things in exchange, or briefly, its purchasing power. Other commodities are valued by some men for what they will bring in exchange, by other men for the satisfaction to be derived from them directly or indirectly. The ultimate cause of the value which men who hold ordinary commodities for sale ascribe to such commodities is the value ascribed to them by those who will use them in the satisfaction of wants. There are practically no men who ascribe value to money as a means of direct satisfaction. In this respect, accordingly, the value of money is a unique phenomenon, requiring special explanation.

10. *The value of money is measured by its power to command commodities in general.*

The value of money, then, is its purchasing power. How is this power to be measured? Evidently not by reference to any particular commodity. A dollar may buy one and one quarter bushels of wheat to-day and only one and one fifth bushels to-morrow. We should not say that the value of money has declined, but that the price of wheat has risen. For there are probably many other commodities in respect to which the purchasing power of money has increased. To form a true estimate of the value of money we must consider its power to command commodities in general. In order to measure changes in the value of money we may form a list of the principal commodities, showing how much of each a dollar will command at different dates. By the method of averages we can then ascertain whether the general purchasing power of money has changed. This method has long been employed by economists, and it has been shown that through long periods of time the value of money fluctuates widely. A dollar bought in 1914 twice as much as in 1922. Very likely a dollar will buy much more in 1932 than in 1922.

11. *Changes in the supply of money tend to bring about changes in the value of money.*

The factors which determine the value of money, and hence the general level of prices, are so numerous and complex that only a provisional account of them can be given in this work. It is quite generally agreed that, other things equal, the greater the volume of money there is in the world, the lower will be the value of any unit of it. It is, of course, true that there are in operation many influences affecting prices besides changes in the volume of money. Hence we cannot say that if the volume of money, twenty years hence, shall be twice as great as it is to-day, prices will be higher than they are to-day. Yet this fact does not make it the less important for us to gain a clear view of the effect of a change in the volume of money.

Let us suppose that through the discovery of a new gold field the world's supply of that metal is perceptibly increased: $100,000,000 worth of gold, let us say, is taken from the new mines every year. Some of the new gold may be used in the arts, but the greater part of it will find its way to the mints of the nations, and issue thence as coin.

The only use which money subserves is that of purchasing other commodities. The fortunate owners of the new mines will therefore enter the market as purchasers, either of consumable commodities or of capital goods or rights to capital goods — stocks, bonds, etc. There is no reason why the production of goods, whether consumable goods or instruments of production, should at once increase upon the discovery of gold. We may think of the supply of such goods as substantially unchanged. Now, new purchasers, with $100,000,000 to spend, appear upon the market. It is quite evident that competition for commodities will increase, and hence prices will rise.

Let us assume, for the moment, that the rise in price of the commodities purchased by the first owners of the new gold has no effect in stimulating the production of such commodities. The enterprisers engaged in the production of these commodities, then, will enjoy abnormally large money incomes as a result of the high prices at which they sell their products. They will have more money to spend on other classes of commodities for their own use. As the production of these, we assume, has not yet been affected, they also must rise in price. And so the new gold will percolate from one economic stratum to another, everywhere raising prices.

Our assumption that the production of the commodities demanded by the original owners of the new gold remains unchanged is purely arbitrary. The rise in prices would probably lead enterprisers to enlarge their mills, or to run them overtime, and this would require more laborers and more capital. The total supply of labor and capital at the command of society has not, however, been affected by the increase in the volume of money. The only way, then, in which an enterpriser can secure additional labor and capital is by enticing these agents away from the employment of other enterprisers. And this, it is evident, must raise the rates of wages and interest in the district where the expansion of enterprise occurs.

After the rise in wages, each laborer has more money to spend; he will therefore seek to increase his purchases of the commodities suitable for his use. The supply of these, however, has not yet increased; their price is, therefore, forced to a higher level. Similarly the increased money income of the capitalists raises the prices of commodities taken by the members of that class. Eventually not only the price of all finished products, but the price of all raw materials and other capital goods, and of all labor, will be affected.

The new gold may be first used to purchase consumable goods, or it may be used to purchase stocks or bonds. In the latter case, the first effect is an increase in the price of these securities. But the sellers of the securities will use the money to buy other things. Eventually the effect must be felt in the market for commodities and labor.

12. *The issue of paper money by a government, if conducted with moderation, affects prices in the same way that an increase in standard money affects them.*

Instead of assuming that the supply of money is increased through new gold discoveries, we may assume that such increase in the money supply is brought about through an issue of a moderate amount of paper money by the government. Suppose that the United States Government, in order to finance projected irrigation works, issues $100,000,000 in paper money. This money will find its way into circulation through the purchase, by the Government, of additional supplies and the payment of wages to new employees. The supply of steel, cement, and other commodities needed by the Government, however, is not increased at once by the issue of new money; hence the price of these supplies must rise when the Government enters the market as an unanticipated purchaser. Similarly, wages are forced up by the new demand for labor created in this way. Through attempted expansion of business and through increased liberality of expenditure, the enterprisers and laborers first affected by the increase in the money supply transmit its effects, in the form of increased prices, to men engaged in other industries. In the end general prices and general costs are on a higher level than they would otherwise have been.

If, however, a government falls under control of men who are willing to carry the issue of paper money to extremes, its value is determined on quite different principles. The announcement that new issues are contemplated causes a rapid fall in the value of money and a corresponding rise in general prices even before a single new note has been issued. On the other hand the announcement that no more paper will be issued for, say, six months, causes an instant rise in the value of the money. Rumors indicating the fall of the issuing government would cause a great decline in the value of its money, quite irrespective of the demand for money as a medium of exchange.

13. *The employment of substitutes for money in effecting exchanges operates as an increase in the supply of money.*

Not all exchanges are effected through the medium of money. Barter exists even to-day, although this form of exchange may be ignored, as of very slight importance. Many exchanges — indeed, much the greater number, in a society like our own — are effected through the medium of various substitutes for money. Let us suppose that A, a person of unquestioned financial standing, buys of B commodities worth $100, and instead of paying cash, gives a promissory note, due in six months. B in turn may buy $100 worth of goods from C, paying for them not with cash, but with A's note, properly indorsed. C may use the same note to effect a purchase. At any given time a vast number of such notes may be at work effecting exchanges, although each one may be transferred only two or three times before its maturity. The effect of the use of such notes as a means of exchange is the same as that of an increase in the supply of money. A man who can use a note in this way is enabled to enter the market for the purchase of goods as he could not have done if sellers all insisted upon cash payment. The effective demand for commodities, therefore, is increased, just as it would be by an increase in money. We need not at this point carry further the analysis of the effects of the introduction of such substitutes for money, as these effects will receive full discussion in the next chapter.

14. *Changes in the volume of business affect the value of money.*

The value of money, as we have seen, is affected by changes in the volume of money and in the use of substitutes for money. It is also affected by changes in the volume of business to be transacted through the use of money. Where most men produce for themselves the principal commodities which they need, exchanging only their surplus for luxuries, a very little money will meet the requirements of trade. Where, on the other hand, men produce almost exclusively for sale, a large volume of money or of substitutes for money is required. If we imagine that men suddenly change from the system of production for immediate consumption to the system of production for the market, without any change in the volume of money and of its substitutes, we can easily see that the price level must be lowered. Where one commodity under the earlier system was offered for sale to the possessors of money, one hundred may be offered under the later system. Some sellers of commodities would then find that at the scale of values originally existing they would be unable to find purchasers with money to pay. They would accordingly reduce prices, and so attract to themselves a part of the money supply. This would leave other sellers without buyers, and these in turn would lower prices. Thus the price level would fall or, what amounts to the same thing, the value of money would rise, until all sellers could find buyers at the prevailing prices.

The assumption that the system of production could change thus rapidly without a change in the volume of the media of exchange involves unrealities, as we know that exchange and the medium of exchange must evolve together. Yet it points to a real fact: that exchange may expand more rapidly than the volume of the media of exchange, necessitating a lower price level.

15. *An increase in the supply of money tends to raise prices; but there is no definite relation between the degree in which the money supply is increased and the degree in which prices rise.*

It must now be evident that changes in the volume of money are not alone sufficient to explain changes in the value of money, or price changes. The development of substitutes for money and changes in the volume and character of business transactions must also be taken into account. Therefore, although we may say that an increase in the volume of money will, other things equal, raise general prices, we cannot say in what degree any specific addition to the money supply will raise prices. A doubling of the money supply of the world might conceivably double prices. In all probability, however, prices would be increased by less or by more than one hundred per cent. For the readjustments consequent upon such an extraordinary expansion in the volume of money would probably result in vital changes in the volume and character of business, the nature of which it would be impossible to predict. The reader is cautioned against the view that an increase in the money supply, brought about in any way that is known to practical experience, can leave the industrial mechanism unchanged while changing the scale of prices.

We may also say that, other things equal, all prices will be raised by any important increase in the volume of money. But we cannot say that all prices will rise in the same proportion. Indeed, this is something that a little reflection on business conditions shows to be impossible. The supply of some commodities is easily increased, while the supply of other commodities can be increased only after the lapse of considerable time. If the new money is spent largely on commodities of the first class, the attendant rise in prices is quickly counteracted, in some degree, by increase of production. If it is spent on commodities of the second class, there can for a time be no such counteracting influence. We can imagine that the first impulse of the beneficiaries of "easy money" is to acquire high-priced automobiles. This would raise the prices somewhat, but production would increase and prevent the prices from going to immoderate heights. We can also imagine that this first impulse is to acquire antiques and Old Masters. There is no assignable limit to the possible rise in prices of such goods.

16. *Changes in the volume of money give rise to practical economic questions of the greatest importance.*

The fact that not all prices rise in the same degree, and the fact that some classes of business relations cannot be immediately adjusted to price changes, renders the question of increase or decrease in the volume of money of vital practical importance. Some social classes are affected favorably and other classes are affected adversely by such changes.

When general prices are rising, the wages of labor also tend to rise. But it may take some time after prices have begun to rise before enterprisers decide to extend their business operations. The demand for labor, accordingly, does not for a time increase and wages remain unchanged. The laborer receives no higher wages per week or month; the commodities he buys with his wages have risen in price. It follows that the command of the laborer over the necessaries and comforts of life is for the time diminished. Eventually, to be sure, enterprisers will endeavor to enlarge their businesses, and wages will rise. But if the prices of commodities continue to rise, it may well be that for a long period of time the rise in money wages will not be an adequate offset for the increased expense of living. It is a well-known fact that during the Civil War the prices of commodities rose far more than the price of labor. American wages kept closer to the general price level during the Great War, chiefly because the special position of the United States made possible an enormous increase in production from which both wages and return to capital could be increased. Nevertheless, although labor was more fully employed in 1918 than in 1913, the purchasing power of the average yearly wages declined by about five per cent.

For many services compensation is fixed by law or by custom. The salaries of public officials remain fixed through long periods of time, notwithstanding changes in the price level. The postal employee receiving $2000 a year is seriously injured if prices of commodities rise, since years may elapse before the Government grants him an increase of salary. Physicians' fees, in most cases, are regulated by custom and can seldom be increased on account of an advance in general prices.

The business relations most seriously disturbed by price changes, however, are those of creditor and debtor. Let us suppose that a farmer has borrowed $10,000, agreeing to pay off the loan in ten years, together with annual interest at six per cent. After the contract has been made, general prices, we will assume, rise twenty per cent. The farmer does not have to pay more than $600 interest each year, although the purchasing power of that sum has declined twenty per cent. At the end of the ten years, he will not need to pay more than $10,000, although this sum, for the same reason, represents a lower value. The creditor has been injured through the change in the price level just as much as he would have been if the debt had been arbitrarily scaled down to $8333, prices remaining unchanged. The farmer, on the other hand, has gained materially. He receives higher prices for what he has to sell, and so is enabled to pay the annual interest and the principal when due with much less sacrifice than would otherwise have been necessary.

It has already been indicated that the relations of debtor and creditor are thrown into confusion by such extreme fluctuations in the value of money as followed the Great War, especially in Central Europe. In large part the creditor class was simply eliminated. Persons who lived before the war on interest from government bonds and on the returns from mortgage loans and the like were thrust into the ranks of the propertyless.

Enterprisers as a class are benefited through a rise in general prices. What they have to sell commands a higher price; their costs of production increase, but not proportionately. Mention has already been made of the fact that wages may not rise so rapidly as prices. Furthermore, most enterprisers have some charges to meet that remain unchanged from year to year. If they occupy buildings and land not owned by themselves, these are probably held under long time leases. Until it is necessary to renew such leases, the rental cannot be adjusted to the change in the price level. Most enterprisers are heavily in debt, and the rise in the level of prices has the effect of reducing the burden of such debts, as in the case of the farmer of our illustration. A period of rising prices, to the active business man, is, therefore, a period of prosperity, whether it is a period of prosperity to the people as a whole or not.

We have only to reverse our argument to show that in a period of falling prices, or rising value of money, the wage earners as a class gain, because wages do not fall so rapidly as prices, unless, as is not unlikely to happen, the attendant industrial depression produces general unemployment; those receiving salaries fixed by law or custom gain yet more, because a readjustment of such incomes to the new scale of prices is long delayed; creditors gain through increase in the purchasing power of the interest and principal due them. The enterprisers as a class find profits succeeded by losses, and complain bitterly of business depression.

17. *A monetary standard of fluctuating value results in serious hardships; it is therefore natural that efforts should be made to render the standard more stable through governmental action.*

The value of money can neither rise nor fall without inflicting unmerited hardship upon some members of society. Any change in the value of money, therefore, is an evil. The evils of a rise in the value of money are, however, more easily perceived than the evils resulting from a fall in the value of money. When money rises in value — or, what amounts to the same thing, prices fall — enterprisers incur losses, and restrict their operations, reducing their working force as far as possible. Many debtors find themselves unable to sustain their burdens, and become bankrupt. The hardships of unemployment and bankruptcy quickly attract public attention. The hardships arising from a fall in the value of money, or rising prices, are more widely diffused and less patent to the eye of the observer. Wage earners and the recipients of fixed incomes, whether from labor or from loaned capital, encounter greater and greater difficulty in making ends meet, but this fact receives little attention at a time when enterprisers great and small are enjoying prosperity. Accordingly, it is quite natural that when prices are falling men should endeavor to mend matters through the action of government, while the evil effects of a general rise in prices are usually left to mend themselves. Or if the rise in prices is so rapid that the majority suffer keenly under the increased cost of living, the evil is usually assigned to other causes than the true one. The enterprisers and all the series of dealers between them and the consumer are accused of joining in combinations to hoist prices and of profiteering. In countries of fluctuating paper standards the first evidence of declining money value which the ordinary consumer encounters consists in the marking up of prices by the retail dealer. That looks like an arbitrary practice, designed to extort profits out of the consumers, and consequently often produces rioting, or at least an enraged public sentiment which forces the government to take action looking to price control. Such action seldom achieves its purpose. It serves only to divert attention from the true cause of the difficulty.

18. *In order to check the fall of prices which occurred in the period from* 1874 *to* 1897, *it was urged by many that silver should be restored to free coinage, so as to increase the money supply of the world.*

In the period from 1874 to 1897 the prices of commodities steadily declined. In 1897 a dollar would purchase approximately the same amount of commodities that $1.50 would have purchased in 1874. Many classes of producers were seriously injured by this decline in prices; business depression appeared at times to threaten widespread ruin. The debtor classes in all modern countries were seriously burdened, and in some parts of the United States, especially in the newer agricultural states of the West, a popular demand arose for an increase in the supply of money through the restoration of silver to free coinage at the ratio of 16 to 1 — the ratio prevailing in the United States prior to 1873.

19. *The adoption of free silver in* 1896 *would probably have expelled gold from circulation in the United States. It would have reduced the value of gold and would have raised the value of silver.*

In 1896 the market value of silver had fallen so low that an ounce of silver was worth less than one thirtieth of the value of an ounce of gold. Consequently, if silver had been admitted to free coinage, it would have been very profitable to buy up uncoined silver, both in America and in other countries, present it at the mints, and exchange the coined silver for gold, so long as any gold coins remained in circulation. It would obviously have been only a very short time before gold would have disappeared entirely from circulation.

The great demand upon the silver supply that would thus have been occasioned would no doubt have increased the value of that metal. The gold displaced from the American coinage would have been thrown upon the markets of other countries, and would have reduced the value of gold there. Nevertheless, an ounce of gold would probably have continued to command more than sixteen ounces of silver — perhaps twenty ounces. A silver dollar would then have been worth less than a dollar in gold, even though gold had fallen. Measured in commodities, the depreciation of the dollar would have been still greater. That is, general prices in the United States would have been forced to a higher level.

20. *An international agreement for the universal adoption of bimetallism might have prevented freely coined silver from expelling gold from the currency.*

Many persons who shrank from a policy which would probably have substituted a silver standard for the gold standard in the United States, nevertheless favored the adoption of free coinage of silver if the other commercial nations could be induced to follow the same plan.

If all the countries of the world had agreed to coin silver and gold freely at the same ratio, it is quite possible that coins of both metals would have continued to circulate side by side. The chief reason why gold would leave the circulation of a single country, if placed at an unfavorable ratio with freely coined silver, is that in other countries it is given a higher coinage value. More gold would be used in the arts, perhaps, but much of it would remain in the coinage if all countries gave it the same coinage value, relatively to silver.

21. *Rise in prices in the period beginning with 1897 checked agitation for the free coinage of silver.*

The adoption by the chief nations of free coinage of silver would no doubt have resulted in a higher level of prices. Other forces affecting prices had, however, begun to operate while the free-silver movement was still gaining strength. The production of gold was steadily increasing; in the decade 1890 to 1900 the amount of gold produced exceeded that of any earlier decade in the history of the world. The annual production steadily increased down to the time of the Great War. In 1913 the output of gold was over twice as great as it was in 1897. It fell off during the war and the years immediately after its close, but not seriously. This increase in the supply of gold must have had a tendency to reduce its value, or, what amounts to the same thing, to raise the prices of commodities. When it became evident that the rise in prices was likely to continue, agitation for the adoption of the policy of free coinage of silver practically ceased.

22. *A government may raise or lower the value of money by increasing or reducing the amount of paper money in circulation.*

The evils of falling prices are so readily perceived by almost every one, that in times of falling prices plans are usually put forward for releasing the price level from the uncertainties attendant upon the production of gold and silver by supplementing metallic money with paper money issued by government. Advocates of such plans usually propose that whenever general prices are found to be falling, the government shall issue additional paper money. When prices are rising, paper money received at the public treasury, it is proposed, shall be destroyed, until a reduction in the money supply checks the rise in prices.

In practice, paper money, when issued, usually takes the form of notes, issued in behalf of the government and alleged to be payable at the treasury on demand. But a government of a sovereign state cannot be compelled to meet its promises unless it chooses to do so. Hence the person who receives such a note must take it with the intention of parting with it in the purchase of goods or in the payment of debts, not of presenting it at the treasury for specie. These notes therefore represent a net addition to the money supply.

In order to give such notes currency, the government endows them with the legal tender quality. If the volume of paper money is narrowly limited, it may circulate at par. It is always good in transactions with the government, such as payment of taxes, and so long as the average citizen does not have to carry more in his purse than he could presumably use in such ways, there is no reason why he should discriminate against it. In a country like the United States, where over five billions of dollars must be paid in taxes, federal, state and local, some hundreds of millions of paper would circulate even without formal arrangements for redemption.

If, however, an enormous amount of paper money is issued by the government, so that we are all likely to receive more of it in exchange than we can certainly use at par, we begin to look upon it with suspicion. We exchange it, if we can, for "hard money" — gold or silver; if possible, we stipulate that we shall be paid in hard money for our commodities or services, offering our goods, if necessary, at lower prices than we would accept if paid in paper. Relatively to gold, paper depreciates. If there is very much of it issued, no one pays gold if he can avoid it, but uses paper instead. Thus specie disappears from circulation, and paper becomes the only money in use. Under the circumstances it is the worst possible kind of money: it fluctuates wildly in value, falling with rumors of additional issues, rising when it is rumored that the government intends to redeem it. At every change in its value some men gain unmerited profits and others suffer unmerited losses.

If, as has been said, a government exercises great moderation in the issue of paper money, depreciation will not necessarily occur. The increase in money will tend to raise prices, but not in very great degree, and if prices are tending downward this effect may be beneficial. Why, then, do practically all students of monetary science agree that paper money is always a dangerous expedient? Because governments almost never exercise moderation in the issue of paper money. They resort to paper money in time of need, usually while carrying on war. Thus they obtain funds without burdening the people with taxation. As the expenses of the war increase, more and more paper money is issued, until hard money is driven out of circulation, and the redundant paper currency falls lower and lower in value, as evidenced by constantly rising prices.

During the Great War every belligerent nation except Japan and the United States resorted to the issue of paper money either directly or through unsecured bank note issues endowed with legal tender quality. And in not a single case did the government arrest the process of issue before gold had been excluded from the circulation and the paper had depreciated seriously. The British currency suffered least, falling off only about twenty per cent from its gold value. The currency of Russia, at the other extreme, was inflated by issues running up into the trillions of rubles, with the result that a hundred thousand ruble note, nominally the equivalent of fifty thousand dollars, would barely command a square meal. The experience of Europe in the war and the post-war period proves quite conclusively that paper money is like a habit-forming drug, requiring constantly increasing doses.

While it would be theoretically possible to regulate prices by a scientific plan of increasing or reducing the volume of paper money in circulation, actual experience demonstrates conclusively that no such plan will work in practice. It would be a simple matter to increase the volume of paper money when prices are falling. The government would print the money and spend it, no doubt to the satisfaction of a public which observed public works being undertaken without any increase in the burden of taxation. But the plan would break down when an attempt was made to check rising prices by withdrawing paper from circulation. Before the government could withdraw the money it would have to take it away from the citizens through taxation. And increased taxes having no other object than that of keeping prices down would be so unpopular that no political party desiring to remain in power would be willing to propose them.

Might there not be some way of taking the regulation of the supply and value of money out of politics and of subjecting it to expert control?

In recent years an active campaign for the stabilization of money has been conducted by a number of American economists under the leadership of Professor Irving Fisher. The scheme of regulation proposed by Professor Fisher turns upon varying the amount of gold entering into the "dollar." The business world is already habituated to the use of certificates for gold deposited, instead of the gold itself. There is no compelling reason why the gold held against certificates should always remain the same. When prices are rising relatively to gold, let the treasury require an increased amount of gold before delivering, say, a twenty dollar certificate. When prices are falling relatively to gold, let the amount of gold required for the delivery of a twenty dollar certificate be reduced. To-day a twenty dollar certificate represents 416 grains of gold, nine-tenths fine. Under the stabilization scheme it might represent at one time 400 grains, at another time 425 grains. A body of expert price statisticians, aloof from the political fortunes of the government, would determine what the gold content of the dollar should be. Perhaps they could not establish perfectly stable prices. But there is every reason to believe that a far more stable medium could be established in this way than by the ordinary play of supply and demand under gold monometallism. The chief obstacle to the application of the plan is not any valid criticism that has been brought against it, but the inherent conservatism of the financial classes, who fear that any tampering with the gold standard may bring consequences wholly unforeseeable.

23. *A currency based upon gold or silver freely coined displays a tendency toward reasonable stability of value under modern conditions.*

So long as the production of the precious metals was dependent upon the activity of men of small capital, working on their own account, only the richest fields could be worked, and these only for a limited period of time. The supply of precious metals depended, therefore, upon the chance discovery of new fields, and was consequently very irregular. At present the principal supply of the precious metals comes from the reduction, by large scale enterprise, of low grade ores, which are found in large masses in many parts of the world. If the supply of gold increases so rapidly that the value of gold money falls, or, what amounts to the same thing, general prices rise, the production of gold is discouraged through the rise in price of labor and the materials and appliances used in gold production. If the supply of gold does not keep pace with the demand for it, and general prices fall, the production of gold is encouraged by the decline in wages and in the prices of goods used in the production of gold. We see, then, that there are forces at work which restrict fluctuations in the value of money. We must not, however, exaggerate the potency of these forces. Within limits which are not so narrow as would be socially desirable, the value of freely coined money fluctuates from year to year and from decade to decade.

24. *Summary.*

Whatever men regularly accept in payment for their services or in exchange for their goods, with the sole purpose of exchanging it for other services or goods, is money. The primary function of money is that of a medium of exchange; money serves also as a means of storing value, as a standard of value, and as a standard of deferred payments.

In order that money may be uniform in value, its issue must be regulated by government. As a rule, a standard form of money is established, and the government merely certifies the weight and fineness of metal contained in this form of money. Other forms of money are issued in limited quantities, and it is the aim of a well-regulated government to maintain these forms at a parity with the standard form. If there is more than one standard form, maintenance of parity between them is difficult, if not impossible. When a government fails to maintain its various forms of money at a parity, the less valuable forms tend to displace the more valuable forms from the circulation.

The value of money is measured by its purchasing power. The purchasing power of money is continually fluctuating, owing to changes in the supply of and the demand for money. Changes in the supply of money may be due to changes in the output of the metal from which standard money is made, or to changes in the volume of non-standard forms issued by government. Changes in the demand for money may be due to changes in the general character of business, or to increase or decrease in the volume of substitutes for money.

A rise in the value of money is tantamount to a fall in prices; a fall in the value of money, to a rise in prices. General changes in the price level inflict serious injury upon some classes and give unmerited gains to other classes. Hence a popular demand for governmental regulation of the price level through expansion or contraction of the money supply. The free silver movement of the end of the last century is explainable upon this principle. The adoption of free silver by the United States would probably have raised the world level of gold prices; it would have placed prices in the United States upon a silver basis.

Under ideal conditions, general changes in the price level might be prevented through the issue or retirement of paper money. Under existing conditions, since the pressure for higher prices is always stronger than the pressure for lower ones, a consistent policy of issue of paper money is impracticable. It is conceivable that a plan of regulation through varying the gold content of the "dollar" might bring a fair degree of stability. In default of the application of such a plan, the only practicable corrective of rising prices is the automatic reduction in the output of gold resulting from the increased cost of extracting gold from the ore, just as the only practicable corrective of falling prices is the automatic increase in the gold supply resulting from lower cost of gold extraction.

CHAPTER XVII

FINANCIAL INSTITUTIONS: THE BANK

1. *An important function of the modern economic organization is the placing of the control of capital in the hands of those who can use it to the greatest advantage.*

In a complex industrial society it is natural that there should be some men possessing capital who are unable or unwilling to employ it in business undertakings under their own management. Some men, while able to use part of their capital in the conduct of business under their own control, are unable to use all of it advantageously. And some men, while able to use all their capital part of the time, fail to find use for it during some weeks or months of the year. On the other hand, there are those who have not enough capital of their own for the proper exploitation of the opportunities for its employment which they command, and still others, while having capital enough during the greater part of the year, require an additional amount during certain seasons.

Accordingly, one of the functions of the modern industrial organization is the transfer of the control of capital from those who have a superfluity of it to those who can use it profitably. This function, which in view of the enormous amount of capital to be thus transferred is one of vast importance, may be designated by the term "finance." Institutions designed primarily to effect the transfer, or "placing," of capital are known as financial institutions. It is to be noted that we are here using the word "finance" in a sense in some respects more restricted, in some respects broader, than is usually conveyed by the term. But we are justified in this by the analogies of such words as "capital," "rent," "labor," etc., which have one meaning in economics and a slightly different meaning in popular language.

2. *The transfer of the control of capital may take the form of a loan, of a partnership agreement or of the purchase of shares of stock.*

Let us suppose that a mine operator holds a lease of advantageously situated coal lands. To develop these lands he needs, we will say, a capital of $100,000. A retired merchant in the vicinity has $100,000 from which he desires to get an income without the labor of managing a business on his own account. The mine operator may borrow the $100,000, agreeing to pay a stipulated rate of interest. On the other hand, he may be willing to form a partnership with the owner of the capital, agreeing to share the profits in fixed proportions. In either case the capital is virtually placed under the control of the mine operator. From a legal point of view the distinction between the two methods of transfer of capital is clear. If the transfer is effected through a loan, the mine operator becomes the legal owner of the goods in which the capital is invested, subject to the claims of the lender for interest and principal. The lender has no voice in the management of the business. If the transfer of capital is effected through a partership agreement, the capitalist becomes part owner of all the capital goods employed in the business, and is entitled to a voice in the management of it. From an economic point of view, the chief distinction is that in the case of a loan transfer of capital, the capitalist receives a fixed income, not affected by the vicissitudes of the business, while in the case of the partnership transfer, the capitalist receives a share of the proceeds of the business, fluctuating with the alternation of prosperity and depression.

Instead of making himself partner in the mining enterprise, and assuming all the liabilities of partnership, the retired merchant may induce the coal operator to form a corporation with a share capital of, say, $200,000, of which the operator retains one half and the merchant takes the other half in exchange for his $100,000. As stockholder, he is part owner, just as he would be as partner; the income that he will receive, under the form of dividends, fluctuates with the prosperity of the business. If the business fails, the merchant loses his investment in it, but no matter how severe the failure, he can not be made to make good its liabilities out of other resources he may have, as he could be made to do under a partnership agreement.

3. *A productive loan is the transfer of capital, reduced to terms of money value, usually under a definite agreement as to charges for its use and as to time of repayment.*

In its simplest form a loan is a transfer of a sum of money from one person to another, with the stipulation that a certain return shall be paid for its use and that at some future time, usually specified, an equivalent sum of money shall be repaid. The borrower naturally transforms the money thus obtained into goods at the earliest possible moment. If the goods purchased are designed for sale or for use in further production, the loan is virtually the transfer of capital. Such a loan is called a productive loan. If the money is spent for commodities for consumption, the loan is called a consumer's loan. The productive loan is by far the more common, and we shall concern ourselves chiefly with it.

4. *A loan may be disguised under the form of a sale.*

Very frequently loans are disguised under the form of sales "on credit." The seller, instead of demanding spot cash for his wares, may agree to wait for a certain period of time — say, three months — before demanding payment. In this case the seller really lends the buyer a sum equal to the price of the goods. A company engaged in the manufacture of agricultural implements sells a self-binder to a farmer. The latter has not the ready cash to pay for it, but expects to have the necessary sum four months later, when he sells his crops. He may borrow the money from a neighbor, giving his note, payable in four months, with interest. Or, instead of borrowing the money and paying cash for the machine, the farmer may buy it "on time," agreeing to pay for it at the end of four months. In this case we sometimes say that the farmer has purchased the machine with his credit. If we analyze the transaction into its elements, we shall see that this expression is inadequate. The company has not merely sold the machine; it has also, in effect, loaned the farmer the money with which to pay for it. Moreover, it has made provision for interest on the loan, in the form of a higher price on a credit sale than on a cash sale. Every sale "on time" or "on credit" is a double transaction, involving a sale, in the proper sense of the word, and a loan of the capital represented by the goods sold.

5. *Lenders intrust the control of their capital only to those who have "credit"; that is, reputation for honesty and ability to meet their financial obligations.*

It is, of course, obvious that loans, whether productive or consumer's, will be made only to persons who have "credit"; that is, to persons who are regarded as sufficiently honorable and efficient to be willing and able to repay the sums loaned when they fall due. A man's credit may rest upon his reputation for personal integrity and business capacity; more commonly it rests, in part at least, upon the fact that he has property which, under the law, can be seized by his creditors in case of default in payment of his debts.

There are some writers on economics who regard credit as a mysterious productive instrument, a form of capital, or at any rate a substitute for capital. The illustration given in section 4 shows that this view has no justification. What the farmer cuts his wheat with is a capital good, embodying capital furnished either by his neighbor or by the agricultural implement company. This capital existed before the farmer gained possession of it, and would doubtless have been employed productively by other persons if the farmer had not decided to buy a machine. The fact that he buys the machine with borrowed capital shows that he believes that he can make this capital yield more than the interest which he must pay for its use. His "credit" enables him to procure capital to use in an employment which he believes to be superior to the average in productivity. If he is right in his opinion, he is able to keep for himself a part of the product of this capital, as a profit. But the profit is not produced by his credit, any more than the wheat is cut by it.

6. *A document in which the claim of the lender upon the borrower is reduced to written form is known as a credit instrument. If the claim thus reduced to writing can be sold and purchased, it is known as a negotiable credit instrument.*

The contract between the lender and the borrower is sometimes merely oral, and rests for its fulfillment upon the honor of the borrower. In a larger number of cases, the lender enters the sums due him upon his books, and claims thus entered are usually collectible through the courts. This is the common form of loans effected under the guise of credit sales. The creditor may draw up a form instructing the debtor to pay the sum due at a specified time. Such an instrument is known as a "draft" or "bill of exchange." The borrower may, at the time of raising the loan, sign a form which specifies the terms of the contract. Such an instrument is known as a "promissory note." The borrower may specify, along with the general terms of the contract, certain property belonging to him upon which the creditor will have a special claim in case of default in payment. A note thus accompanied by the pledge of property is commonly known as a "mortgage."

The claim of a creditor upon his debtor is regarded in law as a form of property, and may ordinarily be purchased and sold like any other form of property. Claims represented by promissory notes, due bills, and bills of exchange are very frequently purchased and sold, or "negotiated." They are therefore called "negotiable credit instruments," or simply, "negotiable paper." Transfer of such instruments is commonly effected by indorsement; that is, the original claimant signs an order upon the back of the instrument, instructing the debtor to pay the sum due to a third party named in the order.

7. *Under modern conditions there is a demand for and a supply of loanable capital for short periods of indefinite duration, for short terms and for long terms. Corresponding with these conditions are call or demand loans, short term loans and long term loans.*

Capital loans display wide variation in the length of time for which the lender surrenders control of his capital. Sometimes the lender retains the right of calling for his capital at any time he desires. Such a loan is known as a "call" or "demand" loan. Sometimes the date when the debt falls due is fixed at thirty, sixty, or ninety days. Such a loan is known as a short term loan. Sometimes the loan runs for five, ten, or fifty years. In this case the loan may be called a long term loan. This variation in the life period of loans is a reflection of the economic situation of the various classes of lenders and borrowers.

At any given time there are men who have more capital than they need immediately; they cannot tell, however, how soon they may need all they have. On the other hand, there are men who can use capital profitably for an indefinite period of time, who can yet return it to its owner whenever it is demanded. Thus a man who deals in stocks and bonds may find exceedingly profitable employment for capital in the purchase of such securities when prices are rising. If he is operating with borrowed capital, he can sell the securities at any time when payment is demanded, and so restore the capital to its owner.

Again, there are men who can safely part with the control of their capital for a definite period of time — say, from one to six months. Corresponding with this class of lenders is a class of borrowers who cannot agree to pay off a loan on demand, but who are able to make arrangements for payment at a definite date some weeks or months after borrowing the capital. The merchant will serve as a type of this class. He can safely purchase a stock of goods with the proceeds of a three months' loan, feeling quite sure that within the three months he will be able to sell the goods and so gain possession of the means of repayment.

Finally, there is a class of lenders who have no desire for the early repayment of their capital. With satisfactory arrangements made as to the rate of interest to be paid, they may be willing to transfer control of their capital for a period of ten, twenty, or fifty years. There is a corresponding class of borrowers, who desire capital for investment in land, buildings, and permanent equipment, and who would be greatly embarrassed by the necessity of early payment.

There are, then, three distinguishable sources of supply of loanable capital, and three corresponding sources of demand for it. In practical life, of course, with highly developed financial institutions, there is a certain degree of interchangeability in the different funds of capital. Let us suppose that lenders of the first class place their capital in a bank, reserving the right of withdrawing it at any time. Experience shows that while some lenders withdraw their capital each day, new lenders will each day offer capital at the bank. Thus the bank has a permanent fund of capital which it may lend to business men for stated periods of time. Men who wish to lend their capital for long periods of time may place it with a bank, which may use it in short term loans, experience showing that when one business man repays a loan of this kind another will be ready to borrow the capital.

8. *The principal functions of the bank are the collection of funds of loanable capital that are available for short periods only, and the employment of such funds in call and short term loans.*

The bank proper is chiefly engaged in providing business men with demand and short term loans. The capital employed in this way is in part the bank's own, and is permanently devoted to the purpose. By far the greater part of the capital, however, is supplied by other persons, who loan their surplus funds to the bank, receiving for its use either interest or some other form of compensation. Provision for long term loans is usually made by various other financial institutions, such as the savings bank, the insurance company, the investment company, the farm loan bank, and the exchanges. Our present concern is the economic nature of the transactions in which the bank proper is engaged.

Let us suppose that a bank is established in a town which up to the present has had no similar institution. As the bank has doubtless better means for keeping money safe than are to be found elsewhere in the town, we may suppose that many persons will be glad to deposit with it any money which they do not immediately need, reserving the privilege of withdrawing it whenever they need it. On pay days salaried employees will deposit most of their month's earnings, expecting to withdraw the money day by day to meet their current expenses. Similarly, capitalists will deposit their annual or semi-annual interest receipts, to be withdrawn in like manner for current expenditures. Merchants will deposit surplus cash which they will not need to reinvest in stock for some days or weeks. Lenders whose loans have been repaid will deposit the money until they find another satisfactory opportunity for lending. Thus a great part of the community will use the bank in greater or less degree for the storing of surplus funds. The sums so deposited are credited to the depositors on the books of the bank.

The use of checks, or written orders for the transfer of funds, greatly increases the usefulness of the bank as a repository of funds of this kind. The depositor, instead of going in person to the bank to withdraw money for a purchase, may give a check for the sum involved in the transaction. The recipient of the check may present it at the bank for payment, carrying away the sum in money. If he is in the habit of depositing his own surplus funds in the bank, he is more likely to deposit the check, instead of cashing it. The sum called for in the check is then transferred, on the books of the bank, from the account of the one person to the account of the other. Thus payment is effected without the handling of money by any one. When the check system is well developed funds deposited with the bank may change owners scores of times without ever leaving the vaults.

The cash intrusted to the bank may amount to a very considerable sum. At one time such deposits may aggregate $50,000, at another time $75,000. Experience may show that the volume of deposits never falls below $40,000. This sum of $40,000 may be regarded as a perpetual fund intrusted to the bank by the body of depositors, although actual ownership of each part of it is continually changing.

The bank is, of course, under no obligation to keep in its vaults the money that has thus been intrusted to it. All that the bank is required to do is to hold itself in readiness to pay the money on demand. So long as it does this, it may use the deposits in any way that it may find profitable — observing, of course, such restrictions in the use of its funds as the law prescribes. And this fact indicates the economic nature of such deposits. They are loans, payable on demand, the depositor being the creditor, the bank the debtor.

Up to the present point we have been concerned with the bank as a borrower of capital. We have now to consider its position as a lender of capital. Let us suppose that one of the inhabitants of the town is a manufacturer of hardware, who sells his products "on time" to jobbers. This manufacturer has sold, let us say, $10,000 worth of products, receiving in lieu of payment notes for $10,000 at three months' time. This means, as we have already seen, that the manufacturer has made a disguised loan of capital to the jobbers. The manufacturer, however, needs his capital in order to continue his business of manufacture.

He may, if his credit is good, borrow $10,000 from the bank, agreeing to repay the loan in three months. When his debt falls due, the notes of the jobbers will also fall due; accordingly, he will find himself in an excellent position to cancel his debt. Other business men will borrow from the bank under similar conditions as large a portion of the capital deposited with the bank as can safely be loaned. When one set of borrowers repays the sums borrowed from the bank, another set can easily be found. Thus the bank has a permanent volume of loans, as well as a permanent volume of deposits, although the borrowers, like the depositors, are continually dropping out and being replaced by others.

9. *A bank loan may be regarded as the purchase of a credit instrument, such as a promissory note or bill of exchange.*

In the foregoing section it was assumed that men who wish to secure capital from a bank borrow it directly; and this, indeed, is often the case. When a business man borrows for the purpose of recovering the control of capital which he has loaned, under the form of a sale to other persons, he is more likely to take the notes received from the latter to the bank for sale. In buying the notes, the bank substitutes itself, as creditor, for the business man who first held the notes. If the notes bear no interest, the bank, in purchasing them, will deduct from their face value interest for the time that will elapse before the notes "mature," or fall due. This process of deducting interest in advance is known as "discounting." In the language of the banking business, the purchase of a note is commonly spoken of as the discounting of a note, and notes purchased are called "discounts." Discounts are evidently nothing but loans.

When a person desires to borrow capital from a bank, he offers his own note, which the bank usually discounts in the manner described above. We may think of the borrower as offering his own note to the bank for sale. Thus the whole volume of bank loans may be regarded as investments in credit instruments.

10. *A bank must invest funds intrusted to it in such a way that it can quickly regain possession of such funds if necessary.*

While the volume of funds intrusted to a bank may, under ordinary circumstances, remain fairly constant, owing to the fact that new deposits offset withdrawals, it would be unwise for the managers of a bank to invest such deposits in ways that would make early payment of depositors impossible. At any time depositors may lose confidence in the stability of a bank and demand the sums due them. Let us suppose that such a panic of the depositors or "run on the bank" occurs, and that the bank has invested the funds intrusted to it in suburban real estate. This property may not be salable, and all the bank can do is close its doors until such time as it can dispose of its real estate holdings and pay off its depositors. This would, of course, mean the ruin of the bank, even though the real estate sold eventually at an advance.

The bank may invest the funds deposited with it in government bonds. These always find a market, but their price fluctuates, and the bank might incur some loss in disposing of its holdings in order to meet the pressing demands of its depositors. Moreover, such bonds yield a very low rate of interest.

The notes that are created in ordinary commercial transactions are one of the most satisfactory forms of bank investments. They are usually drawn for brief terms — thirty, sixty, or ninety days — and such notes are usually given in payment for goods which are salable in a reasonable time. Thus there is reason for believing that the notes can be met when due. If the depositors of a bank press for payment, so that the bank cannot await the maturity of the notes it holds, it can usually sell them to other banks and thus secure the means of immediate payment.

In the United States national banks are limited by law to such investments as short term notes, bills of exchange, and government bonds. Investments in real estate, except for use in connection with the business operations of the bank, are prohibited. State banks are also more or less narrowly restricted in their investments.

11. *Under modern conditions the greater part of the volume of bank deposits arises out of the process of making loans.*

It has been assumed, in the foregoing sections, that the principal business of a bank is the lending of deposits intrusted to it in the form of spare cash. It is only under simple conditions that this is a fair representation of the business of a bank. In a modern industrial and commercial city the deposits of cash represent a very small part of the volume of deposits that figure on the books of a bank.

Let us suppose that a bank commences business with a capital of $100,000, consisting entirely of cash. Part of this sum — say $10,000 — is spent in acquiring a suitable building. The remaining $90,000 is held in the safe of the bank, to be loaned to business men who can offer adequate security.

A manufacturer offers at the bank acceptable notes amounting to $10,000, and gets them discounted. He may, if he chooses, carry away with him the cash represented by the discounted value of the notes. This, however, he is not likely to do. What he wants the money for is to make purchases of materials, to pay salaries and wages, and to meet other business expenses. The most convenient method of payment is by checks drawn on the bank. So instead of carrying the money away from the bank he is likely to leave it as a deposit, subject to withdrawal on demand. Of course there is no reason why the bank should go through the form of counting out the cash to the manufacturer if it is to be redeposited in this way. What it does is to credit the manufacturer with a "deposit" equal to the discounted value of the notes which he has transferred to it.

Let us follow in imagination the history of the manufacturer's deposit. In the course of a month he may draw in payment of wages and other expenses checks aggregating a sum equal to the deposit credited to him. These checks may be redeposited with the bank by the manufacturer's employees and the merchants who furnish materials and other supplies. The employees and merchants draw checks upon the bank to cover their expenses, but these checks may also be redeposited. It is possible that the notes originally discounted will fall due and be paid before the bank is compelled to surrender any considerable amount of cash on account of the loan which it made in discounting the notes.

Let us suppose that the bank has discounted notes amounting to $90,000 — a sum equal to its original cash holdings. In discounting these notes the bank has credited its customers with deposits amounting, we will say, to $89,000. As these deposits are drawn upon, the checks drawn are largely deposited with the bank under other accounts. Very likely not more than $4000 out of the $89,000 in deposits is withdrawn from the bank in the form of cash. We see, then, that if the bank were to limit its loans to the amount of cash actually on hand, the greater part of this cash would remain in the bank idle.

Accordingly, it is natural that the bank should try to get a return from its cash by making additional loans. If it lends $200,000 on a basis of $90,000 in cash, crediting the borrowers with deposits amounting to $195,000, the chances are that a larger amount of cash will be withdrawn by depositors than if its loans amounted to $90,000 and the deposits to $89,000. Yet the withdrawals of cash may amount to only $15,000, leaving the bank still with a large amount of idle cash. It can safely increase the volume of its loans and the resultant deposits. As the volume of deposits increases, a point must eventually be reached where the cash on hand is just sufficient to meet all probable demands. At this point the bank must cease to make further loans.

12. *Every bank receives in the course of its business checks drawn upon other banks. Through the clearing system the checks received by a bank are balanced against checks drawn upon it and deposited with other banks, so that little cash is withdrawn from it in the settlement of claims of other banks.*

One reason why a bank can extend its loans far beyond the volume of the cash in its possession is that checks drawn upon it are likely to be deposited with it, instead of being cashed. If checks drawn upon one bank are deposited with another bank, withdrawal of cash would appear to be inevitable, since one bank does not, except under special circumstances, keep a deposit with another bank.

Let us assume that in a town there are several banks which we may designate as A, B, C, etc. Some of the citizens of the town will deposit their funds with bank A, some with B, some with C. Often a man will use his check, drawn on bank A, in making a payment to a man who keeps his deposit with bank B or C. The recipient of the check might of course take the check to bank A, obtain cash for it, and deposit the money with his own bank. It is more convenient, however, for him to transfer the check, by indorsement, to his own bank. The bank then credits him with the sum represented by the check, and assumes the trouble of collecting the sum from bank A. And so every day, we may suppose, checks drawn on bank A are deposited with banks B and C; checks drawn on these banks are deposited with bank A. At the end of each business day a clerk in the employ of bank A takes the checks drawn on B and C and presents them for payment at those banks. Similarly a clerk from bank B presents for payment checks deposited with that bank, drawn upon A and C. One can easily see that such a method of settlement involves some waste of energy. While a clerk of bank A is presenting for payment at bank B checks drawn upon that bank, a clerk of bank B is presenting for payment at bank A checks drawn upon the latter bank. Money is being carried from A to B at the same time that money is carried from B to A. Obviously some method of balancing can be devised which will save the unnecessary labor and risk of thus carrying money to and fro. Especially would this be necessary in a large city, where there are scores of banks.

In every important center the banks form an association which provides a building or a hall known as a clearing house, where representatives of the several banks meet daily for the settlement of the claims of each bank upon the other banks. The claims of each bank upon all the others are set off against the claims of all the other banks upon it. When this has been done, it will be found that some of the banks have a balance in their favor, while others have a deficit to make good.

Each debtor bank then pays a single lump sum representing its indebtedness to all the associated banks; each creditor bank receives a lump sum representing the balance of its claims upon all the banks. By this method the transfer of cash from bank to bank is reduced to the lowest terms.

13. *The cash kept on hand by a bank to meet probable cash demands is known as the reserve. The laws regulating banking require the banks to maintain reserves amounting to a certain proportion of the deposits and other demand liabilities.*

If banks are free to extend their loans at will, the amount of cash kept on hand to meet the possible demands of the depositors will vary according to the banking habits of the business community and the temperament of the bankers. In highly developed commercial communities, very little cash is used in effecting exchanges; reliance is placed almost entirely upon the use of checks. In such a community a bank may extend its loans, and the attendant volume of its deposits, almost without definite limit. If it keeps on hand $10 in cash for every $100 of deposits, it will probably be able to meet all cash demands without difficulty. Banks have been known to conduct a successful business with only $5 in reserve for every $100 of deposits.

The smaller the proportion of the reserve to the deposits, however, the greater the chance that a bank will be unable to meet demands for cash from its depositors and other creditors. Failure to meet such demands may cause great embarrassment to the customers of the bank. If a man cannot draw upon his bank deposit, very likely he will be unable to meet his own obligations; his creditors, in turn, are embarrassed in meeting their obligations, and so the evil extends in ever widening circles throughout the business community. The depositors of other banks, fearing that their banks will likewise fail to pay cash on demand, withdraw their deposits until, at times, it becomes impossible for those banks to continue to pay cash.

It is natural that legislatures should attempt to reduce the chances of such a calamity by regulating the business of the banks. A favorite device is to fix by law a minimum reserve to be maintained by each bank against its deposits. In the United States the minimum reserves in national banks formerly were fixed at twenty-five per cent for the chief cities and fifteen per cent for smaller places. At present the banks are required to keep reserves in the federal reserve banks ranging from seven to thirteen per cent, besides whatever money in their tills that may be required to meet current demands for cash.

Bank reserves, while they may be ample in ordinary times have often proved inadequate in times of crisis. If suspicion, however groundless, falls upon a bank, there may be a "run," which quickly reduces the reserve below the legal limit and may if unchecked wipe it out altogether. Before the enactment of the Federal Reserve law of 1913 such emergencies were usually provided for by mutual aid among the banks. If withdrawals of deposits from one bank became too heavy, that bank would transfer some part of the notes in its portfolios to other banks, receiving in return cash items to replenish its reserves. If all the banks of a given city or section of the country found themselves embarrassed by excessive withdrawals, they made similar arrangements with banks in other parts of the country whose reserves remained strong. And in times of general commercial crisis the banks of the country formed temporary associations whose object was to present a united front against panic. The force impelling to mutual aid was the common danger. For if one bank in a city is forced to suspend, the contagion of suspicion is likely to be transmitted to other banks and lead to heavy withdrawals of cash. If in time of crisis one bank failure after another is reported, a point is soon reached in which the public loses confidence in all banks, and even the strongest incurs the risk of being deprived of its reserves by the run on deposits.

It was primarily to meet this condition that the Federal Reserve system was instituted. Under this system all national banks and such state banks as wish to meet the requirements as to reserves, etc., are grouped in twelve systems, each with a federal reserve bank at its head. This bank derives its capital from subscriptions by member banks, amounting to six per cent of the capital and surplus of each bank. The principal part of the reserves of the member banks are kept in the federal reserve banks and may be drawn on when required. Moreover, any member bank may take notes from its portfolios and transfer them — "rediscount" them — with the federal reserve bank, receiving in return credits to be drawn upon or bank notes with which to meet the demands of its depositors. So long as a member bank has sound paper in its portfolios, it is in no danger of being forced to suspend for want of currency to pay off its depositors. Under the Federal Reserve plan the banking system of the United States proved able to weather safely all the stresses of war and post-war depression.

14. *The chances of ultimate loss to the depositor of a well conducted bank are very small.*

It may seem that even when a bank keeps a reserve amounting to twenty-five per cent of its deposits, the depositor is in danger of loss. What if more than twenty-five per cent of the deposits should be demanded on any one day? The bank would, of course, be unable to make payment immediately.

If a bank is not grossly mismanaged, it has property worth at least one dollar for every dollar figuring in its deposits. When it makes a loan of $10,000, thus creating a deposit amounting, we will say, to $9700, it receives from the borrower notes amounting to $10,000, which must be set against the $9700 which it owes its depositors. If the notes are good, at their maturity the bank will receive more than enough cash to cancel the deposits created when the loan was made. Every part of the volume of deposits is covered in this way by notes, bills of exchange, etc., in the vault of the bank.

These notes, etc., usually run for short periods, seldom extending over six months, and frequently maturing in less than thirty days. Even if the bank fails to meet its obligations on demand, the worst that the depositor usually has to fear is that he will have to wait some weeks or months until the bank can collect the sums due it.

But suppose that the notes in the bank's vaults are worthless; that the bank will be unable to collect the sums due. In that case, the bank's own capital must be used to meet the claims of the depositors. If the volume of worthless notes exceeds the amount of the bank's capital, then the depositor may suffer loss.

It is, however, rarely the case that a bank discounts any large number of worthless notes. A bank accepts only such notes as there is reason to believe are good. Bank officials are in an excellent position to judge of the business standing of the bank's customers. Checks used by these customers in payment of their obligations pass through the bank; checks received by them are deposited with the bank. Thus it becomes fairly easy for competent bank officials to ascertain whether a business man is prospering, or operating at a loss. In the latter case, the bank forces the payment of notes when due, and refuses to make new loans. Thus bank loans are, as a rule, restricted to those members of the business community who are able to keep themselves in a position to pay their debts.

In some instances, to be sure, banks are ruined through fraud. Bank officials may embezzle the funds or may extend loans to personal friends to be employed in risky ventures which result in total loss. The laws of most states are stringent enough to reduce losses through fraud to a minimum. And the federal banking laws are so stringent as to reduce the chance of failure very near to zero. In 1920, for example, there were 8,019 national banks with deposits aggregating $15,142,000,000. There were ten failures, with liabilities aggregating $3,350,000. And even of this insignificant sum, a large part was covered by assets that could later be liquidated.

15. *Bank notes are claims upon the bank that are essentially of the same nature as deposits.*

In the foregoing discussion it has been assumed that the transfer of claims upon the bank is made through checks, drawn upon a deposit, and redeposited by the holder. A man who receives a check may, however, transfer it, properly indorsed, to another man, who in turn may transfer the check to a third person. Each holder of the check becomes in turn the creditor of the bank. When the check is at last deposited with the bank, the claim upon the bank is formally transferred on its books. But it is obvious that the claim on the bank is just as certainly transferred whenever the check changes hands.

Such a check could not pass through many hands, because only those persons knowing the credit of the drawer would be willing to accept it. There are men who draw checks on banks where they keep no deposit; if you are offered a check drawn by some one you have never heard of, how do you know that it will be honored by the bank?

A person wishing to use checks as a means of payment among persons who are not certain of his credit may take the checks to the bank and have the cashier certify upon their face that they represent a deposit, and will be honored by the bank. Such checks — known as certified checks — may circulate as freely as money in the community where the bank's standing is known. It is clear, however, that a certified check is a claim upon the bank of the same nature as an ordinary check drawn upon a deposit.

Instead of certifying checks drawn upon a deposit, the bank may give the customer who wishes means of ready payment a parcel of its own notes, payable to the bearer on demand. The customer is then the creditor of the bank for the amounts stated in the bank notes in his possession. As soon as he uses the notes for the purchase of supplies, etc., he transfers the claim upon the bank to the seller of the supplies. Such notes may pass from hand to hand for years, each successive holder of a note becoming the creditor of the bank.

Obviously it makes little difference to the bank whether a business man who discounts a note is credited with a deposit on the books of the bank or takes the bank's notes in the same sum. The deposit represents a right to cash on demand; the bank notes represent exactly the same thing. The deposit may pass from owner to owner through checks drawn upon it and redeposited with the bank; the note passes from owner to owner without the formality of a transfer on the books of the bank. Any one of the series of owners of the deposit may demand cash at any time; the same is true of any one of the series of holders of a bank note. For some classes of transactions, it is true, a deposit subject to check is the more convenient means of payment, while for other classes of transactions bank notes are the more convenient.

16. *The issue of bank notes is usually hedged about by legal restrictions designed to protect the note holder from loss.*

The issue of bank notes is usually carefully regulated by government, so as to safeguard the holder of notes against loss. Now, we have seen that the positions of the note holder and the depositor are analogous. Both are creditors of the bank; both have a right to cash on demand. Why then should the government take greater pains to insure the note holder against loss than to insure the depositor?

The depositor usually lives in the city in which the bank which holds his funds on deposit is established. He is therefore in a position to know something of the standing of the bank. If he has reason to believe that the bank is not well managed, he can at once withdraw his deposit. On the other hand, bank notes often find their way to distant cities. The holders of such notes can know nothing about the credit of the issuing bank. For this reason it is only just that their interests should be protected by the government.

Various methods are employed by the different governments to protect the note holder against loss. In some countries the volume of notes that a bank may issue is limited to a certain proportion of the capital of the bank; in case of failure the note holders have a prior claim upon all the resources of the bank; furthermore, each bank is required to contribute to a fund for the immediate payment of notes of banks that have failed.

In the United States the privilege of note issue is practically restricted to national banks; other banks may indeed issue notes, but are taxed so heavily on their notes that issue is unprofitable. A national bank which avails itself of the privilege of issue must purchase, and deposit with the United States Treasury, United States bonds the par value and the market value of which is equal to the value of the notes issued. In case the bank fails, these bonds are sold, and the proceeds used to redeem the notes. Thus it is quite impossible for the holder of bank notes to suffer loss, even if the bank of issue fails.

Besides the ordinary national bank note we have in circulation two other kinds of notes, the federal reserve bank note and the federal reserve note. The federal reserve bank note is secured, like the national bank note, by government bonds deposited in the treasury by the federal reserve bank. The federal reserve notes are issued on the basis of ordinary commercial paper, rediscounted with the federal reserve banks. But the credit of these notes is supported by all the assets of the federal reserve banks and ultimately by that of the whole system. Only a universal financial disaster could destroy the value of these notes.

17. *Bank notes and bank deposits serve as currency, and reduce the amount of money needed for effecting exchanges.*

In the United States bank notes are used in effecting exchanges in the same way that money is used. Every one knows that the note holder is absolutely insured against loss; consequently no one takes the trouble to present bank notes at the issuing bank for redemption in money. Were the issue of bank notes prohibited, a large volume of exchanges now effected through their use would have to be effected by means of money. We should need a much larger amount of money than we now possess to carry on the existing business of the country.

Bank deposits serve in a similar way as a means of effecting exchanges. A deposit, we have seen, is not a definite sum of actual money, kept safe in the vaults of a bank. It is a right to demand money at the bank. When a man pays for goods by means of a check drawn on such a deposit, he simply transfers his claim upon the bank. Such a claim may be transferred again and again, effecting scores of exchanges.

It has been estimated that in the great commercial centers of the United States fully ninety-five per cent of the total volume of purchases and sales is effected by means of the transfer of claims upon banks. Money plays a relatively more important part in the lesser towns and the rural districts; yet even here bank notes and deposits effect a larger volume of exchanges than does actual money.

18. *Summary.*

The principal function of finance is the transfer of capital to those who can use it most advantageously. The transfer of capital most frequently assumes the form of a loan, either recognized as such, or disguised under the form of a credit sale. We may look upon the lending of capital as the purchase of such credit instruments as the promissory notes given by borrowers.

The function of the bank is primarily the borrowing of sums of capital available for short periods of time and the investment of such sums in short term credit instruments. The sums borrowed by the bank are known as "deposits"; the investments of the bank, since they represent for the most part the face value of the credit instruments purchased, less interest to maturity, are known as "discounts." In practice, when a business man sells a note to a bank, he leaves the proceeds of the note as a "deposit" in the bank, subject to withdrawal by check. In modern banks by far the greater part of the volume of deposits is created in this way, and not by the deposit of cash.

While the bank is compelled to pay out its deposits on the demand of the depositor, it is rarely the case that many depositors demand cash at any one time. This is partly due to the convenience of payment by means of checks. A depositor who wishes to make a payment draws a check in favor of his creditor; and this check is likely to be deposited in the bank by the payee; thus the payment is effected without any withdrawal of cash from the bank. The system of clearing protects each bank against serious drains upon its cash holdings through checks drawn upon it and deposited in other banks.

While little cash is withdrawn from a bank under ordinary circumstances, it is nevertheless necessary for a bank to keep on hand a considerable amount of cash, to safeguard itself against unexpected demands. The cash thus kept on hand is known as the reserve. The amount of the reserve should bear a proportion to the deposits which varies according to the character of the community in which the business is carried on. In the United States a minimum reserve is prescribed by law. The ultimate solvency of a bank does not depend upon its reserve, but upon the character of the notes in which the bank invests its funds. These are, as a rule, sound, and the chances of bank failure, except through fraud, are small.

The notes issued by banks are demand liabilities not essentially different from deposits. Since notes wander far from the bank of issue and are offered in payment to persons who can know nothing of the credit of the issuing bank, special regulations are adopted by governments to insure their payment.

Bank notes and bank deposits fulfill the functions of currency. The amount of money necessary for carrying on exchanges is greatly reduced by the use of a deposit and note currency.

CHAPTER XVIII

OTHER FINANCIAL INSTITUTIONS

1. *The making of permanent and long term investments may be regarded as the flow of funds from the capitalist class to the enterpriser class.*

The chief function of the bank, as we have seen, is the supplying of the demand for short term loans, through the accumulation and placing of capital which is available for use for short periods of time. The creditors of a bank and its debtors are, as a rule, members of the same economic class — men actively engaged in trade and industry. Each man is, in turn, borrower and lender. In the present chapter we are concerned with the investment of funds in credit instruments that run for long terms, or are perhaps even perpetual. It is plain that we are here dealing with the relations of two fairly distinct economic classes. Men who, for one reason or another, take no active part in business, place their funds with active business men. The former class corresponds roughly with the capitalist class of economic theory, the latter, with the enterpriser class. We may, therefore, regard the placing of capital in permanent and long term investments as a flow of funds from the capitalist to the enterpriser.

2. *The principal sources of demand for long term investment funds are* (1) *the purchase and improvement of real estate;* (2) *the financing of large corporations; and* (3) *the extraordinary needs of government.*

Throughout the country there is a constant demand for capital for the purchase and improvement of real estate. Men with small capitals of their own desire to buy farms or building lots; men who possess land desire to prepare it for cultivation or to equip it with the necessary stock or buildings. Those with insufficient capital — and they are many — enter the capital market as borrowers. They expect such capital as they may raise through loans to be productive, but they cannot be sure that they will be able to restore it to the lenders for several years. To meet the needs of such borrowers, lenders must surrender control of their funds for a considerable period of time — five, ten, or fifteen years.

A second source of demand for capital arises from the needs of the modern large scale business enterprise. In many forms of business the capital necessary for effective operation exceeds the amount that an ordinary enterpriser owns, or can raise through personal loans. The number of million-dollar enterprises in the United States vastly exceeds the number of millionaires. Accordingly, it is necessary to transfer to a single active enterpriser the capitals accumulated by numerous individuals.

A third source of demand for capital — and the last with which we need concern ourselves — arises from the extraordinary needs of government. Under ordinary conditions the expenditures of most governments are met by current revenues. Owing to unforeseen circumstances, revenues may be less than were anticipated, while expenditures may prove unusually heavy. As it takes time to revise a revenue system, a considerable deficit may appear, which involves borrowing under one form or another.

A much more important cause of public borrowing is the enormous expense entailed by modern warfare. No great war can be carried to a successful issue without the employment of far greater resources than any practicable system of taxation will afford. Recourse must therefore be had to loans. Government loans thus arising cannot quickly be paid off. Often loans are negotiated for ten, twenty, or thirty years; and even at the expiration of the period for which they are contracted, they are frequently paid out of the proceeds of new loans. Before the outbreak of the Great War most of the debt of the United States was a legacy from the Civil War; much of the debt of Great Britain originated in the wars of Napoleon. Large as those debts seemed in 1914, they have been wholly dwarfed by the debts created in the course of the Great War. In many European countries the debts exceed all practical possibility of repayment. That is not true of the debt of the United States or even of that of Great Britain. But there is no probability that the American debt will be paid off within a generation, nor that the British debt will be visibly reduced in that period of time.

Again, governments may borrow money for the purpose of carrying out a policy of permanent improvements. The United States, for example, raised the funds for the construction of the Panama Canal through loans. Before the war European governments borrowed vast sums for the purpose of purchasing and constructing railways. Cities are continually borrowing money for similar purposes. Especially where the policy of municipal ownership finds favor, the demand for capital for public use is enormous.

3. *The principal sources of supply of capital for long term investments are:* (1) *private fortunes accumulated in business, whose possessors desire freedom from the labors of active management;* (2) *the funds of endowed institutions;* (3) *the funds accumulated from private incomes and kept as a reserve against contingencies.*

Just as there are always men who are entering business life, so there are always men who are retiring from active business affairs. Men of the latter class desire to obtain an income from their accumulations without the labor that personal management entails. Universities, hospitals, and other institutions receive money endowments, which must be invested in such a way as to yield a steady income. Wage-earners and professional men are under the necessity of putting by a part of their incomes as a reserve against sickness and old age, or as a provision for their dependents in case of death. Capitalists who look forward to increasing burdens save part of their interest receipts; active business men save part of their profits. Of these savings some part is reinvested in their own business by the men who save. A great part of the total fund of savings must, however, be placed under the control of other persons, if it is to yield a considerable income.

We have now a view of the work that the financial mechanism must perform. It must gather together the funds of free capital and place them under the control of those who can make best use of such funds. We may next proceed to a study of the methods by which this work of placing capital is performed.

4. *The typical instruments employed in the effecting of long term and permanent investments are mortgage notes, bonds, and stocks.*

The transfer of capital for long terms implies the creation of various instruments which serve as evidence of the claims of the capitalist. The simplest type of such instruments is the promissory note secured by the pledge of property, such as houses and lands. Where the sum to be raised by a loan is very great, as in the case of corporation loans, the resources of numerous lenders must be drawn upon. Instead of executing a great number of separate notes, representing the amount borrowed from each person, the corporation may execute a note, secured by the pledge of property, covering the whole sum, and deposit it with a trustee. The trustee then prepares certificates representing shares in the loan, and delivers them to lenders as evidence of the sums loaned. Such certificates are known as "bonds." A government may issue similar certificates of indebtedness without executing a note representing the entire loan. Such bonds are seldom secured by the pledge of property. In any case it is clear that government and corporation bonds are merely forms of promissory notes.

Instead of raising money through an issue of bonds, a corporation may sell shares of stock which entitle the owner not only to an income, but to a share in the management of the enterprise. In law the position of the stockholder is very different from that of the bondholder. The former is a partner in the business undertaking; the latter is a creditor of it. In practical life the ordinary stockholder has little to do with the control of a corporation. He purchases stocks for the income they yield, just as he would purchase bonds for their income. The bondholder is a preferred claimant; therefore bonds, as a rule, offer a more certain income. The different classes of bonds vary widely in security, however, and many are inferior to certain classes of stocks in this respect.

Such instruments — promissory notes, bonds, and stocks — are clearly not capital, but merely evidence of ownership of capital. We may, however, think of the purchase and sale of such instruments as the purchase and sale of capital, since the ownership of the underlying productive goods is transferred with the transfer of such instruments. For convenience we may speak of notes, bonds, and stocks as "investments." Bonds and stocks are commonly called "securities."

5. *Investments vary greatly in respect to security.*

Investments of this character, as has been said, differ widely in security. The long term notes of business men are usually secured by the pledge of tangible property of some kind, but the property pledged may represent a more or a less adequate guaranty of repayment. A loan secured by the pledge of land in a semi-arid region is not so safe as a loan secured by the pledge of land in a locality where crop failures are unknown. A series of dry years may depopulate the semi-arid district, and practically destroy the value of land there. Loans secured by suburban real estate are not, as a rule, so safe as loans secured by business property in the heart of a city. The bonds of a government like that of the United States are to-day generally regarded as safer investments than those of Great Britain; the bonds of the latter country are regarded as safer than those of France, Belgium or Italy. Corporation bonds similarly vary widely in security. Experience has shown that corporations frequently become bankrupt, and in such cases the bondholders may lose part or all of their invested capital. Stocks, as a rule, are yet more uncertain investments. When a new interurban railway is constructed, no one knows certainly that the business which it will carry on will yield a fair return on the capital invested; if it does not do this, dividends on its stock will be low. Even in the case of an established business, changed conditions may annihilate profits and cause a suspension of dividend payments.

6. *Investments vary in their transferability.*

Suppose that an investor in New York holds a note secured by a mortgage on a farm in one of the western states. In some of the states such a note is not transferable at all. Even if the laws are such as to permit the sale of the note to a third party, the holder would find difficulty in disposing of it. The buyer would need to know something of the value of the property pledged as security and this he might be unable to ascertain without examining it himself. The bonds of a small manufacturing or mercantile corporation in one of the minor cities would more easily find buyers in distant financial centers. Even these, however, would ordinarily be difficult to dispose of. The bonds of a great railway or of an industrial consolidation always find a ready sale. One who invests in a Pennsylvania Railway or a United States Steel Corporation bond knows that he can at any time find some one who will be ready to buy it from him.

7. *The productiveness of an investment is measured by the ratio between its return and its market value. Different classes of investments vary widely in productiveness.*

It is, perhaps, straining the meaning of words to speak of a mortgage note or a corporation bond as being "productive." There is, however, reason to distinguish between the securities that yield an income and those that yield none, and the business world has drafted the words "productive" and "unproductive" into this service. We may safely accept the terms, as we are in no danger of falling into the error of regarding notes and bonds as actually productive, in the physical sense of the term.

We must distinguish between nominal productiveness and real productiveness. A bond of $100 face value may yield $4 per annum. The nominal productiveness of capital invested in such a bond is four per cent. But perhaps the bond may be purchased in the market for $80. In such case the real productiveness of capital invested in the bond is five per cent. A $100 share of stock paying dividends of ten per cent on its par value may sell at $200. The real productiveness of capital invested in such a stock is no greater than that of capital invested in the four per cent bond.

We need not concern ourselves here with nominal productiveness. Whether such productiveness is high or low is a matter dependent upon the volume of securities covering a specific earning power, and this volume is arbitrarily fixed. Real productiveness varies widely. Some investments yield only two per cent; some yield ten per cent or even more.

8. *The principal cause of variation in the productiveness of investments is risk, real or imagined.*

The bonds issued by the United States government yield only a little over three and one half per cent on the capital represented by their market value. Bonds issued by the government of Santo Domingo, before the time of American intervention in the affairs of that country, often yielded as much as twelve per cent on their market value. Practically the only reason for the great difference in productiveness was the difference in security. The bonds of the several states vary considerably in productiveness, and the bonds of municipalities display yet greater variety. The greatest variations in productiveness are to be found in corporation stocks, for here risk is greater than in the case of most classes of bonds.

Although there may be no real difference in risk between two investments, if it is commonly believed that there is such a difference, this belief is reflected in the productiveness of the respective investments. The bonds of Japan may be as safe as those of the United States; but this is not generally believed to be true. For this reason investments in Japanese bonds are more productive than investments in United States bonds.

9. *The productiveness of investments varies with their degree of transferability.*

As a rule, the greater the transferability of a form of investment, the lower will be its productiveness. Few investors are absolutely certain that they will not at some time desire to regain control of their funds. They will therefore take at par a bond that is easily disposed of rather than one of equal security and equal nominal productiveness which they might find difficulty in selling. Consequently, the price of bonds of the former class will generally be higher than that of bonds of the latter class. A hundred dollars invested in the former class of bonds will yield a lower rate of interest than a hundred dollars invested in the latter class.

The bonds of a great industrial corporation are usually less productive than those of a small one, on account of the greater transferability of the securities of a well-known business concern. Most classes of bonds furnish less productive investments than small real estate mortgages, because the latter can be transferred only with difficulty.

10. *The placing of capital may be effected by direct arrangements between the capitalist and the enterpriser or through the intermediation of a broker or other middleman.*

Where economic conditions are simple, as in an agricultural district or in a small town, the placing of capital may be effected through direct arrangements between those who need capital and those who have it to spare. The moral character and business capacity of an enterpriser is easily ascertained by those who wish to place their capital. A man who wishes to borrow capital can easily establish relations with those who have capital to lend. Even in such simple conditions, however, the individual borrower or lender is often at a disadvantage.

The former may fail to meet the men who are ready to lend at the lowest interest rate; the latter may fail to find the safest and most productive investments for his capital. Hence the need for a middleman, to bring together borrower and lender, enterpriser and capitalist. As industrial conditions become more complex, the need for the middleman becomes more intense. It would be quite impossible for the small capitalist of a city like New York or London to search out the most productive investments afforded by the business of such a city, were there no men who made it their business to bring capitalist and enterpriser together.

The men who perform this function may employ either of two methods. They may act as mere agents, in behalf of lender or of borrower or of both. Thus in some towns there are men who undertake, for a fee or "commission," to place any man who wishes to borrow in relations with men who have capital to lend. The function may, however, be performed in another way. Men with some capital of their own may hold themselves in readiness to borrow any capital that is offered for a definite period of time, trusting to the chance that they will be able to lend it again on more advantageous terms. The difference between the interest received and the interest paid represents the profits of the middleman. This, we have seen, is the method employed by the bank in its proper field.

The distinction which we have drawn between the two methods of placing, or marketing, capital, finds its analogue, we readily see, in a similar distinction in the methods of marketing commodities. A manufacturer may employ an agent, at a fixed commission, to bring his wares before the consuming public, or he may sell them to a merchant, who undertakes the responsibility of disposing of them to consumers.

11. *In the great modern commercial centers the placing of capital is effected largely through the stock exchanges — markets for the purchase and sale of securities.*

Under modern conditions an enormous amount of capital is represented by the bonds of nations, states, and municipalities and of private corporations, as well as by the stocks of corporations. A government may issue several hundred millions in bonds, all yielding the same return and having the same security, and private corporation issues of bonds and stocks are sometimes of equal magnitude. A person wishing to invest in a particular issue of government or corporation securities leaves an order with a broker to purchase such securities for him. A person wishing to regain control of capital invested in securities leaves them with a broker with orders to sell them. Naturally, the brokers dealing in stocks and bonds establish the custom of meeting at a fixed place, where those who have orders to buy may meet those who have orders to sell. Such a meeting-place, or market, is known as a stock exchange. For convenience, each exchange makes rules which brokers doing business there must observe. In their details these rules do not concern us here; in principle they are designed to insure effectiveness and fair dealing.

12. *Since securities dealt in on the exchanges fluctuate in value, profits may be secured through buying when such securities are cheap and selling them when dear. Business of this nature is termed speculation.*

Practically all the securities dealt in on the exchanges are constantly fluctuating in price. The bonds of a country like the United States are unusually stable in value, yet a hundred-dollar bond is somewhat cheaper at one time than at another. When a nation becomes involved in a war, the price of its bonds declines, because of the probability of vast new issues and the possibility that the war will drag on to the point of bankrupting the nation. Even the rumor of a war, however slight its foundation, may affect adversely the price of a nation's bonds. The bonds of a city may decline in value if the city government announces its intention of undertaking improvements on a large scale, or if it falls under the control of an extravagant administration. The price of bonds of railway and industrial corporations is affected by every change in business conditions. Price fluctuation is still more common in the case of stocks. It is not unusual for the price of a given stock to decline from $150 per share to $60 per share within a single year. Suppose that a company has been formed to exploit gold mines in Alaska. Its shares are offered on the market; we have read glowing accounts of the prospects of the company, but whether these accounts are reliable or not we cannot say. The company may earn enough to pay enormous dividends; it may earn nothing. What is more natural than that opinion as to the value of the stock should fluctuate accordingly?

In view of the constant fluctuation in securities, it is natural that some men should make it their business to buy stocks when they appear to be cheap, with the purpose of selling them when prices rise. This is one of the numerous forms of speculation. The buyers of stocks and bonds are commonly divided into two classes — investors and speculators. The former class buy chiefly with the purpose of enjoying a permanent income from the securities purchased; the latter, chiefly with the hope of profiting from a rise in price of the securities.

13. *The speculator provides enterprises which have not yet demonstrated their power to yield an income with the capital necessary for carrying on business.*

Naturally, the speculative buyer deals commonly in the securities that show great fluctuations in price, while the investor prefers the securities that have a comparatively steady price. Now, it is the securities of new companies that are most likely to fluctuate in value. After a company has been in operation for a number of years, its normal earning power becomes established, and the real value of its securities becomes fairly well settled. Thus there is a constant progress of securities from the speculative class to the investment class.

We can now see what one of the economic functions of stock speculation must be. So long as the success of a company is in doubt, the cautious investor will have nothing to do with it. Men who are willing to take risks — speculators — buy the securities of such a company, with the expectation of selling them later at a profit. In so doing they furnish the company with the funds necessary for carrying on business operations. If the company succeeds, and demonstrates its power to produce a large and steady income, its securities acquire a stability of value fitting them for purposes of permanent investment. The speculators, in such cases, gain large profits. If the company is a failure, the speculators bear the loss.

It is of course true that stock speculation offers great opportunities for sharp practice. A group of speculators holding the stock of a gold-mining company may succeed in placing in circulation deceptive accounts of the prospects of the company, and so manage to dispose of their holdings to the unwary at unreasonably high prices. A group of speculators, desiring to purchase certain stocks at a low price, may circulate rumors of impending disaster, and so create a panic among holders of stocks. Nevertheless, it is to be borne in mind that the speculative buyer of stocks performs a very important economic function in furnishing capital for enterprises the success of which is still in doubt, but which may eventually prove to be highly profitable. The speculator stands in the position of a middleman between the company which needs capital and the cautious investor.

14. *When a company seeks to raise capital through an issue of securities, it may place orders with brokers to sell the securities for what they will fetch, or it may make, with an association of financiers, an agreement according to the terms of which the association assumes responsibility for the sale of the securities at a definite price. Such an association is called an underwriting syndicate.*

Let us suppose that a great railway desires to raise about $50,000,000 by a new issue of five per cent bonds. It may place orders with brokers to sell the bonds at whatever price they will command. The bonds of the railway which are already outstanding may be selling above par, but no one can say exactly what effect on the price of bonds the new issue will have. Possibly the bonds will be taken by investors at par; possibly the price will fall to $85 per hundred dollar bond. Moreover, it may take a long time before all the bonds are taken by speculators or investors. The railway company, however, desires a definite amount of capital at a definite time, and cannot afford to experiment. So its agents may make an arrangement with a group of financiers whereby the latter agree to insure the sale of the entire issue at $95 per hundred dollar bond. The bonds are then placed on sale at, say, \$100. If the investing public takes the bonds at this price, the group of financiers, or "underwriting syndicate," gains a profit equal to the difference between the price to the public and the price agreed upon between the railway company and the syndicate. If the public refuses to buy, the syndicate is compelled to take the issue of bonds at the price agreed upon — \$95. Possibly the syndicate will be able to dispose of the bonds later on favorable terms; possibly it will in the end be compelled to sell them at less than the price it has paid.

Where the securities underwritten by a syndicate are of a more speculative character, as for example the stocks of a new industrial corporation, the difference between the price placed upon securities offered to the public and the price to the syndicate is much greater. The possible profits of the syndicate are much greater; but so also are the possible losses.

15. *An investment company is a company which purchases and holds stocks, bonds, mortgages, etc., the income of which is distributed as dividends among its own shareholders.*

A company may be formed for the sole purpose of dealing in the securities of other companies. Such a company — which we may call an investment company — places its stock upon the market, and invests the proceeds of the sales of such stock in the stocks and bonds of banking, railway, franchise, and industrial corporations, in government bonds, or in real estate mortgages. The interest and dividends from such investments make up the gross profits of the investment company. From these profits are deducted the expenses of administering the company; the remainder may be distributed among its stockholders as dividends. The advantages of such a company are obvious. It can employ men who are thoroughly familiar with the securities market to purchase stocks and bonds when the condition of the market is favorable. Since it purchases on a larger scale than the ordinary investor, it may participate in underwriting syndicates, and so obtain securities at a lower price than the outside investor must pay. It may distribute its investments so that when some of them fail to yield the expected returns, others may yield unusually large returns. Thus the stockholders of the investment company are made more certain of a steady income than they would be if they invested their funds directly.

Further, the investment company may deal in securities of undoubted value, which are nevertheless not well enough known to be easily transferred. There is no reason why the investment company should ever part with such securities. It may purchase mortgage notes which never would find a purchaser on the general market. As we have seen, the non-transferable investments yield, as a rule, higher returns than those that are easily transferred. Accordingly, the man who invests his funds through an investment company enjoys the higher income that non-transferable investments yield; at the same time, he can at any time regain control of his funds through the sale of his stock in the investment company.

16. *The savings bank performs the same function for the small investor that the investment company performs for the large one.*

It is only persons possessing at least a moderate amount of free capital who can purchase with advantage investment company shares. Persons who have no other resource than their daily labor need to save some part of their income against sickness, old age, or unemployment; and these savings should be placed where they may at once begin to earn interest. The artisan who saves $5 a month cannot be expected to keep the money on his premises until he has accumulated enough to buy a share of stock. This would involve keeping part of his savings idle for perhaps twenty months. It would, moreover, expose such savings to the recurrent temptation to spend. Hence the need of an institution which will accept savings deposits, however small, paying interest on them from the beginning, and which will return them to the depositor upon reasonable notice. Such an institution is the savings bank.

Unlike the commercial bank, described in the last chapter, the savings bank can depend upon a certain permanence of deposits. Men who intrust their funds to such an institution do so, as a rule, with the expectation of leaving them for an indefinite time, to earn interest. The rules under which a savings bank operates may of themselves insure a reasonable degree of permanence of deposits. Depositors are often required to give some days' or weeks' notice of intention to withdraw deposits. Furthermore, interest is usually allowed only at the end of six months' periods; withdrawal at any time within such periods involves the forfeiture of accrued interest.

Some part of the deposits of a savings bank must be kept as a cash reserve, to meet possible withdrawals, but this reserve need not be large. The remainder of the deposits may be invested. State laws generally specify the classes of investments that a savings bank may make, with a view to insuring the depositor against loss through insecure investments. Real estate mortgages, federal, state, and municipal bonds, are the favorite investments of such institutions. The real estate mortgages present the advantages of security and high degree of productiveness; government bonds, while yielding low returns, are easily convertible into cash whenever an unusual volume of withdrawals renders this necessary.

Savings banks may be organized as mutual associations, in which case all the profits from investments are distributed among the depositors as interest. They may be organized as joint stock associations; in such case the excess of earnings above stipulated interest to depositors is distributed among the stockholders as dividends. The mutual form of organization prevails in the northeastern states; in the western states provision for savings is usually made through savings departments in the ordinary commercial banks. In many foreign countries the place of the mutual savings bank is taken by municipal and postal savings banks and in the United States since 1910 the post office has conducted a savings bank with branches distributed rather irregularly over the country. In general, it is recognized that the proper function of the savings bank is to promote thrift among the poorer classes, not to afford an opportunity for profit to the well-to-do. Hence the small depositor is frequently given the preference over the large depositor, receiving a higher rate of interest. In many cases the size of the individual deposit is narrowly limited. In the postal savings system of the United States the maximum individual deposit is $1000.

17. *The building and loan association is a form of investment company which limits its field to small loans on real estate security.*

A financial institution which in some parts of the country takes the place of the savings bank in promoting saving among the working classes is the building and loan association. Each member of the association purchases a certain number of shares of "stock," paying for them in monthly installments. If at any time he wishes to withdraw, the association returns to him the sums which he has paid in, with or without interest, according to the time that has elapsed since his first payment. If a member desires to build a house, he may borrow from the association a sum not exceeding the par value of the stock in the association which he holds. As security for the loan, he gives a mortgage upon the house which he builds with the aid of the loan. He further binds himself to make monthly payments to the association which represent interest on the loan, plus some part of the principal. Without entering upon the details of the organization of such an association, we can see that its object is to collect sums of capital from persons of small means, with the purpose of loaning them to other persons of small means who desire to own homes. The latter class pay the interest that the former class receive.

18. *The Land Bank is an investment company designed to facilitate the flow of capital into agriculture.*

Agriculture, especially when it is conducted under the system of relatively small holdings operated by the owner, presents peculiar problems of financing. When a farm changes hands the buyer is usually not in a position to pay down the whole purchase price, but buys under mortgage. Accordingly the load of indebtedness of the typical agricultural community is heavy. Until recently in America the mortgage loan ran for periods ranging from two to five years. Such periods were insufficient to permit the accumulation of earnings sufficient to pay off the principal of the debt. In most cases the loan might be extended at maturity, but the debtor always ran the risk that payment would be insisted on, and that unless another creditor could be found, he might be deprived of his holdings through foreclosure proceedings. Rates of interest were often unfavorable, since farm mortgages were largely restricted to the local market; frequently the burden upon the debtor was increased through commissions upon the negotiation or renewal of the loan. In contrast, farmers in most European countries enjoyed low interest rates and long term loans, through the operation of various forms of land banks.

In 1916 Congress enacted a law providing for the organization of federal land banks, national farm loan associations and joint stock land banks. The land bank is a corporation with capital subscribed partly by individuals, partly by the federal government. Provision is made for one such bank for each of twelve divisions of the country. The minimum capital is $750,000. The farm loan associations consist of groups of ten or more borrowers, each of whom assumes a liability for all debts of the association equivalent roughly to the amount of his borrowings. When a loan is desired, the loan committee of the association appraises the security and recommends it to the federal land bank, which again appraises the security. The association indorses the mortgage which it receives from the borrower and conveys it to the federal land bank, which then advances the funds sought to the association, which in turn advances them to the borrower. The federal land bank then issues its own debentures in an equal sum and sells them in the investment market. This is the economic kernel of the whole transaction. The land bank exchanges its credit, known universally to be good, for the mortgage secured credit of the borrower, known only locally. Even with the added expense of conducting so complicated a system, the borrower secures his capital at a much lower rate than formerly.

Besides, the loans made under the system run for longer periods, from five years to forty, with the influence of the banks exerted in favor of fixing the term at thirty-five years. Every year the borrower pays, along with interest on the loan, a fixed percentage which goes to the repayment of the principle. Say that he pays five per cent interest: he is required to pay one per cent in addition, which will amortize or extinguish the principal in thirty-five years. Thus he is never put to any serious strain in meeting payments due. After five years he may, if he chooses, extinguish any part of the loan for which he has funds available.

19. *From the financial point of view, the life insurance company is a modified form of investment company. The returns from investments are for the most part made over to the policy holders.*

One further institution requires notice here: the life insurance company. From a financial point of view, the life insurance company is a device for accumulating savings which shall be returned, either to the man who saves in the form of an endowment, or to his heirs at his demise. Some of the insured, it is true, die long before the sum of the premiums they have paid equals the sum that the insurance company has agreed to pay at their death. On the average, however, the insured live long enough so that their premiums, together with the earnings of the capital which those premiums form, are at least equal to the sums which the insurance company pays out in death claims.

It is obvious that in a country like the United States, where life insurance is exceedingly common, immense sums of money must be collected by the companies every year, to be held as a reserve against death claims. As the business of life insurance is steadily growing, the funds accumulated by these companies are also increasing. The annual receipts of all the important life insurance companies exceed the annual disbursements. Accordingly, a life insurance company may invest its funds without much regard to the possibility of turning its investments into cash at short notice. It is important, however, that the business should be conducted in a conservative manner, since the failure of an insurance company would be a more widely felt calamity than the failure of almost any other business enterprise of equal magnitude. The loss would be borne in the end largely by the dependents of propertyless men.

The reserves of life insurance companies are invested chiefly in real estate mortgages, in state and municipal bonds, and in the bonds of railway, commercial and industrial corporations. Stock investments have often been made by insurance companies, but the practice is now generally regarded with disfavor, since the values of stocks are likely to show a wide range of fluctuation.

20. *The mechanism for bringing investor and enterpriser together necessarily becomes more complex as industrial operations increase in magnitude.*

In a small village, the investor and the enterpriser enter into direct relations with each other. In a larger town, funds flow from the investor to the enterpriser through the intermediation of a broker. In a great city funds flow from the investor to the enterpriser through the intermediation of a series of brokers and a series of speculators; often other functionaries, such as the underwriter and the investment company, insert themselves in the chain connecting the two primary financial classes — the investor and the enterpriser. We shall understand this flow of funds better if we construct a diagram representing it: —

	STOCKHOLDER	DEPOSITOR	POLICY HOLDER
	↓	↓	↓
Independent Investor	Investment Co.	Savings Bank	Insurance Co.
	↓		
	(Broker)		
	↓		
	Speculator		
	↓		
	(Broker)		
	↓		
	Underwriting Syndicate		
	↓		
	Industrial Enterprise		

In our diagram the broker is placed in parenthesis, because he is nominally an agent for the investor or the speculator. The diagram is less complex than the reality, because it assumes that only one speculator figures in the chain, when in fact a security may pass from one speculator to another for years before its value becomes sufficiently stable to attract the interest of investors.

21. *Summary.*

In modern economic society there is a constant flow of funds from the capitalist class to the enterpriser class. The purchase or improvement of real estate, the financing of large business enterprises, and the extraordinary needs of governments give rise to the demand for long term investment; men retiring from active business life, endowed institutions, and persons accumulating capital against future needs furnish the supply of such funds. This flow of capital may be represented as the purchase and sale of stocks, bonds, and mortgage notes.

Long term investments vary widely in security and transferability. As a rule, the greater the degree of security and transferability, the less the productiveness of an investment.

The placing of capital may be effected through direct arrangements between the capitalist and the enterpriser, or through the intermediation of a broker or other middleman. The broker may carry on his business independently, or he may join with other brokers in organizing a stock exchange. The purchasers of stocks and bonds may hold them for the income which they yield, or for a rise in price. In the former case the purchasers are classed as investors, in the latter, as speculators. When an enterprise is new its securities are chiefly held by speculators; when its business is well established, the securities are likely to pass into the hands of permanent investors. Thus the speculator appears in the light of an intermediary between the enterpriser and the ultimate investor.

Investment may be made through various institutions, instead of directly by the capitalist. The most important of these are the investment company, the savings bank, the building and loan association, and the life insurance company. These institutions are adapted to the peculiar needs of different classes of investors. They share in common the advantages of expert skill in the making of investments and of power to distribute investments in such a way as to minimize risk.

CHAPTER XIX

INTERNATIONAL TRADE AND FOREIGN EXCHANGE

1. *All permanent trade rests upon differences in productive powers.*

From early modern times, when men first began to think systematically upon economic subjects, a great deal of attention has been bestowed upon the exchange of goods between persons living under different governments, or international trade. It was for a long time believed (and it is still widely believed) that such trade differs radically in its nature from trade that is carried on within the limits of a single country. While the latter, it is generally admitted, is an unmixed good, and ought to be encouraged, or at any rate granted the most perfect freedom by government, the former, many believe, is often a doubtful blessing and ought to be closely scrutinized and regulated, and, under many circumstances, discouraged or even prohibited. Whether there is any justice in this distinction between the two branches of trade is a question that we must defer to the next chapter. For the present, we are concerned with the conditions giving rise to international trade and the mechanism by which it is carried on.

All permanent trade is based upon differences in character of productive powers. To employ a simple example, drawn from the field of local trade, if A can make three pairs of shoes in a day while B can make only two, and B can cut two cords of wood in a day while A can cut only one, the basis for permanent trade between them exists. It will pay A to get all his wood from B, exchanging shoes for it. The assumed difference in character of productive powers may have originated in differences in natural aptitudes or in differences in training. In either case the difference in productive powers is the essential basis of a continuous interchange of commodities.

But suppose that A can not only make more shoes in a day than B can make, but can also cut more wood. Does this supposition preclude the possibility of a permanent interchange of products between A and B? Not at all. Suppose that A can make three pairs of shoes in a day or cut two cords of wood, while B can make only one pair of shoes, or cut only one cord of wood. With two days' work B can produce as much wood as A can with one; with two days' work he cannot produce as many shoes as A can with one. Accordingly, it would pay him to offer A the product of a little more than two days of his own work at woodcutting, in exchange for the product of one day of A's work at making shoes. And it would pay A to accept the offer. B suffers under a disadvantage in either occupation, but his disadvantage is less in woodcutting than in shoemaking. A enjoys an advantage in either occupation, but his advantage is greater in shoemaking than in woodcutting. Common sense, then, urges B to confine himself to cutting wood, A to making shoes.

What A would say, in explaining the reason why he procured his wood from B, is that his "time was too valuable" to spend on wood cutting. It is too valuable, in fact, solely because it can be put to better uses. We need not go back to primitive conditions to see this principle in action. Why does an able-bodied lawyer hire a more or less decrepit workman to mow his lawn? Because the lawyer's time is too valuable to be put to such uses as mowing lawns. In a very large proportion of cases, we hire work done, or buy the products ready made, not because we could not do the work ourselves in average time or less, but because we have more profitable uses for our time.

In the trade between inhabitants of one part of the earth's surface with those of another part, differences in personal aptitude and training of the kind assumed in the foregoing example are supplemented by differences of a more general nature. One region may have excellent mineral deposits but lack fertile land for the growing of food; another region may be quite devoid of minerals, but abundantly supplied with rich lands. Capital may be plentiful and cheap in one region and scarce and dear in another. In this case industries requiring vast capital can be operated to greater advantage in the former region than in the latter. Land may be plentiful in one region, relatively to the population, and scarce in another. Industries requiring an extensive use of land will find their natural habitat in the former region. The populations of two regions, though differing little in fundamental character, may differ widely in their attitude toward particular forms of toil. They possess different habits, or, more properly, traditions of workmanship, which fit the one better for one kind of labor, the other for another. So long as any of these differences persists, there is obviously reason why there should be differences in the industries of the two regions. With adequate means of communication, trade between the two regions naturally arises.

2. *Economically considered, trade should be classified as local and interregional, not as domestic and international. The latter classification may, however, be regarded as practically equivalent to the former.*

We have spoken of differences between regions, not differences between nations. From a purely economic point of view, trade is either local or interregional, not domestic or international. The trade between Belgium and the adjacent *départements* of France is economically of the same character as the trade between Rhode Island and Massachusetts. The trade between California and Hawaii is of the same essential character as the trade between New York and Santo Domingo. From an economic point of view local trade is that which originates in such differences in natural aptitudes and industrial training as may for a long time persist on the same soil. Differences in natural endowment, in general character of population, in rates of wages and interest, characterize interregional trade. As a rule, however, international trade is also interregional; hence the principles that apply to the latter may without serious qualification be applied to the former. Since the classification of trade as domestic and international is widely used, we shall accept it in the following pages.

3. *Trade between two regions or nations may be based upon the fact that each one produces goods of a kind that cannot be produced within the boundaries of the other.*

In some cases the products of two regions are quite dissimilar. Neither region can produce the commodities which it receives from the other. Thus in the Middle Ages an important trade was carried on between Northern Europe and the Indies. The former region furnished furs and amber, the latter, spices and gems. A modern example of the same sort of trade is the exchange of iron and steel products for teas, coffee, and spices between England and the East Indies. In general, the trade between countries in the temperate zone, on the one hand, and countries in the torrid zone, on the other, is largely of this character. Trade having this basis is naturally permanent; with every reduction in costs of transportation it tends to increase. Decline in railway and ocean shipping charges places more and cheaper tropical products in our hands, and places more of our products in the hands of the inhabitants of the tropics. Furthermore, we are, as a people, gradually learning to appreciate the good qualitites in tropical products that a short time ago we held in slight esteem; and we may assume that a corresponding evolution is taking place in the tastes of the inhabitants of the tropics.

4. *Each one of two trading nations may be able to produce all classes of commodities that are the objects of exchange between them. In this case, the one is likely to enjoy greater relative advantages for the production of one class of commodities, the other for the production of another class.*

More commonly one of the trading regions, or both, can produce both classes of commodities exchanged. The United States can produce both sugar and pork; so also can Cuba. But the United States possesses exceptional advantages for the production of pork; for the production of sugar it is not especially well adapted. Cuba, on the other hand, has unsurpassed advantages for the production of sugar, but can produce pork with only a moderate degree of success. It is, therefore, natural that an exchange of products between the two countries should take place. Were there no artificial hindrances to such exchange, we should adjust our production in such a way as to produce all the pork that Cuba needs, and Cuba would devote more of her productive resources to the growing of sugar for our consumption.

5. *Trade based upon differences in productive power arising from differences in the character of two populations is permanent in character and tends to increase with improvements in transportation.*

Among the conditions upon which international trade is based, we mentioned differences in the essential character of the populations of trading regions. Such differences in character are difficult to define, since the characters of nations, as of individuals, are always thickly overlaid with custom and habit. Nevertheless, we may be quite sure that such differences exist. The Frenchman is not exactly the same kind of man as the Englishman, even if due allowance is made for acquired traits. Still less is the Japanese the same kind of man as the American. It is therefore safe to assume that in some of the manifold branches of industry the Frenchman will be superior to the Englishman, while in some he will be inferior. We may certainly assume that in some branches of industry the Japanese will be more successful than the American, while in other branches he will be less successful.

Cotton can be grown successfully by the native population of Central Africa. The tedious labor under a tropic sun is more easily borne by the native blacks than it would be by persons of European descent. The manufacture of cotton cloth by modern methods requires a higher degree of intelligence, perseverance, and responsibility than the native African population possesses. This branch of the industry may better be carried on in a country like England, where the population has the required traits in a high degree of development. Accordingly, there is a natural basis for permanent trade between England and Central Africa. Trade based upon such essential differences in national character also tends to increase in importance with improvements in the means of transportation and communication.

6. *International trade based upon differences in relative supply of land eventually loses a large part of its importance on account of the movements of population.*

Trade based upon differences in relative supply of land attained extraordinary proportions during the nineteenth century. The Old World, for the most part, was densely peopled; in the New World population was sparse. It is a well-known fact that the largest output per workman of agricultural products is attained through the superficial cultivation of large areas. England may have lands that are naturally better adapted for the growing of wheat than the lands of Argentina. But it is hardly possible for one man cultivating twenty acres in England to produce as many bushels of wheat as one man cultivating two hundred acres in Argentina.

In manufactures, on the other hand, density of population, instead of reducing productive efficiency, tends to increase it. Men who live in constant association are better fitted for the organized activity of the modern factory than are men who pass their lives in the isolation of the frontier. Hence an exchange of agricultural products for manufactures between the New World and the Old was in the natural order of events.

During the greater part of the nineteenth century trade between the United States and England was chiefly of the character just described. The United States possessed vast tracts of land for extensive cultivation; England had a dense population well fitted for factory labor. Hence we exported foodstuffs and raw materials and imported manufactures.

While trade upon this basis tends to increase with reduction in costs of transportation, there is a counter tendency at work which in time checks it. Immigration flows into the regions rich in land; the natural increase of population in those regions is likely to be rapid. In the end such regions lose their peculiar advantages in the production of foodstuffs and raw materials, and gain in power to produce manufactures cheaply. Trade of the character under discussion may continue for centuries, but ultimately it decays. At the outbreak of the Great War the United States, while still an exporter of foodstuffs, was moving rapidly toward a condition in which the national consumption of food absorbed the whole production. The war, with its huge waste of foodstuffs and its disorganization of agricultural production in Russia and the Balkans, gave a new stimulus to American agricultural exports. As the economic state of the world returns to normal, we may expect American exports to assume prevailingly the form of manufactured products. There is no reason for forecasting a time when the United States will be absolutely dependent on foreign supplies of food, but incidental imports of food will more than balance exports of food before another quarter of a century has elapsed.

7. *International trade based upon differences in relative supply of capital can not long persist if capital flows easily from country to country.*

So long as England was *par excellence* the land of capital, and so long as English capitalists were unwilling to invest their funds in foreign lands, there were many branches of manufacture that could be prosecuted to greater advantage in England than in other countries. In practically every branch of manufacture, in fact, the interest on capital makes up a far larger proportion of the total expenses than in grazing, agriculture, lumbering, etc. It is easy to see, then, that English manufacturers, with interest at five per cent, enjoyed a decided advantage over American manufacturers, with interest at eight per cent. The English farmers and stockmen, it is true, also had an advantage in interest rates over their American competitors. But the advantage was of less relative importance and more easily offset by other factors in which the Americans enjoyed an advantage, such as cheaper land.

Under orderly international conditions no country can long hold a branch of trade merely through cheapness of capital. Like labor, capital tends to migrate to the less developed regions of the world; its migration involves far less personal sacrifice and far less cost. Furthermore, capital increases rapidly in the newer lands. If interest rates were much higher in the United States than in Great Britain, British capital would steadily flow into the former country; and this influx of capital, added to the new capital constantly accumulating here, would tend to depress interest rates, until there remained no perceptible difference in the rates prevailing in the two countries.

There have always been countries, however, in which capital failed to find adequate security. Before the Great War the Balkan states, and some of the Latin American republics were generally regarded as especially perilous fields of investment. At any time war or revolution might destroy factories and machinery and other concrete forms of capital. Since the war practically the whole of Central and Eastern Europe has come to be regarded as a field in which the investor incurs great risks.

In such conditions of excessive risk, local accumulation of capital will not be active, nor will capital flow in from foreign countries. Production will therefore be confined chiefly to the industries requiring a modest investment, such as grazing and agriculture. Manufactures, at least in their more elaborate forms, will have to be imported. The exchange based upon such differences in security for capital may be relatively permanant.

8. *International trade based upon differences in traditions of workmanship often manifests a high degree of permanence.*

In a region that has long been devoted chiefly to a given branch of industry, something that we may call a tradition of workmanship evolves. The best type of iron worker is not developed in a single generation. The mill that is manned with workers whose fathers and whose fathers' fathers were reared in a world of iron manipulation possesses a decided, though indefinable, advantage over the mill that is manned with workers whose antecedents are of the field or forest. Costly experiments in settling urban stock upon farms have lent color to the popular view that it takes generations to make a farmer. Still more important is the tradition of workmanship in industries requiring a high degree of taste and skill. Where is the Occidental who can produce a true Oriental rug?

When other conditions are ripe, the population of any region may develop the tradition of workmanship necessary for the successful prosecution of any specific branch of industry. But no region can be expected to gain a superiority in all lines. We may at some future time be able to make gowns as well as the French, and ivory toys as well as the Japanese. But there will always be objects of taste which we must buy from the French and the Japanese. Trade based upon such differences may, therefore, be treated as permanent in character.

9. *Fluctuations in the value of money may give rise to trade of a transitory character.*

In the nineteenth century trade between gold standard and silver standard countries was often stimulated or depressed by changes in the relative values of the monetary media. The Oriental or Latin American producer of export goods found himself in a position to earn exceptional profits when silver declined. His products were valued abroad in gold, but his costs were measured in silver. In such a situation, the producer would in the long run have to raise wages to counteract the effect of the declining value of silver. But wages and other factors in cost readjust themselves slowly. In the interval there are great profits for exporters, and naturally an increased volume of trade.

Still more striking have been the effects of depreciating paper currencies since the Great War. Down to 1922 the currencies of almost every state of Central and Eastern Europe steadily sank in value, until the German mark, once worth a quarter of a dollar, came to be worth half a cent, and the Russian ruble, once worth half a dollar, came to be worth one-thousandth of a cent. Wages, though steadily rising, could not keep pace with the rising prices of commodities. The producer for export therefore enjoyed a special advantage. He paid his wages, interest on loans and rent on buildings in the depreciated domestic currency and got for his exports some international medium that had not been affected by depreciation. That left in his hands a margin of net profits that was often very considerable.

It is to be observed that the process of depreciation must be continuous if it is to exert a continuous effect on exports. If the German mark, after falling to half a cent, remained steadily at that point, wages and other factors of cost would gradually readjust themselves, until the German exporter found himself in the same relative position as before the decline in the mark.

We have only to reverse the foregoing argument to make clear the effect of a rise in the value of currency.

Suppose the German mark rises to one cent, two cents, then three. How would that affect the exporter? Wages and other factors in cost would not adjust themselves immediately. The German producer would incur the same cost in marks as before, while such international currency as he received for his product would buy fewer marks. Thus his margin of profit would be cut down, or even wholly eliminated.

10. *The foreign trade of modern nations is based upon a combination of differences, some of a permanent and some of a transitory nature.*

In the foreign trade of a great country like the United States or Great Britain it is natural that we should find one part having one underlying basis, another part another basis. In many cases the exportation or importation of a commodity arises from a combination of several of the causes which we have described as bases of trade. The exportation of iron and steel products from Great Britain to India is based upon the fact that Great Britain has vastly superior deposits of iron ore and coal, cheaper capital, and a population better fitted than that of India for metallurgical industry and possessing a superior tradition of workmanship. The exportation of wheat from the United States to England is based upon the greater abundance of land, and the extensive use of agricultural machinery. The importation into the United States of French articles of taste may be due in part to superiority of the French national character, in this respect; but it is undoubtedly due in large part to a superior tradition of workmanship on the part of the French. With the lapse of time we shall cease to export many of the commodities we now export; many of the commodities which we now import will be produced in this country.

11. *A country may import commodities for the production of which it is better fitted by nature than are the countries which export these commodities. Such a proceeding is economical when the first country enjoys even greater advantages in the production of other commodities than the other countries enjoy.*

We have, hitherto, considered only cases in which each one of two trading regions possesses unique, or at any rate superior, advantages in the production of the commodities which it exports. Under certain conditions trade may be advantageous even when this is not the case. To use a time-honored illustration, let us suppose that the United States, by reason of its natural wealth and the character of its population, is in a better position to produce both wheat and steel than England. A day's labor will produce more of either commodity in America than in England. Yet it may be profitable for the United States to buy its steel from England, giving wheat in exchange. We will assume that in America a day's labor will produce four bushels of wheat or two hundredweights of steel, while in England a day's labor will produce one bushel of wheat or one hundredweight of steel. Disregarding the costs of transportation, it would be profitable for America to offer England three bushels of wheat in exchange for two hundredweights of steel, and it would be profitable for England to accept the offer. America would thus obtain two hundredweights of steel for three fourths of a day spent in wheat growing, instead of spending a whole day's labor in making the steel. England would obtain three bushels of wheat through two days' labor spent in steel making, instead of spending three days' labor producing the same amount of wheat. America possesses an advantage in either industry, but her advantage is greater in wheat growing. England is at a disadvantage in either branch of production, but her disadvantage is less in steel making. It is therefore natural, under the assumed conditions, that America should make a specialty of wheat production, England of steel making, and that the two countries should carry on a mutually profitable trade.

This case is obviously analogous to the case of exchange between shoemaker and woodcutter which we employed in the early part of this chapter. But while any person of ordinary intelligence can see how it may be profitable for an efficient shoemaker to hire a man less fitted than himself for woodcutting to supply him with wood, it appears to be beyond the comprehension of most ordinary men, and many extraordinary ones, that a country can profitably pursue the same business policy. Since a day's labor does actually produce more steel in the United States than in England, many men believe that it must be unprofitable for us to buy steel from England. Obviously, they fail to consider the possibility that we may have other industries so much more productive than those of England that we cannot afford to divert our labor to the making of steel.

12. *From the fact that a country has greater natural advantages for the production of a commodity than other countries enjoy, it does not necessarily follow that the money cost of the commodity is lower in the former country than in the others.*

Let us look at the matter from another point of view — that of prices and money cost of production. The men who engage in the business of importing and exporting commodities do not inquire into underlying bases of trade. Their inquiries begin and end with prices. Is steel cheaper in England than in America? If so, and if the difference is great enough to pay the cost of transportation, they import the steel, unless they are prevented by government from doing so. Is wheat cheaper in America than in England? If it is enough cheaper to pay the costs of transportation, they export it.

But why should steel be cheaper in England than in America, while wheat is cheaper in the latter country? Prices, we know, tend to equal money cost of production; therefore we may assume that it costs less to produce steel in England, wheat in America. Our inquiries cannot stop here, however, for we must know why it costs more to produce the one commodity in the one country, the other commodity in the other country.

Ask a steel manufacturer why it costs more to produce steel in this country than in England, and he will probably reply, "Labor is dearer." The pay of English steel workers is, indeed, lower than that of steel workers in America, but so also is the pay of English agricultural laborers lower than that of farm hands in America. It is, therefore, plain that it is not the low wages, absolutely considered, that give the British steel manufacturer an advantage, but the low wages, relatively to the productive efficiency of the workmen. Low wages do not make British agriculture prosperous, because the productive efficiency of laborers in that industry is low, relatively to wages. The disadvantage of the British steel industry as compared with the American is less than the disadvantage of British agriculture as compared with American.

13. *It is profitable to import a commodity whenever labor and capital engaged in its production yield less than the same agents would yield in other fields.*

We shall get a clearer view of the situation if we recall the principles determining cost of production. Wages and interest are the chief constituents of cost of production;

but we will fix our attention upon wages alone. In earlier chapters we saw that wages are determined by the marginal productivity of labor. Now, let us suppose that one trading region has a vast extent of fertile land and a sparse population. Only the best lands are tilled and these in a superficial way. Add a thousand laborers to the population. How much can they produce? Perhaps five bushels per man a day. This amount of wheat, or the price of it, they can demand as wages; all other equally efficient workmen will get as much, but no more. Another trading region has, let us say, a dense population and little land. All the good lands are carefully tilled; most of the poor lands also are under cultivation. Add a thousand men to the working population. It is highly improbable that these men will increase the product by five bushels per man per day. Rather, we may assume that the daily product of a man is only one bushel. And this, or its price, is all that any equally efficient laborer in the society can get.

If the two regions are in easy communication with each other, the price of wheat in the one will be the same as the price in the other, allowance made for the cost of shipping wheat from the one to the other — a few cents per bushel, we will assume. This means that money wages will be much higher in the region which is sparsely settled than in the region where population is dense.

Now, let us suppose that each region possesses ores and coal, but that the deposits of the sparsely settled region are so much the richer that a day's labor will produce from them twice as much steel as a day's labor will produce from the deposits of the densely settled region. Enterprisers of the former region will have to pay miners, furnacemen, etc., at least as much as they could earn in agriculture — the price of five bushels a day. Enterprisers in the region of dense population will also pay wages gauged by the returns to agricultural labor — the price of one bushel a day. A simple calculation will show that steel manufacturers in the region of dense population can produce steel much more cheaply than their competitors in the other region.

In order to make our example correspond more closely with reality, we should need to substitute, for steel making only, a wide range of industries, mainly manufacturing; for wheat raising we should substitute a wide range of industries, mainly extractive. We might then say, with perfect truth, that in a sparsely settled region the marginal productivity, and consequently the wages of labor, are likely to be so high that manufactures cannot be carried on profitably in competition with a densely settled region, where the marginal productivity of labor, and hence wages, are low. American manufacturers of iron and steel products have for a century been forced to pay higher wages than English manufacturers, largely because the productivity of labor in agriculture was so much higher here than in England.

It is of course possible that in the end methods will be found for increasing the productivity of the high priced labor of one country so that the wages element in cost will be less than in countries of low wages. Well-paid labor is likely to be physically more fit and more alert mentally. It is better adapted to systematic organization and to the operation of complicated machinery. As a fact, the American iron and steel industry long ago overcame the disadvantages of high labor cost. The actual cost of most of the important products of the industry is no higher than in other industrial countries.

14. *Trade between different countries originally took the form of barter.*

In early times, interregional trade, like all other forms of trade, was carried on through barter. The Phœnician merchant carried to each port commodities that he thought would be in demand there, and bartered them for commodities which he desired. In a later stage money was employed, but chiefly for effecting exchanges within a single locality. The artisan merchants of the mediæval Hanse towns trading with England carried cloth and other wares to London and exchanged them for wool and other English products. Doubtless when in England the Hanse merchants often first exchanged their wares for local money, and exchanged the money in turn for goods to carry back to Germany. From the point of view of the two trading regions, the trade was an exchange of goods for goods, or barter, in spite of the employment of money in England.

After the Great War, in countries where the currency had become badly disorganized, international trading transactions returned in some instances to their primitive character. Any merchant who sent goods to Russia or Rumania, Poland or Jugoslavia, naturally sought to take in exchange some kind of goods which could be sold in the world market. The currency of those countries would not serve his purpose, since it fluctuated wildly in value and might turn out to be utterly valueless. He could not accept lands or houses or other immovable goods, because he could not have any assurance that some political overturn might not result in confiscation. If, then, he sold goods for currency it was with the intention of turning the currency immediately into goods.

The character of international trade as barter is only slightly obscured where the currencies of both trading regions, though fluctuating with respect to each other, command a fair degree of confidence. During the Great War and the post-war disorders, gold, which had been the basis of the currencies of all the important commercial nations, was displaced through almost all Europe by paper currencies. The only commercial powers of the first rank that maintained the gold standard through that period were the United States and Japan. In Great Britain, France and Italy, the money in daily use was paper, which fluctuated considerably in value. Accordingly, any American exporter to one of those countries had to take either goods in payment or paper that might sink enough in value to wipe out his profit. Of course it might also rise enough in value to double his profit. To sell his goods for currency thus involved a speculative element in addition to the possible fluctuations in the prices of the goods he exported. And the ordinary exporter is not prepared to engage in currency speculations.

In every great commercial center, however, there is to be found a body of men whose business is to speculate in fluctuating values, foreign currencies among the rest. Say that an American exporter ships a hundred thousand pounds of cotton to a customer in France, taking in return two hundred thousand paper francs. Within the month the franc may sink to seven cents or it may rise to nine. Its current value in the speculative market is, we will say, $8\frac{1}{2}$ cents, and the merchant has only to sell his francs to translate the value into American money. The speculator may lose on the transaction, but on the other hand he may gain. He is doing business with his eyes open.

But what becomes of the francs in the speculator's hands? He certainly does not intend to hold them until that remote time when he might send them to France and obtain their face value in gold. He holds them merely until a customer appears to buy francs at what seems to him a good price. Say that an American house wishes to import goods from France. Or that an American wishes to buy a house in France, or provide for the expenses of a protracted sojourn there. He buys francs; perhaps from the identical fund created by the export of cotton to France.

American trade with a country which employs a paper currency is, in the large, barter. We exchange American goods for French goods of equivalent value. The intervention of speculators in currency may obscure the relation slightly. For several months we may export more to France than we receive in exchange in the form of goods, in the meantime heaping up the supply of francs in the hands of the speculators. Or we may sell goods in France on credit, in terms of dollars, leaving it to our French customers to run the risk of a decline in francs which makes dollars ruinously dear when they have to make good on their contracts. In either case, if the volume of excess claims on France becomes too heavy, the American price of francs is likely to decline. This makes it easier to pay for imports from France and harder to sell exports there advantageously. Thus forces are set in operation which tend to restore the equilibrium of exports and imports.

Where both trading countries employ the gold standard the relation between imports and exports may drift farther away from the equilibrium represented by direct barter. An exporter sells his goods for what they will fetch, taking the price in gold. He may carry the gold back to his country, if he chooses, have it recoined at the mint without cost or at nominal cost and use it like any other money. Here it looks at first as if no necessary relation existed between exports and imports. We shall examine into the case in detail, because it is typical of normal economic conditions. There may be protracted periods of disturbance like the present when each nation has its own special currency, fluctuating in value according to its own laws. But sooner or later the normal condition of interchangeable standards will return.

15. *The use of gold in international payments is largely obviated by the employment of bills of exchange.*

Let us suppose that A, an American exporter, has sold 50,000 pounds of cotton to X, a Japanese importer, at the price of 20 cents a pound. If he wishes the $10,000 delivered to him in America in gold, he must, of course, pay freight and insurance on it. This will cost about $1 for every $100, or $100 for the entire sum.

But suppose that after shipping the cotton, and before giving orders for the delivery of the gold, he meets B, an American importer, who is about to order $10,000 worth of silks from Y, a Japanese exporter. If B were to ship the $10,000 in gold to Japan, it would cost him $100 for freight and insurance. Now, if A will give B an order instructing X to pay Y the $10,000, instead of remitting it to himself, B can pay A the $10,000 that he would otherwise have remitted to Y. Both debts will be extinguished by such an arrangement, and both A and B can save $100 by it.

Such an order as we have assumed that A gives to B, requesting X to pay Y a certain sum originally due to A, is known as a bill of exchange. Such a bill may be payable as soon as it is presented to the person upon whom it is drawn, or it may be payable after the expiration of a period of time — twenty, thirty, sixty days. In the former case it is a "sight bill," in the latter, a "time bill." Time bills usually bear interest — a fact that assimilates them to other credit instruments, but has no bearing on the principles of exchange. We shall therefore assume that bills of exchange are sight bills only.

In our example it appeared that both A and B gained $100 by the arrangement. Now, if B had been unwilling, for some reason, to give A $10,000 for the latter's bill of exchange, A might have taken less. It would have been more profitable for him to take $9910 than to incur the expense of importing the gold. If B had offered $9900, it would have been a matter of indifference to A whether he sold his bill to B or imported the gold. $9900 is evidently the very lowest price at which the bill would be sold. On the other hand, if A had been unwilling to part with his bill for just $10,000, B might have offered more, for he could better have afforded to pay $10,090 for the bill than stand the expense of exporting gold. If A had demanded $10,100, it would have been a matter of indifference to B whether he bought the bill or shipped the gold. $10,100 is, then, the very highest price that a $10,000 bill can be made to fetch.

16. *Bills of exchange sell at par when the supply of them just equals the demand. When the supply is less than the demand, they rise above par; when the supply exceeds the demand, they fall below par.*

When a bill of exchange sells for just its face value, it is said to be at par; when for more or less, it is above or below par. We have now to inquire under what conditions bills will be at par, or above or below par.

If the importer whom we designated as B thinks that the chances are good that he can find other exporters besides A who wish to dispose of bills of exchange, he is likely to offer less than par for A's bill. If one of the holders of bills will not sell at a low price, another probably will. If, on the other hand, A thinks that he can easily find other persons besides B who have payments to make abroad, and who wish to purchase bills for the purpose, he is likely to hold his bill at a price above par. In general terms, when the volume of bills offered for sale appears to exceed the volume of remittances to be made to a foreign center, bills fall below par. When the volume of bills appears to be inferior to the volume of remittances to be made, bills rise above par. In the former case, each holder of a bill knows that some bills cannot be sold at all; their holders will have to go to the expense of importing specie. Rather than be left in this position himself, he is willing to sell his bill at less than its par value, provided that the price offered is not so low that to bear the cost of importing specie would be a lesser evil. In the latter case each person having remittances to make knows that some men will have to go to the expense of exporting specie. Hence each one will offer more than its par value for a bill of exchange.

17. *Whether bills are at par or above or below par depends on the total volume of payments between trading regions.*

We must now endeavor to determine the conditions under which the volume of bills equals, is superior to, or inferior to, the volume of remittances. We shall assume that the relations between the United States and Japan are carried on without regard to relations with other countries.

The United States, we will assume, exports in one year products worth $200,000,000 to Japan, and Japan exports products worth $350,000,000 to the United States. Under the head of exports and imports, we shall have bills on Japan aggregating $200,000,000, and remittances to make aggregating $350,000,000.

The Japanese government and its nationals owe considerable sums to citizens of the United States; citizens of the United States owe lesser sums to citizens of Japan. Interest on these debts will be transmitted by way of exchange. Let us say that Japan must pay us $25,000,000, while we must pay Japan $5,000,000. This will add $25,000,000 to the total volume of bills, and $5,000,000 to the aggregate of remittances.

Some Japanese borrowers are paying off their debts to American capitalists; others are borrowing fresh capital. The sum of payments we will assume is greatly inferior to the sum of new loans. We will put the former at $5,000,000, the latter at $25,000,000. Under this head, then, we may add $5,000,000 to the volume of bills, $25,000,000 to the volume of remittances.

Americans living or traveling in Japan must have their incomes sent them from here; Japanese living or traveling here must have their incomes sent from Japan. Let us suppose that we must send $15,000,000 to our citizens in Japan; Japan must send $5,000,000 to her citizens here. This would add another $5,000,000 to the volume of bills, $15,000,000 to the volume of remittances.

Most of our trade with Japan is carried on by Japanese ships. We must, of course, pay for the service, and our payments must be sent to Japan. We will place the aggregate at $25,000,000. What we carry for Japan may be put at $15,000,000. So we must add $25,000,000 to the volume of remittances and $15,000,000 to the volume of bills.

DUE THE UNITED STATES		DUE JAPAN	
Exports	$200,000,000		$350,000,000
Interest	25,000,000		5,000,000
Proceeds of new loans,	25,000,000	Repayment of old loans	5,000,000
Japanese travelers' expenses	5,000,000	American travelers' expenses	15,000,000
Payment for ocean transportation	15,000,000		25,000,000
	$270,000,000		$400,000,000

Footing up the assumed items of indebtedness, we find that the United States can draw bills to the amount of $270,000,000, and must make remittances to the amount of $400,000,000. Exchange on Japan will be above par under these conditions.

If the United States and Japan formed a closed trading circle, having no other relations with other countries, exchange would rise to the point where it paid to ship gold to Japan, and it would continue at this point until enough gold had been shipped to cover the excess of debits over credits.

18. *The price of exchange on any country depends upon the balance of indebtedness between that country and all other countries, not upon the balance of indebtedness between that country and any particular country.*

For simplicity we assumed that the exchange relations between the United States and Japan were not complicated by relations with other countries. This assumption we must now abandon. Japan buys manufactures from England. England buys wheat from the United States. Now, it is evident that Japanese exporters to America will be glad to accept from American importers bills of exchange drawn on England, as these bills will be in demand among Japanese importers of British manufactures.

And so, even though Americans have to remit $400,000,000 to Japan, while Japanese have to remit only $270,000,000 to America, American exchange may still be above par in the Japanese market. Japan may have imported from England, France, Germany and Italy an excess of imports greater than $130,000,000, her excess of exports in the American trade, and exchange on America will serve to pay off debts to the European countries, which in turn will use the claims acquired from Japan to pay for excess imports from America.

19. *If other items of international payments remain unchanged, the price of bills of exchange is lowered by an increase in exports or a decrease in imports; it is raised by a decrease in exports or an increase in imports.*

If we assume that other items of international payments (transmission of capital, interest payments, travelers' expenses, payments for ocean transportation) remain constant, fluctuations in exchange will always follow fluctuations in exports and imports. If we increase our exports, imports remaining unchanged, the supply of bills increases, and their price tends to fall. If we increase our imports, exports remaining the same, the volume of remittances to be made increases, and exchange rises in price.

20. *Fluctuations in the rate of exchange tend to bring about a balance of international payments, through stimulating exports and discouraging imports, when exchange is above par, and through discouraging exports and stimulating imports when exchange is below par.*

When bills are above par, it is more than usually profitable to export goods. Let us suppose that in America the price of cotton is twenty cents a pound, while in Japan the price is twenty-five cents. If it costs four cents a pound to ship cotton from America to Japan, the exporter will make $1,000 on a 100,000 pound shipment, if exchange is at par. If exchange is at its maximum above par, the exporter will be able to sell his $25,000 bill for $25,250, thus adding $250 to his nominal profit of $1,000. If exchange is at its minimum below par, the exporter can get only $24,750 for his $25,000 bill, thus losing $250 of his nominal profit of $1,000. If a profit of $1,000 on 100,000 pounds of cotton is just sufficient to induce exporters to ship cotton, no cotton will be shipped if exchange is below par.

When exchange is below par, it is more than usually profitable to import goods. Let us suppose that it barely pays to import a certain kind of Japanese silks when exchange is at par; that under these conditions the importer makes only $100 on a $10,000 shipment. If exchange is at its lowest price, the importer can pay for his goods with a $10,000 bill costing only $9900. Thus he adds $100 to his profits. If exchange is at its highest price, and the importer must pay $10,100 for a $10,000 bill, the importer's anticipated profit is entirely wiped out.

It follows that there is a tendency for an excess of either exports or of imports to check itself. If our exports increase, other things equal, exchange falls, and this discourages further exports, but encourages imports. If our imports increase too rapidly, exchange rises, and this discourages further imports and encourages exports.

The fluctuations of the rate of exchange, then, have a tendency to create a balance of exports and imports — allowance made for other items of international indebtedness. Exports and imports, in the long run, must increase or decline together.

21. *If the difference in the general price level between two countries is so great that fluctuations in the price of bills of exchange cannot bring about a balance of payments, gold flows from the one country to the other until the price level becomes practically the same for both.*

But suppose that the margin between prices in two countries is so wide that it pays to export in spite of a low price for exchange, or to import in spite of a high price. In the former case, gold must be imported to pay for the exports; in the latter, gold must be exported to pay for the imports. Now, we saw in an earlier chapter that an increase in the supply of money tends to raise prices; a reduction of the money supply causes prices to fall. If, then, our prices are so low that men find it profitable to send an excess of commodities abroad for sale, to be paid for in gold, the condition must be transitory. For as the gold flows into the country, prices rise, and the exporters' gains grow smaller and smaller. If, on the other hand, general prices here are so high that it pays importers to bring into the country vast amounts of goods, to be paid for by exportation of gold, the condition must be equally transitory. With the efflux of gold, prices fall, and the profits of importers dwindle away. In the end more of our commodities become cheap enough to export; and so the balance between exports and imports is restored.

There are men who hold that the United States should endeavor to increase its exports, but systematically discourage importation. It is obvious that such a policy would be futile. If our exports increase, our imports will necessarily increase also, and *vice versa*. The fluctuations in the price of foreign exchange, and the effects of influx or efflux of gold, insure this result. Exports and imports are indissolubly united by natural law; governments can destroy both, but no policy can be successful which aims to foster the one while persecuting the other.

22. *Summary.*

Trade, both domestic and international, is based upon differences in productive powers. The trade between two nations may arise from the fact that each possesses exclusive powers of producing certain commodities; or it may arise from the fact that each is superior to the other in some particular branch of production. The differences in productive powers upon which international trade is based may be due to differences in the character of population, differences in traditions of workmanship, differences in natural endowment, or differences in supply of capital. Of these differences some tend to disappear with lapse of time, while others constantly increase in importance.

A country may profitably import commodities for the production of which it possesses natural advantages superior to those of the exporting country. This is often the case when the marginal productivity of labor and capital, and hence money cost of production, is higher in the former country than in the latter.

The trade between two countries is carried on through the mechanism of exchange. Gold payments are reduced to a mere settlement of balances; hence it may be said that international trade is essentially barter.

When exports exceed imports, other things equal, exchange falls below par; and this tends to encourage importation and discourage exportation. When imports exceed exports, exchange rises above par; and this tends to encourage exportation and discourage importation. Thus fluctuations in the rate of exchange tend to bring about an even balance of exports and imports. If for any reason the balance of trade inclines persistently in one direction or the other, gold is imported or exported, and this, through affecting prices both domestic and foreign, ultimately establishes an even balance of international exchange.

CHAPTER XX

THE REGULATION OF FOREIGN TRADE

1. *Foreign trade is subjected to governmental regulation chiefly under the form of taxation.*

Since early modern times a great part of the energy of governments has been expended upon the regulation of international trade. The reason for such regulation has been twofold. In the first place, there is a deep-rooted belief in the people of every nation that the national prosperity may be furthered by restrictions upon trade with foreigners. In the second place, such trade has long been recognized as a convenient and appropriate source of public revenue.

A century ago the policy of prohibiting the importation of some classes of goods, and the exportation of other classes, was widely followed. By the middle of the nineteenth century this policy had fallen into disuse, except in countries in a low stage of economic development, like Russia and some of the Balkan states, where the exportation of foodstuffs was prohibited in times of scarcity, in order to reduce the risks of famine. The Great War produced a reversion to an earlier stage of history in many parts of the field of trade. Every belligerent state prohibited the export of various commodities deemed essential to national security, and most of them prohibited the importation of various unessential commodities, as involving a strain upon the national credit resources. After the war prohibition of imports and exports was freely resorted to in central and eastern Europe, as an instrument for coercing an unfriendly neighbor. Omitting such abnormal cases, however, we may say that the regulation of foreign trade is everywhere carried on under the guise of taxation. If we wished to prohibit the importation of cotton from Egypt, we should place such high taxes upon imports of Egyptian cotton that no one would find it worth while to import it.

Taxes on foreign trade may be levied upon either imports or exports or upon both. Export taxes are generally unpopular, because of the common belief that it is a good thing to export as many goods as possible. During the Great War and for several years after, England levied heavy export duties on coal and secured considerable revenues from this source. In the United States export taxes are prohibited by the Constitution. We shall therefore confine our study to taxes on imports.

2. *Import taxes, or "duties," may be levied for the sole purpose of raising a revenue, or for the purpose of raising the price and thus discouraging the importation of commodities of classes that can be produced within a country. Taxes levied for the former purpose are called revenue duties; taxes levied for the latter purpose are called protective duties.*

All the tea used in the United States comes from foreign soil. A tax or "duty" of, say, five cents a pound would raise the price by five cents, but this would check importation in only a slight degree. Most of us would use as much tea, even at the higher price. A duty of $20 a ton on steel, on the other hand, would practically prohibit the importation of steel. For our own steel industry can produce steel almost, if not quite, as cheaply as that of any foreign country. Suppose that we can produce steel at $20 a ton while in some foreign country it can be produced at $17. If the cost of bringing steel from the foreign country is $2 a ton, foreign producers can sell steel here at lower prices than our own producers can afford to take. But if foreign steel is compelled to pay a duty of $20 a ton, none of it can be sold here, unless the American producers combine and force steel up to the price of $39 a ton. Such a duty, since it "protects" domestic producers against foreign competition, is known as a protective duty.

All duties levied upon imported goods of a character that cannot be produced in a country may be classed together as pure revenue duties. All duties levied on goods of a character that can be produced in a country are protective duties. Of course a duty the aim of which is the raising of revenue may be incidentally protective. Thus if we were to levy a duty on imported coffee, it would "protect" the coffee growers of Porto Rico. On the other hand, protective duties may incidentally yield a revenue. In the case employed above, if the duty on foreign steel had been $1 instead of $20, foreign steel would have continued to be imported, and thus a revenue would have been obtained. At the same time the foreigner would have been prevented from underselling the American; accordingly, the latter would have been "protected." Most of our duties are protective, but incidentally yield a revenue, as they are not high enough to prevent importation altogether.

The schedule of all duties levied by a country is known as the "tariff." A tariff consisting of duties whose main object is the raising of a revenue is known as a revenue tariff. Such a tariff has long been in force in England. It must necessarily be confined to a small number of items, since there are very few commodities that cannot be produced in a country of varied resources like the United States. Tea, spices, natural camphor, rubber, cocoanuts and similar tropical products are commodities that would be suitable for revenue duties. A protective tariff consists of duties whose main purpose is the protection of domestic producers against foreign competition. Such a tariff has been in force in the United States since early in the nineteenth century; its character has been most strongly marked since the Civil War.

3. *Revenue duties on imports are among the most convenient and most popular forms of taxation, partly because the taxpayer does not realize how heavy the taxes are, and partly because of the common belief that such taxes are borne by the foreigners who export the goods.*

Every government needs large funds for the maintenance of the numerous corps of officials and servants making up its civil and military establishments and for the meeting of other expenses incurred in the discharge of its various functions. These funds must be obtained chiefly through taxation. Two methods of raising taxes are open to the government. It may send its officials to each man's house, and levy upon his income or property. In this case it is said to levy direct taxes. The government may, on the other hand, impose taxes upon salable commodities as they are found in the hands of producers or dealers. The latter then add the tax, if they can, to the selling price of the commodities taxed. If the tax is very light, or if the producer is a monopolist who is already fixing prices at as high a point as the consumers will endure, it may be impracticable thus to shift the tax to the consumer. But in the case of all commodities produced under competitive conditions, the tax operates like an addition to costs and it reappears in the price. The buyer of the commodities thus bears ultimately all or the greater part of the tax. Such taxes are said to be indirect.

For such obvious and imperative needs of government as the construction of highways, the maintenance of courts and schools, the average citizen is willing to pay direct taxes, although he usually quarrels with the amount imposed upon him. When a war is to be financed, or preparations are making for a war that seems imminent, direct taxes, however onerous, will be borne without murmur. During the Great War income taxes in America were raised to a point where they absorbed over one-half of the income of many individuals, yet there was comparatively little outcry. After the war opposition to the high rates became more and more vigorous. Any new service to be undertaken at the expense of the treasury was resisted. And that may be said to be the normal condition. It is hard to finance through direct taxes scientific inquiry, public health inspection and the thousand and one inconspicuous but valuable creative activities of government. For this reason, national governments rely in normal times largely upon indirect taxes. The average citizen has no very clear idea as to the amount of taxes he pays in this way. Whenever you buy a pound of imported sugar (and most of our sugar is imported) you pay a tax. Whenever you buy English woolens or cottons or French silks, you are taxed. If you use tobacco in any form, you pay taxes on it. And so with a host of other commodities. How great is the aggregate yearly sum that you contribute to government in indirect taxes? You probably have not the least idea. But this is certain; if the entire amount were collected from you in cash at one time, you would be much less complacent about government enterprises involving heavy expense.

Of all indirect taxes, those levied on foreign trade are the most convenient. All foreign goods must cross the national frontier, where there are always officials and soldiers whose services can be employed in preventing goods from being secretly carried into the country. A few points through which such goods must pass may be designated; a comparatively small body of officials may be stationed at these points to levy and collect the taxes.

Another reason for the popularity of taxes on imports is that many persons believe that such taxes are borne by foreigners. If we tax British woolens, French silks, and German sugar, are we not compelling the British, French, and Germans to help pay the expenses of conducting our government?

4. *Import duties are, as a rule, borne by the consumer, not by the importer nor by the producer.*

Let us say that a given grade of woolen goods is produced in England at a cost of fifty cents a yard. Under the laws of competitive industry, the cloth sells in England for very nearly fifty cents. If the cost of bringing it to this country is one cent a yard, and there is no tax to pay on imports, the cloth will sell here for about fifty-one cents. Now if we place a duty of fifty cents a yard on the cloth, none of it will be sold here for less than the British price plus the cost of transportation plus the tax, or a dollar and one cent. The man who buys the goods for use pays the tax, in the last instance. And so with most import duties. Even those who talk most loudly about taxing the foreigner make haste to supply themselves with such imported goods as they may require in advance of any proposed increase in duties. They know by experience that the price will rise when the duties go into effect.

But will the price rise by the whole measure of the duty? That will depend on circumstances. After the Great War American manufacturers of coal tar dyes declared that even a high schedule of duties would not protect them against German competition, because the

German exporters would absorb the tax and sell dyes here as cheaply as before, rather than permit the development of an American dye industry. No doubt this danger was exaggerated. But the point is of some importance, nevertheless. A business which derives a large part of its income from foreign sales, if it possesses monopoly powers and can stand the loss, may assume all or a part of the duty levied upon its goods by a foreign government.

Again, when an industry is largely dependent upon a particular foreign market, a duty making access to that market difficult may produce a general reduction in the costs of that industry, and so make possible the resupplying of the foreign market at a price less than the original cost plus the duty. The raw silk industry of Japan is dependent, we will say, on the American market for a great part of the demand that sustains the value of its product. Suppose that we place so heavy a duty on raw silk as greatly to curtail its use in manufacture. The Japanese industry would find its products accumulating in its hands. There would be a slump in values, which would be reflected back in a reduction in the return to capital of the industry, and hence in a scaling down of capital values. There would also be a reduction in the wages of laborers engaged in the industry. Let us say that the duty in question amounted to fifty per cent on the value of the silk. It is possible that the readjustments in profits and wages would reduce costs by twenty-five per cent. In that case we should find that the fifty per cent duty, instead of raising prices by fifty per cent, was raising them by only twenty-five per cent. Our consumers and the Japanese producers would be dividing the tax between them.

We see, then, that there is a theoretical possibility of making the foreigner pay a considerable fraction of certain import duties. We should not, however, overrate this possibility. There are very few foreign industries so dependent on a particular foreign market as in our hypothetical case. British industries, for example, look to a world-wide market. If we make their access to the American market more difficult through increased duties, they sell more in other countries and less here, until we are willing to pay a price nearly equal to the old price plus the duties. Thus we pay practically the whole tax ourselves.

5. *Protective duties are sometimes advocated as a means of keeping money at home.*

While the raising of a revenue is an important object of every tariff, it is not the primary object of American tariff policy. That object is protection. A protective tariff is designed to foster domestic industry at the expense of the business of importation. Whether it does this or not is a question of great importance. We must see exactly how such a tariff affects, not merely isolated branches of industry, but the industry of a nation as a whole.

There is a very primitive view, unfortunately yet far from extinction, that it is an evil thing to buy anything from foreign producers — even the things that cannot be produced in the country at all. Those who hold to this view imagine that we must send abroad money to pay for all purchases, and money, they say, should be kept at home. We saw in the last chapter that the medium through which international payments are effected is, in normal times, bills of exchange. The shipping of gold from country to country is reduced, by the mechanism of exchange, to very small proportions. Now, the bills of exchange with which we pay for our imports are really due bills, representing the value of commodities that we export. We saw also that if a country for a time imports more than its exports will pay for, bills on foreign points rise in price, and this discourages further importation and encourages further exportation, until the proper balance between imports and exports is again restored. Accordingly, we may cheerfully proceed to import as large a volume of commodities as we may require. We shall not thereby run the risk of a serious drain upon our money supply; we shall merely make preparations for an unusually large and profitable export trade in the near future.

6. *There is no sound reason for discouraging importation from countries which do not take commodities in exchange.*

Some men who have advanced beyond the view that all importation of commodities is an evil yet cling to the belief that importation from countries that do not buy as much from us as we buy from them is to be discouraged. They argue that such trade must leave a balance which we must pay in gold, and this they regard as a net loss. About twenty-five years ago one of the administrative departments of our national government published a report containing the statement that our losses from trade with South America, during the preceding half century, had exceeded the cost of the Civil War. For we had purchased from those countries billions of dollars' worth of commodities in excess of their purchases from us. Of course, the facts in the case are, not that we sent billions of dollars in gold to South America, but that we paid the balance in bills on England. England was then buying more from us than she sold to us, and in her turn, was selling more to South America than she bought from that region. How could it have made any difference to us whether the goods with which we paid for South American products were actually consumed in South America or in England?

We buy more from Japan than we sell to Japan. Japan

buys more from the rest of the world than she sells. That means that in England, Italy, Germany, India and China, wherever Japanese purchases are in excess, there is a possible market for American goods. This market would not exist if we placed an embargo on trade with Japan the moment our imports from Japan exceeded our exports to that country.

The principle involved is that by its imports a nation helps to create a demand for its exports, and by its exports it finds means for financing its imports. This principle has been strikingly illustrated by the economic depression following the Great War. Because Russia had very little to export, she could import little, and the export industries of England and Germany suffered severely in consequence. Because Germany was unable to find satisfactory foreign markets for her industrial products, she could not import raw materials and foodstuffs so liberally as her natural requirements demanded. Hence low prices for American copper, cotton and agricultural products.

Thus we see not only that our own exports are dependent on our imports but that the prosperity of our foreign trade depends on that of all the countries associated in commercial intercourse. Russian exports decline; accordingly Russian imports decline. Although we have never had an important trade with Russia, our own trade suffers through the effect of Russian commercial collapse upon our customers in western Europe. International trade to-day ought to be looked upon as a vast coördinated movement, which brings prosperity or depression to all the countries that engage in it. Nothing could be more stupid than the practice of isolating certain elements in the trade of a particular nation and judging them good or bad without reference to their place in the general movement of international trade.

7. *The argument that the national wealth is necessarily reduced when one purchases from abroad commodities that can be made at home is fallacious.*

Slightly less shallow is the view that one should not buy from foreigners commodities that he can obtain from his fellow-citizens, even if the latter demand higher prices than foreigners are content to receive. If you wish to buy an automobile, it is urged, you should buy one of American make, even if you can get a better one of French make at the same price. By so doing you will increase the prosperity of the American automobile industry. You will enable the industry to employ more men at higher wages, and to pay higher dividends to those who have invested their capital in the industry. And if you are not sufficiently moved by patriotism to favor the industry of your fellow-citizens over that of foreigners, it is right that the government should compel you to do so, through the imposition of heavy duties.

The ulterior effects of a policy that compels American buyers to patronize the home industry are no less happy (so runs the familiar argument). The laborers and capitalists, being more prosperous, have more to spend on products for their own use. The capitalists erect mansions and the laborers build cottages, and this creates employment for carpenters, masons, and other craftsmen in allied trades. These in turn have more money to spend, and increase their purchases of clothes, provisions, and other articles of use. And so the beneficent effects of confining one's purchases of automobiles to the American industry are widely distributed throughout society.

In a similar way it is urged that we should buy all our sugar from our own producers. There is not much doubt that in ten years we could extend our production of sugar sufficiently to cover the demand for it, if we would but pay a sufficiently high price to tempt labor and capital into the industry. Instead of sending $100,000,000 abroad to fructify Cuban industry, we could keep it at home among our own workingmen and capitalists.

Let us see whether the foregoing argument will bear close examination. Assuming that we import $100,000,000 of sugar in a year, how do we pay for it? Not with gold, but with bills of exchange representing the value of commodities that we export.

Now suppose that we place so high a duty on sugar that importation ceases altogether. The immediate effect would be a reduction in the demand for foreign bills aggregating $100,000,000 per annum. Bills would, of course, fall below par; men exporting wheat and meat and cotton would get less for their products in consequence. The importation of commodities other than sugar would be stimulated, as we have seen, by the low price of bills. Exports and imports would have to be brought to a balance again, and this would come to pass through a shrinkage of exports and an increase of imports other than sugar. Perhaps we should buy annually $50,000,000 more of these other imports than we did before, and export $50,000,000 less of wheat, meat, and cotton than we formerly exported. The producers of sugar are indeed benefited by the elimination of foreign competition, but the producers of wheat, cotton, etc., are injured by the reduced prices of exports, and the producers of other commodities of which part of the supply is imported, are injured by the increase in importation of those commodities. Obviously enough, the evil ulterior effects of the losses of these two classes of producers cancel the beneficent ulterior effects of the gains of the sugar producers. The one effect of the duty that stands out without any corresponding offset is that we shall pay a higher price for sugar — certainly a result that no one can ardently desire.

8. *Protection of all industries is an impossibility.*

But suppose that the government places prohibitive duties on all imports. Will not this place all industries in a position where they may enjoy higher prices? A protective system, it is often said, is unjust when it singles out a few industries and grants them special favors. But it is just if it favors all industries equally.

An obvious objection is that if this were possible, if each industry were enabled to charge prices one hundred per cent higher, and each person, accordingly, received twice as large an income as he would otherwise have received, no one would secure any real benefit at all. If the income of each of us should be doubled, and we had to pay twice as much for everything that we buy, we should be no better off than we are now. But a more serious objection is this: no protective policy can raise the prices of all commodities. A duty can raise the prices only of articles that we are in the habit of importing. Now, if we import anything, we must export something to pay for it, and the export commodities must ordinarily represent as great a volume of values as the import commodities. Exports may exceed imports if a nation is making investments abroad; they may be inferior to imports if a nation is borrowing from abroad. But in the long run such operations do not destroy the fundamental relations of exports and imports. Sooner or later the lending nation will have to take back an excess of imports, and the borrowing nation will have to find an excess of exports.

Now, the price of a commodity that we export must be lower in this country than in the countries to which it is sent. The prices of wheat and cotton in America must be less than the prices of the same articles in England, since we are constantly exporting them. It is manifestly absurd to suppose that by placing duties on wheat and cotton imported into the United States we can raise the price of those commodities. Who would wish to import them into the United States? The duty on any export product is utterly ineffective.

We have seen that restrictions on our imports restrict our exports also. They do this by making it hard for foreign customers to pay for our goods. And this restriction on exports necessarily depresses their prices. An "all round" system of duties, in spite of itself, imposes a positive burden on as large a volume of industry as that which enjoys special favors under it.

9. *A plausible but fallacious argument for protection is that high wages in America cannot be maintained in free competition with low-wage countries.*

Another argument for protective duties runs as follows: The American laborer requires a greater measure of the necessaries and comforts of life than the laborers of any other country. His wages must therefore be higher. It follows that American enterprisers, having higher wages to pay, are at a disadvantage as compared with their foreign competitors. They must therefore sell their goods at higher prices; and this they would be unable to do if the foreign producer could bring his goods here without payment of duty. From this point of view the tariff is regarded as the bulwark of the American standard of living.

This argument can no more bear analysis than the preceding ones. All the export industries are able to pay the American scale of wages, and yet undersell their foreign competitors on foreign soil. These industries are hampered, not aided, by the protective system. Apart from the injury inflicted upon them by the restriction of the markets for their products entailed by import duties, these industries are rendered less profitable by the fact that many of their expenses are increased by the tariff.

Wheat and cotton growers are compelled to pay higher prices for agricultural implements, lumber, fertilizers, and other supplies because of the protective duties. The duties on iron and steel increase the costs of railway building and are reflected in higher freight rates, which represent a deduction from the net gains of the producers of the commodities that are carried to the ports by rail. If restrictions on imports reduce the amount of freight carried to this country from Europe, many ships are compelled to cross the ocean in ballast to carry away our exports; and this means that the exports have to pay ocean freights covering the costs of a return voyage, instead of a single passage of the ocean. Now, when we consider that in spite of all these disadvantages the export industries can retain the home market and invade foreign ones, we see clearly that a protective tariff is not needed to maintain the American rate of pay in all industry, although it may be necessary to maintain that rate in special industries — industries in which our advantages for production are less telling than they are in those industries that have succeeded in conquering a place for themselves in foreign markets.

10. *A policy which draws labor from the fields that are of greater natural productiveness to fields of lower natural productiveness tends to reduce wages.*

In order to gain a clear view of the relation of a protective duty to the rate of wages we must return to fundamental principles. In any country, as was shown in earlier chapters, wages are determined by the marginal productivity of labor. We will represent the various opportunities for employment that a country like the United States affords by the symbols A, B, C, and D. A may stand for a group of industries in which we have exceptional advantages over foreign countries. B stands for a group of industries in which our advantages are less, C one in which they are still less, and D the group of industries in which they are least of all. When our population is so small that all our labor can be engaged in the group represented by A, wages will be at their maximum. When our population increases so that some of the labor will have to be set at work in group B, the wages of all labor must decline to the level of productivity in that group. We will suppose that population has increased up to a point where the opportunities represented by A and B are fairly well manned, and wages are determined by the productivity of labor in B.

With wages thus determined, it is clear that no employer, without governmental aid, can afford to hire labor to exploit the opportunities represented by C and D. This would necessitate paying labor in C and D as much as it produces in B, and that, by hypothesis, is more than it produces in C and D.

Now let us suppose that a political party is in power which holds the belief that we should produce everything that we consume — that is, that the opportunities represented by C and D should be exploited as well as those represented by A and B. Labor must be drawn away from A and B and set at work in C and D. This involves the necessity of compensating enterprisers in some way for the disadvantages under which they will operate in C and D. Either wages must be reduced in A and B, or some form of subsidy must be granted to C and D.

The commodities that the industries composing C and D will produce have been hitherto, we assume, obtained from abroad through exchange for commodities produced by A and B. The government now renders this difficult by placing high duties on the former class of commodities. This means that producers in the groups A and B — both employers and workmen — must pay higher prices for what they buy. They do not receive higher prices for what they sell; in fact, they receive lower prices, as this, we have seen, is the effect of protective duties on export industries. It appears, then, that part of the disadvantage of producers in C and D is removed by reducing wages (estimated in purchasing power) in A and B.

After the duty has gone into effect and the prices of commodities that can be produced by C and D have risen sufficiently, enterprisers will be able to hire labor at the wages prevailing in A and B, and establish industries in C and D. So far as the remaining laborers in A and B buy the products of C and D, the difference between the price which they pay for those products and the price that they would pay if they were permitted to import those products duty-free is a tax paid not to the government, but to the producers in C and D, to enable the latter to remain in business. It is an uncompensated deduction from the natural earnings of the laborers in A and B. Their wages have been reduced; nor are the workers in C and D paid as much, estimated in purchasing power, as they would have received if they had been allowed to remain in A and B under the earlier conditions. The net effect of the imposition of the duty has been to saddle the self-supporting industries, A and B, with the support of the pauper industries, C and D. Yet the inventors of this policy have the effrontery to tell laborers in A and B that this policy is the bulwark of their high rate of wages!

The principles involved in the illustration may be stated in the following general terms: Wages in any country will be at the highest point when all the labor of that country is concentrated in the industries in which its relative advantages over other countries are greatest. If there are no protective duties whatsoever, employers will, as a rule, seek out the industries in which their country has the greatest relative advantages. Protective duties enable other industries to exist, but only through taxing the more productive industries for their support. Protection as a permanent policy means a slight reduction of money wages, and a greater reduction of wages estimated in purchasing power. Instead of a bulwark of the standard of living, protection is a serious menace to it.

11. *The strength of the protectionist policy consists largely in the fact that the good effects of the policy are more easily perceived than the evil effects.*

The arguments for protection that have been discussed so far are all manifestly fallacious. They are not therefore to be despised, since to hosts of men they appear to be absolutely irrefutable. And this, as Bastiat, a great French economist, was wont to say, is because the average man is unable to weigh the unseen effects of an economic policy against the effects that are seen. If we place a high duty on imported fabrics, the resultant high prices enable a new industry, employing thousands of workmen, to be established. This is the effect that is seen, and considered in itself, is wholly good. Every purchaser of the fabrics throughout the land is compelled to pay higher prices for them; but this effect is only dimly seen, if at all. In itself, it is wholly evil. Since part of what the new industry receives in this way from the public merely compensates that industry for the natural disadvantages under which it labors, it follows that the aggregate net gain to the industry is less than the aggregate net loss to the public. Again, the national production of wealth is increased by the amount that the new industry adds, and this effect of the duty is one that is seen. The national production is reduced by the amount that the labor and capital diverted to the new industry would have produced elsewhere; this effect is not seen. Yet the reduction in national production that the duty entails is greater than the increase due to it, since labor and capital are diverted from the branches of production enjoying greater natural advantages to branches enjoying lesser advantages.

12. *Protection increases the productiveness of labor and capital if it drives labor and capital out of the less productive into the more productive fields.*

In the foregoing discussion the assumption has been made that when left to themselves enterprisers will seek out the industries enjoying the greatest natural advantages. On this assumption, all that government can do is to force industry into the less productive fields — a policy that can result only in reducing the national production.

Now, while the assumption is ordinarily defensible, it is not universally valid. Enterprisers do not always know what fields offer the highest rewards. Furthermore, even if an enterpriser suspects that a given field, hitherto unexploited, would offer rich returns, conservatism may deter him from abandoning a field in which he is already gaining profits for a field in which he may gain larger profits, but in which he may also incur losses.

The men who govern a nation may be more far-sighted and more progressive than the business men of the same nation. The former class of men may become convinced that certain fields of production will be profitable long before the latter class will venture into those fields. The government, by placing duties upon the products that those fields might yield, makes success a certainty. Once the new industries are established, the duties can be removed without destroying them. The industry of the nation is enriched by the addition of fields of employment that are as good or better than those already under exploitation.

It must, of course, be borne in mind that this case is a rare one. It is not often that the statesman knows more about business than the body of business men themselves. Where, however, the government is manned by officials of a race intellectually superior to that of the governed, the national industry may be furthered in the way described.

13. *Protection may enable an industry of more than normal productiveness to surmount initial obstacles to success.*

Even when there exists no superiority of foresight on the part of those who make up the government, a government may often succeed in diverting industry from fields in which the natural advantages are less to fields in which they are greater. The United States has always possessed great natural advantages for the production of iron and steel. What it lacked, in its early period, was training in the art of working metals. The enterpriser was unacquainted with the best processes, and he had to use labor that had not acquired the skill and the traditions necessary for efficient production.

Now, the only way to acquire an art is to practice it. We had to make iron for a long time before we could become adepts in the art. A generation might have sufficed for establishing the industry in a particular locality; but what enterpriser would have undertaken to produce at a loss through a generation in order that some other enterpriser might ultimately conduct the business with a profit? Obviously, the case demanded governmental aid; and the government did indeed come to the aid of the industry, through the imposition of duties on imported iron and iron wares.

Long before the end of the nineteenth century the iron industry had become well established in certain parts of the East. It was still a new industry in the South and in Colorado. Although the Pennsylvania industry might have been able to get along without duties, it was urged that the newer centers still required protection. Was it not better to over-protect the established centers than to expose the newer centers to the full effects of foreign competition?

14. *When an industry is well established within a country, protection becomes unnecessary.*

After an industry has been well established within a country, it migrates without great difficulty to other parts of the same country, if natural conditions warrant. When the iron industry has been established in Pennsylvania, it readily migrates to Alabama or Colorado, if natural conditions are as good as they are in Pennsylvania or better. Processes that are in use in Pennsylvania can be transferred without cost to the other regions; a body of workers can be induced, without great difficulty, to migrate with the industry. There is far less reason for giving governmental aid to the newer centers than there was for giving it to the original one. Accordingly, we may say that it may be advantageous to protect an industry until it is well established within the national domain; if it is of a character that fits it for existence there, it will extend itself to other regions even if protection is withdrawn.

15. *In practice it is difficult to determine when protection should be withdrawn from an industry.*

When an industry has become firmly established, further protection is inexpedient and unjust, as it enables the industry to levy upon other industries that are self-supporting a tribute that it does not need. Here a practical difficulty arises. How can we determine just when an industry has passed through the period of infancy, and therefore should be left to shift for itself? We cannot find out from those who are engaged in the industry, since they are naturally desirous of a continuance of public aid, even though they do not need it; and those who are not engaged in the industry cannot tell.

At the annual banquets of the various manufacturers' associations, the boast is frequently made that we can manufacture more cheaply than any other nation on earth. But if Congress proposes to reduce duties, the same men soberly declare that our industries will be ruined if this is done. And shall Congress, in its search for truth to enlighten it, appeal from the manufacturers pleading soberly the handicaps under which they labor to the manufacturers off their guard and intoxicated with success? The fact is, it is almost impossible for a government to determine just when a protective duty can be removed. As a result every nation retains many such duties long after they have lost all efficacy for doing anything but harm. Accordingly, there is good reason for the view that reckless experimentation in the establishment of new industries is to be avoided.

16. *The establishment of industries that will never be able to maintain themselves without protection should be avoided.*

A stronger reason for cautious action lies in the fact that an industry established by the aid of a protective duty may never develop sufficiently to maintain itself without governmental aid. The natural conditions upon which it is based may be so unfavorable, relatively to the conditions in other countries, that the industry, if established, will be destined to remain forever a burden upon the public — a pauper industry. Let us suppose that in a given branch of industry a commodity can be produced here at a cost of $1, while it can be obtained from abroad for fifty cents. Without government aid, no enterpriser can afford to undertake its production. Now, let us assume that a statesman, eager to see the United States producing every possible kind of goods, succeeds in placing a duty of fifty cents on the imported article. The price to consumers must then rise to $1, a price sufficient to induce American enterprisers to produce the goods.

After all the initial difficulties, such as training a force of men, establishing market conditions, etc., have been overcome, the cost of producing the article may fall to seventy-five cents, and remain there. This is the natural American cost of it. If the duty is removed, the foreign article will again be sold for fifty cents. The men who have put their capitals into the industry will have to close down their plants and discharge their workmen. The buildings and machinery used in the industry will probably be worth almost nothing for any other purpose. The skill acquired by the workmen, at great cost of time, perhaps, will be equally worthless. The removal of the duty, therefore, involves the ruthless destruction of what to those who have put their capital and skill into the industry are bona fide means of wealth production, although from the national point of view the industry makes no net addition to wealth, but rather leaves us poorer than we should be if the industry were dismantled.

The question naturally arises, is it right to call an industry into existence by governmental action, and later abandon it to the mercies of foreign competition? There can be but one answer: It is not right. The government did wrong in calling into existence an industry that would never be able to survive unaided. It does wrong again when it abandons this ill-begotten industry to die of starvation. If, however, the industry is not abandoned, it is a perpetual expense to the self-supporting industries of the country. A human pauper dies in the end, but a pauper industry may live on forever.

17. *Protection may serve a useful purpose in encouraging the development of industries that make no drain upon the natural resources of a country, and retarding the development of industries that destroy such resources.*

A protective tariff may sometimes be defended on the ground that it preserves the natural resources of a country against wasteful exploitation. If the government does not restrict international trade, we may, as a rule, assume that enterprisers will seek out the fields in which a given quantity of labor and capital will produce the largest amount of value, or the fields in which our advantages over foreign countries are greatest. Let us suppose that one of those fields is the growing of wheat. In most parts of the United States wheat culture represents a heavy drain upon the fertility of the soil. Land devoted to constant wheat cropping becomes almost exhausted in a generation. Accordingly, when one sells a bushel of wheat, he sells not only the product of his labor and capital, but a part of the natural heritage of his country. But why should he care? After his field is worn out, his years will probably be few. The next generation may be left to repair the wastes of this generation.

Let us assume that coal and iron mining and the production of petroleum are other industries in which we have great natural advantages. Enterprisers, if left to themselves, would employ vast amounts of labor and capital in exploiting these natural resources. Every year we should send away from our country these commodities, representing not merely the annual product of our labor and capital, but also a part of our irreplaceable natural wealth. In a few generations we should be, as a nation, impoverished.

We have seen that protection places a burden upon the

industries in which we have, for the present, great natural advantages, in order to build up industries in which our natural advantages are less. If the industries that are naturally most productive are of the kind that waste the natural wealth of the country, it is a statesman's proper policy to impose burdens upon them and so reduce the extent to which they are carried on, in favor of industries which involve no waste of resources, even though the annual production of wealth is thereby diminished for a time.

The same argument, of course, condemns protection under other circumstances. According to conservative official estimates, we are using up, each year, four times as much lumber as we are growing. The rising price of lumber stimulates the activity of the woodsman to greater and greater remorselessness. Our mountains are denuded, and the waters, formerly held back by the forest covering and allowed to feed the rivers with regular flow, now sweep down the slopes in devastating flood. Obviously, we should endeavor to stimulate importation of lumber; if necessary, we should give a bounty on imports, that the price of lumber might be reduced and our few remaining forests saved. But the destroyers of our natural heritage demand protection in their pernicious pursuit, and we accord it to them.

18. *Protection may serve the purpose of encouraging the development of industries that are favorable to the health of the laborer.*

If extractive industries, prosecuted too relentlessly, waste the natural wealth of a country, manufacturing industries, prosecuted in the same way, waste its men. The population of a manufacturing center does not usually compare favorably, in health and vigor, with the population of rural districts. Indeed, it is doubtful whether an exclusively urban, manufacturing population can in the long run escape physical degeneration. It might therefore be good policy in a country so largely devoted to manufactures as England to impose protective duties on imported agricultural products, with a view to increasing the proportion of the population employed upon the land. This would indeed burden the manufacturing population; it would for many years reduce the product of the national industry. But in view of the ultimate effect upon the character of the population, this policy might be a good one from the point of view of the statesman, who must consider not merely the prosperity of this year and next, but also that of the remotest generations.

19. *A country should be able to provide itself with means for producing commodities essential to the successful conduct of a war; and in many cases can make such provision most conveniently through protection.*

A protective duty is defensible when it serves to maintain facilities for the production of articles of national necessity, the supply of which might be cut off by war. War vessels can be built in Great Britain at far less cost than in the United States. In time of peace we should make important savings by having our war vessels built in Great Britain. If we were engaged in a war, however, we could not have warships built in Great Britain, whether that country were hostile or neutral. Yet it is precisely at such a time that we should most need to increase our navy. Prudence therefore demands that we should provide ourselves, in time of peace, with establishments capable of turning out warships; and this involves giving them work to do.

It is a moot question whether the creation of facilities for constructing merchant ships stands on the same footing. In former times, certainly, a merchant fleet was an indispensable auxiliary to a fighting fleet. The merchant fleet furnished trained seamen, and many merchant vessels were capable of speedy transformation into warships. In the Great War some fast merchant ships were pressed into service as auxiliary cruisers, and vast numbers served as transports and supply ships.

It is, however, a relatively small proportion of commercial shipping that is adaptable to use in war. Obviously public aid based on motives of national defense should be narrowly restricted to shipping of this character. Moreover, the tendency of the times is toward the restriction of naval warfare. At a time when the chief naval powers join in agreements to sink a considerable part of their war vessels, there is something illogical in a policy of public aid for the construction of ships that might serve as auxiliary war vessels.

Many industries that are not designed directly for the supply of articles of military necessity may be placed in the same class. In order that we may have high explosives in sufficient quantity for war, it is necessary to develop our facilities for making coal tar dyes, which are based on the same material as high explosives. In order that we may be able to construct ships and produce guns and other instruments of war, we must have men who are trained in metal working; and if there is no other way of maintaining such a force of workmen, we should create and maintain an iron and steel industry through protective duties. It is, however, to be borne in mind that the maintenance of an industry large enough to cover all the demand for iron and steel in time of peace cannot be urged on grounds of national defense.

20. *A policy which aims to make a country completely independent of the products of other countries is more likely to create weakness than strength in war.*

There are some writers who extend the principle of national self-sufficiency to an unwarranted extreme. They would have every nation produce practically every article that it consumes, in order that in time of war there might not be the least interruption of supplies. These persons exaggerate the dependence of one country upon any other country against which it may at some time wage war. England, every one knows, does not produce enough grain to feed her population. And this fact exposed her to great danger during the Great War. There were indeed times, during the period of greatest submarine activity, when no one could be absolutely certain that England would not be forced out of the war.

Yet the difficulty was overcome. The technical abilities at the command of a modern nation at war are so great that the appearance of any new weapon of offense quickly evokes means of defense to neutralize it. England found means in the end to assure herself of adequate supplies, in spite of the submarine. Germany, though cut off from vital sources of supply, did not succumb for that reason, but through want of military resources adequate to withstand her increasing number of enemies.

The strength of a nation in time of war does not depend upon its ability to produce everything that its inhabitants consume. Rather, it depends upon the valor and number of its men, and upon its general wealth. Other things equal, a rich nation will overcome a poor one in war. Great Britain has proved formidable because of her wealth. Now, the endeavor to make a nation absolutely self-sufficing would end in making it much poorer than it would be if it used its resources in a more economical way. If England had pursued throughout the nineteenth century a policy of self-sufficiency, she would have been forced to content herself with a limited population and a modest industry. Instead of holding the rôle of the most powerful European state, she would be little more than a satellite of the more populous states of the mainland.

21. *Duties imposed by way of retaliation are seldom advantageous to the country that imposes them.*

One further possible justification of duties designed to discourage importation requires examination. Other countries impose duties upon American products crossing their borders. Therefore, it is said, we should impose import duties on the products of such countries, by way of retaliation. Let us see whether this position is tenable.

If England were to place a high duty on American meats, the persons who would be injured most seriously are the English consumers of meat. The English producer of meat would gain an advantage, but this, under ordinary circumstances, would not be commensurate with the loss to the English consumer. The world demand for American meat would be somewhat reduced, and this would reduce the price of it slightly. A small injury, therefore, would be inflicted upon the American producer of meat.

Now let us suppose that in retaliation we levied extraordinary duties on British woolens. The chief sufferer would be the American consumer of woolens. The American producer would gain, but not commensurately. The world demand for English woolens would be reduced, and this would slightly reduce the price of them. Thus, in order to punish England for inflicting a large loss on British consumers and a small one on American producers, we should be inflicting a large loss on American consumers and a small one on British producers.

But retaliation is war, and in war the petty rules of logical conduct are not often observed. The important question is this: would the policy of retaliation effect its purpose? Would it compel England to remove the obnoxious duty? In all probability, no. After the duty on meat had been in force for some time, British producers would increase their facilities for producing that article. To remove the duty and expose to the mercies of foreign competition the men who had invested their capital in good faith would be a policy as unjust as it would be unpopular. Similarly, American enterprisers would extend their facilities for producing woolens, and this would give them an equitable claim to a continuance of the duty. The only result of retaliation is the institution of permanent protection. If permanent protection is desirable, it should be undertaken without reference to the way in which a foreign government conducts its own affairs. If it is undesirable, it should not be undertaken at all.

22. *Summary.*

Protective duties may be defensible (1) when they make possible the introduction of an industry which in a reasonable time will compare favorably in productivity with industries that are already self-supporting; (2) when they preserve the natural resources of a country from wasteful exploitation; (3) when they preserve the vigor and progressiveness of the population through the maintenance of a just balance between manufacturing and agriculture, city and country; and (4) when they make possible the maintenance of industries that add materially to a country's strength in time of war. In any case such duties are a burden upon the national wealth, at the time when they are instituted, and often for an indefinite time thereafter, and whether the benefit to be gained is a due compensation for the burdens involved is a question demanding in each case careful consideration. Duties that are designed to raise wages or to increase the national wealth by building up industries for which we have no special advantages, are founded in a delusion. They are rendered possible only by the fact that the ordinary mind does not weigh their unseen disadvantages against the advantages that are patent to view.

CHAPTER XXI

THE RELATIONS OF GOVERNMENT TO THE ECONOMIC ORGANIZATION

1. *The economic and the legal systems of a country are, in a measure, interdependent.*

The economic world with the study of which we have been engaged is a world of free private enterprise. Its motive forces are the acts of individuals, each seeking to further his own material interests. When such individuals buy or sell material possessions or personal services, they take little thought of the interests of society as a whole, and are little concerned with the wishes or the will of society. Yet the will of society plays a part in all these transactions, for they are shaped with tacit reference to the law. The individual is free to pursue his own interests only within the limits set by the positive law of the land.

If we attempt to contrast the present economic state with the state that would probably exist were there no political organization of society, we shall realize that the will of society, as expressed in the acts of government (employing the term in its broadest sense), has played an exceedingly important part in economic evolution. Without institutions, either customary or legal, assuring to each man the undisturbed possession of material goods acquired in ways recognized as legitimate, economic life could hardly have developed beyond the hunting or, at farthest, the pastoral stage. Without institutions giving binding force to contracts for the future delivery of goods and services, economic life could not have passed beyond the stage in which the small artisan produced goods, on his own account, for a narrow local market. Progress in governmental institutions has been a necessary condition of substantial economic progress. On the other hand, it was in large measure progress in economic life that necessitated progress in governmental institutions. It was the development of trade that broke down the feudal system and made possible, first the absolute monarchy and later representative government. Political institutions may long resist the forces of economic change, but sooner or later they yield. Some of the most serious practical problems of to-day have their origin in the fact that political evolution has not kept pace with economic. Our political machinery, which developed under simpler economic conditions, appears in many instances incapable of maintaining justice under present complex conditions.

2. *The basis of economic policy in almost all modern states is free private enterprise, or laisser-faire.*

A government may limit its economic activities to the defense of private property and the maintenance of the obligation of contracts. It may assume the function of determining the conditions under which economic transactions are carried on, and may even interfere in their terms. It may engage directly in the production of goods and services. In the first case the government is said to pursue a "let alone" or *laisser-faire* policy; in the second case, a regulative or "paternalistic" policy; in the third, a socialistic policy. In general, the basis of modern economic policy is *laisser-faire.* It is true that the regulation of an industry by government is a frequent phenomenon, and the direct participation by government in the production of commodities and services is an important factor in economic life. In Russia under the Soviet government all industry was, in theory, socialized, although practical considerations dictated many concessions to the principles of free enterprise, as for example the recognition of permanent land tenure for the peasants and tolerated "speculation," or trade. Nevertheless, an overwhelming majority of modern economic transactions are carried on by private individuals, subject to no direct interference on the part of the government.

The question may arise whether the existence of protective tariffs in most of the countries of the world does not make it necessary to qualify the statement that *laisser-faire* is the basis of modern economic policy. In effect, the United States government prevents us from buying English steel, and compels us to buy steel of American manufacture. Yet the method by which it does this does not resemble the method of governmental regulation, to be discussed below. The government imposes the condition that every ton of steel crossing our borders shall pay a certain tax. This condition met, the steel becomes an article to be dealt in freely. In buying or selling it men consult only their self-interest. The imposition of the duty creates a steel industry in this country; but the method by which this is done is very different from the method of governmental production. Prices are enhanced; and this leads individuals, in the pursuit of their private interests, to engage in steel production. The government, as it were, creates a favorable soil in which free enterprise may flourish. We may, therefore, say that the existence of customs barriers does not render necessary a qualification of the statement that the economic policy of modern governments is based upon the principle of *laisser-faire*, or free enterprise.

3. *The question whether the system of free private enterprise is conducive to a high degree of human welfare demands consideration.*

The system of free enterprise has been at once the subject of extravagant praise and of savage criticism. Some writers attribute to it all the progress in civilization that the last centuries have witnessed. To these writers every encroachment by government upon the domain now occupied by private enterprise is fraught with grave dangers. Other writers regard the system as wholly corrupt, and hope to see it replaced either by a system under which all economic activities are minutely regulated by government, or by one in which the government itself carries on all production of wealth in behalf of society as a whole.

An exhaustive treatment of these opposing views would carry us far beyond the scope of the present work. We may, however, consider briefly whether, on the whole, the system of free enterprise meets the tests of fairness and of social expediency. If it does this in the main, there still remains a distinguishable field in which individual enterprise should be subjected to governmental regulation, and yet another field in which the government should take a direct part in the production of wealth. A part of our task must be to find the boundaries of the respective fields, if such boundaries really exist.

4. *From the point of view of production the system of free private enterprise has proved highly effective.*

There can be no question that the productive power of man has been immensely increased in the two or three centuries in which enterprise has been accorded a fair measure of freedom by government. Improvements in methods of production and the formation of large accumulations of capital have reduced greatly the amount of toil necessary for the maintenance of human life. The amount of commodities placed at the disposal of the average man has been vastly increased. Relief from toil and command over commodities are not tantamount to well-being; but they serve at least as a basis of well-being.

It would be unjustifiable to ascribe the entire sum of

progress in production to freedom of enterprise. Many other causes have contributed to this progress; but there is no doubt that many inventions have been made with a view to the profits that might flow from them; and the wide introduction of improved processes of production has been largely the result of the pursuit of profit.

Moreover, the relative efficiency of the system of free enterprise, as compared with earlier systems, should not blind us to the fact that it still falls far short of any reasonable standard of production. Waste of natural resources, of capital and labor is present in every industry. Much of this waste may be obviated by more skilful management, but part of it is inherent in the competitive system. Competing enterprisers have two objectives, the one, to supply their consumers, the other, to secure advantages over one another. Often the latter involves the application of labor and capital to unproductive uses.

5. *From the point of view of the distribution of wealth the system of free private enterprise presents grave defects.*

One of the patent results of the system of free enterprise has been the formation of classes differing greatly in their command over wealth. Inequalities in fortune were probably never greater than they are to-day. It cannot be said that the poor are poorer than they were in earlier stages of the world's history, but it is quite possible that the wretchedness of the poor in our great and wealthy cities is greater than was the case in earlier times. It is a fair inference from the law of diminishing utility that a unit of purchasing power in the hands of a rich man does not afford so much satisfaction as an equivalent unit in the hands of a poor man. If our national income were more equally distributed, the sum of our national happiness would be greater, for any given moment of time. Possibly the ultimate result of an equalization of income would be to reduce production and so in the end to impair the incomes of all. In that case there is a contradiction between the interests of the present and the future. We may conclude that as between present inequalities and future economic decay the former is the lesser evil. None the less inequality is an evil in itself, and in each case can be justified only by its specific relation to the release of productive energies, in the present or in the future.

6. *In the apportionment of profits among enterprisers, the relation between inequalities and the interests of production is easily established.*

Under competition any enterpriser may engage in any branch of production, and create and sell wares to his best advantage. Any enterpriser may make a calculation of costs and prices in the various branches of production. If prices are high in one field, relatively to cost, enterprisers in that field reap profits quite out of proportion to any superiority they may exhibit over enterprisers in other fields. That is an evil in itself, but it bears its own remedy with it. New enterprisers press into the field; the supply of the commodity is increased, and its price falls. Thus the high rewards given to enterprisers in the field are an inducement to the expansion of production; the low rewards in another field give warning that less of the product of that field is wanted by society. The unequal treatment of enterprisers is the means by which society compels them to direct their forces in such a way as best to meet society's needs. The inequalities are salutary in their effects; when there is no longer an improper distribution of productive energies, they cease to exist. In some instances, however, the enterprisers succeed in erecting barriers against the entrance of competitors, and thus secure a character of permanence for their high profits. This is the typical case of monopoly. The consumers are forced to pay year after year prices quite high enough to encourage an expansion of production, but no expansion takes place. The evil of inequality persists: the corrective influence is abortive. It is the constant endeavor of a democratic economic policy to do away with conditions making for profits of this character.

7. *Inequalities in wages and interest operate under competition to correct themselves.*

If in any industry wages are above the average, due allowance made for relative agreeableness and safety of employment, labor tends to flow into that industry from industries in which wages are below the average. Wages then fall in the former industry and rise in the latter. The initial inequalities in wages signified that there was too much labor in some fields, too little in the others, and the very fact of inequalities of reward helped to correct this condition. Similarly, there is a tendency toward equality of rewards for invested capital.

But just as enterprisers may corner a field and fix profits at a permanently high level, so a labor organization may raise barriers to prevent the natural flow of labor into a fruitful field, and an organization of financiers may establish a high rate of interest in a fruitful field of investment. Such labor and capital monopolies are more difficult to maintain than monopolies engineered by enterprisers. In so far as they exist, they defeat the trend toward equal rewards for equal services, and are socially injurious.

8. *When general profits are high forces are set in motion which tend to reduce them. Similar corrective influences operate against high interest and wages.*

In times of rising prices it often happens that practically all enterprisers, not merely those who are unusually efficient, reap important profits. Such general profits are in the nature of a windfall, and correspond to no additional service performed. They emphasize economic inequality, an evil in itself. But they lead to an attempt on the part of every enterpriser to increase his production, in order to participate more freely in the common good fortune. The result is a competitive bidding for labor and capital and a forcing up of wages and interest.

Similarly, if the scarcity of capital or the opening of new opportunities for investment raises interest to a high level, forces are set in motion that tend to draw it back. Saving is stimulated even among those who are not immediate beneficiaries of the high rates of interest and those who are beneficiaries have increased incomes out of which to make new savings. Unusually high wages draw immigrants into a country, and if continued through a generation, may affect the natural increase in population.

It is on the basis of such considerations that it is often argued that no political intervention is necessary even if profits or interest are inordinately high. Say that they are oppressively high; yet the vice carries its own correction with it. This argument has much to commend it when it is applied to normal conditions. Under abnormal conditions, as for example during a war or in the economic disorders following a war, the correction often lags too far behind the evil. At such times the regulative powers of the state are often required to control prices and incomes and to prevent the development of socially injurious inequalities.

9. *When the parties to a contract are unequal in skill and strength, injustice is likely to result.*

An economic system based upon free enterprise will be just and socially expedient only when the parties to each contract stand on a footing of substantial equality. In the first place, the buyer must know the properties of the goods offered to him as well as the seller knows them; the laborer must know the risks and inconveniences attaching to a given employment as well as the employer knows them. When an unscrupulous horse dealer foists upon an unsuspecting buyer an animal with a hereditary taint of character or defect of body, the social welfare is in some degree reduced. The seller receives wealth, not for his services, but for his rascality; the buyer parts with his money, not for utilities, but for "experience." If all trade were of this nature, as much of it was among the ancient Greeks, we should, like the ancient Greeks, regard trade and piracy as twin callings.

10. *Free enterprise results in approximate justice only under competition.*

In the second place, the buyer must be in a position to deal with any one of several sellers, each acting independently of the others, and the seller must be able to offer his wares to any one of several independent buyers. The laborer must have the option of selling his services to any one out of a number of independent employers, and the employer must have the option of selecting from among a number of workmen. In other words, competition must exist on both sides. Otherwise the seller or the buyer, the laborer or the employer, is in danger of being forced to accept terms that are manifestly unfair.

Of the two conditions stated, the latter — the existence of competition — is the more important. If competition is active, the seller of wares will point out their good qualities, and his competitors will point out their bad ones. Even an ignorant buyer is thus in some measure protected against injustice. When one party to a contract has no competitors to fear, knowledge on the part of the other is of little avail. There is a certain town which I can reach only by traveling over a particular railway line. The line is in very bad shape; the ties are rotten and the rails are light; the cars are old and unsanitary. Travel on this line involves an unduly large measure of danger and discomfort. Yet I must buy tickets over the line, because I have no alternative.

11. *The government must regulate the conditions and terms of economic contracts when its failure to do so results in substantial injustice.*

Now, if there were merely sporadic cases in which contracts are made under conditions that make possible a wide departure from fairness, there would be little need for governmental intervention. But when there is an extensive field in which such conditions prevail, the need for governmental intervention becomes imperative.

In early times the producer and the consumer were, as a rule, neighbors. The tailor and his customer lived in the same village. If the tailor worked under unsanitary conditions, the customer had a chance of knowing it. If the tailor substituted inferior materials, trusting to the customer's ignorance, the deception was likely to make itself known in the wearing of the garments, and react unfavorably upon the tailor's business reputation. Fair dealing, under the circumstances, was a prerequisite of business success, and the man who dealt dishonestly sooner or later reaped the due harvest of his misdeeds.

To-day the man who makes your clothes may live a thousand miles away from you. He may be suffering from an infectious disease as he works upon your garments. You cannot know it. The milk that you drink may come from a dairy one hundred miles away, where no attempt is made to prevent its contamination with the germs of disease. The appearance of the milk gives you no warning of the fact. Only an expert can tell you whether the goods you buy are honest and sanitary; and you can probably ill afford to employ a corps of experts to investigate the hidden qualities of the things you buy.

The workman in a large factory is in a similar position of helplessness. He cannot estimate the degree of danger that unfenced machinery represents. He cannot tell whether ventilation is adequate, or whether dust and noxious gases are properly disposed of. Furthermore, he is often unable to judge correctly as to the number of hours that he can toil daily without undermining his health.

Not less significant than the separation of consumer from producer has been the development of combinations of producers. In many fields, buyers have virtually only one seller to deal with. In this state of affairs, there is no way in which the consumer can enforce a demand for wares of good quality, if wares of poor quality are more profitable. The employee of a monopoly may know that unsanitary conditions prevail in its shops, but he may be unable to find other employment. Furthermore, the prices of monopolized products are likely to be unreasonably high, and this means that the monopolist takes from the aggregate income of society a larger share than his services warrant.

12. *The government may be called upon to regulate the quality of goods or of services.*

Governmental regulation of the quality of commodities was exceedingly common in the Middle Ages. The weight of the loaf of bread, the width and quality of fabrics, were determined by public authority. With the development of modern industry much of this regulation fell into disuse. Competition was permitted to regulate the quality of commodities as it regulated their prices. The mediæval kind of regulation has, however, survived in a few instances, where the retention by a country of a valuable branch of trade forbids individualistic tampering with the traditional standards of quality. The Persian government endeavors to suppress the use of aniline dyes in the manufacture of rugs, on the ground that the employment of these dyes will ultimately destroy the foreign demand for Persian rugs. The Japanese government inspects all mattings produced for export, and regulates their quality.

The regulation of the quality of goods in most modern states has for its chief purpose the preservation of the public health. The use of certain ingredients in foods is forbidden; the use of other ingredients is limited to certain fixed proportions. An attempt is made to insure the production of many classes of goods under conditions limiting the risk of transmission of disease from worker to consumer. Some modest efforts are made to protect the consumer against the grosser kinds of fraud, such as short weights and measures. In the United States oleomargarine may not be palmed off on the consumer for butter. But cotton and shoddy may freely be sold for wool; paper may be freely substituted for leather in shoe soles. There is so much difficulty in administering laws directed against such practices that the government usually follows the easy rule, *caveat emptor*, "Let the buyer look out for himself."

The regulation of quality is carried farther in the case of certain goods and services furnished by enterprisers enjoying a monopolistic position. The quality of gas to be furnished to the inhabitants of a city by a private company is commonly prescribed by public authority. The service of passenger transportation by street and steam railways is often subject to regulation as to quality. In these cases regulation is usually defended on the ground that the enterprises are of a *quasi*-public nature. But any enterprise which obtains a monopoly of a branch of production is, from an economic point of view, in the same position. If a powerful monopoly controlled the iron and steel business of the United States, it might find it profitable to use ores rich in phosphorus or sulphur in the production of iron destined to be transformed into steel rails. This would result in the frequent breaking of rails and menace the safety of all travelers; it would therefore be necessary in the end for government to regulate the quality of steel produced.

There is, of course, a danger that the government may go so far in the regulation of quality as to check legitimate improvements. It is seldom expedient to leave much latitude of judgment to administrative officials. That would be to open the door to corruption. Accordingly fairly rigid standards must be laid down, and these will resist change stubbornly. The progress of science is continually elaborating new tests of quality, and the best type of producer applies them as soon as they are known. Such tests would come into operation, in administrative practice, only after much time had elapsed. Obsolete tests and "red tape" would somewhat slow up the progress of industry. But in spite of this danger it must be admitted that the principle of regulation of quality is salutary, and that the scope of regulation is destined to extend itself in future.

13. *A government may regulate the prices of commodities or services.*

Governmental regulation of the prices of commodities and services was also exceedingly common in the Middle Ages. In modern times such regulation is normally limited to the field of the so-called *quasi*-public enterprisers. The charges of railway companies, of gas and electric light companies, of telephone and telegraph companies, and even of such petty enterprises as the carriage of passengers in cabs and similar conveyances, are commonly regulated by law. Such regulation is not actually based upon any economic ground, but upon the legal ground that the enterprises in question perform functions that the state has often performed, use the public highways, or employ public powers in obtaining rights of way.

From an economic point of view, all the enterprises mentioned except the last ought to be subject to governmental price regulation, because they are monopolies. Without such regulation, a railway company might, if it chose, levy such heavy charges upon the carriage of goods away from and into a particular locality as to destroy the business of that locality and reduce the value of property situated there to almost nothing. If the railway is the only means of transportation from a mining district, by raising rates it can reduce the profits of mine owners to *nil* and force the closing of the mines. It can then buy up the mines at a very low figure, and operate them profitably on its own account. True, this is an extreme case; yet it illustrates very well the evils that an unregulated monopolistic determination of transportation charges would entail.

If a monopolistic combination succeeded in gaining complete control of the business of mining coal, its powers for extortion would be as great as those of the railway in our example. What would one give rather than pass a Northern winter without coal? Not all that one has, but a good part of it. If we must inevitably see an extension of monopolistic enterprise, as many believe, it is inevitable that we shall see an extension of the principle of governmental price regulation.

In time of war the policy of price regulation is applied over a wide field. In the uneasy state of the public mind buyers' panics are easily engineered, and may result in enormous losses to the public through inflated prices. Most governments, during the Great War, had to intervene for the control of the prices of various necessaries of life. Bread, sugar, and coal were among the commodities most generally subjected to pirce control.

14. *A government may regulate the conditions under which labor is performed.*

So long as economic organization remained simple, there was comparatively slight need for governmental regulation of the conditions under which labor was performed. A large proportion of those who toiled were their own employers, and these could be counted upon to keep their work places in tolerably sanitary condition, and to limit their hours of labor and the intensity of their exertion to the degree that considerations of health demanded. Those who worked for wages enjoyed, as a rule, conditions as favorable as those of the workmen who were their own employers. The advent of the factory system changed conditions materially. Men, women, and children were congregated in great masses, under the supervision of overseers, many of whom were bent upon getting the maximum possible service from the workers under them at whatever cost to the worker's health and happiness. Machinery took a place in the productive series, and the workers were forced to adapt themselves to the speed of the machines. Competition between manufacturers led to a longer and longer working day, and to greater and greater intensity of effort. The worker, seeking employment, was in no position to stipulate that the working day should be limited to a reasonable number of hours, or that the labor should not be so intense as to be destructive of the health of the laborer.

Society, it is clear, cannot afford to see the vitality of its working classes sapped in an effort to raise to its maximum the immediate production of wealth. An individual employer may profitably pursue the policy of hiring a set of workmen, wearing them out in a few years, and replacing them by another set. From the viewpoint of society this policy is as wasteful as it is cruel. The daily exertion of each man should be restricted to such measure that he may live a life of normal length, enjoying the normal number of years of health and usefulness.

When laborers are associated in strong unions, they may be able, without governmental aid, to reduce the hours of labor to the measure that is desirable from a social point of view. Each organization is composed of workers of various ages, and there is a natural tendency to maintain a pace that is not too rapid for the older workers, hence not so rapid as to destroy the physical health of the younger men.

But strong trade unions control only a small part of the economic field. Such associations are especially weak in industries employing large numbers of women and children, and these are precisely the classes that are most seriously injured by long hours of work. Hence it has come to be generally recognized that the conditions under which women and children work in factories ought not to be left to free contract. Hours of labor, for these classes, must be regulated by government.

In almost every modern state some attempt is made to regulate by law the hours of labor of children employed outside of the household. Such regulation has been carried farthest in the states where the system of large scale production has long been established, as, for example, in England. In new industrial states, as in Japan, the regulation of the hours of child labor is only in its inception.

The regulation of hours of labor of women employed under similar circumstances is also a well-established policy in the more advanced states. In the United States the progress of regulation has been slow, partly because of the failure of the public to recognize its importance and partly because the courts have been unfriendly to regulation, as abridging the right of contract. Yet a considerable number of states now have laws limiting the hours of women's work in factories and shops to a specified number weekly — fifty-four hours or less. The regulation of hours of labor of men has as yet made comparatively slight progress; the policy is, however, destined to extend its scope in the future.

The regulation of other conditions of employment — ventilation, sanitation, the safeguarding of the worker against dangerous machinery, etc. — has encountered comparatively few positive obstacles. The field is, however, so wide, and the work of legislatures so slow, that hundreds of thousands of workmen are to-day employed under conditions involving needless risk of mutilation and death. Still greater is the number employed under conditions that predispose the worker to disease. Progress in the direction of regulation of such conditions is steady, but dishearteningly slow.

15. *The government may regulate rates of wages.*

The regulation of wages is a policy very seldom employed in modern times. Doubtless there are many cases in which wages are far below the level of productivity of labor; and in these cases it is manifest that injustice is done. To attempt to fix general wages by law, however, is to encounter grave difficulties. If in any industry wages were fixed at a level that seemed to the workers too low, the latter would feel justified in refusing to work. If the level of wages seemed to employers too high, they would feel justified in closing their shops. To force the laborers to abide by the rate determined by government would be to inaugurate an era of universal serfdom. Men would be compelled to work on terms fixed by others, and this is the essence of serfdom. To force employers to continue production, paying wages that seem to them unduly high, would be to confiscate property. In either case it is likely that economic progress would be checked.

This does not mean that it would not be possible to select certain industries, in which the laborer is most seriously exploited, and establish minimum wages there. If the rate were too low, some of the laborers could seek other employment. If the rate were too high, some of the employers could remove their capital to other industries. With the shrinkage in the volume of the industry, the price of its products would rise, and this would enable the remaining employers to pay the rate of wages fixed. True, some of the workers formerly in the industry would be left without employment. Some means would have to be found for transferring them to other employments. However this might be, such regulation, limited to a few fields, would encounter no insuperable obstacles, and might result in alleviating the distress of some of the most helpless members of society. In a number of states minimum wage laws for women and minors have been in operation for several years in specified industries. The experiments are not sufficiently wide in scope to offer much light on the general problem of governmental determination of wages. They appear to show quite conclusively, however, that a decided improvement can thus be effected in the lot of the class of workers who are commonly most ruthlessly exploited.

16. *Governmental regulation of the relations of capitalists and enterprisers is, in some cases, necessary.*

Regulation of the relations between enterpriser and capitalist, or between borrower and lender, tenant and landowner, has largely fallen into disuse. In modern times the man who borrows capital is usually possessed of some property and of at least a moderate degree of business capacity. It may therefore be taken for granted that he will not subscribe to terms that are not to his advantage. If a man is willing to borrow for business purposes capital at ten per cent, there is good reason for believing that the annual use of the capital is worth to him at least $10 per $100. Accordingly, there is no reason why the public authority should interfere in the transaction. Many of our states do indeed have usury laws, limiting the rate of interest that may be paid. But these laws are seldom appealed to, except in cases involving petty personal loans, which are essentially different in their nature from business loans. Here the need of regulation is obvious. Usually the borrower is poor, often ignorant, and temporarily in great straits. He falls an easy victim to extortion, unless the government intervenes in his behalf.

Where the enterpriser is a corporate body, as is commonly the case in large scale production, the relations between those shareholders who are actually in control and those whose voice in the management is seldom heard, often need regulation. The small investor in a large corporation is often at the mercy of a group of large investors, who manage the property in their own interests, not in those of the entire body of stockholders. Something akin to the confiscation of property takes place when the men in control of a corporation undertake a "shaking out" of the "little men." In the end, doubtless, regulation will come, and the small investor in a corporation's stock will know whether he is buying property or shadowy hopes, and whether or not he will be permitted to keep what he has purchased.

Where a small number of large landholders deal with a vast number of small tenants there is often opportunity for the oppression of the latter. The tenant who brings a tract of land into an excellent state of cultivation should not be evicted by the landowner without fair compensation. Justice demands that he should be permitted to retain his occupancy of the land until he has reaped the fruits of his labor. Upon the renewal of his lease he should not be compelled to pay an additional sum for the use of the productive powers that he has himself created. A wise landlord, it is true, will not deal unjustly with tenants who increase the productive power of his land; but not all landlords are wise. The tenant may, in some measure, safeguard his interests by the terms of the contract under which he enters upon his tenancy; but not all the conditions that may arise during a term of tenancy can be covered by a formal contract. Accordingly, the state, under the conditions assumed, may be called upon to regulate the relations of landlord and tenant in such a way that the latter may proceed confidently with the improvement of the land, knowing that he cannot be deprived of his due reward. No general problem of this nature has arisen in the United States. This is due to the fact that it is easy for any energetic cultivator to acquire land of his own. It is quite conceivable that at some future time, when the rising price of land and the resultant concentration of holdings have given rise to a permanent class of tenant cultivators, the regulation of the relations of landlord and tenant will assume great importance.

Most foreign governments which have occupied themselves with this problem have been forced to the conclusion that no permanent solution is to be found short of the restoration of ownership to the men who actually work the land. This may be effected either through free purchase and subdivision of estates by the government, or by compulsory purchase. In the economic disturbances following the Great War the great estates were subdivided, either by purchase or by confiscation, in almost the whole of eastern Europe.

17. *Governmental regulation does not change the fundamental characteristics of the existing economic system.*

The foregoing survey is sufficient indication of the fact that the regulative activities of government already cover a wide field, and we have excellent reason for believing that the scope of such activities will in the future be greatly extended. In so far, we seem to be drifting away from an economic system based upon free private enterprise. It cannot be said, however, that the essential nature of the existing economic system is thereby altered. That system is based upon private initiative; and though the government may restrict the field in which private initiative finds exercise, it does not bind initiative itself. The government may prohibit the production of certain articles. In so doing it warns private enterprise away from a limited field; but there remain other fields open. The government may fix the price at which a certain article may be sold, but this price must be left high enough to tempt private enterprise into the field; otherwise the article will not be produced. The government may prohibit the employment of certain classes of persons, and restrict the hours of labor of other classes. Private enterprise is still called upon to furnish employment, and the conditions may not be made so onerous as to exclude the possibility of liberal profits. A system of regulated enterprise is none the less a system of private enterprise. A range of choice and an opportunity for gain are left open to the enterpriser, and if enterprise is really active, it is forever creating new opportunities beyond the reach of regulation.

It may appear that while the existing system of economic organization is in no danger of subversion through the extension of governmental regulation, it is in danger of being supplanted by a system of governmental enterprise, or a socialistic state. We have already many examples of direct production of commodities and services by the state; and we may predict an increasing number of such enterprises for the future. Must we therefore believe that a time will come when the state will enter all branches of industry, and organize the whole working population as a civil service corps? We shall get some light upon this question from a study of the reasons that have led to the direct participation of government in industry. From such a study we may draw inferences as to whether or not the same reasons will lead to an indefinite extension of the principle of governmental enterprise.

18. *A government may take over an industry for the purpose of securing a revenue from the profits of the industry.*

In some instances, the production of a commodity or a service is undertaken by government solely with a view to securing a revenue. This is the case with the tobacco monopoly of France and of some other countries, the salt monopoly in British India, and a few other public monopolies. The profits of the business take the place of revenues that would otherwise be raised by taxation. The government of France, instead of operating a tobacco monopoly, might levy duties on the manufacture and sale of tobacco. If the policy of a government monopoly is resorted to, the product is sold to the public at a price exceeding cost of production. Now, the government might, instead, place a tax on the private manufacture of the article. The manufacturers would add the tax to the price paid by the consumers. In either case the government would get a revenue and the consumer would pay a surplus above costs. In either case the consumer would bear the burden. Which is the better policy, then, a government monopoly or a tax on an industry conducted by private enterprise?

It might be that the manufacture and sale of tobacco could be carried on more cheaply by government than by private enterprise. In such a case the government could secure a larger revenue, at the same burden to the consumer, by operating the industry itself. But it is not very likely that the government could produce more cheaply than private enterprises. Men do not as a rule work so hard in public as in private employ, and they usually are paid more liberally.

But tobacco is a product characterized by great differences in quality. It would be extremely difficult to arrange a scheme of taxation which would make each grade pay as large a revenue as it would bear. It is not difficult for a government monopoly to fix the highest revenue price on each grade. This is the paramount reason why the monopoly is favored. It is a better instrument of taxation than any regular tax would be.

19. *The government may assume control of an industry for the purpose of regulating the quality or the price of the product.*

The assumption by governments of the sole right to coin money is an illustration of an industry undertaken by government for the purpose of regulating the quality of the product. Imagine the inconvenience of a currency composed of coins struck by all the private companies that mine gold or silver! Some would be light weight, some heavy; some would have much alloy, some little. Obviously, absolute uniformity and absolute conformity to well-known standards are essentials of a currency employed in a modern state. And such uniformity and integrity of quality can be secured only when the coins are issued by an organ of society which regards the interests of society as paramount. Doubtless it costs more to coin money in government establishments than it would cost in private establishments. But this waste is insignificant as compared with the gains from a currency of unquestioned soundness.

A similar reason has led to the nationalization of the railway in many countries, and to a popular demand for nationalization in other countries. If we could be sure that private railways would furnish good service, at equal terms to all, and at reasonable charges, we should never regard government ownership of railways as desirable. But of this we cannot be sure. We have tried regulation, and are still trying it; and it may be that we shall succeed in our endeavors to secure impartial and reasonable treatment of shippers and travelers. But when it is necessary to carry regulation to the point of fixing rates, quality of service, wages, profits — as we practically do — there is very little room for private enterprise to exhibit its most important virtue, initiative. Yet we cannot regulate less, and make sure of impartial and reasonable charges. It appears probable that we shall in the end make up our minds that the railway is to other business enterprises what the coinage is to other commodities — an essential link in almost every business transaction — and that its social aspects are of such paramount importance that it ought to be operated directly by the government.

A similar argument applies to the so-called municipal monopolies — street railway transportation, the furnishing of water and light, and the telephone service. If it is impossible to regulate the quality and the price of service under private management, public management becomes necessary.

20. *Where the utilities created by an industry are not appropriable, government operation becomes a necessity.*

In the foregoing instances there is no inherent necessity for public operation of industry. In the first case this policy is adopted in lieu of a policy of taxation; in the other cases, in lieu of a policy of regulation. We come now to consider cases in which government enterprise is necessary, because it is the only means of securing certain important utilities for society.

In some branches of industry, practically all the utilities created embody themselves in a concrete form, so that the producer is able to recoup himself for his costs of production through sale of the utilities to those who are to enjoy them. The utilities created by a shoe manufacturer are embodied in the shoes; and the manufacturer can obtain from the user of shoes a price that will compensate him for his expenses. If the consumer will not pay enough to cover costs, the shoes ought not to be made, for there are no utilities arising from their making that the consumer cannot appraise.

We may contrast with the utilities furnished by such an industry the utilities furnished by a lighthouse. These are scattered far and wide over the waters that are rendered safe by the light. They benefit every shipowner whose vessel sails in these waters; every passenger for whom the danger of death at sea is thereby reduced; every shipper who pays lower freights because of the smaller chance of the foundering of ships. In a year's time the utilities contributed by the lighthouse may far exceed its cost of maintenance. But if you or I were to erect a lighthouse, how would we collect pay for these utilities from the beneficiaries? Clearly, this is no field for private enterprise, and yet it is a field in which labor and capital may produce greater utilities than elsewhere. The government, as the representative of society, can alone afford to exploit this field.

Again, an industry may produce some utilities that are concrete and appropriable, and some that are elusive, flowing freely to persons who cannot be made to pay for them. In a very slight degree this is true of all industries; but we are concerned only with cases in which this differentiation of utilities is well marked. We may take as an example common school education. The children who receive instruction are the immediate beneficiaries; they, or their parents, could be made to pay something for it. But all of us who wish a government of officials selected by intelligent voters; all of us who prefer intelligent and efficient employees to ignorant ones; all of us who wish to enjoy the products of a rich and varied national production, — are the indirect beneficiaries. A great part of the total benefit from educating a child is reaped by persons not connected with him by ties of blood or personal interest.

Now, if the benefit to the child is so great, and so clearly appreciated by him or by his guardians, that the entire expense of education can be met by tuition, we who are also beneficiaries may take our gains gratis. But if this is not the case — and, as a rule, it is not — we should be very shortsighted if we refused to contribute our share to the expenses of his education. From a social point of view the benefits of popular education far outweigh the expenses of it; the expenses cannot in each case be assessed upon the beneficiaries; therefore the production of the utilities in question must be undertaken by government.

In the foregoing cases the utilities created, though real, are not tangible, nor are they capable of definite measurement. There are other cases in which the utilities created are measurable, but yet can not be appropriated by the producer. Near one of our large cities there is an island which is capable of providing building lots for a large population. Until recently comparatively few persons could make the island their home, on account of the uncertainty and inconvenience of passage to the city. A ferry service existed, but the boats were small, old, and slow. The owners of the ferry line could not furnish better service, however, because the increase in fares would not cover the increase in expense.

The introduction of an efficient ferry service would have greatly increased the value of land on the island; it would have furnished an outlet to some of the surplus population of the city, and diminished the evils of overcrowding in tenements. These utilities might very well have been of sufficient annual value to offset the increased cost of service. But the private ferry company could collect no charge for them; therefore it could not make the improvement. The city, on the other hand, could very well afford to establish a satisfactory service to the island, since the city as a whole would get most of these elusive benefits, in addition to the fares it would collect from passengers.

It is obvious that the same principle may be extended to a great many enterprises — street railways, steam railways, etc. At any given time most of the utilities produced by such an enterprise as a street railway system may be of such a character that a price can be charged for them. As the city grows in size and questions of transportation assume greater and greater importance, the utilities that are not appropriable increase in number and in value. In the end, these utilities may come to be of such significance that the transit system ought to be managed chiefly with reference to them. When this is the case public ownership ought to take the place of private ownership.

Now, as population increases, the industries producing non-appropriable utilities, along with those that are appropriable, become more numerous — or, more exactly, the non-appropriable element in utility production becomes more important, relatively to the appropriable element.

Accordingly, an expansion of public enterprise, in this direction, seems inevitable.

21. *When private enterprise is too weak to enter upon a productive field, government enterprise is sometimes necessary.*

One further case in which public enterprise may enter the field of production may here be touched upon. Sometimes private enterprise is not sufficiently daring or skillful to enter upon the supplying of utilities even when there is no obstacle in the way of charging a price for them. The government, if under the control of able administrators, may then increase the social welfare by undertaking production directly. When a country, long habituated to one mode of economic life, is suddenly compelled to adapt itself to new conditions, this superiority of public to private enterprise may manifest itself. In the last half of the nineteenth century many enterprises were undertaken by the Japanese government, in fields ordinarily left to private business. As a class of enterprisers developed, the control of such business was gradually transferred to them. When, on the other hand, private initiative dies out in a people, owing to the weeding out of the more intelligent and enterprising elements in the population, the government may gradually assume control of production and trade. Something of this nature occurred in the later years of the Roman Empire and in the declining period of Venetian history.

So long as there remains in society a large class of persons possessing enterprise and ingenuity, there is little reason for believing that the extension of the field of public enterprise will really narrow the field of private enterprise. For the boundaries of the latter can be extended indefinitely outward, so long as men have wants that remain unsatisfied. Public enterprise will wholly supplant private enterprise only when the latter has become impotent to direct the supplying of the needs of society.

22. *Summary.*

The basis of the modern industrial system is free private enterprise; such apparent violation of the principle as a protective tariff represents does not alter its fundamental truth.

The system of private enterprise has proven highly effective in the field of production; in the field of distribution it is impossible to give an unqualified opinion as to the justice and expediency of the system. Unregulated private enterprise gives rise to serious evils which demand governmental intervention.

In general, wherever gross inequality appears in the bargaining power of parties to contracts, governmental regulation is necessary. The government may be called upon to regulate (1) the quality of commodities and services; (2) the price of commodities and services; (3) the conditions of labor; (4) the wages of labor; (5) the relations between capitalist and enterpriser.

Governments often participate directly in industry. The purpose of public enterprise may be merely the securing of a revenue. This end may usually be better attained through taxation of private industry; hence extension of governmental enterprise to this end is improbable. The government may take over an industry in order to regulate effectively the quality or the price of the product of the industry. Public enterprise having this object is likely to become more common with the development of society. The government may take over industries, the utility-product of which is not readily appropriable. Public enterprise of this nature is also likely to increase in importance. The government may found industries when private enterprise is lacking in efficiency.

INDEX